WHITHER SOCIALISM

Quest For a Third Path

WHITHER SOCIALISM

Quest For a Third Path

Editors

K. K. Sinha

Uma Sinha

Priyam Krishna

SERIALS PUBLICATIONS

NEW DELHI

First Published - 2008

ISBN : 978-81-8387-171-6

Published by

SERIALS PUBLICATIONS
4830/24, Prahlad Street, Ansari Road
Darya Ganj, New Delhi-110002 (India)
Phone : 23245225. Fax : 91-11-23272135
E-mail: serials@satyam.net.in

A humble academic exercise to interpret
Indian Society and its Spirituality
–offered to the cause of a great
ongoing national and
spiritual movement
after

Swami Ramdeo

स्वामी रामदेवाय समर्पये।

In Memory of

A SOCIAL LEGEND

Babu Brajendra Bahadur; (1905-1998);
Elected Chairman Chapra Muncipal Board (1941-1962) for 5 terms
Member Legislative Council Bihar, (1952-1962);
Remembered for spirituality and service to the poor.

CONTENTS

PART - 3
JAN SAMAJVAD
(The Third Path)

INTRODUCTION

ON SOCIALISM OF AN INDIAN MAKE

There has been an intense quest for some alternatives to capitalism and socialism, quite marked after the early nineties when these systems showed grave signs of break-down and increasing poverty. India did borrow these systems in parts from the West but this thwarted any indigenous and more real system to grow to suit its rural and colonial set up of chronic poverty. The hybrid of capitalism and socialism adopted in India after its Independence acquired dubious faces which have eventually turned into a neo-rich and privileged polity fed by corruption and black money and by a parliamentary system where the poor do not matter.

A silent reaction to it is however discernible in India when State socialism was challenged while market capitalism had become too corrupt to trickle down to rural areas. It was in this period that intellectuals wrote widely in newspapers how India was fast losing its spiritual fervour and succumbing to a material order of the West. It was the 100th year of Vivekananda's Chicago speech made in 1893, when V.K.R.V. Rao wrote a paper on Spiritual Socialism, once talked by Vivekananda himself. It was also in this period that poverty economics was being studied with some Gandhian moralism and Vedantic colour of Dharma. The prevailing systems borrowed from the West seemed alien which India had to get rid of. The present book tries to collect such papers of the period which talked much about the indigenous contents of socialism, or a socialism of Indian make so that the form developed in western countries could be soon dispensed with.

The Part–1 of the present book therefore highlights such papers of the period which were discussed in light ofVivekananda's Chicago speech on Hindu religion. Dharma is interpreted as a uniting force and not at all as any short-cut equalizer. In fact, of the three ideals of the French Revolution in 1789, Liberty or freedom was opted to crush equality and later equality was preferred to choke freedom. This left out the third, fraternity, which was never achieved but which actually was the strongest uniting factor, what Indian Vedanta treated as Dharma.

The first part of this book brings Dharma as the most important constituent of spiritual socialism of an Indian make. The papers might speak out that Unity is the most important factor for a system and this alone can ensure both Freedom and Equality, not vice-versa. It is why Dharma is brought in as the strongest factor in making a system cohesive and compact. Here different interpretations of the Chicago speech have been given to recreate an awareness about true Religion. Unity in diversity could be achieved only in a garden of flowers and not in a zoo of caged animals. That flagrance of flowers in diversity is Dharma.

Some misunderstanding about culture and its 'oldness', about nationalism and love for the country and lastly about the Humanism or the human elements of Dharma are given to the various paper writers to settle. Some of the papers would say that a single language for the country can work as a great uniting factor while some other say that Human love with God above, could treat the country as one common unit of everybody's love and could solve most of the problems of the material systems invented in the West. In fact some systems in the West cracked for want of the feeling of its nationhood. Service of the living gods [poor men] is the socialist Dharma of Vivekananda's system.

The purpose here is not to enter into comparative religions and their common good factors. The norm of all religions here is only to move from lower truths to the higher truths of love and compassion, a system not religious but spiritual. As Vivekananda said India needs a Vedantic brain and an Islamic body. Here again Vedanta is not specific to the Hindus but is all-inclusive, and the problem of religions is not only to tolerate other ones but to accept them. What Sister Nivedita summerised about such a system, it was a "Love India" system. Here there is no suggestion at all of any Hindu Nationalism or Hindu Dharm. If these terms are in usage they have no other meaning than Love for India and Vedanta or the ultimate knowledge of the divine spirit in Man. Nationalism here is no chauvinism or a

Nation-State but only a love of the nation and its people. There may be some Hindu religion for name sake but there cannot be any Hindu Vedanta as Vedant addresses all human beings.

In the second part of the book, we collect articles showing the cracks in the material systems of the world, capitalism, socialism and lastly communism, which vaguely tags socialism with small communes or groups of people as the best organization in place of the State, Thus all these systems virtually rest on least governance by State, but they have actually fortified themselves as war groups or warring states. Here we have collected some reflections on Gandhism and its Swadeshi elements, which has at least the merit of being indigenous and moralistic though least worked out as economics. But ideas beyond economics or with less economics, do not mean bad economics. In fact the articles of the book treat abstract economics or fully theorized economics of Smith or Marx as unreal and in many cases faulty too. Some reflections on the abstractions of modern economics have been discussed as examples.

The Last Part (Part 3) tries to make a compendium on what actually poor man's Socialism would mean for India. Does it mean more of spiritualism and less of economics for the poor or the other way round, that is, more of economics and less of Religion or Dharm. Will it be a Dharmic order, what follows from most of the Vivekananda's utterings or it will be some market order with a righteous and moral state craft and people's democracy. Jai Prakash Narain speaks of an Indigenous Socialism; Gandhi talks of Sarvodaya which is no Ism or state order but a self-government of small people. Curiously this concept has radical import, more radical than any of the borrowed systems of socialism adopted in India since Independence. But the radicalism envisaged in the Gandhian system has a moral force of Truth (Dharma) and Ahimsa (Non-violence) which is more a tactics than just religion. Will perfecting the Gandhian system with a spiritual awakening create the new third path for India?

But how will the powerful state wither away? It has fortified itself too strong to go. This may require a continuing struggle of people vis-a-vis the state, some sort of enlightened anarchism.

METHODOLOGY OF THE BOOK

The collection of papers has been more a chance than a strived effort. But what made this book strongly thematic was a curious stream of intellectual thinking in early 1990s expressed generally in national Dailies, which is often thrown out as a scrap of paper. We felt the other way round. These ideas were so current and so spontaneous that they could not be reproduced in books unless collected. It appears that every Indian in the period had started seriously thinking of a radical change in the system and a third path which was more Indian.

Of course it was great courtesy of various news papers, who had no objection to the use made of their published papers written by most noted thinkers in the country. Most of the authors showed personal interest in the present work too and sent me personal copies of the prints. It is obvious that if you could collect 60-70 articles in this way, for any selected theme which shows some periodical upsurge of ideas, you could create an invaluable volume on a current problem. The office of the revered Dalai Lama could not locate the valuable article which His Holiness had written 13 years back on eve of Mahatma Gandhi's birth day. But this has become an invaluable part of a big theme.

We feel our effort is a honey bee's, getting the fragrance of the flowers freely with so little effort. Of course intense involvement in the subject and interactions with many authors during writing and research might have given some insight for the work, but using Dalies as valuable sources of research on practical problems might open up new dimensions of debate and thinking.

In the scheme of the Book, we had to change the printed titles of the papers, so as to show the relevance of our choice for them, but even these titles occur somewhere inside the papers.

ACKNOWLEDGEMENT

Our association with Vivekananda Kendra, Kanyakumari since 1990 as one of the Bihar convenors (jointly with Gen. S.K. Sinha, now Governor of J & K) of the centenary convention of Vivekananda's Chicago speech brought us close to the subject. Sister M. Laxmi, the then President of the Kendra was a great source of inspiration and so was A. Bala Krishnan, General Secretary of the Kendra who both visited us at Patna and gave lectures to students in colleges here. Prof. Amiya Majumdar was another erudite scholar at Calcutta who was himself devoted to Swami Vivekananda, and appreciated our efforts. Prof. Brahmananda, the great economist with whom the senior editor was associated for 30 years as a contributor in Indian

Economic Journal actually gave him personally his print on Service Socialism, and to our great grief, he died only a few days after it. Prof. S.B. Mehta of Gujrat was also very much interested in contributing for the Book like Sister M. Laxmi of Vivekananda Kendra herself.

An Emeritus fellowship award by the UGC, Delhi, gave the senior editor an opportunity to take up the current thinking on economics of poverty and this brought him close to the recent stress on Morals in economics and in its academic character. (Ref. his recent Book–Poverty of Economics).

The co-editors organized Part 1 and 2 of this work, related to religion and political systems and their break-down, as this has been their area of study and research, and reviewed it in light of a poor man's world in a Gandhian setting.

We must thank our family members for their academic contributions (Uma Sinha and Pravir Krishna) and for keen interest, shown by a galaxy of them with high accomplishments in life, for making this work readable and fruitful as a tribute to their mentor, Brajendra Babu. He was a saint in public service and his wife, Jaidevi, a spiritual soul behind him. We hope, this work will be a befitting tribute to their memory.

We owe great debt to the contributors in the book, some of whom we never met, and to the editors of the papers but we value them as most significant for the present work.

We feel, if Religion is brought near economics, the poor will become the main beneficiary in such a system of economics and not the wealthier, stronger or learned people or the priests who try to grab all privileges.

K.K. Sinha, Uma Sinha and
Priyam Krishna

N-28, Twadiyam,
Chitragupta Nagar,
Patna-800020

OUR CONTRIBUTORS

(In Order of Papers)

Sister Nivedita; Miss Margaret E. Noble, the Irish disciple of Swami Vivekananda got the significant name, Nivedita parading the dedicated one from her Guru. Her service to India in the field of education and science, religion and philosphy, art and culture, freedom movement and national consciousness, is immense. She was a powerful writer on Swamiji's ideas, contained in her Memories of her Guru and Collected writings.

Priyam Krishna; She is the co-editor of this book and is presently working as Research Assistant at Gandhi Samiti and Darshan Samiti, New Delhi.

Rajni Bakshi; A noted journalist and author.

Nitish Sengupta; An erudite professor of Calcutta and an authoritative writer on Swami Vivekananda.

Arvind N. Das; A prolific writer and author of the famous book- The Republic of Bihar.

Acharya Ramamurti; One of the brilliant living Gandhians and a prolific writer and orator. He was decorated with Padma Shree for his social works. He was closely associated with J.P. and is the author of "JP Ki Virasat" along with many others.

Maulana Wahiduddin Khan; Erudite Scholar on Islam and a theologian, also popular Indian writer on religion and Vivekananda.

T.K. Oommen; A noted writer and journalist from Kerala.

Swami Vivekananda; The great disciple of Ramkrishna Paramhans and a world figure for his views on the Hindu Religion. His

Chicago speech in the Parliament of Religions in 1893 was epoc-making. His ideas are contained in 10 volumes under Collected works. He is the main subject of the present Book, along with Mahatma Gandhi.

S.B. Mehta; Professor of Economics, Gujrat University.

Ramendra; Professor of Philosophy, Patna University and editor of a Journal Budhivadi. He is associated with the Radical Humanism of M.N. Roy.

H.H. Dalai Lama; A world figure and a Noble Lauret for Peace. His association withGandhi and his love for India is as deep as is India's love for Budhism.

R.M. Pal; A radical humanist and noted writer.

M.N. Srinivas; A noted Sociologist and author.

V.P. Verma; Erudite scholar of Political science and Religion. Was Head PG. Deptt. of Pol. Sc. in Patna University and is author of various research books.

Mulkraj Anand; Noted Art writer and author.

Rasheeduddin Khan; An authority on Sufism and Sufi literature.

Ehsan Ashraf; Professor of Philoisophy in Magadh University and a UGC Professor.

Vinod P. Singh; Retd. Professor in Delhi University and a noted soialist and author.

Rammanohar Lohia; A noted socialist writer and activist and a prolific writer on Gandhi, Marx, and the propounder of Sapta Kranti. Also a great parliamentarian.

V.M. Takunde; The noted justice of Bombay High Court, An Associate of M.N. Roy and J.P. and a social activist and thinker.

Kashiram Sharma; Noted writer and journalist.

J.D. Sethi; Noted political thinker and author and one of the most brilliant writers on Gandhi.

Sachchidanand Sinha; A socialist thinker and writer, Associated with Acharya Narendradeo Study Centre, Muzaffarpur.

Ashok Mehta; Noted socialist writer and parliamentarian and ex-vice chairman of planning commission.

Pravir Krishna; Indian Administrative Service, presently Jt. Secy. Health, Govt. of India, Delhi.

Nikhil Chakravarty; A noted journalist and author.

K.K. Sinha; Editor of the present work, Emeritus Professor, U.G.C.

Khalid Mirza; Professor of Pol. Sc. in Patna University and a noted writer.

Uma Sinha; Retd. Professor of Economics, M.U., Patna and convenor of women's cell of Vivekanand Kendra at Patna; Co-editor.

Prabhawati Sinha; Professor of Pol. Sc., Patna University.

Abu Abraham; A noted free lance journalist.

Prakash Louis; A socialist writer and Director, Bihar Social Institute Patna.

Dattopant B. Dhengadi; Associated with the Swadeshi Bachao movement and a prolific thinker on Hinduism and writer of the "Third Path".

B.R. Nanda; A renowned writer on Gandhi.

Vijay Kumar; Professor of Pol. Sc., Patna University.

P.R. Brahmananda; Professor of Economics of Bombay University and widely known economist for his "Wage Goods Model" and economic ideas.

Jai Prakash Narain; The noted socialist thinker, switching from Marxism to Democratic Socialism and finally to Bhoodan and Sarvodaya–The propuner of partyless democracy and Total Revolution in the best Gandhian traditions.

Amiya K. Majumdar; Professor of Philosophy in Calcutta University and a devoted writer on Vivekananda.

M. Laxmi Kumari; A scientist turned spiritualist in the Vivekananda Kendra, Kanya Kumari, presently.

Swami Budhananda; A widely traveled Sanyasin of the Advait Ashram, Mayawati, Pithoragarh, Himalayas and writer of a brilliant book on Vivekananda–Can One Be Scientific And Yet Spiritual.

Hiranmaya Karlekar; Noted journalist and writer.

V.K.R.V. Rao; Noted Economist, Former Director, Delhi School of Economics.

खण्ड-1

धर्म तथा समाज

(A Debate on Unity Versus Equality)

1

HUMANITY AND TRUTH

(धर्म में मानवीयता तथा सत्य)

Sister Nivedita

We know that all religious alike, from the lowest fetishism to the highest absolutism, are but so many attempts of the human soul to grasp and realize the Infinite. So we gather all these flowers, and binding them together with the cord of love, made them into a wonderful bouquet of worship.' To the heart of this speaker, none was foreign or alien. For him, there existed only Humanity and Truth.

Of the Swami's address before the Parliament of Religions, it may be said that when he began to speak it was of 'the religious ideas of the Hindus', but when he ended, Hinduism had been created. The moment was ripe with this potentiality. The vast audience that faced him represented exclusively the occidental mind, but included some development of all that in this was most distinctive. Every nation in Europe has poured in its human contribution upon America, and notably upon Chicago, where the Parliament was held. Much of the best, as well as some of the worst, of modern effort and struggle, is at all times to be met with, within the frontiers of that Western Civic Queen, whose feet are upon the shores of Lake Michigan, as she sits and broods, with the light of the North in her eyes. There is very little in the modern consciousness, very little inherited from the past of Europe, that does not hold some outpost in the city of Chicago. And while the teeming life and eager interests of that centre may seem to some of us for the present largely a chaos, yet they are undoubtedly making for the revealing of some noble and slow-wrought ideal of human unity, when the days of their ripening shall be fully accomplished.

Such was the psychological area, such the sea of mind, young, tumultuous, overflowing with its own energy and self-assurance, yet inquisitive and alert withal, which confronted Vivekananda when he rose to speak. Behind him, on the contrary, lay an ocean, calm with long ages of spiritual development. Behind him lay a world that dated itself from the Vedas, and remembered itself in the Upnishads, a world to which Buddhism was almost modern; a world that was filled with religious systems of faiths and creeds; a quiet land, steeped in the sunlight of the tropics, the dust of whose roads had been trodden by the feet of the saints for ages upon ages. Behind him, in short, lay India, with her thousands of years of national development, in which she had sounded many things, proved many things, and realized almost all, save only her own perfect unanimity, from end to end of her great expanse of time and space, as to certain fundamental and essential truths, held by all her people in common.

These, then, were the two mind-floods, two immense rivers of thought, as it were, Eastern and modern, of which the yellow-clad wanderer on the platfrom of the Parliament of Religions formed for a moment the point of confluence. The formulation of the common bases of Hinduism was the inevitable result of the shock of their contact, in a personality, so impersonal. For it was no experience of his own that rose to the lips of the Swami Vivekananda there. He did not even take advantage of the occasion to tell the story of his Master. Instead of either of these, it was the religious consciousness of India that spoke through him, the message of his whole people, as determined by their whole past. And as he spoke, in the youth and noonday of the West, a nation sleeping in the shadows of the darkened half of earth, on the far side of the Pacific, waited in spirit for the words that would be borne on the dawn that was travelling towards them, to reveal to them the secret of their own greatness and strength.

Others stood beside the Swami Vivekananda, on the same platform as he, as apostles of particular creeds and churches. But it was his glory that he came to preach a religion to which each of these was, in his own words, only a travelling, a coming up, of different men, and women, through various conditions and circumstances to the same goal'. He stood there, as he declared, to tell of One who had said of them all, not that one or another was true, in this or that respect, or for this or that reason, but that 'All these are threaded upon Me, as pearls upon a string. Wherever thou seest extraordinary holiness and extraordinary power, raising and purifying humanity, know thou that I am there.' To the Hindu, says Vivekananda, 'Man is not traveling from error to truth, but climbing up from truth to truth, from truth that is lower to truth that is higher.' This and the teaching of Mukti–the doctrine that 'man is to become divine by realizing the divine', that religion is perfected in us only when it has led us to 'Him who is the one life in a universe of death, Him who is the constant basis of an ever-changing world, that One who is the only Soul, of which all souls are but delusive manifestations'–may be taken as the two great outstanding truths which, authenticated by the longest and most complex experience in human history, India proclaimed through him to the modern world of the West.

For India herself, the short address forms, as has been said, a brief Charter of Enfranchisement. Hinduism in its wholeness the speaker bases on the Vedas, but he spiritualizes our conception of the word, even while he utters it. To him, all that is true is Veda. 'By the Vedas,' he says, 'no books are meant. They mean the accumulated treasury of spiritual laws discoverd by different persons in different times' Incidentally, he discloses his conception of the Sanatana Dharma. 'From the high spiritual flights of the Vedanta philosophy, of which the latest discoveries of science seem like echoes, to the lowest ideas of idolatry with its multifarious mythology, the agnosticism of the Buddhists, and the atheism of the Jains, each and all have a place in the Hindu's religion.' To his mind, there could be no sect, no school no sincere religious experience of the Indian people–however, like an aberration it might seem to the individual–that might rightly be excluded from the embrace of Hinduism. And of this Indian Mother-Church, according to him, the distinctive doctrine is that of the Ishta Devata, the right of each soul to choose its own path, and to seek God in its own way. No army, then carries the banner of so wide an Empire as that of Hinduism, thus defined. For as her spiritual goal is the finding of God, even so is her spiritual rule, the perfect freedom of every soul to be itself.

Yet would not this inclusion of all, this freedom of each be the glory of Hinduism that it is, where it not for her supreme call, of sweetest promise: 'Here, ye children of immortal bliss! Even ye that dwell in higher spheres! For I have found that Ancient One who is beyond all darkness, all delusion. And knowing Him, ye also shall be saved from death.' Here is the word for the sake of which all the rest exists and has existed. Here is the crowning realization, into which all others are resolvable. When, in his lecture on 'The Work Before Us', the Swami adjures all to aid him in the building of a temple wherein every worshipper in the land can worship, a temple whose shrine shall contain only the word Om, there are some of us who catch in the utternace the glimpse of a still greater temple–India herself, the Motherland, as she already exists–and see the paths, not of the Indian churches alone, but of all Humanity, converging there, at the foot of that sacred place wherein is set the symbol that is no symbol, the name that is beyond all sound. It is to this, and not away from it, that all the paths of all the worships and all the religious systems lead. India is at one with the most puritan faiths of the world in her declaration that progress is from seen to unseen, from the many to the One, from the low to the high, from the form to the formless, and never in the reverse direction. She differs only in having a word of sympathy and promise for every sincere conviction, wherever and whatever it may be, as constituting a step in the great ascent.

The Swami Vivekananda would have been less than he was, had anything in this Evangel of Hinduism been his own. Like the Krishna of the Gita, like Buddha, like Shankaraharya, like every great teacher that Indian thought has known, his sentences are laden with quotations from the Vedas and Upanishads. He stands merely as the Revealer, the Interpreter to India of the treasures that she herself possesss in herself. The truths he preaches would have been as true, had he never been born. Nay more, they would have been equally authentic. The difference would have lain in their difficulty of access, in their want of modern clearness and incisiveness of statement, and in their loss of mutual coherence and unity. Had he not lived, texts that today will carry the bread of life to thousands might have remained the obscure disputes of scholars. He taught with authority, and not as one of the Pandits. For he himself had plunged to the depths of the realization which he preched, and he came back like Ramanuja only to tell its secrets to the pariah, the outcast and the foreigner.

And yet this statement that his teaching holds nothing new is not absolutely true. It must never be forgotten that it was the Swami Vivekananda who, while proclaiming the sovereignty of the Advaita Philosophy, as including that expereince in which all is one, without a second, also added to Hinduism the doctrine that Dvaita, Vishishtadvaita, and Advaita are but three phases or stages in a single development, of which the last-named constitutes the goal. This is part and parcel of the still greater and more simple doctrine that the many and the One are the same Reality perceived by the mind at different times and in different attitudes; or as Sri Ramakrishna expressed the same thing, 'God is both with form and without form. And he is that which includes both form and formlessness.'

It is this which adds its crowning significance to our Master's life, for here he becomes the meeting-point, not only of East and West, but also of past and future. If the many and the One be indeed the same Reality, then it is not all modes of worship alone, but equally all modes of work, all modes of struggle, all modes of creation, which are paths of realization. No distinction, henceforth, between sacred and secular. To labour is to pray. To conquer is to renounce. Life is itself religion. To have and to hold is as stern a trust as to quit and to avoid.

This is the realization which makes Vivekananda the great preacher of Karma, not as divorced from, but as expressing Jnana and Bhakti. To him, the worship, the study, the farmyard, and the field are as true and fit scenes for the meeting of God with man as the cell of the monk or the door of the temple. To him, there is no difference between **service of man and worship of God,** between manliness and faith, between true righteousness and spirituality. All his words, from one point of view, read as a commentary upon this central conviction. 'Art, science and religion,' he said once, 'are but three different ways of expressing a single truth. But in order to understand this we must have the theory of Advaita.'

The formative influence that went to the detrmining of his vision may perhaps be regarded as threefold. There was, first, his literary education, in Sanskrit and English. The contrast between the two worlds thus opened to him carried with it a strong impression of that particular experience which formed the theme of the Indian sacred books. It was evident that this, if true at all, had not been stumbled upon by Indian sages, as by some others, in a kind of accident. Rather was it the subject-matter of a science, the object of a logical analysis that shrank from no sacrifice which the pursuit of truth demanded.

In his Master, Ramakrishna Paramahamsa, living and teaching in the temple-garden at Dakshineshwar, the Swami Vivekananda–

'Naren' as he then was–found that verification of the ancient texts which his heart and his reason had demanded. Here was the reality which the books only brokenly described. Here was one to whom Samadhi was a constant mode of knowledge. Every hour saw the swing of the mind from the many to the One. Every moment heard the utterance of wisdom gathered superconsciously. Everyone about him caught the vision of the divine. Upon the disciple came the desire for supreme knowledge 'as if it had been a fever'. Yet he who was thus the living embodiment of the books was so unconscious, for he had read none of them! In his Guru, Ramakrishna Paramahansa, Vivekananda found the key to life.

Even now, however, the preparation for his own task was not complete. He had yet to wander throughout the length and breadth of India, from the Himalayas to Cape Comorin, mixing with saints and scholars and simple souls alike, learning from all, teaching to all, and living with all seeing India as she was and is, and so grasping in its comprehensiveness that vast whole, of which his Master's life and personality had been a brief and intense epitome.

The Shastras, the Guru, and the Motherland–are the three notes that mingle themselves to form the music of the works of Vivekananda. These are the treasure which it is his to offer. These furnish him with the ingredients where of he compounds the world's heal-all of his spiritual bounty. These are the three lights burning within that single lamp which India by his and lighted and set up, for the guidance of her own children and of the world in the few years of work between September 19, 1893 and July 4, 1902. And some of us there are, who, for the sake of that lighting, and of this record that he has left behind him, bless the land that bore him and the hands of those who sent him forth, and believe that not even yet has it been given to us to understand the vastness and significance of the message that he spoke.

[From sister Nivedita's Introduction to the Complete Works of Swami Vivekananda]

2

CHICAGO SPEECH—ITS SOCIALIST CONTENT
(शिकागो भाषण: इसके समाजवादी तत्व)

Priyam Krishna

It was a speech made in parts during the 17 days of the convention of the Parliament of Religions at Chicago by the 30 year young Sanyasin of India–Vivekanand. The convention started on the 11th September, 1893 and the Swami while introducing Indian religion to the West, addressed the Parliament with the words 'sisters and brothers of America. This is said to be the shortest description of the Indian mind and the Vedanta. His calling Hinduism as the mother of all religions only indicated the immense love Indians have for other religions which developed in course of time. They were all like the pearls in the garland. (mai sarvamidam protamsutre munigana iwa') It was India which nurtured different religions in her lap when they were banished from their homeland, as a mother does. To a Vedantic mind no religion was exclusive or had any isolated existence excluding others. They were all like rivers merging ultimately into the ocean of spiritual unity of mankind. 'We (Indians) accept all religions as true' declared Vivekanad. He further observed that 'I fervently hope that the bell that tolled in the convention may be the death knell of all fanaticism, of all persecutions with the sword or with the pen and of all uncharitable feelings between persons wonding their way for to the same goal.

He hit at the fanatics by comparing them with the frog of the well which did not like to come out of the well to see the vast expanse of water of the sea. Hinduism, christianity or Islam lose their worth if they start thinking about themselves in isolation and not in cooperation with others. Religions created wells as well as oceans. The ocean is created when they all come together.

Vivekananda elaborated the Indian view in his own unique way on the 19th Sep. 1893. Stating the history of religions he felt that the pre-historic religions of the Hindus, Jews and Parsis have survivived in spite of severe onslaughts and have proved their metal. Hinduism adopted all of them and many others which developed on Indian soil itself. It was an oceanic expanse where all the rivers became one. What gave such an oceanic vastness to the religious beliefs in India? The Swami redefined the Vedic religion as not a book but a treasure house of spiritual thoughts brought out by different persons over time. This gave the essence of the Vedas, the Vedanta. This religion was a realisation of the spiritual oneness of mankind, a truth not bound by time, a xperpetual truth. Such realisation was by sages in ancient India and they were not men only but women too.

It was in this sense that a supreme truth is established which gives the science of religion, a truth which has no beginning nor end. The creation is similarly without beginning or end and runs parallel as a non-spiritual physical object, perishing and changing forms. But the spiritual is the inner 'self', not the created body. This inert consciousness is not something which is born or which dies. It is common and the same in each creature and when it is so realised, the self mingles in the 'whole' as drops merge in the ocean. The supreme self is thus nothing but the sum total of all soul. Such realisation is attaining perfection, attaining God or becoming Brahma itself.

The Swami elaborates that the realisation of the 'self' is manifested in the very physical base which it defies or transcends. The relation of the self with the body is one of lotus leaf with water. It is doing the duty with the body but without thinking of the reward, good or bad. Thus Vivekannda treats each soul as divine and when divinity is realised, the physical self vanishes and soul attains Mukti or freedom from imperfection, death, birth and fear.

The Swami poses a question–Why should one believe that the self is different form the body and how should one realise it, if at all it is so. The answer here is that God alone knows it, not man, and only by His grace one would realise it. It is here that spiritualism by passes logic and self-deceipt which a person with body and mind tends to develop. Thus spiritualism is not a mere belief but a state of development from simple truth to higher truth and ultimately an experience of the realisation of oneness with Brahma, of loss of duality (dvait). Every science has to reach a unity solution. What stays is not matter but energy and there must be a basic energy to which other elements are 'related'.

Vivekanand accepts the difference of religions so far as their form is concerned. Mosques, churches, cross, idols, sun or moon only refer to symbols but they are static. What is dynamic is to grow. From worship one has to grow to prayer and ultimately to the realisation of the untiy with the supreme truth. It is a process of growing from the lower to the higher truth. Swamiji poses another question–why religions differ. The variety is natural and formal but the unity is real. It is a unity in diversity, like pearls in the garland. The Budhists and Jains scrapped God as a concept but Vivekanand points out that when they see divinity in man, it is seing God all around and it is this which is the essence of religion, not God as such.

If there could be a universal religion it must transgress all boundaries of time and place, 'which would belong neither to Brahmans, nor Budhists, Christians or Muslims but to all, low or high. It will see divinity in all including the non-believers. Swami Ji was critical of religions when it was criticising othr religions in order to prove that it was only true, but he adored them when they had appreciation and positive outlook to other ones. Here he quotes the Brahma Sutra–'There are perfect men outside our race and community' ('antara chaapi tu taddrishtah'). Though a Hindu, I am a Budhist, said Swamiji on the 16th day of the convention. Hinduism and Budhism had the same relation as Judaism and Christianity. Christ was a jew and Budha was a Hindu but where as the Jews Crucified Christ, the Hindus accepted the Budha as an incarnation. What is needed is a Brahmanical mind and a Budhist heart.

Vivekanand who declared later that he was a socialist, asked the Chicago convention (the Christians particularly) not to preach their religion to the Indians in poverty and hunger as they had enough of religion. They needed bread and preaching religion was an insult to them. A little of bread could awaken this power store of divinity. He emphasised that all religions are true and if anybody dreams of the exclusive survival of his own religion, he should be pitied and on his banner of religion should be written–

"Help and Not Fight, Assimilation, Not Destruction, Harmony and Peace and Not Dissension'

Swamiji had initiated the concept of practical Vedant as the religion of the world, which did not distinguish between men nor acknowledged any privilege to one to oppress the other, be it muscle, money, learning or even spiritual. This was spiritual socialism in the offing and Vivekananda was churning out a Vedantic cream out of the milk of all religions for the happiness of human being. The Chicago convention was held 10 years after the death of the great humanist Marx and Swamiji gave an alternative system which the present world is evaluating more intensively today than it did hundred years ago.

By Courtesy, Rotary Club, 1994, Patna.

3

RELIGION AND SPIRITUALITY
(धर्म और अध्यात्म)

Rajni Bakshi

> *"At Cape Comorin sitting in Mother Kumari's temple, sitting on the last bit of India rock–I hit upon a plan: We are so many sanyasis wandering about, and teaching the people metaphysics–It is all madness. Did not our Gurudeva use to say, "An empty stomach is no good for religion'?*
>
> ***—Swami Vivekananda***

The athlectic young sanyasi sat perfectly still on an off-shore rock at Kanyakumari. Steeped in deep meditation he seemed to have reached a realm beyond time, space and the tingling salt spray of crashing ocean waves. This image, of Swami Vivekananda at the rock that now bears his name, is one of modern India's most endurng legends.

The glare of adulation has tended to obscure the tumultuous human struggles of that legendary persona. And these struggles are the clue to why, a century later, Swami Vivekananda and his plans for India inspire people across the ideological spectrum.

"Let us journey back a hundred years to see what bothered Vivekananda and served as an impetus for his sense of mission.

Wandering as a pilgrim, from the Himalayas to India's southernmost tip, Swami Vivekananda saw: "A country where millions of people live on flowers of the mohua plant, and a million or two of sadhus and a hundred million or so of Brahmins suck the blood out of these poor people, without even the least effort for their amelioration–is that a country or hell? Is that a religion, or the devil's dance?"

So he resovled to undo these injustices and revitalise India by saving religion from those who made it a "devil's dance". But this ambitious aspiration had to contend with global forces that were beyond any single man's influence.

Looming large over the threshold of the 20th century, Swami Vivekananda saw "modern western science dazzling the eyes with the brilliancy of myriad suns and driving in the chariot of hard and fast facts". By the late 19th century western materialism and colonialism had come to dominate the world. By comparison the Indian civilisational endeavour seemed to have atrophied. The colonial encounter had the self-confidence of Indian society as never before.

In addition the efforts of Christian missionaries to convert "heathens" had triggered anxieties within sections of Hindu society. Swami Vivekananda's self-defined task was to simultaneously eliminate the evil in Hindu practice and also reaffirm the value of the tradition. Thus he felt compelled to assert that "Hinduism is not a mistake". Herein lay one of his most intense struggles. As a disciple of Sri Ramakrishna Paramahamsa and a diligent spiritual aspirant Swami Vivekananda sought the essentials of Hindusim in pure spirituality. As an activist entangled in the throes of history, he sought the common bases of Hinduism in order to unify its diverse strains. The insights of Vedanta provided these common bases and gave the Swami a means of synthesising his inner quest and his worldly mission.

The essence of this mission was to demystify spiritual truths–bringing them out of the monastries and the hold of priestcraft. Since the objective was to retrieve the highest ideals of the existing religion. Swami Vivekananda placed the greatest onus for this revitalisation on orthodox Hindus. He held them responsible for the fact that essential principles had languished over the centuries and decayed internally. What were these essentials?

Religion, Vivekananda said over and over again, is realisation. Rituals, colours, 'mantras' and idols may help, but these were not the essentials of a spiritual life. For, he said, "if your heart has not opened, if you have not realised God, it is all in vain". And purification of the heart requires "worship of the Virat–of all those around us".

Religion and spirituality, so defined, was in Vivekananda's view the common ground for the amalgam of cultures in India. And restoring health to these essentials of religion was, for the Swami, a necessary prerequisite for the rejuvenation of India.

All these convictions added up not to one but many 'plans'. There had to be a "man-making" education, both spiritual and scientific, that would give strength to the people. Additionally, for the making of a great future India required "organisation, accumulation of power, coordination of wills".

But when he arose from his meditation on th rock at Kanyakumari the high tide of ideas was also accompanied by a dogged restlessness. He was not sure exactly how all this would add up to both, filling empty stomachs and saving religion. Besides, all plans demanded selfless dedicated workers and funds. The wandering endicant had a few followers but no funds. So he decided to go to America to spread the message of Indian spirituality and earn money.

Behind the glitter of western affluence Swami Vivekananda sensed another kind of decay and crisis. So he saw himself as a missionary who must seek a mutually enriching synthesis of eastern and westrn thought. But would preaching "the incomparable glory of the Vedas and the Vedanta" necessarily be compatible with his goal of fostering universal religion? For Vivekananda the two were one and the same. His notion of "conquering" the world with spirituality was based on the faith that "love must conquer hatred, hatred cannot conquer itself."

Thus bursting with "a tremendous power and energy" Vivekanand set forth on the solitary voyage to America and the Parliament of Religions where history waited to test his faith.

II

The cyclonic sanyasi knew he would not live to be 40. So the remaining nine years, following his instant fame at the Parliament of Religions, were spent in a whirlwind of activity. Travelling widely acoss America and Europe he taught, learnt and persued his spiritual quest with intense vigour.

These encounters with diverse cultures confirmed Swami Vivekananda's view that religion had given humanity both "the intensest love" and "the most diabolical hatred". So he set out to explore if this corrosive virus of religious fanaticism could be neutralised. Was a universal religion, a brotherhood of different faiths, at all possible?

Let us begin, Vivekananda suggested, by recognising that there cannot be, and ought not to be, a uniforn :ty of philosophy, mythology and symbol. "For I know that this world must go on working, wheel within wheel, this intricate mass of machinery, most complex, most wonderful. What can we do then?" asked the Swami. "We can make it run smoothly, we can lessen the friction... By recognising the natural necessity of variation."

This requires us to "learn that truth may be expressed in a hundred thousand ways, and that each of these ways is true as far as it goes". The vision of God may vary in every case, Vivekananda said, "yet he is one.... this is only recognition of universality that we can get."

Countless saints and seers in cultures across the world have reiterated this elementary truth for centuries. Why then have most efforts for a brotherhood of religions failed? Swami Vivekananda felt that this was due to the lack of a practical plan which would show people the point of union with all other faiths without destroying the individuality of any religion.

Over the years Swami Vivekananda worked out the rudiments of such a plan and anchored it with the maxim, "Do not destroy". He urged people to build instead of pulling anything down. "Help if you can; if you cannot, fold your hands and stand by and see things go on. Do not injure, if you cannot render help."

"Take a man where he stands and from there give him a life," the swami suggested. "If it be true that God is the centre of all religions, and that each of us is moving towards Him along one of these radii, then it is certain that all of us must reach that centre. And at the centre, where all the radii meet, all our differences will cease."

This poses a demanding challenge to the self-doubting and ever sceptical nature of much of 20th century humanity. For Swami Vivekananda is not only saying that all of us can reach the centrs but that we can teach ourselves to get there. "None can make a spiritual man of you... your growth must come from inside."

Such growth and evolution of human beings is, according to Swami Vivekanda, the only way to check the latent 'tiger' in us. The most terrible weapons of this fanatical tendency are not swords but contempt, social hatred and social ostracism. Thus the fanatic is know to hurl abuse at all those who do not think just as he does.

On the other hand, the rational man is glad that others do not think exactly as he does. For, thinking beings must differ. Therefore,

Vivekananda insisted. An absence of sects would only bring "the peace and harmony of the grave. But so long as mankind thinks, there will be sects. Variation is the sign of life, and it must be there."

A celebration of this variation would be universal religion. the ideal may seem elusive but Vivekananda believed it to be inherent to all human striving. "If the priests and other people that have taken upon themselves the task of preachig different religions simply cease preaching for a few moments, we shall see it is there. They are disturbing it all the time, because it is to their interest."

These were the elements that Swami Vivekanand challenged within his own faith. And the central mission of the Swami's life was within the Hindu fold. In the Chicago address he had said that the Hindu had always recognised that unity in variety was the plan of Nature. But in practice bitter sectarian disputes and layers of superstition had obscured these universalist principles. Vivekananda struggled to retrieve them.

This was simultaneously an effort to creatively locate Hinduism, as a cohesive body of thought and practise, amid the turbulent change of the modern era. Swami Vivekananda belived that a blossoming of the finest and most humane principles of Hindu spirituality was essential not only for the future of Indian society but for humanity at large.

This in turn meant an internal struggle against the prejudices and inequities in contemporary Hindus practice. It was in this context that Vivekananda called Buddhism "the fulfillment of Hinduism". He urgd that the Brahmin intellect must join "with the heart, the noble soul, the wonderful humanising power of the Great Master (Buddha)".

Swami Vivekananda's mission to galvanise Hindus and make Hindu society dynamic was a multi-dimensional endeavour. But at its core was the exhortation for this "fulfillment" to become a part of living practice.

Then it might be possible for Hinduism to actually embody the ideal of universal religion as Vivekananda had defined it in the Chicago address:

> *"It will be a religion which will have no place for persecution or intolerance in its polity, which will recognise divinity in every man and woman, and whose whole scope, whose whole force, will be created in aiding humanity to realise its own true divine nature."*

On the basis of such strengths, the Swami believed that human civilisation could deal with modernity positively rather than defensively. For instance, it could be possible to learn from western materialism without succumbing to its evils. And the West would gain from eastern spirituality without diminishing its worldly vigour.

Since the Swami was a man of action, and not just ideas, his own vigour was over-taxed in the decade leading up to his 'mahasamadhi'. The challenges which he took up often led him into situation of conflict. He was showered with adulation in his own life time but also did not lack adversaries. But it was the magnituge of his self-defined spiritual, social and organisational mission that drove him at a pace which made fatigue inevitable.

But the Swami's disciples believe that exhaustion alone could not overcome that superhuman will. They recall his guru Sri Ramakrishna Paramahamsa's prediction that Naren would leave his body the day he realised his true self. Perhaps it was that realisation which allowed the Swami to slip away one evening in 1902. He had often visualised his own departure from the body murmuring "Hara, Hara (The free, the free)."

Yet the words which resound through his life journey, and perhaps make a fitting epithet, are these:

> *"Love never fails, my son; today or tomorrow or ages after, truth will conquer. ...Believe in the omnipotent power of love."*

(Writer's brilliant columns on 'Quest of a Universal religion' and 'A plan for India'–By Courtesy, Times of India (26 Sept. 1993) with gratitude)

4

RELIGION AND SOCIETY
(धर्म तथा समाज)

Nitish Sen Gupta

The centenary year of the 1893 Chicago Parliament of Religions is an appropriate occasion to recall Swami Vivekananda's message to India and the world and to be amazed at how relevant it is even after a century. Vivekananda was just not a religious saint, but a Vedantic teacher propounding the concept of a universal religion, India's first socialist, a firebrand nationalist and yet a true internationalist who was ahead of his time, a social reform activist, an educationist and, above all, a humanist who believed in the innate greatness of human beings. In his clarion call at the Chicago Parliament, he emphasised the fundamental unity of all religions deprecating the prevailing tendency to emphasise the greatness of one's own religion and decry other religions. He urgd followers of various religions to be true to their fundamental tenets, and not to emphasise "secondary details."

One cannot but recall his stirring words, "The Christian has not to become Hindu or Buddhist, nor a Hindu or Buddhist to become Christian. But each must assimilate the spirit of the other, and yet preserve his individuality and grow according to his own law of growth. Every religion has produced men and women of most exalted character. If in the face of this evidence anybody dreams of the exclusive survival of his own religion and destruction of the others, I pity him from the bottom of my heart."

This Vedantic concept of eternal universal religion could not be the exclusive property of the Hindus. Believing in the unity of all mankind and the same God manifesting himself through all beings, he felt that Islam as a religion had gone the farthest in ahieving this Vedantic concept of equality of mankind. "How I would long to see my India as an Islamic body with a Vedantic head (letter to a friend, Sarfaraz Khan)." Again, "If you are born a Christian be a good Christian. If you are born a Hindu, be a good Hindu. If you are born a Muslim be a good Muslim."

For a generation which is troubled with the Ayodhya phenomenon, these are indeed very comforting words. Different sects fighting for the exclusive right to worship in different names of the same God is contrary to all that Swamiji stood for. Swami Viveakanada would have liked to see both Hindus and Muslims offer prayer to God–called by whatever name–at the same place and in harmony, without disturbing each other. "Advaitism" is the religion of the future enlightened humanity. Yet practical Advaitism which looks upon all mankind as one's own soul was never developed among the Hindus universally. If any religion approaches this equality it is Islam alone."

It was from theVedanta again that several other strands of his thought evolved. He wanted the caste system to be completely eradicated, the poorer sections of the people to be given a fair deal and religion to be freed from priestly tyranny and vulgar ritualism. Man is an incarnation of God. If this is so, if God resides in every soul, there cannot be any high caste, any low caste, any master or slave. For a true Vedantist there is no room for difference or special privileges on the basis of the accident of birth, no room for difference btween nations. Just as a body where blood does not flow through all the limbs equally becomes diseased, the same with the society where large sections of the people are kept backward and deprived of basic facilities and education.

In his stirring words again, "Think of the last 600 or 700 years of degradation when grown up men have been discussing for years whether they should drink a glass of water with the right hand or the left, whether they should gargle five of six times. Our religion is in the kitchen. Our God is in the cooking pot and our religion is "don't touch me, I am holy."

For him the problem of the caste was a part of the greater national problem. To remedy this he suggested free flow of spiritual and secular knowledge among the masses of the people and free flow of opportunities so that all could see the evils of the caste system and resist the humiliation and exploitation. "Religion is neither in books, nor in intellectual consent, nor in reason. Reason, theory, dogmas, doctrines, books, ceremonies are all helps to religion. Religion itself consists of realisation."

For a true Vendantic all these rituals that the priests propagate were meaningless. "For centuries these priests had been doling out ditch water as religion overlooking the eternal fountain of Amrit that lies behind us. I consider the great national sin is the neglect of the masses and that is one of the causes of our downfall. No amount of politics would be of any avail until the masses in India are well-educated, well-fed and well-cared for. If we want to regenerate India we must work for them. So long as millions live in hunger and ignorance, I hold every man a traitor who having been educated at their expense, pays no heed to them. I do not believe in a god who cannot give us bread here, giving me eternal bliss in heaven."

These thoughts were forged in the course of his 14 years of travel on foot across India when he came to know hunger, starvation, shelterless living, the misery of the poor and also their 'great potential.' His prescription was a programme of national regeneration in which education must play a major role. He addressed his appeals to three sections: the youth, the women and the lower classes. He demanded that the task of educating the younger generation should be taken over from the hands of the foreign rulers and from orthodox religious institutions and given to the society as a whole. Also, he considered it necessary that education should be patriotic, useful and that the achievements of advanced technology should be mastered by our younger people.

Again, he attached great importance to professional vocational training and to further education and informal education–ideas which have become fashionable only just now after a century. Also, "spend no more money on the Brahmin's education, but spend all on the Pariah."

"Our aristocratic ancestors went on treading the masses of the country under feet till they became helpless, till te poor people nearly forgot that they were human beings They have been compelled to be merely hewers of wood and drawers of water for centuries, so much so the most demonical and brutal arrangements culled from the crude ideas of hereditary transmission and other such gibberish from the western world and brought forward to brutalise and tyranise over the poor".

He, therefore, wanted the upper classes in India to forget their exclusive privileges and merge themselves with the masses. The new India, according to him, would arise "out of the peasant's cottage, grasping the plough, out of the huts of fishermen, the cobbler and the sweeper, the grocer's shop, from the oven of the fritter seller, from the factory, from the mart and from markets, from the forests, from hills and mountains."

Vivekananda was by far the first in India to call himself a socialist. In his remarkable pamphlet "I am a Socialist" he did not quite preach an armed struggle between the classes but surely, advocated a complete fusion of all classes and castes. According to him, the world having passed through the Brahmanic age, the Kshatriya age, and the Vaishya age, it was inevitable that the Shudras will take over. Few, at that time, understood the significance and value of labour and propagated their upsurge through education and mass upsurge.

The state of a civilistion is to be judged by the way it treats its women. He also attached tremendous importance to women. "If I get 500 motivated men it will take me 50 years to transform India. If I get 50 motivated women it may take only a few years."

In his programme of national regeneration he attributed tremendous significance to mass education, the education that is not religious in the conventional sense but both spiritual and scholarly, at the same time scientific and cosmopolitan. All the reform movements in India, in his opinion, failed to succeed because they were confined only to the 0.5 percent of the people, he upper class, and so long as that they are made to believe that they are born as slaves, hewers of wood and drawers of water. With all our boasted education of modern times, if anybody says a kind word for them, our men shrink at once from the duty of lifting them up–these poor downtrodden poeple. Not only so, but I also find that al sorts of the masses of the people were not transformed through education, these reform movements were bound to be confined to a very narrow base.

Seeing the Roop Kanwar incident and the like, even in today's India one cannot but endorse this assessment. Today, a century after the Parliament of Religions, it is important to recall Swamiji's stirring message. He did not surely preach nationalism as such, but when he preached freedom, the need for emancipation from all bondage, and to be fearless against all oppression, including domination by foreigners, he surely laid the foundation of a great nationalistic movement that arose a few years after him.

Let us recall his words from his famous address at Lahore in 1897, "so give up being slaves. For the next 50 years that alone should be our keynote, our Mother India. Let all other vain gods vanish for the time from our minds. This is the only God."

"If the generation that followed saw, three years after Vivekananda's death, the revolt of Bengal, the prelude to the great movement of Tilak and Gandhi, if India today has taken part in the collective action of organised masses, it is due to the message from Vivekanada," said Romain Rolland. His chosen instrument for transformation was the youth. He wanted to organise a hundred thousand strong brigade of educated young men and women to "send them like waves all over India bringing comfort, morality, religion, education to the doors of the meanest and the most downtrodden." These would be gigantic waves and no thing could resist these young people "with muscles of iron and nerves of steel inside, whose life is one of burning love, self reliances, meeting death face to face, if necessary." That task remains unfulfilled even after a century. It is for our generation to fulfil this task and build a new India and a new world.

Writer's Column 'A century after Chicago'–By Courtesy Hindustan Times Feb. 14, 1993 with gratitude of the editors.

5

PSEUDO—RELIGION DEBASES SPIRITUALITY
(धर्म बनाम अध्यात्म)

Arbind N. Das

India does not lack simple-minded souls. There are many today who spout a simplistic religiosity–a caricature of the immensely complex traditions of Indian philosophical thinking–in the faith that their put-on religion encapsulates the commonness of common sense. Indeed, there are many born-again pundits who peddle religion now with the same zeal with which they earlier propagated hard-headed, this worldly, a religious realpolitik. It is no surprise, therefore, that in the hands of such fair-weather preachers of theocracy, the very Ram of the Ramcharitmanas is distorted and Goswami Tulasidas himself is turned into a two-dimensional cardboard character.

That there is not only literary richness but also an eclectic and even syncretic splendour in Tulsidas is cynically brushed aside as the short-sighted plans of bringing India under a theocracy are prepared. Tulasidas himself would have had little patience for such atavistic narrow-mindedness which characterises today's burgeoning bazaar clergy.

EVIL PRACTICES

In his Kavitavali, Tulasidas himself exposes the ugly underbelly of Hindusim as it actually exists in society. Even an article in Organiser, the otherwise unabashed medium of hindutva myth-making, notes, "From his verses in Kavitavali, we get a lot of information about the then prevailing caste barriers, evil practices in Hindu society, the degeneration of high caste Brahmins especially of Kashi (now Varanasi) and the sufferings undrgone by him for rendering the Ramayana in fok language and for his unorthodox ideas."

Among the "unorthodox" ideas of Goswami Tulasidas were cultural syncretism and disregrd of the sectarian bigotry of those who appoint themselves as arbiters of "correct" socio-religious practice. In one poem, Tulasidas not only rejects being tied down to a fixed place in the caste and even religious matrix but also describes his own peaceful abode in a mosque, a structure just like the one which has been demolished by those who today take his name in vain. *"Dhoot kaho, avadhoot kaho, rajput kaho, julaha kaho kovoo/Kahoo ki beti se beta na beyahab; Kahoo ki jaat bigaar na sovoo/Tulasi sarnam ghulam hai Ram ko; jako ruchai so kahe kachhu vohoo/Maang ke khaibo, masjid mein soibo; laibe ko ek na daibe ko dovoo."* (Let anyone call me either a cheat or a mendicant, a rajput or a (Muslim) weaver/I have no son to marry to anyone's daughter and (thereby) defile his caste/ Tulasi is well-known as the slave of Ram; everyone is free to call him by any name the chooses/He lives by begging for alms; he sleeps in a mosque and is free from any kind of obligation, either to give or to take).

Today however, not only has the bhakti of Tulasidas been defiled by an artifical and aggressive hindutva but the very flexibility of Ram himself has been ended by fossilising him into a stylised icon. It is well-known to those who are familiar with the cultural traditions of India without subscribing to the narrow-minded bigotry of political pseudo-religion that, in deference to the wishes of others, Ram himself took on different forms (roop). The Balkand of Ramcharitmanas describes how when he incarnated himself in the form of the four-armed Vishnu with all his weapons, Kaushalya entreated him to become a child: "Keejay shishoo leela, ati priyasheela" and Ram obliged. Similarly, when Tulasidas refused to bow to his Krishna form *(Ka varnau chhavi aap ki, bhale bane ho nath/Tulasi mastak tab navey, dhanush baan lehu haath), the icon changed: Kit murali kit chandrika kit gopiyan ke saath/ Apane jan ke kaarane Sri Krishna bhaye Raghunath.* (For his devotee, Krishna gave up his flute and even his gopis and became Ram).

This flexibility is a far cry from the attempt of today's votaries of political hindutva to freeze Ram into mundane icons of Ramlalla which are surreptitiously installed, removed and re-installed through acts of vandalism.

It is not that Hinduism does not have contradiction but the contradictions within it, which reflect its evolution over time through interaction with various philosophical and ethical systems, give it the intricacy of a richly woven tapestry. Take, for instance, the very concepts of the meaning of action (karma) as outlined in the Gita itself. At one place (2.55), it notes, *"Prajhati yada kaman sarvan Partha manogatan/Aatmanyevatmanaa tushtah sthitprajnastdochyate."* (He who has forsaken all desires, he alone is truly wise). At another place (2.37), however, Arjun is exhorted to indulge in action (war) not with the attitude of one who has forsaken all desires but with the prospect of very real reward: *"Hato va prapsyasi swargam jitva wa bhokshyase mahim/Tasmaduttishthha Kaunteya yuddhaya krittanischayah"* (O Son of Kunti, if you die you will gain heaven; if you win, you will gain a kingdom. You have gain on both sides; hence get up and fight).

CRUSADE (JIHAD)

The simple-minded version of hindutva being currently popularised and politicised ignores such dialectics and complexities. Indeed, as it abuses religion by turning it into a self-righteous crusade, it even ignores the call of Krishna himself recorded in the Gita (18.66), *"Sarvadhaman paritajya mamekam sharanam vraja/Aham tvam sarvapapebhyah mokshavishyami ma shuchah"* (Give up all religion and come to me; I will free you from all your sins). Those who create armies of vandals to fight in the name of a created, constructed and politically contrived dharma obviously have nothing to do with the call to abjure all religion and seek spiritual solace.

The self-appointed soldiers of political hindutva, led by the mendicants who constitute the bazzar clergy, have little realisation and no appreciation of the syncretism of Indian cultural tradition and even of its religious discourse. They fail to catch the echo of *"Buddham sharanam aagachha" in the Gita's "Mamekam sharanam vraja" (Come into my shelter)*. They do not notice the integration of the pre-Vedic Mother Goddess cults into the post-Vedic Hinduism in, for instance, the Durga Saptashati. Even in contemporary and popular Ram worship, they ignore the use of Akbar-esque charactristics of Jharokha darshan, for instance, bestowed by Tulasidas himself on Ram : "Ram jharokhe baith kar sabka muzara leit."

POLITICAL MAXIM

The reduction of philosophy to religion and of religion from the abstract nirgun (formless) to the concrete sagun (with human characteristics) and of even sagun to an uniform moort (iconistic) does not derive from the cultural traditions of India. Indeed, it would not be wrong to say that the vandalism perpetrated at Ayodhya has nothing to do with either culture or civilisation. It models itself only on the political maxim of the Mahabharat *"Anyo dharmah samarthanam birbalanantu chaparah"* (There are separate dharmas for the powerful and the weak) and ignores the teaching ofVyas, the compiler of the Mahabharat: *"Ashtadash puraneshu Vyasasya Vachandwayam/Paropkarah punyay, papay parapidanam"* (There are only two truths in the 18 Puranas : helping others brings merit and hurting others is sinful."

Those who have made it a deliberate political policy to grab power by hurting others, indeed by creating "the other" among Indians, have not only gone against the Constitution and rule of law but also against religion. They have glorified an unfair version of a weak, deceitful and cowardly Ram whom Bali ruefully reproached : *"Dharam hetu avatareu gosain/Marehu mohi vyadh kenain"* (you, who had come for the cause of righeousness, ended up killing me like a cruel, cunning and unfair hunter who hurled weapons while hidden from view)". Even today, vyadhs continue to hit at the vulnerable from behind the smokescreen of dharma.

Writer's paper on Hindutva and Hinduism by Courtesy Times of India, Dec. 28, 1992 with gratitude.

6

INDIAN CULTURE AND COUNTRY
(भारतीय संस्कृति में राष्ट्र बोध)

Vivekanand Kendra Madras

The most important characteristic of a vital culture is a common outlook among people which when faced with difficulty, resistance or adversity generates a collective will to action. That is why संस्कृति is defined as संइति एकीभूय कृति: संधश:–राष्ट्रश: कृति: In other words, the vitality of a culture can be measured by the capacity of the dominant minority. However, they alone cannot help, if the collective will to resist adverse circumstances is weak. In that case, culture becomes decadent and the people begin to disintegrate.

An extraordinary phenomenon has occurred in the world during recent times illustrating the virility and strength of vital culture. Before World War II, Jews lived in many countries all over the world in ghettos and in concentration camps and had, for centuries, been subjected to inhuman persecution and sometimes to mass murders. During world War II, sixty lakhs of Jews were put to death in Nazi camps. In spite of this savage persecution and mass liquidation they had built their life on common traditions and vivid memories of achievements of their ancestors glorified in the Old Testament.

Impelled by a collective will to action these Jews migrated from 73 countries to Palestine. Inspired by the vivid memory of the 'promised land' given to them by Jehova, three thousand years ago, these men and women–barely a million–worked, suffered, fought and died to build a new Israel, They converted deserts and swamps into a land of trees, flowers and farms and, by rare heroism, developed extraordinary defensive might and that is why we say Ben Gurion,

Golda Meir and Moshe Dayan are heroes not of Israel alone but of the entire humanity.

This provides the most brilliant example in history of the collective will generated by a common tradition and a common memory of achievements, ancient though they have been.

ROLE OF DOMINENT MINORITY

With the passage of time and environmental changes, civilization alters its content, and fermentation continues. As a result, culture is subject to pressure and a new crisis develops. When this occurs the best among the society-the dominant minority-face a new responsibility. They have to accept the challenge, adjust their outlook to it and modify their norms of conduct and basic institutions. However, they have to keep in mind basic fundamental values of their own culture.

Every generation will have to differentiate between the eternal and the changeable between श्रुति and स्मृति, Whatever is good should be preserved, whatever is bad should be discarded. Krishna says in the Gita, "Whenever Dharma declines, I reincarnate myself". However, a new incarnation of God will not reset the old order. Re-establishment of Dharma means-the same life principles will be observed but its expressions and manifestations may change.

The earlier man used to worship Indra, Varuna and Agni. Then came the worship of Shiva and Vishnu, followed by the worship of Panchayatan. As time passes, such changes are bound to take place. At the same time there will be superstitions and wrong notions which should be rejected. Even in America there was a famous Court case- "1925 case that rocked the world" about teaching the theory of evolution in contravention of the theory propounded by the Bible; but Americans have not thrown the Bible out.

Untouchability is another unfortunate aspect of our society for which we should lower our head in shame. It was never there. It gate-crashed through sacerdotalism or Brahmanism. Now it has to be jettisoned lock, stock and barrel as it has affected the basic structure of our society. Abraham Lincoln who abolished slavery in America used to say, "if slavery is not wrong then nothing is wrong'. In the same way we must declare that 'If untouchability is not wrong then nothing is wrong in this world."

This is possible only if the dominant minority in the culture group plays its part. In politics, the vote of an illiterate is as good as the vote of a literate and wise man. However, in human affairs, it is the thinking of the active minority which Toynbee calls the 'Dominant Minority' that counts. It alone can develop inspiration and courage in society provided it can renew and modify itself to respond to emerging challenges.[1]

The vitality of a culture lasts only as long as best men (the dominant minority) find self-fulfilment by living up to its fundamental values. These values cannot be handed down from father to son like a legacy. Every generation must recapture them afresh by trying to live up to them after due discrimination and evaluation.

Swami vivekananda used to say that the future should be in accordance with the past. The Ganges is flowing; you cannot reverse it; you can only divert it. So culture too should be adjusted as per the needs of the age.

The values of culture are recaptured by each generation by a subtle process of reinterpretation, reintegration and adaptation. When the culture is living, the promising young men and women of the generation receive the impact of its fundamental values. The sensitive and vigorous among them become a human laboratory, which purifies the fundamental values and relates them afresh to the central idea.

This central idea drives the stream of culture forward between the banks of time, changing its course, throwing up formations, leaving behind weeds, meandering or roaring according to the conditions imposed by the pressure and material equipment of each segment of time. When conditions change, new crests of waves ar formed. But in their essential unity, their characteristic elements and their directions remain the same. In the Gita we say:

आपूर्यमाणम् अचलप्रतिष्ठं
समुद्रम् आप: प्रविशन्ति यद्वत्।

All rivers flow into the ocean which is full and remains unmoved; the same is the case with culture. In spite of changes in civilization and fermentations, culture remains intact.

REASONS FOR THE DECAY OF CULTURE

When the central idea driving and inspiring the way of life ceases to exist, a culture dies along with its adherents.

The culture of Greece died the day the representatives of Greece faild to find fulfilment in living up to its values. The same was the case with Ancient Rome. Its culture died when its society was overwhelmed by the presence of foreign slaves and mercenaries from Gaul and Germany and the best among the Roman youths ceased to worry about the values cherished by their ancestors which had made Rome the Master of the World. Today there are manyAfrican countries but they do not have an African culture.

Kulapati K.M. Munshi writes, surcharged with emotion, in one of his books 'Suppose a time comes in India-God forbid-when our young men and women lose the values and ideals of our culture, our culture would become dead. Then they may become civilized barbarians or second class Westerners but they can never be the torch-bearers of a living Indian culture for the age in which they live or for the future.

NATIONAL PRIDE

Hence an organisation like the Vivekananda Kendra has to play an active role. It is our duty to preserve our ancient heritage, to imbibe good values in our day-to-day life by setting goods examples, to mould Society and especially its dominant minority. Every family has its tradition. The same is the case with a nation. Every nation has its own character. Swami Vivekananda, in his very first public speech soon after arriving in India said, 'Each nation has a destiny to fulfl, each nation has a message to deliver, each nation has a mission to accomplish. Therefore, from the very start, we have to understand the mission of our race, the destiny it has to shape, the place it has to occupy in the March of Nations, the note it has to contribute to the harmony of races.'

So, for understanding our mission, we must identify the foundations upon which our nation has been built, its culture and the salient features thereof.

FACETS OF INDIAN CULTURE

1. Philosophical Outlook

A tree must love the ground on which it stands. This is the land where, like tidal waves, spirituality and philosophy have, again and again, rushed out and deluged the world.

Swami Vivekananda says: "The Indian Nation cannot be killed. Deathless it stands and it will stand so long as that spirit shall remain as the background, so long as her people do not give up her spirituality. Beggars they may remain, poor and poverty-stricken, dirt and squalor may surround them but let them not given up their God, let them not forget that they are children of sages."

This is the theme of Indian life–work, the burden of her eternal song, the backbone of her existence, the foundation of her being, the raison d'etre of her very survival-the spiritualization of the human race.

Perhaps for this reason, Mahatma Gandhi once said: 'I cling to India like a child to its mother's breast because I feel that she gives me the spiritual nourishment that I need."

Our outlooke is deeply ingrained in the Vedic expression "Tat Twam Asi"-That art thou, connection between जीवात्मा and परमात्मा between the individual soul and the universal soul.

We firmly believe in the Vedantic concept 'Each soul is potentially divine ......'We consider ourselves as अमृतस्य पुत्रा: Sparks of the Divine. Each seed is potentially a fruit. So our aim in life is to bcome a man, a better man, a superman, a divine man, a God-man and ultimately to become God–the concept of अहं ब्रह्मास्मि।

This concept of divinity of the soul is the cardinal article of faith. For us the individual is not just an insignificant unit in a larger whole. This is in total contrast to the communist or capitalist thinking of the Economic man or the Abstract man.[2]

This faith helped a Saint in replying to Alexander when he treatened to kill him.

नैनं छिन्दन्ति शास्त्राणि नैनं दहति पावक:।
न चैनंक्लेदयन्त्यापो न शोषयति मारुत:।।2/23

No weapon can cut this soul, nor any fire can burn it, no water can make it wet and no wind can dry it.

We believe in the theory of rebirth-the Karma theory which gives us tremendous confidence. That is why death is a festival of liberation for us.

The 'I' in me being the same as the 'I' in other beings makes me react to the joys and sorrows of my fellow-beings just as I react to my own. This genuine feeling of identity born out of the community of the inner entity is the real driving force behind our natural urge for human unity and brotherhood.

2. Tradition of Tolerance

The outstanding fact about India is its tradition of tolerance. Many Jews driven from their Holy Land, after the destruction of their temple, found an asylum in India and still live here as a community hardly touched by the troubles through which Jewery elsewhere has been passing. Christian communities were flourishing in India in the 2nd century. A.D. and their descendants are living today in the same areas. The Zoroastrians, that is, the Parsis, driven out of their homeland by the sudden impact of Islam found a sanctuary in India and today, though small in number, about one lakh, have made an impact on India's life.

The name of the Holy Book of the Parsis is Khurd Avestha. Khurd means incomplete. Incomplete because they had to run away against the onslaught of Islam. There is a very interesting story about their migration. When they came to India, they reached Gujarat. The King of Sanjan (near Surat) Raja Udaysingh, sent one full cup of milk through his Pradhan, indicating to the Parsis that they were over populated and so there was no place for the migrants. The clever but intelligent Parsis put a spoon of sugar in the cup indicating that they will merge themselves totally in India and will add to the glories of the Nation. Indeed, they have fulfilled their promise! If we go through the annals of the Freedom Movement in India, we will come across the names of towering giants like Dadabhai Naoroji, Madam Cama, Pherozeshah Mehta and others. Even today we find towering giants amongst the Parsis such as J.R.D. Tata, Nani Palkhiwala, Godrej, Field Marshal Sam Manekshaw, the late Homi Bhabha, Sohrab Modi, etc.

All religions have a place in India including Islam professed by about twelve crores of Muslims. India has successfully upheld her tradition of religious and social tolerance by declaring herself a secular, domocratic Republic.

The tradition of tolerance is not an attitude of indifference to others. It is a fundamental postulate of Hindu thought that every way of life has its own contribution to make to human welfare.

एकम् सद् विप्रा बहुधा वदंति।।
आकाशात् पतितं तोयं यथा गच्छति सागरं
सर्व देव नमस्कारं केशवं प्रति गच्छति।।2।।

Ways of worship are different but the ultimate reality is one; Krishna says in the Gita:

ये यथा माम् प्रपद्यंते तामस्तथैव भजाम्यहम्।4/11।

He proclaims a doctrine, which is fundamental to all Hindu thought. For us, Religion is not a matter of exclusive dogma. We give respect to the faith and benefit of others. We are firm in our faith: but are prepared to approach other faiths with an open mind.

Owing to this approach, we are reinterpreting our own doctrines and doing readjustments. For example, we have absorbed Buddhism, though the religion of Buddha vanished from India, a thousand years ago. Its teachings are closely interwoven with Hinduism.

3. Sense of Synthesis

India is something like a subcontinent; but, there exists a unity because of the sense of synthesis. In spite of 'variations in dress, systems, attitudes, customs, rituals, due to our unique culture, we are bound to one another.' The life–long dream of every Indian is to visit Rameshwaram in the South and Banaras in the North. Every Indian wants to take a dip in the Ganga at Banaras and wants to bring the water from the Ganga to the South to perform Abhisehkha to Lord Ramanatha at Rameshwaram. Such rituals help in binding the people together.

Our concept of the joint family is a unique contribution in the history of mankind. Generation after generation we have developed it. At the time of the death anniversary श्राद्ध we start with जंबुद्विपे-भारतवर्षे गंगातीरे...... By this the entire lineage is maintained.

The synthesis of the Aryan and Dravidin cultures is the basis of Hindu civilization. The development of Indian art also bears witness to this great process. The Mauryan art was undoubtedly influenced by Greek culture. Indian painters mastered the paintings of the Persians and a new Indo-Persian school of paintings known as the Moghul paintings, enriched the artistic tradition of India. A similar process of assimilation and synthesis is taking place in every sphere of artistic activity.

A unique example of this genius for synthesis is Mahatma Gandhi, his theory of 'Ahimas' or 'Non-violence'.

It is the central doctrine of Buddhism and Jainism and is also the accepted creed of the Vaishnavas–वैष्णव जन तो तेने रे कहिये। जो पीड़ पराई जाणे रे। However, Gandhi came to the realisation of this essentially Indian doctrine through Thoreau and other Western thinkers and was confirmed in his faith by Christ's Sermon on the Mount. Even many Muslims claim that Islam profoundly influenced Gandhiji's faith. However, Gandhi claimed himself to be an orthodox Hindu and died with the words 'Hey Ram' on his lips. Gandhiji rightly used to define Hinduism as 'Relentless pursuit of truth' ...... Denial of God we have known. Denial of Truth we have not known Perhaps for this reason Shri Ram Manohar Lohia coined the word 'साथी' Saathi for comrade, हम सब साथी हैं-हम् सत् ढूंढने निकले हैं।

In fact, the essence of Vedanta is nothing but a search for this truth. सत्यमेव जयते Truth alone triumphs. Truth is the ideal of our culture.

We never thought of erecting a Berlin wall between us and others. Only diffident people are afraid of the contacts and the thoughts of others and put up a wall around themselves. The greatness of any system is established only when it can hold its head high even while it is in contact with others.

This search for truth makes India the ideal meeting ground for East and West-historically well qualified and spiritually supreme. The rapid transformation of India's economy, no less than of her social structure, also provides unmistakable evidence of the vitality of this movement for the mingiing of the East and the West and the evolution of a new society based on the synthesis of the best in Europe and of the best in Asia.

4. Social Outlook

A significant speciality of our culture is its revolutionary social outlook. It reflects in the very defintion of Dharma.

धारणात् धर्मं इत्याहुः धर्मं धारयति प्रजाः॥1॥

Dharma is the one which holds together the entire Society. This is called Dharana of Dharma.

यतो बुद्धयाः निश्रेयस सिद्धि सा धर्माः॥2॥

i.e., Material welfare along with Spiritual Bliss. This is called Sadhana of Dharma.

The interpretations of the term Dharma given by Western scholars are too narrow and inadequate. The term dharma has a connottion wider than the notions of law, customs, morality, religion, duty, righteous conduct–It is the ultimate source of all values of human society.

We do not talk of मोक्ष alone. Along with it, we have three Purusharthas धर्म, अर्थ व काम Westerners talk of सन्यासाश्रम to show that we are other worldly. No. सन्यास comes only after the completion of the first three Ashramas ब्रह्मचर्य, गृहस्थाश्रम व वानप्रस्थाश्रम।

Sensual enjoyments were allowed. Earning money was not a taboo. In fact ours was the richest country up to the 17th century. Maurya's period was considered to be a golden peiod. English historians are never tired of telling stories of Mohd. Ghazni's loot and plunder and there is a reference to an underground treasure house, measuring 1.5 lakh cubic-feet full of Gold and Silver during Shahjahan's period.

Indians also carried out a highly sophisticated enquiry into sex relations. Vatsayana was the first commentator. It is a tribute to the glory of the Body-synthesis of the sensual with the spiritual.

Westrners say we were conservative. No! Ours was the most liberal society–Women enjoyed all rights. They were equal to men. Ladies like Gargi and Maitreyi made wonderful contributions to our culture.

With all the richness and liberal outlook, economic and social equality was, and is, the burden of our song, right from the Vedic period.

ईशा वास्यनिदं सर्वं यत्किच जगत्यां जगत्।
तेन त्यक्तेन भुंजीथा मा गृधःकस्य स्विदधनम्।।1।।

Everything animate or inanimate that is within the universe is controlled and owned by the Lord. One should therefore accept only those things necessary for himself which are set aside as his quota and one must not accept other things, knowing well to whom they belong.

The same thought is expressed in the Tulasi Ramayana, the Bhagawad Gita and by Shankaracharya, Kabir, etc.

(2) सबैभूमि गोपाल की। सम्पत्ति सब रघुपति के आहीं (रामायण)।

(3) स्तेन एव सः। –गीता
(One who does not distribute wealth is a thief.)

(4) पानी बाढ़ो नाव में, घर में बाढ़ो दाम।
दोनों हाथ उलीचियो, यही सयानो काम।। – कबीर

5. Scientific Outlook

A major aspect of our culture is its open attitude towards science. Westerners feel that Indians look upon the world as 'Maya'-i.e., illusion and therefore, they are not concerned with the facts of the material world. However this word 'Maya' is grossly distorted.

The reason for the scientific outlook is the enquiring mind. Nachiketa symbolises this mind. The entire Vedanta is a search for truth.

6. Love towards Nature

We consider ourselves as sons of Mother Earth.

माता भूमीः पुत्रोहम् पृथ्वीव्याः

Naturally we start of our day before getting up from the bed by praying .... and chanting.

गंगेच यमुने चैव गोदावरि सरस्वति
नर्मदे सिंधु कावेरि जलेस्मिन् सन्निधिं कुरु।

We call our rivers by suffix ekrk&xaxk ekrk] xks ekrk (our love for animals) etc.

The Advaitic outlook "living in time with Nature" is nothing but spiritualisation of Science and Technology. It may be termed as Ecological Yoga.

7. Role of Sanskrit

संस्कृति संस्कृताश्रयाः

Our Culture and language (Sanskrit) go hand in hand. It is the mother of all languages of the world ...Max Muller says – "I opend my happiest hours in reading Vedantic books. They are like the light of the morning, like the pure air of the mountain. So pure so true."

8. Artistic heritage

The sense of beauty and power it conveys has placed Indian artistic heritage among the major cultural legacies of the world.[3]

9. Universal Outlook

Our culture is universal as it is based on Vedanta which is a Universal Religion. The way of life proposed by this culture is acceptable to entire mankind and can be briefly described by a few quotations from early Indian literature.

(a) एकम् सत् विप्राः बहुधा वदंति।
That which is, is one; wise men speak of it in many ways.

(b) May He direct our thoughts.

(c) We preach उपेक्षा, मुदिता, करुणा, मैत्री, Ignore evil, cultivate graciousness, develop universal love and do active good to all.

(d) Daily in the evening, we pray:
सर्वे भवन्तु सुखिनः सर्वे सन्तु निरामयाः

Let everyone be happy. Let everyone be free from all ills.

(e) The sentiments of Vedic prayers are echoed in the heart of every modern man. May he be an India, Russian, American or Chinese–of any caste, creed or religion.

He is asking the Almighty to lead him from the unreal to the real, from darkness to light from death to immortality.

असतोमा सद्गमय - तमसो मा ज्योतिर्गमय।

मृत्योर्मा अमृतम् गमय, ॐ शांतिः शांतिः शांतिः॥

This is our culture and our philosophy. In the world, we are not a good for nothing race. Arnold Toynbee says: 'The world is at the point of annihilation and only Indians can show the Path.'

NOTES

1. 'महाजनो येन गताः स पन्था' is the Indian version of this idea.
2. पाश्चात्य अर्थशास्त्र में 'आर्थिक मनुष्य' बाजार के कार्यकलापों में सुख पाने वाला एक जंतु मात्र होता है।
3. In each and every field of Art, – Architecture, Sculpture, Painting, Dance Drama and Music, we were the leaders.

(विवेकानंद केन्द्र प्रकाशन, मद्रास 1990 के सौजन्य से साभार)

7

राष्ट्रीयता तथा संगम संस्कृति

आचार्य राममूर्ति

राष्ट्रीयता को जन–आन्दोलन का विषय बनाया गाँधीजी ने। आजादी के बाद तक यह राष्ट्रीयता रही, जो गाँधीजी ने पैदा की थी। सन् 1950 में जब नया संविधान लागू हुआ 26 जनवरी को, तब उसमें एक नयी चीज जुड़ी–बालिग मताधिकार। कोई शर्त नहीं, जो भारत का नागरिक है, उसे वोट देने का अधिकार होगा! इतिहास में जो ज्यादा-से-ज्यादा साहस-भरे कदम बताये जा सकते हैं उनमें भारत के हर बालिग को वोट का अधिकार देना माना जायेगा। हजारों वर्षों की परम्पराओं से अलग जाकर संविधान सभा ने व्यक्ति की इस रूप में प्रतिष्ठा मान्य की। बड़ा साहसिक कदम था!

आज हर जाति, सम्प्रदाय अपनी संख्या गिनता है और उस संख्या के अनुसार सत्ता में अपनी भागीदारी-हिस्सेदारी का दावा करता है। संख्या की शक्ति लोगों के दिमागों में घुस गयी है।

अब सामान्य-से-सामान्य आदमी यह सवाल उठाता है, कभी उसको प्रकट करता है, कभी उसके मन में मन्थन होता है कि 'हमको वोट का अधिकार है, तो हमारा राष्ट्र कहाँ है? भूमिहीन पूछता है कि हमारे पास तो जमीन का एक टुकड़ा नहीं, भूखा आदमी पूछता है कि हमारा पेट खाली है तो हमारा राष्ट्र कहाँ है? इस सवाल का जबाव हम टाल नहीं सकते। जन-जन को यह बताना पड़ेगा कि तुम्हारा राष्ट्र यह है। वह राष्ट्र को अपनी जमीन, अपने दाल-भात और सबसे ज्यादा अपनी इज्जत के रूप में देखना चाहता है।

वोट राजनैतिक सम्मान का चिन्ह बन गया है। इससे बहुत कुछ खराब भी निकलता है, लेकिन जो बड़ी चीज निकलती है वह यह कि अब इज्जत की लड़ाई

लड़ी जायेगी और जीती जायेगी। हम इस लड़ाई में किस तरफ होंगे? हम इस लड़ाई में शरीक होंगे या नहीं? यह निर्णय का वक्त है कि आजादी के गर्भ से निकली हुई यह जो इज्जत की लड़ाई है, उसे हम अपनी लड़ाई मानते हैं या नहीं। इस लड़ाई के पीछे राष्ट्रीयता की एक नयी परिभाषा है। पुरानी परिभाषा से संतोष नहीं, इसलिए नयी परिभाषा की माँग है।

इस गोष्ठी के सामने यह प्रश्न है कि हमारी राष्ट्रीयता की परिभाषा क्या है? वह, जिससे 1883 में कांग्रेस शुरू हुई थी, या वह, जिससे 1920-21 का असहयोग आन्दोलन शुरू हुआ था, या वह, जिससे 1947 में आजादी मिली थी, या वह जिसका बीज हमारे संविधान ने बोया था? और उस परिभाषा के परिणामों को झेलने के लिए हम कहाँ तक तैयार हैं?

राष्ट्रीयता एक भावना है। अब अगर हमारे करोड़ों भाई-बहन कहते हैं कि हम तुम्हारी इस भावना में शरीक नहीं है तो हमें यह मान लेना चाहिए कि वह भावना कमजोर पड़ गयी है।

आज भारतीय जनता पार्टी ने एक नया रूख अपनाया है राष्ट्रीयता के प्रति। कहते हैं कि मीनाक्षीपुरम् ने हमारी आँखें खोल दीं। यदि इसी तरह हिन्दू मुसलमान होते चले जायेगे तो एक वक्त ऐसा आयेगा जब हिन्दू अल्पमत में हो जायेगा और मुसलमान बहुमत में हो जायेगा। जिस 'सेकुलरिज्म' (धर्मनिरपेक्षता) की आड़ में हिन्दू मुसलमान बनता चला जाय, वह 'सेकुलरिज्म' हमको नहीं चाहिए। यह नकली 'सेकुलरिज्म' है। भारतीय जनता पार्टी के लोग कहते हैं कि इतने प्रबल बहुमत में हिन्दू समुदाय जिस देश में है, उस देश की राष्ट्रीयता हिन्दू राष्ट्रीयता होगी। यदि बहुमत पार्टी की हुकूमत होती है तो बहुसंख्यक की राष्ट्रीयता क्यों नहीं होगी?

हमने तो भारत की संगम संस्कृति की बात कही थी, आज हमसे कहा जा रहा है कि नहीं, हिन्दू राष्ट्रीयता, हिन्दू संस्कृति!

आदिवासी संस्कृति, आर्यों की संस्कृति, शकों, कुषाणों, हुणों की संस्कृति, मुसलमानों, ईसाईयों की संस्कृति-इतनी धाराओं की मिली-जुली संस्कृति, जिसे हमने संगम संस्कृति के रूप में देखा था, वह थी भारतीय संस्कृति। गाँधीजी ने तो यहाँ तक कह दिया कि मैं अच्छा हिन्दू हूँ इसलिए अच्छा मुसलमान हूँ। आज तो इसको न हिन्दू मानने को तैयार होगा, न मुसलमान।

हमने जीवों की एकता, सारी सृष्टि की एकता में विश्वास किया था, एक-एक प्राणी के भीतर राम का दर्शन किया था, ऐसी एकता हमारे अध्यात्म का आधार थी। आज उन सारे आधारों को अस्वीकारा जा रहा है और कहा जा रहा

है कि जो हिन्दुस्तान में हैं, वे सब हिन्दू हैं। हिन्दू की परिभाषा व्यापक की जा रही है, भारतीय की व्यापक परिभाषा छोड़ी जा रही है।

दो सबसे बुनियादी शब्द, जिन शब्दों के आधार पर स्वतंत्र भारत की रचना की गयी थी–समाजवाद और धर्मनिरपेक्षता, इन दोनों की पुरानी परिभाषाएँ अब काम नहीं दे रही है। ये दोनों आधार ढह गये। अब किन आधारों पर राष्ट्रीयता की रचना होगी?

42-43 वर्षों में हम देख रहे हैं कि इस देश में एक दीवाल खड़ी हो गयी है, देश दो टुकड़ों में बँट गया है। एक तरफ 20 करोड़ लोग हैं, दूसरी तरफ 65 करोड़। ये 20 करोड़ लोग सम्पन्न हैं और ये 65 करोड़ लोग विपन्न हैं। एक अमीरों का भारत है, एक गरीबों का भारत है। शिक्षा तक में अमीरों का स्कूल अलग, गरीबों का अलग! अब समाजवाद को माननेवाला आदमी ढूँढता है कि भाई, सम्पन्न और विपन्न के बीच यह दीवाल तो ऊँची होती जा रही है, समाजवाद कहाँ है?

आज हमारी राजनीति कहाँ पहुँची है और क्या है उसकी माँग, उसकी पुकार? कितनी राजनीतिक धाराएँ आज काम कर रही हैं? कांग्रेस (आई) है, भाजपा है, राष्ट्रीय मोर्चा-वाम मोर्चा है। इन सबकी राष्ट्रीयता प्रिय है, धर्मनिरपेक्षता प्रिय है, समाजवाद प्रिय है। इन बुनियादी चीजों से किसी एक को इन्कार नहीं है, फिर भी वोटर के सामने एक दूसरे से बिल्कुल अलग दिखाई दे रहे हैं, भारत की राजनीति में अलग-अलग दिशाएँ बनती जा रही हैं।

कांग्रेस (आई) कहती है परिवर्तन से पहले स्थायित्व। परिवर्तन के सन्दर्भ में स्थायित्व का अर्थ होता है परिस्थिति में कोई परिवर्तन नहीं। जैसे डाक्टर कहता है कि मरीज का दिल इतना नाजुक हो गया है कि इसे हिलाइये-डुलाइये मत, इससे बोलिये मत, चुपचाप लेटा रहने दीजिए, नहीं तो इसके ह्रदयगति रूक जायेगी। पूर्ण स्थायित्व रहने दीजिए, कोई परिवर्तन नहीं!

दूसरे दोनों राजनैतिक संगठन–भाजपा और मार्चे के लोग कह रहे हैं कि परिवर्तन एकता की शर्त्त है। दिल इसलिए कमजोर हुआ है कि यह मरीज टहला नहीं, दौड़ा नहीं, परिवर्तन नहीं हुए। अब भाजपा चाहती है परिवर्तन हिन्दुत्व की दिशा में, और राष्ट्रीयता मोर्चा-वाम मोर्चा गठबंधन चाहता है सामाजिक न्याय की दिशा में। हिन्दुत्व के क्या राजनीतिक फलितार्थ हैं, आयाम हैं, और क्या हैं, सामाजिक न्याय के, यह बात समझने की है।

हिन्दू संस्कृति है, इस्लामी संस्कृति है, ईसाई संस्कृति है, आदिवासी संस्कृति है, इन सब संस्कृतियों का अलग-अलग अस्तित्व है, इनमें कोई मेल ही नहीं है,

कोई आदान-प्रदान ही नहीं है इन संस्कृतियों में, कोई संगम नहीं है इन संस्कृतियों का, तो भारत की एकता को कायम रहने का दूसरा क्या आधार है? क्यों भारत की एकता कायम रहे और कैसे रहे?

भारत के लिए यह कहा गया था कि यह देश अपनी संस्कृति के कारण दुनिया को एक संदेश दे सकता है, वह संस्कृति-संगम संस्कृति-नहीं रह जायेगी तो देश एक नहीं रह जायेगा। टुकड़ों में बँटकर देश की क्या दुर्दशा होगी, किस शक्ति के चंगुल में हम पड़ जायेंगे, मालूम नहीं।

देशवासी दो भागों में बँटते चले जायँ-अमीर का भारत एक, गरीब का भारत दूसरा, 20 करोड़ का भारत एक, 65 करोड़ का भारत दूसरा, तो देश कब तक एक रहेगा? एक भयंकर द्वन्द्व की स्थिति है। खतरनाक स्थिति है। इस खतरे को गाँधीजी ने देखा था, बिनोवाजी ने देखा था, जयप्रकाशजी ने देखा था। दुःख है कि जवाहरलालजी ने नहीं देखा। सबसे बड़ा जो खतरा अन्दर-अन्दर पैदा हो रहा था भारत की एकता, अखण्डता, स्वतंत्रता के लिए, उसको नेहरूजी ने नहीं देखा। इसलिए नेहरू परम्परा में काम करनेवाली राजनीति इस खतरे के प्रति उतनी सचेष्ट नहीं है, जितनी उस परम्परा से हटी हुई राजनीति सचेष्ट है। वह इन खतरों को देख रही है, इसीलिए यह माँग कर रही है कि संघीय व्यवस्था में परिवर्तन होना चाहिए, राज्यों का अधिकार मिलने चाहिए, विकेन्द्रीकरण होना चाहिए, अर्थनीति क्री बुनियादें बदलनी चाहिए, विकास की दिशा बदलनी चाहिए।

समय आ गया है कि बुनियादी आधारों को नयी परिभाषाएँ बनायी जायँ। यह जरूरी है, लेकिन इतना ही काफी नहीं है। राष्ट्र की एकता की रक्षा के लिए आज उसी तरह त्याग-तपस्या की जरूरत आ पड़ी है जिस तरह किसी वक्त आजादी के लिए थी।

स्वैच्छिक संगठनों, रचनात्मक कार्यकर्ता साथियों की समझ में अभी तक यह बात क्यों नहीं आयी कि देश का सबसे बड़ा प्रश्न है राष्ट्र की एकता? अगर राष्ट्र नहीं तो रचना किसकी? अगर एकता नहीं तो दूसरा कार्य क्या?

ऐसे लोग होंगे जो यह मानते हैं कि क्या राष्ट्र की एकता की बात करते हो? आगे आने वाली दुनिया में विश्व-नागरिकता होगी। यह देश और राष्ट्र की बातें पुरानी हैं।

हो सकता है मेरा संस्कार उस जमाने का हो, जब राष्ट्रीयता से बड़ा धर्म नहीं था, राष्ट्र से बड़ा कोई देखता नहीं था। लेकिन उस भावना को जाने दीजिए, आज की राजनैतिक वास्तविकता तो यह है कि दुनिया देशों में बँटी हुई है और दुनिया के लोग राष्ट्रों में जी रहें हैं। आगे कभी आयेगा वह जमाना, जब राष्ट्र की सीमाएँ

नहीं रह जायेंगी, लेकिन अभी तो राष्ट्र की सीमाएँ हैं इसलिए राष्ट्र को ही सामने रखकर हमको अपनी परिभाषाएँ बनानी है, अपने कार्यक्रम तय करने हैं।

हमलोग, जो राजनीति से अलग रहने को ही अपना धर्म मानते आये, नहीं पड़े राजनीति के पचड़े में, यह माना की राष्ट्र की चिन्ता राज्य की चिन्ता, देश की चिन्ता, सेवक की चिन्ता! चिन्ताओं को भी हमने अलग-अलग बाँट दिया। अब वक्त आ गया यह तय करने का कि इसी बँटवारे को मानकर हम काम करेंगे या यह मानेंगे कि देश और राष्ट्र दोनों एक हैं, एक रहने चाहिए?

राष्ट्र की रक्षा के लिए राजनैतिक दलों की राजनीतिक क्रिया ही काफी नहीं है। दलीय राजनीतिक एकता को भी दलीय प्रश्न बना देती है। किसी राष्ट्र की एकता किसी एक दल का प्रश्न नहीं हैं पूरे देश का प्रश्न है।

हमलोग, जो यहाँ बैठे हैं, किसी दल से बँधे नहीं हैं। हम दल को मानते भी हैं तो देश को दल से ऊपर रखते हैं। यह हमारी मूल निष्ठा है। हम इस संकट का मुकाबिला किस तरह करना चाहते हैं?

दलीय राजनीति सत्ता की राजनीति है और सत्ता की शक्ति शस्त्र में है। सत्ता राष्ट्र की रक्षा करेगी सेना की मदद से, शस्त्र की शक्ति से। लेकिन अब शस्त्र की शक्ति किसी भी राष्ट्र की एकता की रक्षा करने में अक्षम सिद्ध हो रही है। भारत सरकार के पास मामूली शस्त्र शक्ति नहीं है, लेकिन कश्मीर में, पंजाब में, असम में क्यों नहीं बात बनती?

भारत की राष्ट्रीय एकता के लिए गैर-दलीय राजनीतिक क्रिया की जरूरत है, दलों के दायरे से बाहर जो राजनीतिक क्रिया हो सकती है उसकी। केवल राज्यशक्ति के भरोसे, शस्त्र शक्ति के भरोसे हम अपने देश की रक्षा नहीं कर पायेंगे। हम गाँधी का वह वाक्य याद नहीं रख पायें जो उन्होंने, जहाँ तक मुझे याद है, चेम्सफर्ड के सामने कहा था। चेम्सफर्ड वायसराय था भारत का, उसने पूछा था, ''मिस्टर गाँधी ह्वाई आर यू इन पालिटिक्स? आप तो महात्मा हैं, धर्म को माननेवाले हैं, आप राजनीति में कैसे दिखाई दे रहे हैं।' गाँधीजी का उत्तर था, 'आई ऐम इन पालिटिक्स बिकाज आई ऐम इन रिलीजन। (मैं राजनीति में हूँ क्योंकि मैं धर्म में हूँ) राम ने जब धनुष उठाया था, तो वह उनकी तबकी राजनीतिक क्रिया थी, कृष्ण ने जब सुदर्शन चक्र उठाया था, तब भी वह उस समय की परिस्थिति में राजनीतिक क्रिया थी। हमें गम्भीरता से सोचना पड़ेगा कि देश की रक्षा के लिए हमारे हिस्से कौन-सी राजनीतिक क्रिया है। हम इससे बच नहीं सकते।

राजनीतिक क्रिया हमारी शुरू होती है नयी परिभाषाओं की रचना से। क्योंकि आज की व्यवस्था जिन विश्वासों पर टिकी हुई है, उन विश्वासों को बदलने की जरूरत है। जयप्रकाशजी ने कहा था कि सम्पूर्ण क्रान्ति में शिक्षण पहला कार्यक्रम है। उस शिक्षण का अर्थ यह था कि जिस व्यवस्था से संघर्ष करने निकले हो वह व्यवस्था जिन विश्वासों पर टिकी हुई है, उन विश्वासों को ध्वस्त करना पहला काम है। यह हमारे लोग-शिक्षण का अर्थ है।

राष्ट्र की रक्षा केन्द्र से ही नहीं होगी, गाँव-गाँव में बिखरा है। राष्ट्र इतिहास साक्षी है कि यहाँ केन्द्रित सत्ता कभी टिकाऊ हुई ही नहीं--न मौर्यों का साम्राज्य, न गुप्तों का साम्राज्य, न गुलामों का साम्राज्य, न खिलजियों का साम्राज्य, न तुगलकों का साम्राज्य, न मुगलों का साम्राज्य, न अंग्रेजों का साम्राज्य टिकाऊ रहा। सबसे ज्यादा टिकाऊ मुगलों का साम्राज्य था 1526 ई० से 1707 ई० तक। बस! अंग्रेजों का साम्राज्य तो सौ साल भी नहीं टिका, जिसकी अजेय शक्ति थी। इसलिए उसी पुरानी (साम्राज्यवादी) राष्ट्रीयता के आधार पर चलेंगे, जो राष्ट्रीयता एकता के लिए घातक सिद्ध हो रही है, तो राष्ट्र की रक्षा कैसे होगी?

हम इस राजनीतिक क्रिया में क्रान्ति की बात नहीं कर रहे हैं। हम तो न्याय की बात कह रहे हैं। आज के कानून, आज के संविधान में जो न्याय मान्य है, उसके आधार पर होगी राजनीतिक क्रिया। क्रान्ति के लिए होनेवाली राजनीतिक क्रिया अलग होगी। आज बात है न्याय की, कानून में जितनी समता मान्य है, उसकी। उसे लाने की राजनीतिक क्रिया होनी चाहिए।

संगम संस्कृति की ही बात लें। एक बार यदि हमने मान लिया कि भारत हिन्दू संस्कृति है, संगम संस्कृति नहीं, तो सम्प्रदायवाद का हम चाहे जितना विरोध करें, हम सम्प्रदायवाद को देश के जीवन से निकाल नहीं सकते। हर सम्प्रदाय की अपनी संस्कृति है और अगर वह दूसरी संस्कृतियों को अपनी विरोधी संस्कृति मान ले तो संस्कृतियों की यह लड़ाई राष्ट्र की एकता को टिकने नहीं देगी।

भारत की संस्कृति की विशेषता रही है कि न जाने कितने प्रभाव, कितने प्रभाव इसमें आकर मिले हैं, लेकिन उसका नाम है भारतीय संस्कृति, इरानी संस्कृति, अरबी संस्कृति का नाम तो उसे नहीं दिया किसी ने!

आज विकेन्द्रीकरण की बात होती है। विकेन्द्रीकरण से अच्छा शब्द है संसदीय स्वराज्य। गाँधीजी से पूछा गया था कि क्या अंग्रेजों के जाने के बाद आप भारत में हिन्द स्वराज्य की व्यवस्था लायेंगे? तो गाँधीजी ने कहा था कि 'नहीं', आजाद भारत संसदीय स्वराज्य की व्यवस्था कायम कर ले तो मुझे सन्तोष हो जायेगा।' क्या मतलब है संसदीय स्वराज्य का? स्थानीय जीवन में, गाँव, जिले में

–स्वायत्तता, केन्द्र में संसद। 90 प्रतिशत सवाल हल हो जायेंगे स्वायतता के क्षेत्र मे, 10 प्रतिशत बच जायेंगे संसद के लिए। दिल्ली तब दुश्मन की तरह दिखायी नहीं देगी। आज तो हर राज्य की लड़ाई दिल्ली से है। एक-एक समुदाय को दिल्ली दुश्मन की तरह दिखाई दे रही है। दिल्ली हमारी राजधानी, हमारी आजादी का केन्द्र और प्रतीक है, और वहीं देशवासियों की नजर में हमारी दुश्मन! तब दिल्ली के बल पर हम अपने देश की रक्षा कैसे कर सकते हैं?

जिस राजनीतिक क्रिया की बात हम कर रहे हैं, वह सहमति के बिन्दुओं पर होगी। राष्ट्रीय एकता पर क्या मतभेद है? यदि किसी को मतभेद है तो वह भारत के नमक के प्रति वफादार नहीं है। .... एकता, अस्मिता, नागरिक अधिकार, बुनियादी आवश्यकताओं की पूर्ति, यह सहमति के क्षेत्र हैं। .... कौन कहेगा कि सबकी आवश्यकताओं की पूर्ति नहीं होनी चाहिए? .... सम्प्रदायों के झगड़े हैं, जातियों के झगड़े हैं, अशान्ति है, उपद्रव है अराजकता की स्थिति है। सदियों से हम एक साथ रहते आये, एक सह-अस्तित्व था अस्मिताओं का, आज यह सह-अस्तित्व टूट रहा है, इसकी रक्षा क्या पुलिस करेगी? ये क्षेत्र हैं हमारी राजनीतिक क्रिया के।ख्र हमको ऐसी संघीय व्यवस्था नहीं चाहिए जो स्वायत्तता को छीन ले, हमको ऐसी राष्ट्रीयता नहीं चाहिए जो अस्मिताओं को मिटा दे।

राजनीतिक क्रिया शान्ति के लिए, निरोधक शान्ति के लिए, होनी चाहिए। राष्ट्र के प्रहरी तैयार हों, शान्ति के सिपाहियों का एक जाल बिछाया जाय अपने देश में। तनाव की स्थिति पैदा हो तो ये प्रहरी वहाँ पहुँच जायँ। 10 हरिजन जला दिये गये तो वहाँ पाँच सौ शान्ति-प्रहरी पहुँच जायँ जलने के लिए, तब राष्ट्र के जीवन में एक बिजली दौड़ जायेगी, जलानेवालों के हाथ रूक जायेंगे। सत्याग्रह का यही तो रास्ता है।

हमारी राजनीतिक क्रिया का ध्येय यह नहीं है कि सत्ता हमारे हाथ में आ जाय, हमारी राजनीतिक क्रिया का ध्येय यह है कि राज्य-शक्ति और लोक-शक्ति का मिलन-बिन्दु निकल आये। .... दलीय राजनीतिक क्रिया संसदीय मोर्चे पर, गैरदलीय राजनीतिक क्रिया लोक-पक्ष के मोर्चे पर!

हमारी राजनीतिक क्रिया का दायरा सहमति का है। सहमति का दायरा हमें राष्ट्रनीति की तरफ ले जाता है–राजनीति से आगे जाकर। इस भूमिका को लोगों के सामने प्रस्तुत करना है–शिक्षण, रचना, संगठन और संघर्ष के द्वारा। आज की व्यवस्था के साथ संघर्ष नहीं होगा, और परिवर्तन भी व्यवस्था में हो जायेगा, यह माननेवाला वास्तविकता को नहीं पहचानता। ख्र क्योंकि अत्यन्त गम्भीर, खतरनाक, द्वन्द्व की स्थिति आज पैदा हो गयी है, 20 प्रतिशत और 65 प्रतिशत के बीच।

लोकतन्त्र की प्रक्रियाओं द्वारा अगर इस द्वन्द्व का समाधान निकल आता है तो यह देश गृह-युद्ध से बच जायेगा।

राष्ट्र के जीवन में जितने द्वन्द्व के बिन्दु हैं उनको पहचान कर एक सम्पूर्ण कार्यक्रम बनाने की जरूरत है। अपने-अपने दायरों से बाहर निकलने की जरूरत है। हम भारतीय हैं और हर भारतीय से भारतीयता के नाते मिलना चाहते हैं और उसके साथ काम करना चाहते हैं भारत के लिए। इस व्यापक भूमिका में चिन्तन और चेष्टा का वक्त आया है।

राष्ट्रीय बिरादरी बुलेटिन-1, श्रमभारती संगोष्ठी, अप्रैल 1991 के सौजन्य से साभार

8

राष्ट्रीयता का संबंध देश से-धर्म से नहीं –एक विपरीत पथ

मौलाना वहीदुद्दीन खान

विभाजन ने मौलाना अबुल कलाम आजाद को गहरा आघात पहुँचाया था। उन्होंने सही कहा था कि यह फैसला दश के लिए घातक होगा और वह एक ऐसी बर्बादी के समान होगा जो सदैव के लिए भारत की इस नई आजादी को ग्रस लेगा।

यह विभाजन अवश्य ही उनके विवेक के प्रतिकूल हुआ था। चूंकि वह बतौर एक नेता मोहम्मद अली जिन्ना के सामने निस्तेज से हो गए थे। 1947 से पहले मुस्लिम मामलात में उनका कोई खास असर नहीं था। जब 1947 में तेजी से बदलती परिस्थितियों में वह एक बड़े नेता बन गए और सारी मुसलमान जनता मार्ग निर्देशन के लिए उनकी ओर देखने लगी, उस समय कहानी कुछ और ही होनी चाहिए थी लेकिन आजादी के पूर्व ऐसे सक्रिय नेता बाद में कुछ उदासीन से हो गए और अपने अनुगामियों का कोई स्पष्ट मार्ग निर्देशन करने में विफल रहे। विभाजन के बाद मौलाना 11 साल जिए पर वह अपने लोगों के सच्चे नेता हरगिज न बन सके। दो और प्रभावकारी नेता मौलाना हुसैन अहमद मदनी और मौलाना हिफजुर ओहारवी विभाजन के बाद 15 सालों तक जीवित रहे। इसमें कोई संदेह नहीं कि भारतीय मुसलमानों को सुरक्षा प्रदान करने में उन्होंने बड़ी महत्वपूर्ण भूमिका निभाई लेकिन बदले हुए समय में मुसलमानों को स्पष्ट व सकारात्मक नेतृत्व करने में वे भी नाकाम रहे। उदाहरण के तौर पर बंटवारे से पहले मौलाना अहमद मदनी, मौलाना अबुल कलाम आजाद, मौलाना हिफजुर रहमान तथा अन्य कई नेता यह मानते रहे कि किसी भी देश का आधार उसकी सीमाएं हैं, राष्ट्र एक

भूमि है, इसलिए हिन्दू व मुस्लिम दो राष्ट्र हैं, इस धारणावश अलगाववादी प्रवृति जोर पकड़ रही थी, पर उसे समाप्त करने के लिए इन लोगों ने कोई आंदोलन नहीं शुरू किया। उन्होंने मुसलमानों में यह भावना प्रबल करने की कोई चेष्टा नहीं की कि हालात बिल्कुल बदल जाने के कारण जो बड़ी अहम जिम्मेदारी सामने आ गई है, उसका वे भी हिस्सा हैं। यदि इन नेताओं ने इस काम को अंजाम दिया होता तो वे भारतीय मुसलमानों की विचारधारा को एक नई व सही दिशा दे सकते थे। इससे मुसलमान इस दश में अपनी मजहबी जिंदगी को एक स्वस्थ आधार देने के लिए जरूर तालमेल अवश्य बिठा देते।

मौलाना आजाद व अन्य नेताओं की इस निष्क्रियता का यही नतीजा हुआ कि बंटवारे के बाद के समय में भी मुस्लिम उसी विचारधारा पर चलते रहे जिसकी नींव जिन्ना ने रखी थी व शायर मोहम्मद इकबाल ने जिसका समर्थन किया था। बाद में ऐसे भी नेता उभरे जिनकी सोच अलग थी, पर वे कद में छोटे थे और वे जिन्ना-इकबाल विचारधारा से मुस्लिम सोच को मुक्त कराने में असमर्थ थे। ज्यादातर मुसलमान आज भी उसी विचारधारा से प्रभावित हैं।

जिन्ना की गलत सोच

जिन्ना और उन्हीं की तरह के मुस्लिम नेताओं ने अपने समर्थकों के मन में दो राष्ट्रों के सिद्धांत को इस प्रकार बिठा दिया था कि यह भावना स्थायी बन गई। इससे मुस्लिम हिन्दुओं से दूर हो गए। वे उसी वक्त हिन्दुओं के सम्पर्क में आए जब विरोध-प्रदर्शनों व अपनी मांगों के कारण हिन्दुओं से उनके संघर्ष की नौबत आ गई। अपने अवसरों को नकारने और अपनी समस्याओं को उजागर करने की मुस्लिम समुदाय को आदत-सी पड़ गई। उन्होंने केवल मांगें रखने के अलावा कोई भाषा नहीं सीखी। जिन्ना के गलत नेतृत्व के कारण ही मुसलमानों ने हिंदुओं को अलग राष्ट्र समझने की भूल की। 1947 के बाद भी सही नेतृत्व के अभाव में वे उन्हें अलग राष्ट्र मानते रहे। इसका कारण यह था कि जिन्ना ने उनके मन में यह कूट-कूट कर भर दिया था कि दो राष्ट्रों वाला भारत, दोनों के लिए एक धरती होने पर भी, कभी उनकी मातृभूमि नहीं हो सकता। मुसलमान कमोबश इसी ढर्रे पर सोचते रहे। उनके चेतन-अवचेतन मन में यह बात बैठ गई कि भारत उनका वास्तविक देश नहीं है। इस प्रकार अपने ही देश में मुसलमान मनोवैज्ञानिक रूप में बेघर हो गए। मेरे विचार में मुस्लिम नेतृत्व, चाहे वह मजहबी हो या उदारवादी, हर दृष्टिकोण से जिन्ना के ढंग को ही आगे बढ़ा रहा है। हर नेता दरअसल वह दोहरा रहा है जो जिन्ना पहले ही कह चुके हैं। इकबाल भी इसी विचारधारा के

थे। दोनों नेताओं में बस फर्क था तो केवल शब्दों का, मूल रूप से वे एक एक ही बात करते थे।

मुसलमान हिन्दुओं की तरह ही भारतीय

हमें यह याद रखना चाहिए कि बंटवारे के हादसे से कुछ साल पहले तक मुसलमान पिछले एक हजार सालों से भारत को अपना दश मानते आ रहे थे। शुरू में उनकी संख्या बहुत कम थी और आज बढ़कर 15-20 करोड़ हो गई है। ये मुसलमान कौन हैं? इनमें अधिकांश लोग पहले हिंदू थे और आज भी ये लोग (मुसलमान) उतने ही भारतीय हैं जितने कि हिंदू। पंडित जवाहर लाल नेहरू ने इस बात का अपनी पुस्तक 'डिस्कवरी ऑफ इंडिया' में स्पष्ट उल्लेख किया है। उन्होंने लिखा है कि पिछले एक हजार साल में हिंदुओं ने यह कभी नहीं कहा कि अकेले वही भारतीय हैं तथा मुसलमान भारतीय नहीं हैं। हिंदू मान्यता के अनुसार सभी धर्मों में सत्य निहित है, इसलिए जब कोई हिंदू मुसलमान बना तो उसने अपनी आस्था के अनुरूप एक को छोड़ कर दूसरा धर्म उसी सत्य को पाने के लिए अपनाया। वास्तव में चूंकि वंश परम्परा में वह भी उसी जाति से आया था, इसलिए उसकी भारतीयता पर उन्होंने कभी संदेह नहीं किया। 1940 में जब जिन्ना ने पहली बार अपनी दो राष्ट्रों की धारणा रखी थी, तब भारत के इतिहास में एक नया मोड़ आया। जिन्ना ने इस बात पर जोर दिया था कि राष्ट्रीयता का संबंध देश से नहीं धर्म से है और चूंकि हिंदू वह मुस्लिम अलग मजहबों के हैं इसलिए वे अलग राष्ट्र हैं। अपनी इस दो राष्ट्र वाली धरणा के आधार पर जिन्ना ने दोनों धर्मों के लिए अलग-अलग देशों की मांग रखी थी। जिन्ना के इस प्रचार की ही प्रतिक्रिया में हिंदूओं ने मुसलमानों को अपने से अलग मानना शुरू कर दिया था। कट्टरपंथी हिंदुओं ने अब भारत के प्रति मुसलमानों को विदेशी कहना शुरू कर दिया और यह नाम उनके साथ जुड़ ही गया। यहाँ तक कि एक मुस्लिम देश (पाकिस्तान) के खिलाफ युद्ध के दौरान बिग्रेडियर उस्मान व हवलदार अब्दुल हमीद की अद्भूत कुर्बानियां भी इस धारणा को मिटा नहीं सकी कि मुसलमान भारत के प्रति वफादार नहीं है। जिन्ना की सोच से उभरी यह धारणा उसके विपरीत एक बलशाली विचारधारा द्वारा ही मिटाई जा सकती थी लेकिन 1947 के बाद जिन्ना की विचारधारा को निरस्त करने में सक्षम कोई भी जोरदार बुद्धिजीवी आंदोलन नहीं उभर सका। भारत के लोगों का सदा ही यह विश्वास रहा है कि राष्ट्र का अर्थ मातृभूमि ही है, जो एक भूमि के हैं वे एक ही राष्ट्र के हैं लेकिन जिन्ना के दो राष्ट्रों वाले सिद्धांत के प्रभाव में हिंदू यह विश्वास करने लगे कि हिंदू

व मुस्लिम अलग मजहबों के हैं इसलिए वे बिल्कुल अलग राष्ट्र हैं। किसी भी बुद्धिजीवि आंदोलन की सफलता के लिए परिस्थितियों का अनुकूल होना आवश्यक है। ईश्वर की कृपा से 6 दिसम्बर 1992 की घटनाओं के बाद जिन्ना की विचारधारा से मुक्त होने के लिए इससे बढ़िया स्थितियां नहीं हो सकती थीं। इसमें संदेह नहीं कि बाबरी मस्जिद के गिरने के साथ-साथ अगर जिन्ना की विचारधारा भी नष्ट नहीं हो जाती तो मैं घटना को गहन अंधेरे में रोशनी की एक किरण मानता। इस बेहद दुर्भाग्यपूर्ण हादसे का भी एक उजला पहलू है।

जापान से सबक सीखें

द्वितीय विश्व युद्ध के बाद जापान में एक आंदोलन शुरू हुआ जिसे 'विपरीत पथ' नाम दिया गया। इसका पहला उद्देश्य यह था कि विश्व युद्ध से पहले की जापानियों की विचारधारा विश्व युद्ध के बाद भी जारी न रहे। इस दिशा में प्रयास किया गया कि कहीं विश्व युद्ध में हार और पिछली सोच नकारात्मक असर न डाल सके तथा प्रगति थम जाए। दूसरा उद्देश्य था विश्व युद्ध के पूर्व की विचारधारा के बदले सकारात्मक व रचनात्मक विचारधारा अपनाने की दिशा में काम करना। ईश्वर की कृपा से भारत में भी हिंदूओं व मुसलमानों में उसी तरह की 'विपरीत विचार धारा' की प्रक्रिया शुरू हो गई है।

अब हमारे लिए यह वक्त आ गया कि हम भारतीय मुसलमानों को यह विश्वास दिलाएं कि हिंदू व मुस्लिम दो नहीं बल्कि एक राष्ट्र हैं और नफरत के बदले प्यार दिखलाएं। मुसलमानों को यह समझा दिया जाना चाहिए कि संघर्ष व टकराव की नीति के बदले वे समझौते की नीति अपनाएं। उन्हें यह अहसास कराना चाहिए कि नए भारत में उनका बराबर का हिस्सा है, पर उनके हाथ यह हिस्सा योग्यता के ही आधार पर आएगा, किसी आरक्षण या मांग के आधार पर नहीं।

पंजाब केसरी, 27 जुलाई, 2004 के सौजन्य से साभार।

9

NATION STATE—UNITY AND DIVERSITY
(एकता का तत्व-भाषा)

T.K. Oommen

The rupture between citizenship and nationality has assumed immediacy in the world with the collapse of the Soviet Union and what is happening in East Europe. The problem is even more vexatious in South Asia, given its bewildering cultural complexity and long history. In realtively homogeneous societies, it is possible to fuse citizenship and nationality but any such attempt will spell disaster for heterogeneous societies such as India. And yet, this is precisely what the nation of 'cultural nationalism' advocated by the ideologues of Hindutva would imply.

SACRED RIGHT

It was only by the end of World War I that the idea that every nation should have its own state and every citizen in this state should have full political rights, got crystallised. By the 1940s, citizenship became a sacred right everywhere thanks to World War II and the Great Depression, both of which legitimised the need to regulate foreign migration. Today, single citizenship is a near-universal principle although some states do permit dual citizenship. But the emergence of the European Community and a common citizenship for members of the E.C. go against the conventional idea of fusing citizenship and nationality.

As nations started to constitute themselves into states, as political entities, in Western Europe, following the maxim, one-nation one-state, a new socio-political formation emerged and the hypernated term 'nation-state' came into vogue. However, even in Western Europe the maxim was never fully actualised and it is often forgotten that the nation-state implies a process. It is possible and historically true that the process can even be reversed: not only can a nation be constituted into a state, but a state can dismantle and destroy nations. Further, a state can create a new nation, in that it can accelerate the process of endowing a people with nationhood.

It seems the eclipse of the nation as a cultural entity is almost complete and it has invariably come to mean a political entity. Yet, it is necessary to place the notion in its historical context so as to understand the difference between nation and state. *Further it is necessary to rehabilitate nation as a cultural entity particularly in culturally plural societies so as to maintain collective identities.*

Broadly speaking, three prominent factors create the disjuncture between citizenship and nationality. These are "race" (used loosely to refer to distinct physical features), language (including dialect) and religion (including sect and denomination). If everybody living in the territory of a given state belonged to the same race, professed the same religion and spoke the same language the resulting situation would be one of fusion between citizenship and nationality. Should the combination vary in some form, there would be predictable tension because one or another collectivity may feel deprived objectively or subjectively (even when an objective basis does not exist) that one or another of their identities is invoked to block their full participation in the economy, polity and culture.

The territory, under the jurisdiction of the Indian state contains by far the most culturally complex situation in the world. But India's governability is further complicated by the fact that several of our neighbouring states have populations which share the same socio-cultural and 'racial' features. India with a predominantly Hindu population (83 per cent), and the Hindu Kingdom of Nepal have substantial societal similarities, sharing a common and long religious-historical tradition. Although the Nepali language and culture and distinct, the presence of a substantial number of Indian citizens of Nepali origin makes it difficult to distinguish clearly between Nepali and Nepalese and Indian Nepalese except in purely legal terms. The Nepali citizens who migrate to India expect and may find that the Indian citizens of Nepali origin are their natural allies and protectors. And, both belong to the same society not withstanding the fact that they are drawn from two different states.

CULTURAL HERITAGE

Bengali society envelops the inhabitants ofWest Bengal,Tripura and Bangladesh having a common language and being participants in a shared cultural heritage even as they profess different faiths. At any rate, Bengali Muslims of West Bengal and Bengali Hindus of Bangladsh do participate in a society and culture beyond their respective state boundaries. Yet, those Bengalis who inhabit West Bengal and Tripura are Indian citizens and those who live in Bangladesh are non-Indians.

The Tamils inhabiting Sri Lanka are categorised into three based on their citizenship status: (a) Sri Lankan Tamils, (b) Indian Tamils and (c) those who are not accepted as citizens either by Sri Lanka or by India. Yet the three categories belong to Tamil society along with the Tamils of Tamil Nadu in India. The Punjabi Hindus and Muslims have a common language and culture. But they are citizens of two states, with the former predominantly found in India and the latter in Pakistan.

The territory inhabited by several tribal groups in noth-eat India is divided between two or more states, which in turn fragmented their societies and rendered them citizens of different states. And yet they are members of a society which cuts across international borders. The Kashmiri Muslims of Kashmir valley and their counterparts in 'Azad Kashmir' show a common culture and society and yet they are citizens of two different states.

DISJUNCTURE

These examples clearly point to the disjuncture that exists between citizenship and nationality in South Asia, a product of a long historical process brought about by conquest, colonialism and immigration. As a corollary to this we find that the internal situation prevailing in these countries represent the same disjuncture, India's being the most complex case.

Broadly speaking, discrimination based on 'race' is not obvious or rampant in India although there is prejudice based on colour. As this writer has argued religion cannot be the basis of nation-formation. That leaves us with language as the basis of building the 'nations which compose the Indian polity, the rationale of which cannot be gone into here for reasons of space. But it is possible to enunciate the First Principles if we want to find a lasting solution to reconcile the competing demands of identity and equality.

These are basically three. First, the explicit recognition of the fact that India is a polity, that is a collective of citizens, in which numerous societies and cultures co-exist and that the identity of each of these should be carefully nurtured and not be liquidated or even assimilated into an artificially contrived cultural mainstream. Second, that all Indians are citizens of the same state, with equal rights, even as they belong to different 'nations' (that is societies) and should justly feel proud of it. Third, the fact that they belong to the same polity and state, entitles them to be equal participants in the economy. The recognition of these principles and their internationalisation by all Indians are the first steps in building an authentic India.

By Courtesy, Times of India, June 7, 1993 with gratitude.

10

HINDU NATIONALISM–LIBERAL VERSUS FANATICAL–LOHIA'S VIEW

Rajni Bakshi

> *"O INDIA, Mother, give us the mind of Siva, the heart of Krishna, and the word and deed of Ram, create us with a non-dimensional mind and an exuberant heart, but a life of limits."*
>
> *– **Dr. Rammanohar Lohia***

This prayer-like appeal rose from a man who did not believe in God. He wished to be remember as a socialist and an internationlist. Yet Rammamohar Lohia's politics extended to protesting against the "sacrilege" of polluting our rivers. For, he said, "What is in a tirth (pilgrimage)?–only water."

The "disastrous neglect" of Ayodhya, Benares, Rameshwaram, Dwarka and Ajmer alike concerned Lohia, but not in the way that it bothers religious chauvinists. "Any reasonable man," Lohia said, "would campaign for the renovation of the great pilgrim cities of India on grounds of native policies of people's welfare."

Twenty-six years after his death Lohia is a faintly remembered name in Indian politics and social life. Last week, his 83rd birth anniversay slipped by unnoticed.[1] But those familiar with Lohia's writings find his insights looming over our present.

Ganesh Mantri, former editor of Dharamyug, often recalls a press conference at Ratlam in the early 1950s. A journalist asked Lohia how his call for a reunification of India and Pakistan was diferent from a similar demand made by the RSS and Jan Sangh.

Lohia explained that his call for reunification hinged on dignified and friendly relations between Muslims and Hindus in India. Across four decades Lohia's answer still echoes in Mr. Mantri's memory : "Whoever is anti-Muslim (in India) must necessarily be pro-Pakistan," Lohia said, "and anyone who wishes the end of the Pakistan idea must necessarily be pro-Muslim."

This belief was not based on some facile or romantic notions of Hindu-Muslim unity, says Acarya Kelkar, a veteran Lohiaite. Lohia conceded that there were serious differences between Hindus and Muslims but argued that these could be creatively lived with, he recalls.

Lohia was one in a long line of atheist 'insiders' to the Hindu fold who posed questions and challengs to the religious and cultural tradition, demanding progressive change, not whole-scale rejection.

Even the issue of Hindu-Muslim relations was, for Lohia, one more battle in the 'greatest war of Indian history, the war between the liberal and fanatical in Hinduism'. Writing this in 1950, Lohia seems to have anticipated our anguished present and urged that this tussle within Hinduism must be resolved if this civilisation is to survive and thrive.

A glimpse at this essay, titled 'Hinduism', is thus particularly illuminating today when public discourse is thoroughly vitiated by unprecedented polarisation. The common ground of this 5,000 year long feud within Hinduism, Lohia wrote is ..... a whole world of memories and mythology, of philosophy and customs and practices, part of which grossly evil, and another which can be of service of man.'

Today, in the throes of perhaps their most intense battle ever, both the liberal and fanatical within Hinduism agree that tolerance is an unfailing feature of this culture and religion.

"This is not so except in the sense that open slaughter has hitherto been abhorrent to it." according to Lohia. "The fanatical in Hinduism has always tried to establish unity through uniformity, through the suppression of sects and faiths other than the one that was seeking to dominate, but such attempts have never achieved success." For the element of tolerance was 'almost always stronger than the element of coercion."

At the end of the 19th century Swami Vivekananda has urged that the 'watchword' of Hindus must be not mere toleration but an inclusive acceptance. Later Lohia similarly saw the strengths of

Indian civilisation arising out of the belief that 'variations need not necessarily be wrong, but are perhaps different expressions of what is right.'

In contemporary times for forces of 'unity through uniformity' have given themselves the name of 'Hindutva.' It is not incidental that Hindutva leaders are mostly upper caste Hindus. They call for some amelioration of the conditions of the lower castes but not for abolition of the caste system. Their worldview also does not look kindly upon the women's movement's opposition to patriarchal structures.

This would not have surprised Lohia. He believed that 'as long as caste is not completely erased from the Hindu mind or woman treated an an equal being with man, or property dissociated from the concept of order, the fanatical will from time to time play havoc with Indian history and also impart to it a continuing lethargy'.

Is it this trans-generational lethargy that makes it difficult for most Indians to follow actively in the steps of Gandhi and Vivekananda? Is the kar sevak in Ayodhya perhaps an ironic symbol of this same lethargy? It requires very little effort to blame all your ills on some offensive 'other'.

Thus Nathuram Godse's brazen assassination of Mahatma Gandhi. This act, according to Lohia, was 'not so much an episode of the Hindu-Muslim fight as of the war between the liberal and the fanatical in Hinduism. Never had a Hindu delivered greater blows on fanaticism in respect of caste, woman, property or tolerance. All the bitterness was accumulating.'

Sophisticated Hindutva rhetoric is now compelled to under play this part of its heritage, such is the nature of Gandhi's stature. The vandalism in Ayodhya on December 6 is claimed to be part of a groundswell of emerging Hindu unity which alone, they insist, can keep the map of India whole. For Lohia this would have been just a tragic replay of history : "The motives (of fanaticism) have not always been suspect. Its driving power may well at times have been the desire for stability and strength, but the consequences fo its acts hve always been disastrous. ... The upswing of fanatical fervour in Hinduism has always led to the social and political break up of the country, to the disintegration of the Indian people as a State and as a community."

Decades before the events in Ayodhya, Lohia foresaw that fanatical Hinduism may draw sustenance from 'anti-democratic doctrines like communism and fascism'. According to Acharya Kelkar, "Lohia believed that the liberal alone can unite Indian and today once again liberal Hindu thought is on the retreat."

But is a decisive victory at hand for the fanatical?

Himmat Jhaveri, veteran socialist and Lohia associate, cautions against any simplistic division of people at large as 'fanatics' or 'liberals'. More people seem to be rallying around communal forces, Mr. Jhaveri argues, because "Many liberal minded Hindus, who are not positively anti-Muslim, have become critical of secular politics as practised by the Congress, socialists and communists. We have not communicated our ideas properly to the people, there is something wrong with our behaviour that has led people to go to Thackeray and Advani."

This could be a temporary phase, Mr. Jhaveri says, if secular politics corrects itself by being impartially critical of both Hindu and Muslim communalism.

Madhu Limaye, a prominent Lohiaite and former member of Parliament, argues that forces of change are already at work in society which make the final victory of fanatical Hinduism unlikely. The process of reform on the issues of women and caste now being carried forward through a variety of formations, cannot easily be undone.

What would Lohia have done in today's circumstances? Mr. Limaye suggests that "Lohia would not only have expected the State to take all steps to maintain communal peace, but he would have expected neighbours to give a helping hand to victims of mob fury."

Back in 1964 when widespread riots in East Pakistan led to a large influx of Hindus and other minorities into India there were also cases of violence against Muslims in India. At that time, Lohia and issued a statement jointly with Deen Dayal Upadhyaya, general secretary of the Bharatiya Jan Sangh, predecessor of the present Bharatiya Janta Party (BJP).

If the government of India fails in its duty to protect the life and property of Hindus in Pakistan 'it is only natural that people in India will feel angered', the statement began. "Our appeal is that this anger should be turned against the government of India and not in any circumstances should it be directed against Indian Muslims .... their life and property must be protected under all circumstance like all citizens of India... The state which can not protect its citizens and those citizens who cannot protect their neighbours are barbarian. Protection of all sects is our tradition."

Both Mr. Limaye and Mr. Mantri feel that this unique joint issuing of a statement was politically significant at a time when the rant and file of the Jan Sangh was unabashedly willing to justify violence against Muslims. Others have felt that through such actions Lohia, and later, Jayaprakash, lent respectability to the Jan Sangh, RSS and their anti-Muslim ideology.

Across the distance of time and space Lohia can also seem a supremely confident, liberal Hindu, willing to engage the other side in an attempt to set the ground rules of a conflict he wants to settle without bloodshed.

Was the fanatical 'other' ever open to such appeals? More and more the answer seems to be 'no'. The fate of this great struggle within Hinduism then rests with those who, knowing this have the confidence and strength to stand up against all forms of fanaticism and its infectious virus of hate. Those who can share the faith that, at the end of this 'hideous war' lies what Lohia envisioned as a new endeavour of the Indian mind, 'which shall combine the rational with the emotive, which shall make of unity in diversity not an inert but a vital doctrine which shall acept the clean joy of the sensible world without losing insight into the oneness of all life and things.'

NOTE

1. Paper written on 28 March 1993, by Courtesy, Times of India.

11

WORSHIP OF THE LIVING GOD
(मनुष्य की पूजा)

Swami Vivekanand

The greatest misfortune to befall the world would be if all mankind were to recognise and accept but one religion, one universal form of worship, one standard of morality. This would be the death-blow to all religious and spiritual progress. Instead of trying to hasten this disastrous event by inducing persons, through good or evil methods, to conform to our own highest ideal of truth, we ought rather to endeavour to remove all obstacles which prevent men from developing in accordance with their own highest ideals, and thus make their attempt vain to establish one universal religion.

We believe not only in universal toleration, but we accept all religions as true. I am proud to belong to a nation which has sheltered the persecuted and the refugees of all religions and all nations of the earth.

We must not only tolerate others, but positively embrace them, and that truth is the basis of all religions.

Condemn none; if you can stretch out a helping hand, do so. If you cannot, fold your hands, bless your brothers, and let them go their own way. Dragging down and condemning is not the way to work. Never is work accomplished in that way. We spend our energies in condemning others. Criticism and condemnation is a vain way of spending our energies, for in the long run we come to learn that all are seeing the same thing, are more or less approaching the same ideal, and that most of our differences are merely differences of expression.

Indeed, the varieties of religious belief are an advantage, since all faiths are good, so far as they encourage man to lead a religious life. The more sects there are, the more opportunities there are for making successful appeals to the divine instinct in all men.

My Master taught that religion is one; all prophets teach the same; but they can only present the principle in a form; so they take it out of the old form and put it before us in a new one.

In all religions the superconscious state is identical. Hindus, Christians, Mohammedans, Buddhists, and even those of no creed, all have the very same experience when they transcend the body.

The Christian is not to become a Hindu or a Buddhist, nor a Hindu or a Buddhist to become a Christian. But each must assimilate the spirit of the others and yet preserve his individuality and grow according to his own law of growth.

.... Holiness, purity and charity are not the exclusive possessions of any church in the world, and that every system has produced men and women of the most exalted character. In the face of this evidence, if anybody dreams of the exclusive survival of his own religion and the destruction of the others, I pity him from the bottom of my heart, and point out to him that upon the banner of every religion will soon be written, in spite of resistance: 'Help and not Fight', 'Assimilation and not Destruction', 'Harmony and Peace and not Dissension.

If there is ever to be a universal religion, it must be one which will have no location in place or time; which will be infinite like the God it will preach, and whose sun will shine upon the followers of Krishna and of Christ, on saints and sinners alike; which will not be Brahminic or Buddhistic, Christian or Mohammedan, but the sum total of all these, and still have infinite space for development; which in its catholicity will embrace in its infinite arms, and find a place for, every human being, from the lowest grovelling savage not far removed from the brute, to the highest man towering by the virtues of his head and heart almost above humanity, making society stand in awe of him and doubt his human nature. It will be a religion which will have no place for persecution or intolerance in its polity, which will recognize divinity in every man and woman, and whose whole scope, whose whole force, will be centred in aiding humanity to realize its own true, divine nature.

Offer such a religion, and all the nations will follow you.
Characteristics of a spiritual man

The first sign that you are becoming religious is that you are becoming cheerful. When a man is gloomy, that may be dyspepsia, but it is not religion.... Misery is caused by sin, and by no other cause .... if you have a clouded face, do not go out that day, shut yourself up in your room. What right have you to carry this disease out into the world?

The real spiritual man is broad everywhere. His love forces him to be so. Those to whom religion is a trade are forced to become narrow and mischievous by their introduction into religion of the competitive, fighting and selfish methods of the world.

Why do we see wickedness?... We see the world as we are. Suppose there is a baby in a room with a bag of gold on the table and a thief comes and steals the gold. Would the baby know it was stolen? Thief which we have inside, we see outside. The baby has no thief inside and sees no thief outside. So with all knowledge. Do not talk of the wickedness of the world and all its sins. Weep that you are bound to see wickedness yet. Weep that you are bound to see sin everywhere, and if you want to help the world, do not condemn it. Do not weaken it more. For what is sin and what is misery, and what are all these, but the results of weakness? The world is made weaker and weaker every day by such teachings. Men are taught from childhood that they are weak and sinners. Teach them that they are all glorious children of immortality, even those who are the weakest in manifestation. Let positive, strong, helpful thoughts enter into their brains from very childhood. Lay yourselves open to these thoughts, and not to weakening and paralysing ones. Say to your own minds, 'I am He, I am He.' Let it ring day and night in your minds like a song, and at the point of death declare, 'I am He.' That is the Truth; the infinite strength of the world is yours... Let us be brave. Know the Truth and practise the Truth. The goal may be distant, but awake, arise and stop not till the goal is reached.

Do you not know from the history of the world where the power of the prophets lay? Where was it? In the intellect? Did any of them write a fine book on philosophy, on the most intricate ratiocinations of logic? Not one of them. They only spoke a few words. Feel like Christ and you will be a Christ; feel like Buddha and you will be a Buddha. It is feeling that is the life, the strength, the vitality, without which no amount of intellectual activity can reach God.

There are two sorts of courage. One is the courage of facing the cannoe. And the other is the courage of spiritual conviction. An emperor who invaded India was told by his teacher to go and see some of the sages there. After a long search for one, he found a very old man sitting on a block of stone. The emperor talked with him a little and became very much impressed by his wisdom. He asked the sage to go to his country with him. 'No', said the sage, 'I am quite satisfied with my forest here.' Said the Emperor, 'I will give you money, position, wealth. I am the Emperor of the world.' 'No', replied the man, 'I don't care for those things.' The Emperor replied, 'If you do not go, I will kill you.' The man smiled serenely and said, 'That is the most foolish thing you ever said, Emperor. You cannot kill me. Me the sun cannot dry, fire cannot burn, sword cannot kill, for I am the birthless, the deathless, the ever-living omnipotent, omnipresent spirit'. This is spiritual boldness, while the other is the courage of a lion or a tiger. In the Mutiny of 1857 there was a Swami, a very great soul, whom a Mohammedan mutineer stabbed severely. The Hindu mutineers caught and brought the man to the Swami, offering to kill him. But the Swami looked up calmly and said, 'My brother, thou art He, thou art He!' and expired. This is another instance.

WORSHIP OF THE LIVING GOD

The secret of religion lies not in theories but in practice. To be good and to do good – that is the whole of religion. 'Not he that crieth "Lord", "Lord", but he that doeth the will of the Father.'

Be moral. Be brave. Be a heart-whole man. Strictly moral, brave unto desperation. Don't bother your head with religious theories. Cowards only sin, brave men never, no, not even in mind.[62]

If you are really pure, how do you see the impure? For what is within, is without. We cannot see impurity without having it inside ourselves. This is one of the practical sides of Vedanta, and I hope that we shall all try to carry it into our lives.

Doing good to others is virtue (Dharma); injuring others is sin. Strength and manliness are virtue; weakness and cowardice are sin. Independence is virtue; dependence is sin. Loving others is virtue; hating others is sin. Faith in god and in one's own Self is virtue; doubt is sin. Knowledge of oneness is virtue; seeing diversity is sin.

The watchword of all well-being, of all moral good is not 'I' but 'thou'. Who cares whether there is a heaven or a hell, who cares if there is a soul or not, who cares if there is an unchangeable or not? Here is the World, and it is full of misery. Go out into it as Buddha did, and struggle to lessen it or die in the attempt. Forget yourselves; this is the firm lesson to be learnt, whether you are a theist or an atheist, whether you are an agnostic or a Vedantist, a Christian or a Mohammedan. The one lesson obvious to all is the destruction of the little self and the building up of the Real Self.

After so much austerity, I have understood this as the real truth–God is present in every Jiva; there is no other God besides that. 'Who serves Jiva, serves god indeed.'

These are His manifold forms before thee,
Rejecting them, where seekest thou for God?
Who loves all beings, without distinction,
He indeed is worshipping best his God.

You have read–मातृदेवो भव पितृदेवो भव–'Look upon your mother as God, look upon your father as God',–but I say दरिद्रदेवो भव, मूर्खदेवो भव–the poor, the illiterate, the ignorant, the afflicted–let these be your God. Know that service to these alone is the highest religion.

We want to worship a living God. I have seen nothing but God all my life, nor have you. To see this chair you first see God, and then the chair in and through Him. He is everywhere saying, 'I am'. The moment you feel 'I am' you are conscious of Existence. Where shall we go to find God if we cannot see Him in our own hearts and in every living being?

If in this hell of a world one can bring a little joy and peace even for a day into the heart of a single person, that much alone in true; this I have learnt after suffering all my life; all else is mere moonshine.

If you want any good to come, just throw your ceremonials overboard and worship the Living God, the Man God–every being that wears a human form–God in His universal as well as individual aspect. The universal aspect of God means this world, and worshipping it means serving it–this indeed is work, not indulging in ceremonials... Millions of rupees have been spent only that the temple-doors at Varanasi or Vrindaban may play at opening and shutting all day long! Now the Lord is having His toilet, now He is taking His meals, now He is busy on something else we know not what ... And all this, while the Living God is dying for want of food, for want of education! The banias of Bombay are erecting hospitals for bugs–while they would do nothing for men–even if they die! You have not the brain to understand this simple thing–that it is a plague with our country, and lunatic asylums are rife all over.

Look upon every man, woman and every one as God. You cannot help anyone, you can only serve: serve the children of the Lord, serve the Lord Himself, if you have the privilege. If the Lord grants that you can help any one of His children, blessed you are; do not think too much of yourselves. Blessed you are that privilege was given to you when others had it not. Do it only as a worship. I should see God in the poor, and it is for my salvation that I go and worship them. The poor and the miserable are for our salvation, so that we may serve the Lord, coming in the shape of the diseased, coming in the shape of the lunatic, the leper, and the sinner.

The first of all worship is the worship of the Virat–of those all around us. Worship It. Worship is the exact equivalent of the Sanskrit word, and no other English word will do. These are all our gods–men and animals; and the first gods we have to worship are our countrymen. These we have to worship, instead of being jealous of each other and fighting each other?

This is the gist of all worship–to be pure and to do good to others. He who sees Shiva in the poor, in the weak, and in the diseased, really worships Shiva; and if he sees Shiva only in the image, his worship is but preliminary. He who has served and helped one poor man seeing Shiva in him, without thinking of his caste, or creed, or race, or anything, with him Shiva is more pleased than with the man who sees Him only in temples.

A rich man had a garden and two gardeners. One of these gardeners was very lazy and did not work; but when the owner came to the garden, the lazy man would get up and fold his arms and say, 'How beautiful is the face of my master', and dance before him. The other gardener would not talk much, but would work hard, and produce all sorts of fruits and vegetables which he would carry on his head to his master who lived a long way off. Of these two gardeners, which would be the more beloved of his master? Shiva is that master, and this world is His garden, and there are two sorts of gardeners here; the one who is lazy, hypocritical, and does nothing, only talking about Shiva's beautiful eyes and nose and other features; and the other, who is taking care of Shiva's children, all those that are poor and weak, all animals, and all His creation. Which of these would be the more beloved of Shiva? Certainly he that serves His children. He who wants to serve the father must serve the children first. He who wants to serve Shiva must serve His children–must serve all creatures in this world first. It is said in the Shastra that those who serve the servants of God are His greatest servants. So you will bear this in mind. Let me tell you again that you must be pure and help anyone who comes to you, as much as lies in your power. And this is good Karma. By the power of this, the heart becomes pure (Chitta-shuddhi), and then Shiva who is residing in every one will become manifest... And if a man is selfish, even though he has visited all the temples, seen all the places of pilgrimage, and painted himself like a leopard, he is still further off from Shiva.

You are the highest temple of God; I would rather worship you than any temple, image, or Bible. Why are some people so contradictory in their thought?... They say they are hard-headed practical men. Very good. But what is more practical than worshipping here, worshipping you? I see you, feel you, and I know you are God... The only God to worship is the human soul in the human body. Ofcourse all animals are temples too, but man is the highest, the Taj Mahal of temples. If I cannot worship in that, no other temple will be of any advantage. The moment I have realized God sitting in the temple of every human body, the moment I stand in reverence before every human being and see God in him–that moment I am free from bondage, everything that binds vanishes, and I am free.

The next question is to know what comes after realization .... Yet religious realization does all the good to the world. People are afraid that when they attain to it, when they realize that there is but one, the fountains of love will be dried up, that everything in life will go away, and that all they love will vanish for them, as it were, in this life and in the life to come. People never stop to think that those who bestowed the least thought on their own individualities have been the greatest workers in the world. Then alone a man loves when he finds that the object of his love is not any low, little, mortal thing. Then alone a man loves when he finds that the object of his love is not a clod of earth, but it is the veritable God Himself. The wife will love the husband the more when she thinks that the husband is God Himself. The husband will love the wife the more when he knows that the wife is God Himself. That mother will love the children more who thinks that the children are God Himself. That man will love his greatest enemy who knows that very enemy is God Himself. That man will love a holy man who knows that the holy man is God Himself, and that very man will also love the unholiest of men because he knows the background of that unholiest of men is even He, the Lord. Such a man becomes a world—mover for whom his little self is dead and God stands in its place. The whole universe will become transfigured to him. That which is painful and miserable will all vanish; struggles will all depart and go. Instead of being a prison-house, where we every day struggle and fight and compete for a morsel of bread, this universe will then be to us a playground. Beautiful will be this universe then! Such a man alone has the right to stand up and say, 'How beautiful is this world!' He alone has the right to say that it is all good. This will be the great good to the world resulting from such realization, that instead of this world going on with all its friction and clashing, if all mankind today realize only a bit of that great truth, the aspect of the whole world will be changed, and, in place of fighting and quarrelling, these would be a reign of peace. This indecent and brutal hurry which forces us to go ahead of everyone else will then vanish from the world. With it will vanish all struggle, with it will vanish all hate, with it will vanish all jealousy, and all evil will vanish away for ever. Gods will live then upon this earth. This very earth will then become heaven, and what evil can there be when gods are playng with gods, when gods are working with gods, and gods are loving gods? That is the great utility of divine realization. Everything that you see in society will be changed and transfigured then. No more will you think of man as evil; and that is the first great gain. No more will you stand up and sneeringly cast a glance at a poor man or woman who has made a mistake... No more will you think of jealousy and punishments. They will all vanish; and love the great ideal of love, will be so powerful that no whip and cord will be necessary to guide mankind aright.

If one millionth part of the men and women who live in this world simply sit down and for a few minutes say, 'You are all God, O ye men and O ye animals and living beings, you are all the manifestations of the one living Deity!' the whole world will be changed in half an hour. Instead of throwing tremendous bomb-shells of hatred into every corner, instead of projecting currents of jealousy and of evil thought, in every country people will think that it is all He. He is all that you see and feel. How can you see evil until there is evil in you? How can you see the thief, unless he is there, sitting in the heart of your heart? How can you see the murderer until you are yourself the murderer? Be good, and evil will vanish for you. The whole universe will thus be changed. This is the greatest gain to society. This is the great gain to the human organism.

Bring all light into the world. Light, bring light! Let light come unto everyone; the task will not be finished till everyone has reached the Lord. Bring light to the poor; and bring more light to the rich, for they require it more than the poor. Bring light to the ignorant, and more light to the educated, for the anities of the education of our time are tremendous! Thus bring light to all and leave the rest unto the Lord, for in the words of the same Lord, 'To work you have the right and not to the fruits thereof.' Let not your work produce results for you, and at the same time may you never be without work.'

We owe our debt to R.K. Mission Instt. of Culture, Calcutta, for the above extracts, compiled from Swami Vivekananda's collected works, in their book– My India, 1997.

12

NON-RELIGIOUS MORALITY

S.B. Mehta

We are now on the brink of virtual bankruptcy of our moral standards. This brings us to analyse what relation can be there between religion, secularity and economic development.

First of all, what is economic development? Dr. Michael P. Todaro defines economic development as "multi-dimensional process involving the re-organisation and re-orientation of the entire economic and social system .... Economic development during 1970's was redefined in terms of the reduction or elimination of poverty, inequality and unemployment within the context of a growing economy." (Economy Development in the Third World, pp. 56 and 68).

Thus, western multi-dimensional approach leads us only upto these factors, and all through our seven plans, we have forgotten one important dimension of economic development and it is the building up of national character, strong integrity, staunch patriotic fervour and exquisite moral standard, especially amongst the youths, as also in the rest of our countrymen. It seems that our secular democracy has made us consider religion, morality and cultural education as new untouchables! And in doing so, we have also forgotten to invoke our rich and precious heritage of Indian culture and thought.

It is the aim of this paper to remind our countrymen of the true meaning of secularity in the contect of Indian culture, since without integrity, high moral standard and character, no plan or project can be implemented without substantial leakages from plan funds and consequent inefficiency, high cost and low profits or losses in enterprises and intolerable squandering and misdirection of scarce resources, which we can ill-afford.

This is why non-religious morality (secularity) requires to be inculcated in the minds of all of our citizens and in this the author feels stimulated by the views of the great economist Dr. V.K.R.V. Rao, who avers to give a major place to .... "positive secularism and composite Indian culture," as also by the idea of 'civil religion' described by the Chairman of the Minorities Commission though he follows Islam. By these concepts, these experts mean 'pride in their individual religion, esteem for each other's religion and cognition of the universal values that are contained in all the religions." "There is no reason why Indian Muslims should not be proud of their pre-islamic Indian cultural heritage, even as the Hindus are proud of the Taj Mahal, Red Fort," etc. (vide, Indian Economic Crisis 1985 pp. 63 and 67).

Thus, non-religious morality and respect for all the best books, architecture and culture that flourished 5000 years ago in India, should be extensively brought home to all these citizens of India, who now revel in apeing western styles, misculture of terrorism, horror comics, narcotics drug-addiction loose dressings and all sorts of vices. Where in the world will anyone find the exquisite thoughts, cultural traditions that were found in India in her long history of 5-6 milleniums? Why should every Indian not be proud of it and restablish it in the present period also?

> *The above analysis leads us to suggest that for efficient planning, its effective implementation and national character building, what is required is nothing short of a Cultural Renaissance in India. Surely, this cannot be brought about by Government or its agencies. The terms like 'civil religion' or 'positive secularism' or 'non-religious morality' or secularity mean raising the human beings from sub-stratum of animal life to the divine life.' A recent Mahatma Yogeshwarji who realised God after exquisite penance for more than two decades in the Himalayas, gives four stages in the evolution of human race, viz, khar, nara, narottam and Narayana.*

All prophets have aimed at raising the people from animal ass-like-khar-life to Narayana or divine life, but their followers have soon lapsed into sub-human life including our people. Now for Reaissance of all religions in India, we require a concerted effort by all religious leaders and educated, patriotic saints, teachers, professors and preachers. When a person is full of vices, follows his religion only in rites and rituals and is parochial clinging to his caste, community, region, language and hates those belonging to other religion, region, community, etc. and often destroys their life and property and revels in stoning, looting, bourning shops, houses and othr national properties, he is worse than an animal. He is in 'khar' stage of human race. He takes away from and often destroys much more national property and contributes little if any to it.

When a person, following his own religion correctly, respects all other religions, does not harm or harass anybody, he rises to the 'nara' stage or human race. He takes from the nation only as much as he contributes by his labour and intellect. When a person follows his religion and understand and respects truths of other religions and tries to help others by means at this disposal, sometimes sacrificing his own self interst; and his contribution to society is much more than what he earns as remuneration, he is in the 'narottam' stage, or his is an exalted human life.

When a person does not find any distinction between himself and rest of the whole of human race, has his ego sense completely destroyed, is beyond the sense of mine-thine, pleasure-pain, affection-disgust, respect-insult, likes-dislikes, he does not think of harming any person in the world, not even beasts and birds, trees, flora, fauna, he is beyond all dualities and his individual souls is universalised or secularised, he attains the 'Narayana' stage or divine stage of human race. He is then in unison with God, one with God, as many prophets saints and divine souls in various religions were.

Which religion in the world has been successful in bringing about such evolution of human beings turning them from animal life to divine life? Absolutely none, except very few mahatmas, sais, faquîrs, and saints. The vast majority of the followers of all religions may have changed their religion but not their nature and behaviour and this is why we see the world, hanging in balance between the pinnacle of scientific progress and prospects of mass annihilation by nuclear weaponry in a moment.

Now that we are evolving a new education policy, the ideas about Indian culture and non-religious morality should be included in the curricula right from the primary level to post graduate level of teaching. Some text books giving cultural values of India and basic truths of all religious as also national integrity should be compusarily taught to all primary and secondary students. At collegiate levels, history of Indian culture and leaders from ancient times to the present time, should be taught, so that each citizen possesses basic knowledge about the progress of his motherland through 50-60 centuries.

Extensive lectures by true saints in all religions should be arranged in schools and colleges at least one per month an 80 percent attendance of all students in them should be compulsory for passing to upper class.

The radio, television, cinema, video, press all media should be used to inculcate in the minds of our people the main ideas about the secularity, values in life, national character, moral standards, love for humanity, respect for all religions and deep study of one's own religion.

For this we will require patriotic saints in all religions of India and honest and noble teachers in primary, secondary and college education. They should at least have reached the Narottam stage of human evolution as noted above. Since any social, moral and cultural reform and renalssance require best teachers like Maharshi Vyasa and Shukadev in India, Haroonal Rasdin in Arab, Socrates in Greece, Thorou in Germany and Vivekananda and Mahatma Gandhi of our times.

This will add cultural and moral dimensions to our new educational policy and will go a long way in building up national character in all the citizens of India. The policy makers will have rational thinking and the administrators will be honest and efficient in performing their duties, if they are imbibed with fervour of patriotism, service to nation and humanity at large.

Extracts edited from the author's paper graciously sent to us. The author is professor of Economics in Gujrat University.

13

राय का नव मानवतावाद

रमेन्द्र

नव मानवतावाद या रैडिकल मानवतावाद उस सामाजिक राजनीतिक दर्शन का नाम है जो बीसवीं सदी के एक महान स्वतंत्रता-प्रेमी भारतीय विचारक मानववेन्द्रनाथ राय ने अपने जीवन के अन्तिम काल में विकसित किया। राय ने अपने राजनीतिक जीवन की शुरूआत एक लड़ाकू राष्ट्रवादी के रूप में की थी। शस्त्रों की तलाश 1915 में उन्हें भारत से बाहर ले गई। शस्त्र प्राप्त करने में तो उन्हें सफलता नहीं मिली लेकिन उन्हें एक नई विचारधारा अवश्य मिल गई। राय ने मेक्सिको में सोवियत रूस के बाहर विश्व की पहली कम्युनिस्ट पार्टी की स्थापना की। 1920 में राय लेनिन के निमंत्रण पर कम्युनिस्ट इंटरनेशनल के सम्मेलन में शामिल होने के लिए मॉस्को गए। कम्युनिस्ट इंटरनेशनल के नीति निर्धारक संगठनों ने उन्हें महत्वपूर्ण स्थान प्राप्त हुआ। भारत में कम्युनिस्ट पार्टी की स्थापना में भी उनकी महत्वपूर्ण भूमिका थी। 1927 में उन्हें कम्युनिस्ट इंटरनेशनल के प्रतिनिधि के रूप में चीन भेजा गया। लेकिन बाद में कुछ वैचारिक मतभेदों के कारण 1929 में उन्हें कम्युनिस्ट इंटरनेशनल से निकाल दिया गया।

दिसम्बर 1930 में राय के भारत लौटने के बाद जुलाई 1931 में उन्हें गिरफ्तार कर लिया गया। ब्रिटिश सरकार को उखाड़ फेंकने के षडयंत्र के आरोप में उन पर मुकदमा चलाया गया और 6 वर्ष के लिए जेल की सजा दी गई। 1936 में जेल से अपनी रिहाई के बाद राय अपने समर्थकों के साथ भारतीय राष्ट्रीय काँग्रेस में शामिल हुए। लेकिन 1940 में दूसरे विश्वयुद्ध में भारत की हिस्सेदारी के प्रश्न पर मतभेद के कारण राय और उनके अनुयायी भारतीय राष्ट्रीय काँग्रेस से अलग हो गए। दिसम्बर 1940 में अपने भारत लौटने के दस वर्ष बाद राय ने रैडिकल

डेमोक्रेटिक पार्टी की स्थापना की। और इसके साथ ही राय के जीवन के उस अन्तिम चरण की शुरूआत हुई जिसमें उन्होंने नव मानवतावादी दर्शन का विकास किया।

राय के नव मानवतावादी दर्शन का परिचय हमें रैडिकल डेमोक्रेटिक पार्टी द्वारा अगस्त 1947 में जारी किए गए घोषणा-पत्र 'न्यू ह्यूमैनिस्म' से मिलता है। इस घोषणा-पत्र का प्रारूप राय ने ही तैयार किया था, लेकिन जैसा कि राय ने स्वयं 'न्यू ह्यूमैनिस्म' की प्रस्तावना में कहा है इसे अन्तिम रूप देने में सर्वश्री फिलिप स्प्रैट, सिकन्दर चौधरी और वी०एम० तारकुण्डे के सुझावों से राय की काफी मदद मिली थी। इस घोषणा-पत्र में व्यक्त किए गए विचार राय के शब्दों में, **"आलोचनात्मक मार्क्सवादियों और भूतपूर्व कम्यूनिस्टों के एक समूह"** द्वारा विकसित किए गए हैं। इस घोषणा-पत्र की केन्द्रीय विषय-वस्तु राय द्वारा प्रतिपादित और रैडिकल डेमोक्रेटिक पार्टी द्वारा दिसम्बर 1946 में बम्बई में अपने तीसरे सम्मेलन में पारित रैडिकल लोकतंत्र पर 22 सिद्धान्त सूत्र–22 थीसीस है।

22 थीसीस और घोषणा-पत्र 'न्यू ह्यूमैनिस्म' पर आगे चर्चा के आधार पर राय इस निष्कर्ष पर पहुँचे थे कि पार्टी-राजनीति और उनकी कल्पना के आदर्श लोकतंत्र के बीच संगति नहीं है, और अन्ततः दिसम्बर 1948 में रैडिकल डेमोक्रेटिक पार्टी ने कलकत्ता में अपने चौथे सम्मेलन में राजनीतिक दल के रूप में कार्य करना छोड़कर अपने को रैडिकल मानवतावादी आन्दोलन में बदलने का निर्णय लिया। तदनुसार उन्नीसवें और बीसवें थीसीस और घोषणा-पत्र के अंतिम तीन पैराग्राफ को भी संशोधित कर दिया गया। संक्षेप में हम कह सकते हैं कि अपने संशोधित रूप में 22 थीसीस राय के नव मानवतावादी दर्शन का सार और रैडिकल ह्यूमैनिस्ट आन्दोलन की आधारशिला है। राय के नव मानवतावादी दर्शन को समझने के लिए हमें अपना ध्यान 22 थीसीस पर केन्द्रित करना चाहिए।

दिसम्बर 1948 में कलकत्ता में 'इण्डियन रैडिकल ह्यूमैनिस्ट एसोशिएशन' के सम्मेलन में दिए गए अपने अध्यक्षीय भाषण में जाने माने रैडिकल ह्यूमैनिस्ट श्री वी०एम० तारकुंडे ने 22 थीसीस को तीन वर्गों में बाँटा हैं: उनके अनुसार थीसीस संख्या 1 से 6 में रैडिकल ह्यूमैनिस्म के बुनियादी सिद्धान्तों को व्यक्त किया गया है। थीसीस संख्या 7 से 13 में कम्युनिज्म और औपचारिक संसदीय-लोकतंत्र की खामियों का उल्लेख है, जबकि थीसीस संख्या 14 से 22 में सत्ता के विकेन्द्रीकरण और जनता की सीधी हिस्सेदारी पर आधारित रेडिकल लोकतंत्र का विकल्प हमारे सामने प्रस्तुत किया गया है। यह 22 थीसीस को वर्गीकृत करने का एक अच्छा तरीका है।

सबसे पहले हम रैडिकल मानवतावाद के बुनियादी दर्शन को लें, जिन्हें प्रथम 6 थीसीस में व्यक्त किया गया है। राय की प्रथम थीसिस के अनुसार समाज के मूल में है व्यक्ति। यह सही है कि सहयोगात्मक सामाजिक संबंधों से व्यक्ति की क्षमताओं के विकास में सहायता मिलती है, लेकिन सामाजिक प्रगति का पैमाना व्यक्ति का विकास है। किसी समूह के अस्तित्व के लिए व्यक्ति का अस्तित्व आवश्यक है। व्यक्ति से अलग राष्ट्र या वर्ग में सामूहिक अहं के अस्तित्व को मान लेना एक भूल है। व्यक्ति को प्राप्त स्वतंत्रता और सुख से अलग सामाजिक विकास एक काल्पनिक आदर्श है। सामाजिक कल्याण व्यक्ति के कल्याण द्वारा ही सम्भव है।

राय की दूसरी थीसिस के अनुसार स्वतंत्रता की चाह और सत्य की तलाश मानव विकास के बुनियादी प्रेरक तत्व है। स्वतंत्रता की चाह बुद्धि और भावना के उच्च स्तर पर जीववैज्ञानिक अस्तित्व के संघर्ष या जीवन संघर्ष का ही विस्तार है। सत्य की तलाश इस संघर्ष का ही परिणाम है। प्रकृति के अपने बढ़ते हुए ज्ञान की सहायता से मनुष्य प्रकृति और सामाजिक वातावरण की तानाशाही से क्रमशः मुक्ति पाने में समर्थ होता है।

तीसरी थीसिस के अनुसार सभी मानवीय प्रयत्नों का–चाहे वे व्यक्तिगत स्तर पर हों या सामूहिक–लक्ष्य है अधिक से अधिक स्वतंत्रता प्राप्त करना। राय के लिए स्वतंत्रता का अर्थ व्यक्ति के अन्दर मौजूद सम्भावनाओं के प्रकट होने की राज से हर बन्धन का क्रमशः समाप्त होना है। इसलिए राय के विचार में किसी भी सामूहिक प्रयत्न या सामाजिक संगठन की सफलता का मापदण्ड उससे समूह की इकाई व्यक्ति को होने वाला वास्तविक लाभ है।

इस तरह, अगर हम समाज-दार्शनिक दृष्टिकोण से देखें तो राय की प्रथम तीन थीसीस का सार है: व्यक्तिवाद। राय ने समूहवाद के विपरीत व्यक्तिवाद का समर्थन किया है; व्यक्ति, और उसकी स्वतंत्रता को राय ने नव मानवतावादी दर्शन में सर्वोच्च महत्व दिया है। राय ने व्यक्ति और उसकी स्वतंत्रता को साध्य और समाज को इसके लिए साधन माना है। राय के अनुसार सामाजिक-राजनीतिक दर्शन की शुरूआत इस बुनियादी विचार से होनी चाहिए कि व्यक्ति समाज के पहले आता है, और व्यक्ति ही स्वतंत्रता का अनुभव कर सकता है।

थीसीस संख्या 4, 5 और 6 में राय ने इतिहास की मार्क्सवादी व्याख्या या, दूसरे शब्दों में, इतिहास की आर्थिक व्याख्या की आलोचना की है और इतिहास की नई मानवतावादी व्याख्या का प्रस्तुत किया है। 22 थीसीस में व्यक्त नव मानवतावादी दर्शन को स्पष्ट करने के प्रयत्न में राय ने रैडिकल डेमोक्रेटिक

पार्टी के 1946 और 1947 के सम्मेलनों में कई भाषण दिए थे, जो राय की पुस्तक 'Beyond Communism' में संकलित हैं। इन भाषणों में भी इतिहास-दर्शन सम्बन्धी राय के महत्वपूर्ण विचार मिलते हैं। जैसा कि राय ने 'न्यू ह्यूमैनिस्म' के दूसरे संस्करण की प्रस्तावना में कहा है नव मानवतावादी दर्शन का विकास इतिहास की मानवतावादी व्याख्या के आधार पर करना चाहिए। बाद में अपनी पुस्तक Reason, Romanticism and Revolution में राय ने विस्तार से सभ्यता की शुरूआत से आधुनिक समय के इतिहास की मानवतावादी व्याख्या को हमारे सामने रखने का प्रयत्न किया है। संक्षेप में, राय ने नियत्त्ववाद (determinism) के वैज्ञानिक और भाग्यवाद (Predestination) के धार्मिक सिद्धान्त के बीच अन्तर किया है। राय के अनुसार ऐतिहासिक नियतत्त्वाद और संकल्प-स्वातंत्र्य के बीच कोई विरोधाभास नहीं है। राय यह मानते हैं कि इतिहास एक नियत (determined) प्रक्रिया है, लेकिन इसे निश्चित करने वाले कई कारण हैं, जिनमें मानव-संकल्प सबसे महत्वपूर्ण है; और मानव-संकल्प को हमेशा आर्थिक प्रेरणा से नहीं जोड़ा जा सकता है। राय यह प्रश्न उठाते हैं कि अगर इतिहास आर्थिक दृष्टि से पूर्वनिश्चित है तो फिर हम मानव प्रयत्नों द्वारा क्रान्ति कैसे कर सकते हैं। राय के अनुसार इतिहास का निर्माता स्वयं मानव है, क्योंकि उत्पादन के साधन और आर्थिक ढाँचे सहित मानव-समाज एक मानवीय रचना है। राय बतलाते हैं कि आर्थिक नियतत्त्ववाद का परिणाम एक किस्म का आर्थिक भाग्यवाद है।

इसी तरह, राय ने इतिहास के विकास में विचारों के महत्व पर बड़ा बल दिया है। राय स्पष्ट शब्दों में मार्क्सवादी इतिहास की आर्थिक व्याख्या के इस सिद्धान्त को अस्वीकार करते हैं कि विचारधाराएँ और नैतिक मूल्य समाज के आर्थिक ढाँचे की अधिरचना (Superstructure) मात्र है। राय के अनुसार विचारों की उत्पत्ति भी इस भौतिक विश्व की पृष्ठभूमि में मानव मस्तिष्क में ही होती है, लेकिन एक बार उत्पन्न हो जाने के बाद विचारों का अपना स्वतंत्र अस्तित्व होता है, और अपने स्वतंत्र नियम होते हैं। विचारों का विकास और समाज का विकास ये दोनों प्रक्रियाएँ एक-दूसरे के समानान्तर चलती हैं, और एक दूसरे को प्रभावित करती हैं। लेकिन मानवीय विकास की इस समग्र प्रक्रिया में हम किसी भी समय ऐतिहासिक घटनाओं और विचारों के विकास के बीच कारण-कार्य सम्बन्ध नहीं सिद्ध कर सकते हैं। विचारों का विकास अपने स्वतंत्र तार्किक नियमों के आधार पर होता है, और इनका हमारे आचरण पर जबरदस्त प्रभाव पड़ता है। दूसरे शब्दों में, राय ने अपने इतिहास की मानवतावादी व्याख्या में मानव-संकल्प और विचारों

और नैतिक मूल्यों को केन्द्रीय महत्व दिया है, और इन कारणों की अवहेलना करने के लिए इतिहास की आर्थिक व्याख्या की आलोचना की है।

थीसीस संख्या 7, 8, 9, 10 और 11 में मुख्य रूप से कम्युनिस्ट सिद्धांतों और व्यवहार की आलोचना की गई है। यह आलोचना मुख्य रूप से क्रान्ति के बाद के रूसी अनुभव के आधार पर की गई है। इसकी चर्चा राय की पुस्तक 'न्यू ह्यूमैनिस्म' के तीसरे अध्याय "Degeneration of Communist Theory and Practice"—कम्युनिस्ट सिद्धान्त और व्यवहार का पतन–के अन्तर्गत भी की गई है। राय के अनुसार स्वतंत्रता पर आधारित विश्व की रचना के लिए क्रान्ति का समाज के मात्र आर्थिक पुनर्निर्माण से आगे जाना जरूरी है। शोषित और दलित वर्गों के नाम पर सत्ता पर कब्जा कर लेने और निजी सम्पत्ति को समाप्त कर देने से अपने आप अनिवार्य रूप से स्वतंत्रता की स्थापना नहीं हो जाती है। राय कहते हैं कि कम्युनिज्म या समाजवाद कहाँ की स्वतंत्रता के उद्देश्य प्राप्त करने में सहायक हो सकते हैं, इसकी जाँच अनुभव के प्रकाश में की जानी चाहिए। एक ऐसी राजनीतिक और आर्थिक व्यवस्था जो हाड़ माँस के मनुष्य को वर्ग या राष्ट्र जैसे काल्पनिक सामूहिक अहं के अधीन रखे, स्वतंत्रता के लक्ष्य को पाने में सहायक नहीं हो सकती। इसी तरह, किसी भी ऐसे सामाजिक दर्शन या सामाजिक पुनर्निमाण की योजना का, जो व्यक्ति की सम्प्रभुता को मान्यता नहीं प्रदान करे और स्वतंत्रता के आदर्श को एक अमूर्त्त कल्पना कह कर अस्वीकार करे, बहुत ही सीमित प्रगतिशील और क्रान्तिकारी महत्व हो सकता है।

राय ने राज्य की मार्क्सवादी अवधारणा को भी अस्वीकार किया है। मार्क्सवाद के अनुसार राज्य एक वर्ग द्वारा दूसरे वर्ग के शोषण का औजार है, जबकि राय के अनुसार राज्य समाज का राजनीतिक संगठन है। और कम्युनिस्म के अन्तर्गत राज्य के विसर्जित हो जाने की बात एक यूटोपिया या काल्पनिक आदर्श है जो अनुभव द्वारा गलत साबित हो चुकी है। समाजीकृत उद्योगों के आधार पर योजनाबद्ध अर्थव्यवस्था के लिए शक्तिशाली राजनीतिक तंत्र का होना आवश्यक है, और इस तंत्र पर लोकतांत्रिक नियंत्रण के जरिए ही नई व्यवस्था में स्वतंत्रता की गारन्टी हो सकती है।

कम्युनिज्म के अन्तर्गत संक्रमण काल में ''सर्वहारा की तानाशाही'' के विचार को भी राय अस्वीकार करते हैं। राय के अनुसार यह कहना बेकार की बात है कि स्वतंत्रता के निषेध के माध्यम से हमें स्वतंत्रता प्राप्त हो सकती है। तानाशाही में अपने को स्थायी बनाने की प्रवशति होती है। कम्युनिस्ट तानाशाही में कार्यकुशलता, सामूहिकता और सामाजिक प्रगति के नाम पर व्यक्ति की स्वतंत्रता की अनदेखी

की जाती है। परिणामस्वरूप समाजवाद के तहत एक उच्चतर किस्म के लोकतंत्र की बात असम्भव हो जाती है। राय के अनुसार राजकीय स्वामित्व और योजनाबद्ध अर्थव्यवस्था से न तो अपने-आप अनिवार्य रूप से श्रम का शोषण समाप्त होता है और न ही धन का समान वितरण हो जाता है। जिस तरह आर्थिक लोकतंत्र के अभाव में राजनीतिक लोकतंत्र सम्भव नहीं है, उसी तरह राजनीतिक लोकतंत्र के अभाव में आर्थिक लोकतंत्र भी संभव नहीं है। इस तरह, तानाशाही स्वयं अपने लक्ष्य को ही पराजित कर देती है।

जहाँ एक ओर राय ने कम्युनिस्ट तानाशाही की आलोचना की है, वहाँ दूसरी ओर, थीसीस संख्या 12 और 13 में औपचारिक संसदीय लोकतंत्र की उन खामियों की ओर ध्यान दिलाया है जो अनुभव से प्रकाश में आई है। राय के अनुसार संसदीय लोकतंत्र की खामियों का कारण है सत्ता का प्रतिनिधियों के हाथों में सौंपा जाना। लोकतंत्र को कारगर बनाने के लिए सत्ता का हमेशा जनता के हाथों में रहना जरूरी है। और इसके लिए ऐसे तरीके और रास्ते निकाले जाने चाहिए जिससे जनता कभी-कभी नहीं बल्कि रोज-रोज अपनी सम्प्रभुता का कारगर इस्तेमाल कर सके। अलग-अलग व्यक्ति अधिकांश समय सभी व्यवहारिक दृष्टियों से शक्तिहीन होते हैं। उनके पास ऐसा कोई साधन नहीं होता है जिससे वे अपनी सम्प्रभुता का इस्तेमाल करते हुए राज्य मशीनरी पर स्थायी नियंत्रण स्थापित कर सकें। राय बतलाते हैं कि संसदीय लोकतंत्र में उदारवाद की पैरोडी बन जाती है। आर्थिक अहस्तक्षेप (laissez faire) की नीति से मनुष्य द्वारा मनुष्य के शोषण को वैधानिक मान्यता मिल जाती है। दूसरी ओर, आर्थिक मनुष्य की अवधारणा व्यक्तिवाद के मुक्तिदायिनी सिद्धान्त के असर को बेकार कर देती है। आर्थिक मनुष्य की प्रचलित अवधारणा के बदले सहज रूप से बुद्धिसम्पन्न और बुद्धिसम्पन्न होने के नाते नैतिक मनुष्य की अवधारणा को हमें अपनाना चाहिए।

जैसा कि इस निबन्ध में पहले उल्लेख किया गया है, थीसीस संख्या 14 से 22 में राय ने सत्ता के विकेन्द्रीकरण और जनता की सीधी हिस्सेदारी पर आधारित रैडिकल लोकतंत्र का विकल्प हमारे सामने प्रस्तुत किया है। साथ ही यह भी बतलाया है कि इस लक्ष्य को हम कैसे हासिल कर सकते हैं। राय के अनुसार संसदीय लोकतंत्र का विकल्प तानाशाही नहीं, देशव्यापी लोक-समितियों के जाल पर आधारित संगठित लोकतंत्र है। इस संगठित या रैडिकल लोकतंत्र में राज्य का ढ़ाँचा एक पिरामिड की तरह होगा जिसकी बुनियाद लोकसमितियों होंगी। इन लोकसमितियों के जरिए राज्य पर जनता का प्रत्यक्ष नियंत्रण स्थापित होगा।

राय बतलाते हैं कि किसी भी क्रान्तिकारी या मुक्तिदायी सामाजिक दर्शन का कार्य इस बुनियादी तथ्य पर बल देना है कि अपने विश्व का निर्माता स्वयं मानव है, और वह एक चिंतनशील प्राणी और व्यक्ति के रूप में ही विश्व का नवनिर्माण कर सकता है। मनुष्य का मस्तिष्क एक उत्पादन का साधन है और इसमें सबसे क्रान्तिकारी वस्तु का उत्पादन होता है। क्रान्ति के लिए रूढ़िभंजक विचारों का होना जरूरी है। ऐसे व्यक्तियों की बढ़ती हुई संख्या, जिन्हें अपनी सर्जनात्मक शक्ति का ज्ञान हो, जिनमें इस विश्व का नए सिरे से पुनर्निर्माण करने का जबरदस्त संकल्प हो, और जो साहसी विचारों और स्वतंत्र व्यक्तियों के स्वतंत्र समाज के आदर्श से प्रेरित हों, उन परिस्थितियों की रचना कर सकती है जिसमें सही मायने में लोकतंत्र सम्भव होगा।

राय के अनुसार सामाजिक क्रान्ति की विधि और कार्यक्रम को सामाजिक विकास के बुनियादी सिद्धान्तों पर आधारित होना चाहिए। स्वतंत्रता और बुद्धिसंगत सहकारी जीवन के सिद्धान्तों में शिक्षित करने के व्यापक और दृढ़ प्रयत्नों के जरिए ही सामाजिक नवजागरण सम्भव है। साथ ही, क्रान्ति के बाद की व्यवस्था की सामाजिक-राजनीतिक बुनियाद के रूप में जनता को कारगर लोकतांत्रिक संगठनों के माध्यम से संगठित किया जाना चाहिए। सामाजिक क्रान्ति के लिए एक ओर तेजी से बढ़ती हुई संख्या में नवजागरण के मनुष्यों और दूसरी ओर तेजी से फैलते हुए लोकसमितियों की व्यवस्था का अस्तित्व, और दोनों के बीच सहज समन्वय आवश्यक है। इसी तरह क्रान्ति के कार्यक्रम स्वतंत्रता, बुद्धि और सामाजिक सामंजस्य के सिद्धान्तों पर आधारित होंगे। इसका अर्थ होगा सामाजिक जीवन से हर किस्म के एकाधिकार और निहित स्वार्थों को समाप्त करना।

राय का यह मानना था कि रैडिकल लोकतंत्र की स्थापना के लिए मानव द्वारा मानव के शोषण की सम्भावना को समाप्त करने की दृष्टि से समाज का आर्थिक पुनर्निर्माण भी जरूरी है। समाज के सदस्यों के बौद्धिक और मानवीय सम्भावनाओं का विकास हो सके इसके लिए उनके भौतिक आवश्यकताओं की पूर्ति एक आवश्यक शर्त है। स्वतंत्रता के लक्ष्य की ओर आगे बढ़ने के लिए जनता की आर्थिक मुक्ति जरूरी है। इसलिए, मनुष्य के जीवन स्तर को बढ़ाने की गारन्टी देनेवाली आर्थिक व्यवस्था रैडिकल लोकतांत्रिक राज्य की बुनियाद है। रैडिकल लोकतंत्र की अर्थव्यवस्था उपयोग के लिए उत्पादन और मानवीय आवश्यकताओं के अनुसार वितरण पर आधारित होगी। जबकि उसकी संस्कृति ज्ञान के सर्वव्यापी विस्तार के लिए वैज्ञानिक और रचनात्मक गतिविधियों को अधिकतम प्रोत्साहन और न्यूनतम नियंत्रण पर आधारित होगी। वह नया समाज बुद्धि और विज्ञान पर

आधारित होने के नाते योजनाबद्ध होगा लेकिन उसकी योजनाओं का मुख्य लक्ष्य व्यक्ति की स्वतंत्रता होगा। इस तरह, वह नया समाज राजनीतिक, आर्थिक और सांस्कृतिक दृष्टि से भी एक लोकतांत्रिक समाज होगा। एक ऐसा लोकतांत्रिक समाज जो अपनी रक्षा आप करने में समर्थ होगा।

जैसा कि पहले भी उल्लेख किया गया है 22 थीसिस और घोषणा-पत्र 'न्यू हयूमैनिस्म' को रैडिकल डेमोक्रेटिक पार्टी के दस्तावेज के रूप में स्वीकार और जारी किया गया था। लेकिन इनमें व्यक्त विचारों पर आगे चर्चा के आधार पर राय इस निष्कर्ष तक पहुँचे थे कि सत्ता की राजनीति द्वारा रैडिकल लोकतंत्र की स्थापना सम्भव नहीं है।

राय के अनुसार उनकी कल्पना के रैडिकल लोकतांत्रिक समाज का निर्माण स्वतंत्रता के लक्ष्य से प्रेरित ऐसे मनुष्यों के प्रयत्नों से होगा जो जनता के भावी शासक के रूप में नहीं, बल्कि उनके दोस्त, दार्शनिक और मार्गदर्शक के रूप में काम करेंगे। स्वतंत्रता के उनके लक्ष्य को ध्यान में रखते हुए उनका राजनीतिक व्यवहार बुद्धिसंगत और इसलिए नैतिक होगा। स्वतंत्रता और सत्ता के केन्द्रीकरण के बीच तार्किक संगति के अभाव को समझते हुए रैडिकल लोकतांत्रिक सत्ता के अधिकतम विकेन्द्रीकरण के लिए प्रयत्न करेंगे। जनता में स्वतंत्रता की इच्छा के विकास से उनके प्रयत्नों को बल मिलेगा। और अन्ततः प्रबुद्ध जनमत और जनता के बुद्धिमतापूर्ण प्रयत्नों के समर्थन से रैडिकल लोकतांत्रिक राज्य का उदय होगा।

राय बतलाते हैं कि अन्तिम विश्लेषण में नागरिकों की शिक्षा रैडिकल लोकतांत्रिक दिशा में समाज की प्रगति की अनिवार्य शर्त होगी। इसलिए लोकसमितियाँ नागरिकों की राजनीतिक शिक्षा के लिए स्कूल की तरह काम करेंगी। रैडिकल लोकतांत्रिक राज्य का ढाँचा और काम करने का तरीका ऐसा होगा जिससे मानसिक दृष्टि से स्वतंत्र और स्वार्थरहित व्यक्तियों को सार्वजनिक जीवन में आगे आने का अवसर मिलेगा। ऐसे व्यक्तियों द्वारा संचालित होने पर राज्य एक वर्ग द्वारा दूसरे वर्ग के शोषण का औजार नहीं रह जाएगा।

इस तरह अपने नव मानवतावाद में राय व्यक्ति और उसकी स्वतंत्रता को सर्वोच्च महत्व देते हुए एक ओर व्यक्तित्व और सामूहिक जीवन, और दूसरी ओर, आर्थिक नियतत्त्ववाद और विचारों के गति विज्ञान के बीच सामंजस्य स्थापित करते हैं; और इस सामंजस्य के आधार पर हमारे सामने आज के समय के लिए सामाजिक क्रान्ति की एक विधि और कार्यक्रम प्रस्तुत करते हैं।

22 थीसीस के माध्यम से व्यक्त किया गया राय का नव मानवतावादी दर्शन हमारे लिए आज भी प्रासंगिक और प्रेरणादायी है। दरअसल, राय के नव

मानवतावाद का सही मूल्यांकन किया जाना अभी बाकी है। हमें यह आशा करनी चाहिए कि राय के जन्म शताब्दी वर्ष में राय के नव मानवतावाद का संदेश अधिक से अधिक लोगों तक पहुँच सकेगा।

लेखक पटना विश्वविद्यालय में दर्शनशास्त्र के प्रोफेसर हैं तथा 'बुद्धिवादी' पत्रिका के सम्पादक।

14

COMPASSIONATE HUMANISM

H.H. Dalai Lama

LOVE IS NO RELIGION BUT HUMAN
(प्यार धर्म नहीं, मानव स्वभाव)

Mahatma Gandhi was a great human being with a deep understanding of human nature. He made every effort to encourage the full development of the positive aspects of the human potential and to reduce or restrain the negative. I consider myself to be one of the followers of Mahatma Gandhi.

Even as violence seems to be growing around us, we remember that the epitome of non-violence, Mahatma Gandhi was himself assassinated. That act of violence revealed one aspect of the human personality, but we must remember that all of us have a most remarkable potential, the ability to develop infinite altruism and compassion and a brain capable of unlimited knowledge and understanding. This needs to be used in the right way for it is also capable of unlimited destruction.

BE WISELY SELFISH

I consider the cultivation of non-violence and compassion as part of my daily practice. I do not consider this as something that is holy or sacred but of practical benefit to myself. The practice gives me satisfaction, it gives me a peace that is very helpful to have sincere, genuine relationships with other people.

As a human being I love friends, I love their smiles. We most realise that human happiness is interdependent. One's own successful or happy future is related to that of others. Therefore, helping others or having consideration of their rights and needs is actually not only one's own responsibility but a matter of one's own happiness. So I often tell people if we have to be really selfish, then let us be wisely selfish. If we are warm-hearted we automatically receive more smiles and make more genuine friends. We human beings are social animals. No matter how powerful or how intelligent we are, it is virtually impossible to survive without another human being. We need others for our very existence. The practice of compassion and non-violence is in one's own self-interest.

Genuine non-violence is related to one's mental attitude. When we talk of peace we must mean genuine peace, not merely the absence of war. For example, in the last few decades there was relative peace on the European contient, but I do not think it was genuine peace. It was peace that came out of fear as a result of the cold war.

What is the relevance of non-violence and compassion in today's world? Ahimsa or non-violence is an ancient Indian concept which Mahatma Gandhi revived and implemented in modern times not only in politics but in day-to-day life. That was his great achievement. The nature of non-violence should be something that is not passive but active in helping others. Non-violence means that if you can help and serve others you must do that. If you cannot, you must at least restrain yourself from harming others.

The 20th century, I think is the most important century in human history. It has seen many outstanding scientific achievements and yet more human suffering than ever before. The human being in this century is basically the same, as 1,000 or 10,000 years ago. He has had the same negative feelings of anger and hatred but this century has seen an enormous increase in his destructive power. This has produced a desperate situation of fear. With the possibility of nuclear holocaust the picture seemed hopeless and unbearable. The future looked so bleak that it forced and helped the human mind to think of alternatives This gives great hope.

During the fifties and sixties many people felt that the ultimate decision in any disagreement or conflict could only come through war or weapons that were believed to deter war. Today more and more people are realising that the proper way of resolving differences is through dialogue, compromise, negotiations, through human understanding and humility. It is a very great sign.

GANDHIAN PHILOSOPHY

The events and developments of our century have encouraged the human being to become wiser, more mature. In many countries, I think the attraction to Gandhian philosophy is growing. Because the capacity for human destruction is so immense, because the threat to the environment is so great, people are developing a greatr understanding of the meaning of non-violence and of compassion.

Sometimes people feel that human beings are not all that gentle; after all there is so much violence, so many killings, so much tragedy. But if you look closely, of the more than five billion human beings the number who are engaging in negative activities or have negative thoughts is very small. If human nature was so bad I think we would not have had to worry about the population problem.

Compassion and love are not matters of religion, though many religions teach these things. When we are born, we do not have any religion but we are not free from human love and affection. This is not a matter of religion. I believe it is a separate thing. What religions do is try to strengthen these qualities which are already there in human nature from birth.

Why is it necessary to make a distinction between religion and human nature? This is essential because of the five billion or so people on our planet no more than about one billion are "believers" or actively follow any organised religion. We are all members of the same human family. We must find ways of cultivating a deeper awareness of love and compassion, with or without religion. At the same time, we need to understand the negative expressions of the human mind such as anger, hatred and attachment.

COMPASSION THE KEY

What is anger? It is true that sometimes due to some tragedy in our lives or due to frustrated desires we feel negative feelings which express themselves more openly in anger. This may sometimes seem useful. But we must analyse and investigate the value of anger. Anger brings forth extra energy, boldness and determination. It is possible to use this energy to take certain drastic actions. Usually decisions taken when your minds is dominated by anger are wrong decisions which bring unhappiness or regret.

When we face some external problem, it is often possible to escape it and find a solution, but when the anger or the hatred is within, you cannot do so easily. Once you have an understanding or realisation of the nature of your mind, then gradually it will change. As time goes on your attitude, even to the external enemy, will change. With understandng there will be forgiveness and an increase of your inner strength. As a result there will be less fear, less doubt and more self-confidence, tolerance and patience. This is why I consider compassion to be the key.

That is my belief, my daily practice This Buddhist monk, 57 years old now, finds that through my own little experience, through training, through analytical meditation I have changed. If we make the attempt we can change. We can improve ourselves.

We are human beings, our basic nature is that of love and compassion. When we see a tree with some branches dying we are sad. When we see greenery and buds growing into flowers we feel positive and happy. In human nature, there is a natural feeling for living things. I think the time has come to think about the basic cause of our suffering.

Paper on "understanding human nature" by courtesy Times of India, Oct. 2, 1992 with gratitude.

15

RADICAL HUMANISM

R.M. Pal

If an intellectual history of India's freedom struggle is written, M.N. Roy, who was born on March 21, 1887, is certain to find a leading place in it. Roy is generally known as an outstanding Marxist theoritician who founded the first communist party outside Russia and had the courage, when he was in his late twenties, to differ from Lenin on the national and colonial question in 1920. He rose very rapidly to occupy almost all important positions in the Communist Intrnational–membership of the executive, the presidium, the secretariat, the editorial board, chiarmanship of the Eastern Commission, and member-secretaryship of the Chinese Commission. There are, however, other achievements of Roy, more fundamental and more significant–his philosophy of Radical Humanism, of organised democracy and party-less politics. Until a few years ago there used to be at least occasional discussions on an alternative system as propounded by Roy, Gandhi and Jayaprakash Narayan and dismissed by some social scientists as utopian.

Radical Humanism goes beyond Marxism. The spirit of this philosophy is revealed in the following words of Roy: "The old-fashioned revolutionaries thought in terms of freedom. In those days, we had not read Marx. We did not know about the existence of the proletariat. Still, many spent their lives in jail and went to the gallows. They had the human urge to revolt against the intolerable conditions of life. They did not know exactly how these conditions could be changed. But they tried to change them anyhow. I began my political life with that spirit, and still draw my inspiration rather from that spirit than from the three volumes of Capital or 300 volumes by the Marxists."

Broadly speaking Radical Humanism centres round radicalism which aims at bringing about a revolution to attain freedom and justice, and Humanism which aims at seeking knowledge, tolerance and co-operation. Roy proposed organisd democracy and a government based on party-less politics, as against the political practice of liberalism, i.e./parliamentary form of government. He stood for a comprehensive ideal of political and economic freedom. A government under the parliamentary system represents only the ruling party and even the largest party is a small fraction of the people. Very often a party government is ruled by a minority. The individual, in this system, has to be a subservient part of the party machine. Thus, party politics is inconsistent with the ideal of democracy and is bound to degenerate into unprincipled scramble for power.

Roy also offered an economic theory–alternative both to capitalism (liberalism), and state capitalism (socialism)–and he called it coopertive economy. Under this system the means of production would belong neither to the capitalist class nor to the state; they would belong to the people.

While attacking fanaticism and unreason, he wrote: "All saints and seers, modern as well as ancient, are victims of a very complicated type of hysteria. Ramakrishna Paramhansa, for example, lived practically always under auto-suggestions... The quintessence of the dharma of India in her golden age is contained in the Shanti Parva of the Mahabharata. Read it to find how eager even the Brahmins were to acquire worldly goods." In the preface to his book. India's Message Roy wrote, "... a critical examination of what is cherished as India's cultural heritage will enable the Indian people to cast off the chilly grip of a dead past. It will embolden them to face the ugly realities of a living present and look forward to a better, brighter and pleasanter future."

A SHOCK

In 1946 Roy gave a shock to his colleagues and admirers by declaring that the political practice of communism was undermocratic and must be rejected. But the rudest shock that he gave was when after Mahatma Gandhi's assassination. Roy hailed Gandhi as a cosmopolitan humanist and also as one who endeavoured to bring morality to politics.

"My whole political life", Roy said, "has been nothing but a tormented soul's urge and search for freedom. I am afraid I have not been able to impart that urge to many with whom I came in contact."

Paper entitled 'A Tormented Soul's urge for freedom By Courtesy Times of India, March 21, 1993.

16

RENEWING FAITH IN GOD AS A SAVIOUR
(ईश्वर युक्त मानववाद)

M.N. Srinivas

The country is going through a grave and multi-faceted crisis in which the goals which were formulated at the dawn of independence as well as the means used for attaining them have lost much of their sheen though some forces in all the political parties have a vestd interest in their continuance. There is, however, a need to examine critically the entire situation in order to find goals which are in tune with the culture and institutions of the bulk of the people. This task requires that a few old but unfashionable truths be restated.

ROLE OF RELIGION

It needs to be stated clearly, and from the houses tops, that religion plays a vital and pervasive role in the lives of the ordinary people in the country, and that this is true of the followers of all the religions in India. During the last six decades or so, however, a process of "Secularisation" (not secularism) has occurred in all the religions though perhaps far more in Hinduism than in the others. By secularisation I refer to a decrease in the pervasiveness of religion, and its confinement, over a period of time, to specific areas, situations and events. A caution : even within the same religion, secularisation has not occurred uniformly in all the social strata.

Ideas of purity and impurity which were formely so pervasive in the lives of Hindus, have become much weaker as a result of the recent great developments in communications, transport, urbanisation and education. The movement of substantial numbers of Hindus into the middle classes has resulted in a lifestyle in which purity-impurity ideas are becoming confined to the rites of passage, pilgrimage and a few festivals. Further, among the middle classes, the age of marriage has risen sharply, the endogamous circle has widened greatly, inter-caste and inter-regional marriages are occurring frequently, and more rarely, inter-religious marriages.

What I have said of middle class Hindus is true by and large of the middle classes in the other religions in India, the only difference being that purity-impurity ideas were weaker among them initially. In other words, entry into the middle classes involves some secularisation of lifestyle.

It is simplistic to assume an invariant relationship between the middle classes and secularisation. Education, urbanisation and unemployment in the professions may also provide the ideal soil for sowing fundamentalist seeds. Fundamentalism has to be distinguished from orthodoxy for while the latter involves strict adherence to tradition the former reinterprts tradition for political or other purposes.

To return to my main point: India is a religious country par excellence even after taking into account the fact that secularisation has occurred in all the religious groups, with Hidndus being subjected to it far more than the others. Rationalists and un-believers really constitute a minuscule minority but it is difficult to remember this since they more than make up for their lack of numbers by their articulation, their access to the media and to power, Intellectuals in the academia, media and the bureaucracy are the pillars of rationalism, and they enjoy the support of the communist parties even though the latter have recently discovered religion. The DMK, once committed to rationalism and atheism, abandoned both over 10 years ago since the voters were all believers in God. (Decades of atheist propaganda by the dent in Tamil religiosity and this serious study.)

Indian communists have been badly let down by their former patrons and mentors, the USSR, who have also rediscoved religion after seven decades of the most brutal suppression of religion and the state promotion of atheism. I was in Russia seven or eight years ago when our group was taken to an impressive orthodox church service in 'Zagorsk, a town about 60 kilometres from Moscow. And in Samarkhand, we were taken to a sylvan and restful mosque where we met the Imam who hospitality and friendliness did not conceal his fundamentalist inclinations.

MATERIAL SUCCESS

Nehruvian socialism has lost ground with the middle classes because of, among other things, its creation of an over-centralist state, compounded by a powerful planning commission and the inevitable outcome of both, a licence-permit raj which has enabled corrupt politicians and officials to become filthy-rich at the expense of the people. Smugglers, blackmarketeers, and plain criminal elements have been enabled to get a half-nelson on the politico-economic system. Underlying all this is the rule, each man for himself and devil take the hindmost. Material success is the goal.

The kind of consumerism that the media is so frenetically promoting day in and day out is absurdly unrealistic in the sense that most Indians will have to go without the goods and gadgets, considering the fact that India's population will reach a billion in a little over a decade. The only kind of development that India, and indeed the world, can afford is sustainable development. Resources are crushingly finite even granted the inventiveness of scientists and technologists. Sustainable development needs to be underpinned by a proper restraint and that cannot be secular humanism. It has to come from a religious world-view.

There is, however, a basic difficulty in bringing in religion : established religions do divide people into the faithful and unbelievers. Volumes have been written on the harm inflicted by institutional religion. But institutional religion is not the whole of religion. Underlying institutional religion is a universal layer, referred to by the philosopher Leibnitz as "philosophia perenis."

According to Aldous Huxley, perennial philosophy underlines every religion known to humankind. Every religion has its mystics, and it is the latter who articulate the universal element in religion, albeit in the cultural medium of their own particular religion.

SAME LANGUAGE

In a sense, the Upanishadic seers, Bhakti saints, Sufis and Jewish and Christian mystics, all speak the same language. The Bhakti saints are particularly relevant to us today as they rejected caste and gender inequalities, and spoke not only in the language of the people but for the salvation of the hoi polloi, the "ignorant" masses. And an essential lesson to be learnt from the mystics is the primacy they gave to the spiritual over the material. This is particularly relevant in the context of the growing menace of consumerism in the country.

With growing liberalisation and increasing size of the middle class, consumerism is likely to become a Frankestein's monster, if steps are not taken to halt it.

It is in this overall context that the need for a new philosophy and social ethics becomes urgent and imperative. And that philosophy cannot be secular humanism. It has to be firmly rooted in God as creator and protector, and the sustainer of human societies. The fraternity of all human beings cutting across divisions of race, ethnicity, caste, class, religion and gender follows logically from the idea of God as creator. The idea of human free will is in all religions and it provides the basis for individual liberty without which there can be no true democracy.

The idea of God as creator is also a cure to anthropo-centricism, and it requires that man has to be friendly to all nature including animals and birds, and to the environment as a whole. The recent western sensitiveness to the environement and to animal rights needs a firmer basis than calculated human self-interest and that can only come from a religious world-view.

By courtesy Times of India, July 9, 1993 with gratitude.

17

ETHICAL HUMANISM OF VIVEKANAND
(विवेकानन्द का नैतिक मानववाद)

V.P. Verma

Swami Vivekananda (1863-1902) was a mighty majestic and comprehensive personality. Although of athletic muscular build, he had a mystic consciousness like Plotinus and Spinoza attuned with the absolute of the monistic idealists. But simultaneously he was a gignatic intellectual thoroughly at home in the greatest secrets of metaphysical Vedantism, European philosophy and element of modern science and had a burning enthusiasm for the alleviation of human suffering. The person who could perform the collossal feat of mastering the first 11 volumes of the Encyclopaedia Britannica (out of a total 20) had also a luminous and passionate urge to experience directly the ecstatic absorption with the subject objectless (asamprajnata) beatific supernal state. The late Brajendra Nath Seal testifies to the deep and restless passion ofVivekananda to apprehend the highest truth from his early young days. Although the Swami was a reversed teacher of the monistic Vedanta, still the devotional mood-characteristic of the great Vedantic Acharyas like Madhava and Vallabha was also prominent in his person. The world knows him is a gigantic mind who employed his stupendous will-power and energy to bring about a regeneration of India.

The intense nationalism and patriotism of Vivekananda is revealed in this declaration of his: "For the next fifty years... let all other vain Gods disappear for that time from our minds. This is the only God that is awake, our own race. everywhere His hands, everywhere His feet, everywhere, His ears. He covers everything.

All other Gods are sleeping. What vain Gods shall we go after and yet cannot worship the God and we see all round us, the Virat?.... The first of all worship is the worship of the Virat—of those all around us... These are all our Gods—men and animals, and the first Gods we have to worship are our own countrymen... (The Future of India). This monk, social energist and humanist philanthropist waned : as he said, to fall on the society like an avalanche. He was a pilgrim of the city of God and a warrior for the cause of the suppressed. Hence the swami's persoanlty was unique in its comprehensiveness and deep sensitiveness to the evils prevalent in the social economic and moral structure of the country. He preached both monastic asceticism and social service. His intellectual vision was immensely clear and he could penetrate into the currents and cross-currents that were manifested in the history of India. Before his vigorous mind everything from the Rigveda to Kalidasa and Kant and Spencer was clear and luminous. He claimed to have realised the supracosmie truth but still he worked with the strength of a lion. His soul gave one the impression not of the silent Purusha of the Samkhya but of the active Atman of the Vaisesika as also of the Atman of the Upanishads – the supreme energic of the cosmic mamlestation .... It appeared as it the virya and ojha of the Mahabirarata hences and the stalwart protagonists of Hindu imperialism in th days of the Mauryas and the Guptas was combined in his magificent personality, with the spiritual 'tejas' characteristic of the ancient seers of the Veda and Vedanta. Hence the Swami was able to achieve miracles in a short life-time of only 39 years.

The triumphant marches of Swami Vivekananda, the 'Hindu Napoleon' in the American continent and Europe demonstrated to the poeple that Hindusim had grown once more vigorous and was intent upon making a spiritual, moral and cultural philosophical propaganda in the world. The New Imperaialism of America and Europe met with this counter-attack from Asia. Asia had given to Europe the main elements of religion and culture in the past (e.g. Judaism, Christianity, Oriental influences on Roman religion, Islam in the Iberian Peninsula—also the incluence of Vedantic thought on Thoreau and on the transcendental Over-soul of Emerson) and Asia wanted once more to provide moral inspiration to Europe. Vivekananda's powerful and eloquent orations on the stage of the World Parliament of Religions at Chicago in September 1983 gave to our motherland a new self-confidence which is the true psychological precaisor of an independent foreign policy. The nefareous game of the Europeanisation of this land of the sages received a great challence. Hence Vivekanda succeeded in imparting a dynamic and heroic spiritual fervour to the formation of the culture-complex of India. The same vigour which Luther and Calvin had impartd to Western Europe seemed to be infused by Vivekananda and Dayananda in the passive calm of the contemporary Indian civilisation. There is no doubt that the influence of Vivekanada on some of the political leaders of Bengal like Autobindo and Subhas Bose was deep.

The Swami made a distinct and notable contribution to world religion in his championship of Hinduism as a universal gospel of ethical humanism and spiritual idealism. Hinduism had been the subject of intense misrepresentation at the hands of Christian missionaries who sufferred from superiority complex and were actuated with a sense of burden in to "Civilise" the black and men and brown men by clearing the road for the economic exploitation of Asia and Africa (as can be seen from a study of the rise of modern new imperialism from 1870). But Hinduism was, in Vivekananda., a comprehensive gospel which could shelter within its bosom the profound philosophic intellect by its Nyaya, Samkhya and Vedanta, could offer to the psychologist its vast store of psychic wisdom of the Rajayoga, could inspire the devotee with the enchanted hymns of the Samaveda and the devotional songs of Tulsidas or the Alvar and Naynars (saints of the south) and finally could give to the puissant and hectic worker the doctrine of selfless action as enunciated in the celestial song of Sri Krishna. Hinduism did not mean to him the cluster of obscure cults and ritualistic superstitions, orthodox dogmas and primitive ceremonialism which unfortunately the superficial European critic is very keen in observing, but it signified to him a body of moral and spiritual injunctions and primordial supertemporal laws for the uplift of humanity.

To him Hinduism was the mother of religions and this can be, to a great extent, demonstrated historically. The ancient Vedic religion influenced Buddhism, and the latter was possibily a potent factor in the rise of christianity. The order Vedic religion also influenced the religion of Persia and Media and the reformist ethical movement which began in Judea in the 6th century. BC was inspired by some aspects of the western Asiatic religions (of Persia and India) which the Jews came to learn during the Babylonish captivity. The researches that are being carried into the antique history of Egypt and Western Asia are demonstrating the cultural penetration of ancient India religion in far-off lands. In the Tell-el-amarna letter (c. 1380-1350 B.C.) we come across vedic names, e.g. Artamanya which, according to Keith, certainly suggests Ritamanya (A.B. Keith, Indian Historical Quarterly, 1936, P. 573). The Rita is a vital concept of ancient Indian philosophy. The Mittanian gods (referred to in records of abotu 1400 B.C.) have a nomenclature which is definitely Vedic.

Vivekananda was a representative of entire Hinduism from the Vedas to Vaisnavism. He did not emphasize the Sanctity of the Veda to the same extent as did the late great Swami Dayanand. He was impressed greatly by the Jnanakanda of the Upanishads. The universalism of Vivekananda remained one of the catholic culture of Ashoka. He had been brought up under the influence of his teacher Ramakrishna whose whole personality was demonstration and vindication of the inherent spiritual truths in all the various religions. The Swami partly introduced once more the practice of proselytism in Hinduism which was falling into oblivion.

He defined religion as the vital and moral force which gives life to a person or to a nation. In thundering words he said:

> *"Strength is life, weakness is death". Jawaharlal Nehru in his "The Discovery of India" has pointed out that the great refrain of Vivekananda's teaching was abhayam, (fearlessness). Vivekananda wantd to make a harmonious fusion of the Kshattriya manhood and Brahmana intellectualism. He shunned all weakening mysteries. Melamed in his book Spinoza and Buddha wants to differentiate between Hebraism and Hinduism and says that the former is individualistic, theistic, optimistic and presents an anthropocentric view of the world. As distinct from it, the latter is universalistic, pessimistic, cosmocentric and worldnegating. These generalisations are born out of a superficial study of Indian history and philosophy. The creators of Mauryan imperialism and Maratha policy were not vague sentimentalists. Vivekananda; although a monist, always stood for a vigorous and valiant action in the secular sphere and heroically inculcated that absolute bravery and firm bold faith could shake history.*

European critics level the charge against Indian Philosophy of being indifferent to ethics. Dr. A.B. Keith has the boldness to say : "In comparison with the intellectual activity of the Brahmanas the ethical content of the Upanishads must be said to be negligible and valueless... they (the Brahmanas) have completely failed to see that morality is the most objective and essential part of philosophy. "But

Vivekananda and Ram Tirtha have pointed out in their American lectures that the Vedantic metaphysics which teaches spiritual equality is the real guarantee of an equal treatment ot the vast masses of men. The French Revolution taught liberty and equality, but it degenerated into the despotic imperialism of Napoleons I and III. The Russian slogan of the dictatorship of the proletariat is now the slogan of dictatorship of a manipulating group, "the vanguard" because these movements are not ethically inspired. After all, genuine ethics and social morality are meant for good behaviour and the development of freedom, right, self-consciousness and good in the world. The Vedantic metaphysics does not neutralise the subejctive disposition to life because of its Mayavada but strengthens moral action by providing to that a rock-like spiritual foundation.

Vivekananda advocated the monism of the Upnishads as systematised by Badarayana and Samkara. The ever conscient blissful reality was to him the supreme existent and the eternal real and could be realised as a result of philosophic thinking and living. The world, according to the view of Samkara is the vivarta of Brahma, (cp Spino za's theory of "modes" of one infinite eternal, immutable, selfsubsistent, substance, God). Vivekananda did not wholly deny the reality of the cosmos although he was bound to do so philosophically. He was inspired by his great teacher who believed in the "motherhood" of governing principle of universe a tantric doctrine and formula which in its incipient form is also found in the religious systems of the ancient Indus valley and Western Asia.

Vivekananda had a peculiar theory of evolution which has been supposd to supplement the Darwinian formula. The Swami, though admitting Darwin's theory to be sound enough to a certain extent, assailed it with a greater theory, that of Patanjali's "filling in of nature which, he showed, offered the ultimate solution of the causes of evolution". He pointed out that the Darwinian analysis fitted well on the lower plane, but on the higher plane, moral factor had a great hand in giving to man his birthright of perfection and eternal salvation.

Vivekananda's epistemological analysis follows the orthodox Vedantic formula. He pointed out that all the knowledge that we receive from outside is not any external addition.

By Courtesy, Hindustan Times, April 27, 1996 with gratitude.

18

RELIGION AND RIGHTEOUSNESS
(धर्म और न्यायशीलता)

Mulk Raj Anand

In our hectic times, the noise of history drowns thought. And yet it is necessary, if we are to emerge from the atmosphere of querulous words, to ponder on the basic concepts of religion and politics which have been confounded by the shouting of slogans, especially by the protagonists of Hindutva.

It may be possible to achieve some clarity in the ongoing debate between the would be proponents of Hindutva nationhood and the upholders of secular democracy if we recall the role of religion in politics, especially during the time the political state emergd in India. The rule of law, and its breach, were defined by the promoter of the first solid state, Chanakya, in his Arthashastra.

There third century writings laid down the political basis of a stable state in the land system, which ensured the well-being of villagers by the careful conduct of the census of population, the record of livestock, the fixing of revenue, and giving people rights commensurate with their obligations to the state.

Ashoka, the third emperor of the Maurya dynasty, who inherited a fairly well-built empire from his grandfather, Chandragupta, and his father, Bindusara, went further than Chanakya in giving a humanist content to statecraft. In one of his edicts he put forward the philosophy of government in the concept of dhamma–which is the Prakrit variation of the Sanskrit dharma.

Ashoka seems to have understood the word dhamma as righteousness, not as religion. It was to be embodied in laws concerned with the welfare of individuals in society and with their rights and responsibilites as human beings in their relations with one another-defined through their human faculties and impulses which seek to connect human beings with the family, the group, and the larger community.

Tolerance of others was the inner core of Ashoka's will, as he asked for 'consideration towards slaves and servants', 'honour for another man's sect', 'concord.. so that men may hear one another's principles.' In fact, he desired the integration of different peoples to achieve some harmony against discord. Of course, he had come to this human ideal after his repentance for the killings in the Kalinga war.

Is it possible that, when Jawaharlal Nehru advocated the adoption of the four-lion symbol as an emblem of the Indian republic in 1947, he had in mind Ashoka's belief in the universal law of righteousness? The neutrality of the state towards various religions, advocatd by the first Prime Minister of India and his colleagues in the constituent Assembly, is thus not 'pseudo-secularism', as the Hindutva protagonists dub it, but the inheritance of Ashokan grace, which implies a tolerance of the multitudes of faiths of our country.

If our Constitution accords with democratic orders evolved or brought into being in the West in the modern period, that lone is no reason to attribute 'secularism' entirely to western inspiration. Our own inherited dhamma, applied after two centuries of struggles for freedom in an aspiration for a just social order, is not borrowed from western democracies.

Again, if our slogan of liberty harks back to John. Sturat Mill's pamphlet written as a warning against British hierarchical prejudices, our own renascent thinker, Raja Ram Mohan Roy, thought human happiness to be possible in a free society. His ideas coincided with those of Mill and Bentham and other utilitarian philosophers.

The dharma implicit in our Constitution is based on the deepest reverence for human life and is thus a sacred trust for us to preserve and extend. This must be defended against the sectarian assertiveness of the fundamentalism of Hindutva. Dharma, as Chaturvedi Badrinath has recently suggested, is not to be identified with Hindu religion, as some British interpreters have done, and as Hindutva fanatics now tend to do by making it the core of Hinduism.

We might remember that this savant Ram Mohan Roy insisted on being transported to a French ship in Cape Town harbour when he was on his way to London as he wantd to salute the flag of liberty, equality and fraternity adopted after the French revolution against the monarchy in 1787 which had answerd Roy's own projections.

Our 19th century renascent thinkers knew that the writings of Tom Paine had inspired the manifesto of the French revolutionaries, even as they were earlier the basis of the Bill of Rights of the American revolution.

The liberal humanist movement in the West emerged after 500 years of struggle of wars of Reformation, of the Protestant Christians against the patriarchal and monarchist assertions of the Catholic Church.

The Italian renaissance of the 15th century followd Galileo's revolutinary theory that in the beginning there was the act and not the word of God. And there were five centuries of enlightenment through discussions, debates and polemics before the rationalist hypothesis won against obscurantist religious dogmas.

And if some of our humanists like Rabindranath Tagore, Jawaharlal Nehru and M.N. Roy accepted the emphasis on the worth of man and our founding fathers defined egalitarian laws, it is because these principles have answered our own integral aspirations and are not mere transplants from the West.

The dharma impicit in our Constitution is based on the deepest reverence for human life and is thus a sacred trust for us to preserve and extend. This must be defended against the sectarian assertiveness of the fundamentalism of Hindutva. Dharma, as Chaturvedi Badrinath has recently suggested, is not to be identified with Hindu religion, as some British interpreters have done, and as Hindutva fanatics now tend to do by making it the core of Hinduism. In fact, there was no Hindu religion or Hinduism until the word Sindhu was perverted by infiltrates from the 12th century onwards, which later became 'Hindu', a word of contempt for idol worshippers.

If the Constitution of 1947, with its emphasis on human rights, confers on the individual the liberty to profess any faith of his choice, placing religion in his private conscience, the co-existence of different religions is possible with an Ashokan reverence for all faiths.

The assumption of Hindutva nationalists, who proclaim the supremacy of the faith of the majority, Hinduism, and ask Muslims, Sikhs and Christians to consider themselves Hindus because they are mostly converts from Hinduism, smacks of authoritarian arrogance. If Hindutva theocracy comes to prevail, it will spell the same fate for the minorities as in Pakistan, where people professing Hinduism have almost ceased to exist, and Christians and even Qadiani Muslims (who believe there might be other prophets than Muhammad) are also almost eliminated.

The choice before our countrymen then is between the acceptance of our inherited historical humanism and the VHP-majority religion. Accepting the second could mean torture of dissenters, cruel inquisitions, and killings in internecine wars, as happened in Europe.

Let us devise our laws so that in future election sloganeering in the name of temples or mosques or gurdwaras is not allowed, as also votes gathered. through propaganda for a theocratic state in place of democracy built on fundamental human rights.

By Courtesy Times of India, Aug. 29, 1993.

19

SUFISM–UNITING CULTURES

Rasheeduddin Khan

Historically, India has been one of the greatest confluences of cultural strands, a laboratory of racial inter-mixing, of cross-fertilisation of religious ideas and secular thought, of coexistence of languages and dialectics, indeed a veritable microcosm of the globe.

In the dim twilight of history the migration of primordial hordes of ethnic groups mostly from Central, South-Central and North-Eastern parts of Asia that have, wave upon wave, descended into the fertile Indo-Gangetic plains moving south wards to the alluvial Deccan Plateau inhabited by the earliest known indigenous people, provided the first pattern of interethnic mixture in the mighty generous land that was to become one of the biggest crucible of races and cultures in human history.

The Muslim migratory clans of the Uzbeks, the Turkoman, the Turks, the Iranian, the Turanian, the Afghans and the Pathans moved in during the mediaeval times and made Hindustan their homeland. With multi-ethnic migrants came their dialects and belief patterns, social systems and value structures, all contributing to the expanding cultural diversity and societal diffusion in the historic process of the building of what is today the rich continetal plural society of India, comprising a fifth of the total human population.

In terms of cultural depth and intensity and wider social repercussions the two most profound influences on the making of a distinct Indian civilization, are those of the ancient Indo-Aryan and the mediaeval Indo-Muslim segments. The Indo-Aryans contributed to the flowering of Vedic cultural streams that over the centureis have continued to fertilize the body politic of this ancient land, and even today remains the sub-soil of a culture.

The Indo-Muslim strands have woven into the texture of India's national existence a new design of 'composite culture', by intertwining the threads of the Bhakti Marg with the Islami Sufi (mystic) traditions, the Indian social customs with the Turko-Iranian mores of collective life, thereby creating a new inter-cultural synthesis, in which the values of man and social ethics reflected a new ethos.

It is not surprising, therefore, to realize that the composite culture in India orginated in an environment of reconciliation rather than refutation, cooperation rather than confrontation, coexistence rather than mutual annihilation.

It was in the last decade of the 12th century that the first Sufi order was firmly established in India, by the great Chisti saint, Khwaja Muinuddin Hasan Chisti (1143-1234). He was born in Seistan and came to India on the directions of his teacher Khwaja Usman Haruni in 1190 during the reign of Rai Prithvirai, the powerful Chauhan king of Ajmer and Delhi. In his youth he had also visited Baghdad to spend time at the Khanqah of Sheikh Abdul Quadir Jilani, the great founder of the Qadiriah silsila. It is true that before him many Sufi teachers had come to India, like Shaikh Ali Hujjwiri, popularly known as Data Gunj Baksh of Lahore, at whose tomb Khwaja Muinuddin spent much time in meditation, before moving to Ajmer in 1197, as the permanent centre of his activities.

There were also several towns in north India like Multan, Lahore, Badaun, Kanauj, Nagar etc. where Sufi teachings were spreading since the end of the 10th and the beginning of the 11th century. But it was left to Khwaja Ajmeri to go down in history as the 'Sultan-ul-Hindi" (the spiritual sovereign of India) and the 'Naib-e-Rasullulah fil Hind' (the vice-regent of the Prophet in India).

He remains the 'Patriarch saint' of the sub-continent, his main effort was to promote harmony between the Hindus and Muslims, to combat against caste inequalities and other inhumanities by preaching the message of monism, peace and social ethics. His piety, simplicity and sincerity won him many devotees, from different castes and creeds.

Although Abul-Fazl in Ain-i-Akbari mentions 14 Sufi silsilas as active in India by the 16th century, but the fact remains that in terms of their following and better-organisation, only six silsilas should be recognised as active and influential. Of these the Chistiyah, founded in India by Khwaja Ajmeri (though begun by Khwaja Abdul Chisti–d. 966–in Iran) atttracted the largest of devotees, both Muslims and Hindus, and also made a profound impact on the course of the new Bhakti movement among the Hindus that gained momentum in the 14th century, and spread out to many parts of the country in the next three hundred years.

The only other silsilas active in the Sultanate period (126-1526) was the Suhrawardia, with its headquarter in Multan, and later extending to Sindh, which was established in India by Sheikh Bahauddin Zakaria (d. 1192). Then came the Firdausi silsilas, mainly restricted to Bihar, that was founded by Shaikh Badruddin Samarkhandi and was spread by the prolific writer of mystic literature Shaikh Sharfuddin Yahya Muniri around the 13th century, followed by the Qadiriya and the Shuttaria silsila in the middle of the 15th century.

The Qadriya was established in India by Shaha Nayamatullah Qadiri, and the Shattaria by Shah Abdullah Shuttari (d. 1458). the former spread in Uttar Pradesh (UP) and the Deccan, while the latter spread mainly in Madya Pradesh and Gujarat regions. In the reign of Akbar (1556-1605) the last of six major silsilas, the Naqshbandiah was established by Khwaja Baqi Billah (1563-1603) and its most famous saint was Shaikh Ahmed Sirhindi (d. 1625) known as 'Mujaddid Alif Saani' (The Reformer of the 10th century).

In the mominant Chistiyah silsilas, Khwaja Ajmeri (d. 1234) was succeeded by a galaxy of brilliant saints for almost a continuous period of 20 years, whose names still evoke tremendous popular devotion and reverene, and around whom an entire movement of human fraternity was built. These saints of the people rose in public estimation for their message of love, humanism, compassion, and above all for their heroic defiance of autocracy and tyranny, scrupulous dissociation from holding offices of religious affairs under the Sultans, and for keeping distance from the lives and lifestyles of the feudal aristocrats and propertied strata of the mediaeval society.

Khwaja Ajmeri's principle successor, Khwaja Qutubuddin Baktiar Kaki (d. 1235) established the Chisti centre in Delhi. This was the time of recurrent Mongol invasions throughout Central Asia, where many centres of cultural life were destroyed. Scholars, artists, man of skills and crafts were flocking to Delhi, 'which by the end of the 13th century became one of the great centres of Muslim learning.'

Sultan Iltutmish (d. 1236) was such a big devotee of the Khwaja that he built the famous Qutub Minar in Delhi to perpetuate his memory.

Khwaja Qutub had nine successors, among whom the most famous was Baba Fariduddin Masud Gunj Shaker (1175-1265) who moved over to Ajodhya and died in Pakpattan. Baba Farid abjured company and popularity, and preferred solitude and contemplation. He firmly advised his followers: "Do not make friends with kings and nobles. Consider their visits to your home as fatal for your soul," and this despite the great reverance in which Sultan Balban (d. 1287) held him. His khanqah became the refuge of scholars including Hindu yogis and destitutes.

He made a deep impression on the Bhakti saints particularly Sant Kabir and Guru Nanak, the two founders of the KabirPanthi sect and the Sikh religion, respectively. So deep was his influence on Nanak, that the slokas (verses) of Baba Farid have been incorporated in the holy book of the Sikhs, Guru Granth Sahib, and have been sung in the Sikh temples for the last five hundred years. He is regarded as the first Punjabi poet of Sufism, although he wrote in Persian and Arabic, apart from Punjabi and other local dialects.

Of his five well-known successors, the name of Shaikh Nizamuddin Aulia (1236-1325) evokes the greatest admiration. Born in Badaun, after spending few years with his teacher at Ayodhya he returned to Delhi where he dominated the spiritual scene for nearly 60 years. He is recognised by many as "the greatest Indo-Muslim saint of all times", who survived the ups and downs of three dynasties and seven Sultans, without ever visiting a durbar, which he thought was beneath the dignity of a true Sufi.

Yet he had a great fondness for Amir Khusrau, the mystically inclined aristocrat, a versatile genius, who used to spend his days with the Sultans and nights of devotion at the Khanqah of Nizamuddin Aulia. It is in his poems and odes, sung over the centureis by the qawwals (religious singers) that Saint Nizamuddin figures prominently.

Shaikh Nizamuddin's liberal and tolerant outlook, offended the orthodox clergy but helped the spread of his message throughout the country and gained for him the popular title, Mahboob-i-Illahi (the beloved of the God). The tomb in Delhi built by Sultan Muhmammud-bin-Tughlak, (despite the Saints wish: "I want no monument over my grave; let me rest in broad and open plain") remains even after six and a half centuries a constant point of pilgrimage, and of massive congregation of people of all castes and creeds, Hindus and Muslims.

Shaikh Nizamuddin Aulia's successors spread throughout the country–one to Hansi, another to Gulbarga, a third to Bengal, and two remained in Delhi, of whom Shaikh Nasiruddin Mahmud (d. 1356), who was later known as Chirag-i-Delhi (the lamp of Delhi) was a charismatic saint, whose 100 'conversations' (as reported in Khairul Majalis) reflected melancholy at the state of affairs in social and economic life, caused by political upheavals, bad administration, price rise and general anarchy.

With the death of Chirag-i-Delhi, the first phase of Chisti silsila ends. One of his successor was Syed Muhammad Gesu Daraz (d. 1421) who went to Gulbarga in Karnataka at the time when the great Bahmani Sultanate (1347-1484) was established by Hasan Gangu Bahmani in 1347. Syed Gesu Daraz was a prolific writer of over thirty books on Tasawwuf mysticism). His love for the poor and the lowly and his defence of the rights of man earned him the title of Bandanawaz (benefactor of God's creatures).

He was one of the early poets and writers in the Urdu language–a new language that had grown as a synthesis of Persian, Turkish and Arabic on the one hand and of the Indian dialects Khari Boli, Braj and Punjabi on the other, with its base in Sanskrit syntax and etymology drawn from many sources. His famous couplet, that reflects the credo of the mystic and bhakti, was one of the first specimens of Urdu poetry. The ipeccable couplet is "Infidelity is welcome to the infidels and Islam to the Shaikh/But to us lovers, love and the content and harmony of our hearts is enough."

'A new ethos' by the author, By Courtesy, Hindustan Times, Nov. 10, 1991.

20

धर्म, ईश्वर आदि पर अस्तित्ववादी दृष्टिकोण

एहसान अशरफ

(विद्वान लेखक ने पाश्चात्य दार्शनिकों के विचारों का एक बड़ा ही सामयिक तत्त्व इकट्ठा किया है। भारतीय दर्शन में भी इस तरह के दृष्टिकोण कई रूपों में मिलते हैं जिनपर शोध किये जा सकते हैं। यहाँ लेखक के मूल लेख का सरल भावानुवाद किया गया है। **–सम्पादकद्वय**)

आदमी तीन सवालों से परेशान है–मैं कौन हूँ; मेरी बाहरी दुनिया क्या है; तथा सच्चा विश्वास क्या है तथा उसे कैसे पाया जाये। इस बारे में पुराने ग्रीक तथा कुछ जर्मन तथा फ्रांसिसी विचारकों के अस्तित्ववादी (Existentialist) दृष्टिकोण बहुत ही दिलचस्प लगते हैं। इमनें तो कुछ आस्तिक हैं जैसे कर्क, गैड, हर्सल तथा जैस्पर पर कुछ नास्तिक हैं जैसे नित्जे हेन्डेगर तथा शार्वे। इनके दृष्टिकोण हमारे विचारों को एक नई दिशा देते हैं तथा धर्म, नीति और मनुष्य के होने का मकसद आदि सवालों पर सोचने का मौका देते हैं।

अस्तित्ववाद 'मनुष्य क्या है' इसका बोध कराता है। (Existentialism is concerned with all the aspects of man in this world) यद्यपि इन विचारकों के मत विभिन्न हैं पर वे सभी अपने-अपने तौर पर एक जीवन दर्शन देते हैं। जिसका मूल सवाल आदमी के अस्तित्व का पता लगाना है। ये सभी इसका जबाव तर्क या विवेक से नहीं खोजते न ये किसी आदर्श को ही मानते हैं।

इनके अनुसार आदमी दुनिया के सभी जीवों से निराला है। प्रोटीगोरस ने तो कहा कि आदमी ही सभी विश्वासों की कसौटी है। सुकरात (469-399 ईसा पूर्व) ने बताया हर आदमी की अपनी दुनिया होती है तथा वह हर आदमी से चाहता था कि वह अपने को पहचाने (know thyself)। प्लेटो ने बताया कि हर आदमी को भीतर की आवाज सुननी चाहिए जो न किसी समाज से बनती है और

न जिसके लिए कोई तर्क ही है। पास्कल ने इसी आत्मा की आवाज को ईश्वर को सुनने जैसा मानता है। पास्कल की इन पंक्तियों पर ध्यान दें।

'जब मैं अपने जीवन के इतने छोटे काल पर सोचता हूँ, जो मेरे पहले तथा बाद के युगों का एक लेशमात्र है .... तो मैं डर जाता हूँ। हे अभिमानी मनुष्यों, जानो, तुम क्या हो .... ईश्वर को सुनो'।

ग्रीक विचारकों को यह दर्शन ही आधुनिक अस्तित्व याद का पूर्वाभास है। डेनमार्क का दार्शनिक सोने कर्कगार्ड (1815-95) के अस्तित्ववाद का भी केन्द्र बिन्दु मनुष्य ही है। उसने भी वही प्रश्न उठाया–मनुष्य के जीवन का मकसद क्या है, उसका अस्तित्व क्यों है। उसे मनुष्य का चित्र बेकार तथा बेहुदा लगता है पर एक-ब-एक मनुष्य को बोध भी होता है, बिल्कुल अपने तरह का (Subjective) तथा बिल्कुल निजी (inward)। उसके अन्दर एक प्रकार का ईश्वर उदित होता है, पर हर आदमी का यह आत्मबोध उसी को और बिल्कुल अनूठे रूप में होता है। अपने प्रश्नों का हल उसे खुद अकेले करना पड़ता है।

यह सत्य है कि अपने अस्तित्व का बोध मनुष्य को खुद होता है। डसकटंस के अनुसार ''मैं'' का बोध स्वयं सोचने पर हो जाता है। ('I think, therefore I am,') कर्कगार्ड इसी को उलटकर अपने अस्तित्व को सिद्ध करता है–'मैं हूँ इसलिये मैं सोचता हूँ।' इस तरह का आदमी इस दुनिया का एक मूल तत्व है। ''मैं हूँ इसीलिये ये दुनिया है, अथवा मैं हूँ इसीलिये खुदा भी कोई मानी रखता है।''

इसीलिए शार्वे कहता है कि आदमी हरदम कुछ बनने की प्रक्रिया में रहता है, पर वह क्या बनेगा–इसका कोई निश्चित रूप नहीं दिया जा सकता है। हर आदमी का यही अनूठापन उसके अस्तित्व को बतलाता है। हर आदमी भले ही अपने शरीर, दुनिया, इतिहास, संस्कृति से बँधा है पर वास्तव में वह सबसे मुक्त है।

अस्तित्ववादी इस बात पर जोर देते हैं कि आदमी बिल्कुल मुक्त जीव है, उसे केवल अपनी आँखे खोलकर देखना है, वह जो देखता है वही सत्यहै, भले ही कोई-कोई कारणों से लोग उसे न माने। मनुष्य अपनी पसन्द से करने ही के लिये नहीं बल्कि सोचने-समझने के लिए भी स्वतंत्र है। परन्तु हममें अधिकांश गलत विश्वासों में फँस कर पुश्त-दर-पुश्त कुछ लीकों पर चलने लगते हैं क्योंकि हम अपनी समस्याओं से उलझना नहीं चाहते बल्कि उनसे भागते हैं। अगर हममें हिम्मत हो ताकि हम अपनी पुरानी मान्यताओं से मुक्त हों तब हम बहुत से अन्धविश्वासों से बच सकते हैं।

जर्मन विचारक एडमण्ड हासेल (1859-1939) ने इस अस्तित्ववादी धारणा का बड़ा ही मजबूत तथा पसन्दीदा आधार चुना। आदमी को पहले दुनिया तथा

इसके तत्वों के बारे में जो भी धारणायें व मान्यतायें हैं उससे मुक्त हो जाना चाहिए। इस विधि को एक प्रकार के नकारने तथा फिर नए सिरे से सोचने (Phenomenological reduction) की प्रक्रिया कहते हैं। इससे उन वस्तुओं पर सोचने पर कोई अन्धविश्वास या लकीरी की फकीरी नहीं रह जाती। इसके बाद मनुष्य का एक अहं (ego) या आत्म बोध उसके चारों ओर की दुनिया को प्रकाश में लाने लगता है। एक संदेह (doubt) की नजर होते हुए भी मनुष्य का आत्म बोध उसे ऊपर उठा ले जाता है तथा एक शुद्ध चेतन आत्मा का ज्ञान (transcendental ego) होता है।

यही स्वाभाविक आत्म बोध (natural ego) मार्टिन हिडेगर (1889-1976) के दर्शन का केन्द्र बिन्दु बना। हम अपनी स्थिति (existence) को तभी जान सकते हैं जब हम अपने में ही इस दुनिया को सोचे समझे। हम दुनिया के हर पहलू को अलग-अलग समझें और तभी हम अपने अस्तित्व को जान लेते हैं। हेडगर के अनुसार आदमी एक दुखद स्थिति में रहता है और अन्त में बिल्कुल मिट जाता है। इसलिए उसे इस जीवन की निस्सारता (nothingness) तथा मृत्यु के कटु सत्य को हर पहल कबूल करना होगा।

कार्ल जैस्पर के अनुसार भी आदमी पूरब तथा पश्चिम में पिछले तीन हजार वर्षों से इस दुनिया के अन्तिम सत्य की खोज कर रहा है। उसके अनुसार आदमी को किसी न किसी परिस्थिति में रहना पड़ता है पर वह इनसे भाग नहीं सकता और उसकी स्थिति कभी खतरे से खाली नहीं। उसे उनको सहना पड़ता है और उनसे लड़ना भी पड़ता है। अन्त में वह मर जाता है। इसलिये आदमी को अपनी स्थिति से ऊपर उठना (transcend) करना पड़ता है और उसे इस उत्सरण (transcedence) की गहराईयों तथा छिपी हुई भाषा को समझना चाहिये।

स्पोकेन हेरर तथा नित्जे (1844-1900) दोनों यह मानते हैं कि आदमी को जीने के लिए संकल्प (will) की जरूरत है, नित्जे तो इसे जीने का संकल्प (will to live) ही नहीं बल्कि शक्ति का संकल्प (will to power) मानता है। उसे अपनी शक्ति का भरोसा होना चाहिये और इसीलिये नित्जे ने घोषणा की-ईश्वर मर चुका है (god is dead)। उसने ईसाइयत तथा किसी भी गड़ी हुई नीति या मान्यताओं (values) की भर्त्सना की। उसने लोगों को चुनौती दी कि वे अपने जीवन को एक बिल्कुल नया मार्ग दें जिसे वह धर्मों के ऊपर का धर्म (trans valuation of values) का नाम दिया। इसी से आदमी अपनी निराशाओं से बच सकता है।

नित्जे ने आदमी को विशिष्ठ आदमी (superman) का चित्र दिया और उसकी अपार शक्ति को गुहारा जिसके सामने ईश्वर जैसी शक्ति भी झूठी पड़ गई।

शार्त्रे ने नित्जे के अनीश्वरवाद को और भी पुष्ट किया। ईश्वर भला आदमी की क्या मदद कर सकता है। वह आदमी की लाचारी को कबूल करता है पर इसके लिये कर्कगार्ड की ईश्वरीय आस्था (faith) की जरूरत नहीं। कर्कगार्ड भी ईसाइयत का अर्थ कोई धर्म नहीं मानता। मैं ईसाई हूँ–ऐसा कहना एक विचारहीनता है पर मैं ईसाइयत को अपने ढंग से समझता हूँ–एक अर्थपूर्ण बात हो सकती है। ("It is with subjectivity that christianity is concerned, and it is only in subjectivity that its truth exists, if it exists at all. Objectively christianity has absolutely no existence.")

इस लेखक का अपना विचार है कि हिन्दू, इस्लाम अथवा किसी भी धर्म को ऐसी ही नजर से देखना चाहिये, अन्यथा हमारे हिन्दू, मुसलमान अथवा ईसाई होने का कोई अर्थ नहीं है। यह तो केवल अपने दादों परदादों की लीक पर आंख मूंद कर चलना होगा। यह ठीक है कि अपने स्वतंत्र भावों को जगाना सबके लिये संभव न हो पर हर आदमी अकेला व्यक्ति है तथ अपने तरह से सोचने तथा करने की शक्ति रखता है। वह अपनी अन्तरात्मा (inwardness) से प्रेरित होता है। परन्तु काश, मनुष्य यह समझ लेता। वह समूह में भटक जाता है और यह भूल बैठता है कि उसकी भी एक हस्ती है। हम किसी भी सत्य को नहीं समझ सकते हैं जब तक हम उसे अपनी नजर से न देखकर दूसरों की नजर से देखते रहेंगे। सत्य अपने लिए होता है, दूसरों के लिए नहीं, यद्यपि दोनों उसे खोजना चाहते हैं। यही अन्तरात्मा (inwardness) या अपने को खोजना है। (This is what inwardness means.)

पर शार्त्रे के तर्क उसे नास्तिक बना देते हैं जब कि कर्कगार्ड धर्म या ईश्वर को आदमी साख्सियत तथा उसके अपने सोचने का कायल बना देता है। इस तरह सामुहिक धर्म कोई चीज नहीं रह जाता। शार्त्रे अपने उपन्यास नान्सी (Nancee) में अपने पाठकों को अस्तित्ववाद की समस्या से परिचित कराता है। नायक एक भावात्मक स्थिति में फँसा है. एक मुश्किलातों की दुनिया में उसकी हस्ती उलझी हुई है। परन्तु वह अपनी दुनिया का रास्ता खुद खोजता है। तब नायक (रोकेन्टीन) तब नायक (रोकेन्टीन) को महसूस होता है कि पहले वह दुनिया को उसके सही रूप में नहीं देख रहा था बल्कि उस पर कुछ लिखी हुई बातों का पर्दा पड़ा हुआ था। इस दुनिया को समझाना किसी भी भाषा के बूते के बाहर की चीज है। तब नायक अनुभव करता है कि उसकी हस्ती क्या है तथा वह क्या कह रही है।

अपनी पुस्तक 'Being and Nothingness' (कुछ और कुछ नहीं) में शार्वे अपनी चेतन की बनावट पर प्रकाश देता है। आदमी की हस्ती के दो रूप होते

हैं–चेतन और अचेतन। चेतन सत्य है पर अचेतन का अपना कुछ नहीं। वह चेतन पर ही आश्रित है।

'हम कुछ हैं'–के साथ-साथ 'हम कुछ नहीं हैं'–का भी बोध होता है। इस धारणा में शार्त्रे जीवन को एक विडम्बना (pretension) मानता है। हम कुछ होना चाहते हैं; अन्तत: मनुष्य ईश्वर होना चाहता है। पर यह असंभव है क्योंकि खुदा के होने का कोई बौद्धिक आधार (intellectual conception) नहीं। फिर वह क्या हो–ऐसे कशमकश में वह वही करता है जो उसकी मौज (free choice) में आता है।

फिर उसे अपने को देखने की प्रक्रिया होती है। लोग मुझे कैसे देखते हैं– और फिर शर्म, भय, द्वन्द्व आदि उत्पन्न होते हैं। फिर वह अपने जीवन की एक योजना बनाता है ताकि उसका जीवन कुछ सार्थक हो तथा 'कुछ नहीं' की स्थिति (nothingness) से यह बच सके। परन्तु इसी क्रम में अधिकांश लोग अन्धविश्वास की चपेट में आ जाते हैं।

'कुछ और कुछ नहीं' के सम्बन्ध में शार्त्रे कुछ मान्यताओं (values) तथा उनके बन्धनों का प्रश्न उठाता है। जब मनुष्य जगत में आता है इसके बाद ही विश्वास बनते हैं, ऐसा नहीं कि ये विश्वास पहले ही से रहते हों और हमारा इन्तजार कर रहे हों। मनुष्य की स्वतंत्रता ही उसके विश्वासों का आधार बन सकती है (My freedom is unique, foundation of values. It is through me that values exist since I am the foundation of my values, as for the same reason as I am the foundation of my world).

परन्तु शार्त्रे का अस्तित्ववाद मार्क्सवाद का रूप लेने लगता है जो उसकी किताब 'The critique of Dialectical Reason' में दिखाई पड़ता है। इस तरह मुख्तसर में यह कहा जा सकता है कि 'अपने को पहचानों' का उत्तर एक तरफ कर्कगार्ड ने व्यक्तिगत या निजी धार्मिक आस्थाओं से मिलता है तो दूसरी तरफ शार्त्रे के मानववादी विश्वासों से जहाँ धर्म, ईश्वर की कोई जरूरत नहीं। लेखक पाठकों को इन प्रश्नों पर सोचने विचारने का निवेदन करता है क्योंकि आज हमारे सामने कर्कगार्ड का यही प्रश्न मंडरा रहा है। इस बेकार तथा नासमझी की दुनिया में मनुष्य कैसे जिये। (How is a man to live in the irrational meaningless world.)

लेखक, दर्शन विभाग, कॉलेज ऑफ कॉमर्स के पूर्व प्रोफेसर तथा हेड हैं और यू.जी.सी. के सीनियर फेलो हैं।

खण्ड-2

समाजवाद एवं पूंजीवाद का संकट

(Break-Down of the Material Systems)

21

समाजवाद के विवाद
(SOCIALIST DILEMMA)

विनोद प्र० सिंह एवं सुनील मिश्र

भारत के समाजवादी आन्दोलन का सैद्धांतिक पक्ष विवादास्पद विषय रहा है। कुछ लोगों के अनुसार समाजवादी आन्दोलन के बिखराव का कारण सैद्धांतिक एकरूपता का अभाव है। कुछ लोग मानते हैं कि आन्दोलन के नेताओं के विचारों में शुरू से एकरूपता नहीं थी। आचार्य नरेन्द्रदेव और जयप्रकाश नारायण मार्क्सवादी थे, अशोक मेहता फेबियनवादी, लोहिया गाँधीजी से प्रभावित और सम्पूर्णानंद, यूसुफ मेहरअली क्रांतिकारी राष्ट्रवादी। मसानी मार्क्सवादी थे लेकिन बाद में ट्राट्स्की1 से प्रभावित हो गये।

अन्य आन्दोलनों की तरह भारत के समाजवादी आन्दोलन का सिद्धांत भी विकसित हुआ। यह स्वाभाविक प्रक्रिया है। मनुष्य और समाज पर घटनाओं एवं स्थितियों का असर होता ही है। अनुभवों से ही वैचारिक आधारभूमि तैयार होती है। वैज्ञानिक सिद्धांत व्यावहारिक जगत् में संशोधित होता है, लेकिन दुर्भाग्यवश उसके रूढ़िवादी एवं बन्द दिमाग वाले अनुयायी उन संशोधनों को उसी रूप में स्वीकार कर, उस सिद्धांत की अपूर्णता दूर करने की कोशिश नहीं करते बल्कि निर्मित खांचे में उन संशोधनों को ढालने की कोशिश करते हैं और सिद्धांत को हास्यापद बनाने की सीमा तक ले जाते हैं। भारतीय समाजवादी आन्दोलन कम-से-कम इस दोष से मुक्त रहा है।

भारत के समाजवादी आन्दोलन की विचार-यात्रा मार्क्सवादी से शुरू होकर लोकतांत्रिक समाजवादी से होते हुए तीसरी दुनिया के लिए एक नये समाजवादी सिद्धांत के प्रयास में खत्म होती है।

भारत के समाजवादी नेताओं के विचारों में प्रारंभ से ही भिन्नता वाली मान्यता सही नहीं लगती। अपने प्रारंभिक दिनों में सभी नेता या तो मार्क्सवादी थे या मार्क्सवाद से प्रभावित। सन् 1938 में नरेन्द्रदेव, कमलादेवी, अच्युत पटवर्धन एवं अशोक मेहता द्वारा तैयार थीसिस से स्पष्ट कहा गया था कि पार्टी के गठन की पहल उन लोगों ने की जो "मार्क्सवाद के प्रभाव में आ गये थे और जिन्होंने मार्क्सवादी समाजवाद स्वीकार कर लिया था।" स्थापना सम्मेलन के अध्यक्षीय भाषण में नरेन्द्रदेव ने शुद्ध मार्क्सवादी विश्लेषण दिया था। और 'मेरठ थीसिस' में अधिकृत तौर पर कहा गया था कि "पार्टी का कार्यक्रम निश्चित तौर पर मार्क्सवादी होगा ओर केवल मार्क्सवाद ही साम्राज्यवाद-विरोधी संघर्ष को अपने निश्चित लक्ष्य तक ले जा सकता है।" अशोक मेहता की प्रारंभिक रचना, 'गाँधीवाद और समाजवाद' (1935) एवं राममनोहर लोहिया के भाषण, 'स्वराज क्यों और कैसे' (1936) में, घटनाओं का मार्क्सवादी विश्लेषण है। सन् 1938 में लाहौर सम्मेलन के अध्यक्षीय भाषण में मीनू मसानी ने कहा–"इससे अधिक स्वाभाविक बात दूसरी नहीं है कि अपनी नीति निर्धारित करते समय हम मार्क्स और लेनिन द्वारा प्रतिपादित शिक्षण की ओर देखें।"

भारत का तत्कालीन स्थिति में प्रगतिशील तत्वों का मार्क्सवाद के प्रति झुकाव स्वाभाविक था। सन् 1921-22 के आंदोलन और कौंसिल प्रवेश के बाद देश भक्तों की एक प्रतिक्रिया छिट-पुट हिंसक कार्रवाइयों के रूप में व्यक्त हुई थी। 1930 तक आते-आते उसकी निरर्थकता स्पष्ट हो चुकी थी। विश्वव्यापी मंदी के समय रूस में मार्क्सवाद के नाम पर स्थापित सोवियत व्यवस्था की सफलता उसके प्रति आकर्षण का एक प्रमुख कारण था। उससे पहले वहाँ निरंकुश जारशाही के विरुद्ध सफल क्रांति हो चुकी थी। इसके अलावा, ब्रिटेन का रूस-विरोधी होना और सोवियत सरकार द्वारा रूस के उपनिवेशी दावों को खत्म कर देना भी आकर्षण का अतिरिक्त कारण था।

भारत के समाजवादियों में शुरू से ही एक अन्तर्विरोध देखने को मिलता है। 'सर्वहारा के अधिनायकवाद' के बारे में चुप्पी और सोवियत व्यवस्था की प्रशंसा एक तरह का अंतर्विरोध है। मार्क्सवाद के सोवियत संस्करण में 'सर्वहारा का अधिनायकवाद' एक अनिवार्य तत्व है। भारत के समाजवादी शुरू से ही उसे अनिवार्य नहीं मानते थे। सन् 1935 में कां० सो० पा० के मेरठ सम्मेलन के समय का बहुचर्चित विवाद की पार्टी को मात्र 'मार्क्सवादी' कहा जाय या 'मार्क्सवादी लेनिनवादी' और प्रथम के पक्ष में फैसला अर्थपूर्ण है, 'लेनिनवादी' मानने का मतलब होता 'सर्वहारा के अधिनायकवाद' की अनिवार्यता स्वीकारना।

गाँधीजी के नेतृत्व वाली काँग्रेस और राष्ट्रीय स्वतंत्रता संग्राम से जुड़े रहने के कारण भारत के समाजवादी मार्क्सवाद को लेनिनवादी व्याख्या के रूप में पूरी तरह स्वीकार नहीं कर सकते थे। सत्याग्रह के रूप में गाँधीजी ने एक नया हथियार दिया था। जिस जमात के संघर्ष का प्रमुख नजरिया आजादी प्राप्त करना हो, वह अधिनायकवादी व्यवस्था स्वीकार शायद ही कर सकती है। मसानी ने 1938 के अध्यक्षीय भाषण में कहा–"स्वतंत्रता और समानता हमारा आधारभूत सिद्धांत है... मार्क्सवादियों में रूढ़िवादी और अपधर्मी दोनों हैं।" एम. एन. राय से छिड़े विवाद में समाजवादियों ने गुप्त संगठन के बदले खुले रूप में काम करने का समर्थन किया।

मार्क्सवादी के रूप में भारत के समाजवादियों का एक नजरिया 1939-40 के पहले का है। कामिन्टर्न की 1928 की तथाकथित राष्ट्रवादी बुर्जुआ नेतृत्व का पर्दाफाश करने की नीति से लेकर सातवीं काँग्रेस (1936) का उनके साथ सहयोग करने की नीति तक का कोई असर समाजवादियों के रूस के प्रति दृष्टिकोण पर नहीं पड़ा। सन् 1935 में तो जयप्रकाश ने मीनू मसानी का कामिन्टर्न के नेताओं से काँग्रेस सोशलिस्ट पार्टी की सम्बद्धता के लिए बात करने को भेजा। उनकी एकमात्र शर्त यह थी कि कामिन्टर्न भारत की कम्युनिस्ट पार्टी से सम्बन्ध-विच्छेद कर ले।

रूस में जब शुद्धीकरण के नाम पर पुराने क्रांतिकारियों की सफाई हो रही थी, उस समय कुछ समाजवादियों ने तरीकों के बारे में शक जरूर व्यक्त किया लेकिन रूसी व्यवस्था के प्रति मोहभंग नहीं हुआ। यहाँ तक की रूसी मुकदमे पर लिखित अपने लेख के अन्त में लोहिया ने 'रूसी राज्यक्रांति की प्रेरक शक्ति के प्रति अपनी श्रद्धांजलि अर्पित' की थी। इसी दौरान कम्युनिस्टों को काँग्रेस सोशलिस्ट पार्टी में शामिल किया जा रहा था।

रूस के समर्थन का एक कारण तत्कालीन यूरोपीय स्थिति भी थी। जर्मनी और इटली में हिटलर और मुसोलिनी के उदय के साथ फांसीवाद, रूस एवं कम्युनिज्म के प्रतिद्वन्द्वी के रूप में उभर रहा था। ब्रिटेन जैसी पूंजीवादी साम्राज्यवादी शक्तियाँ फासीवाद के तुष्टीकरण की नीति अपना रही थीं। ऐसी स्थिति में ब्रिटेन के साथ आजादी के लिए लड़ने वाले किसी समाज की स्वाभाविक प्रतिक्रिया रूस के प्रति सहानुभूति की होती।

पार्टी के अन्दर कम्युनिस्टों के व्यवहार और अगस्त 1939 में स्टालिन हिटलर के आकस्मिक समझौते ने भारत के समाजवादियों को परेशान कर दिया। द्वितीय महायुद्ध के प्रारंभिक दिनों में रूस द्वारा ब्रिटेन के खिलाफ लड़ने और मित्र राष्ट्रों

द्वारा लड़े जाने वाले युद्ध को साम्राज्यवादी युद्ध करार देने से समाजवादियों को कोई दिक्कत नहीं हुई होगी, क्योंकि उनका विश्लेषण भी वही था, लेकिन हिटलर के साथ समझौते को वे पचा नहीं पाये होंगे। पार्टी में कम्युनिस्टों का व्यवहार जरूर हैरान और परेशान करने वाला था। कां० सो० पार्टी के अधिकतर नेताओं के चरित्र हनन, पार्टी पर कब्जा करने की गुप्त चालों आदि का प्रभाव पड़ा। भावना की तीव्रता, नरेन्द्रदेव द्वारा यूसुफ मेहरअली को लिखे पत्र में मिलती है। नरेन्द्रदेव लिखते हैं–"कम्युनिस्ट लोग सबसे अधिक गैर भरोसेमंद हैं। अब इन लोगों से पूरी तरह अलग हो जाना चाहिए। ऐसे निर्लज्ज और बेईमान लोगों के साथ आगे काम करना असंभव है।

जून 1941 में हिटलर द्वारा रूस पर आक्रमण, रूस का मित्र राष्ट्रों के साथ होने और उसके परिणामस्वरूप कम्युनिस्टों का ब्रिटिश समर्थक बन जाने के बाद समाजवादियों का मार्क्सवाद के रूसी 'मॉडेल' से मोहभंग हो गया।

ऐसे समय में लोहिया जैसे समाजवादी ने मार्क्सवाद के बुनियादी आधार की चुनौती दे डाली। सन् 1942–43 के दौरान लिखित 'मार्क्स के बाद का अर्थशास्त्र' इसका प्रमाण है। लेकिन अन्य समाजवादी नेता मार्क्सवाद के लोकतांत्रिक समाजवादी रूप के पक्षधर बन गये। भारत के कम्युनिस्टों और रूसी 'मॉडेल' को नकारने के लिए उन्हें मार्क्स के बदले किसी दूसरे को खोजने की जरूरत नहीं थी। सन् 1872 में प्रथम इन्टरनेशनल से बाकुनिनवादियों को खदेड़ने के बाद मार्क्स ने इंगित किया था कि यदि सामाजिक संस्थाएँ पर्याप्त लोकतांत्रिक हों तो समाजवाद की स्थापना शांतिपूर्वक की जा सकती है। उसी वर्ष हेग–कांग्रेस के तुरंत बाद उन्होंने तर्क दिया कि विभिन्न देशों को क्रांति की विभिन्न रीतियों की आवश्यकता होती है। ब्रिटेन, अमेरीका तथा संभवतः हालैंड में पर्याप्त राजनीतिक सत्ता के संग्रह में सफलता प्राप्त करने मात्र से क्रांति सम्पन्न हो सकती है। एंगेल्स ने मार्क्स की पुस्तिका 'क्लास स्ट्रगल इन फ्रांस' के 1895 संस्करण की भूमिकामें विद्रोह का महत्व कम कर दिया तथा व्यापक मताधिकार और संसदीय संस्थाओं की उपयोगिता पर बल दिया। भारत में भी सीमित मताधिकारों के बावजूद 1937 में अधिकतर प्रान्तों में कांग्रेस को बहुमत प्राप्त हुआ था और आजादी के बाद जब सार्वभौम मताधिकार का सिद्धांत स्वीकारा जा चुका था, मार्क्सवाद का लोकतांत्रिक समाजवादी स्वरूप पर्याप्त था।

काँग्रेस, गाँधीजी और भारतीय परम्परा के नैतिक मूल्यों का प्रभाव भी समाजवादियों पर पड़ा। सन् 1940 में ही जयप्रकाश ने भावी भारत का जो चित्र प्रस्तुत किया था उसे प्राप्त करने के लिए शांतिपूर्ण तरीकों के इस्तेमाल को स्वीकारा था। नासिक सम्मेलन तक आते–आते उन्हें लगने लगा था कि सशस्त्र

विद्रोह और गुप्त संगठन द्वारा क्रांति की तैयार में झूठ, धोखा बेईमानी आदि शामिल हैं और किसी भी नये समाज का निर्माण ऐसे तत्त्व नहीं कर सकते जो इनका सहारा लेते हैं।

द्वितीय विश्वयुद्ध के दौरान कम्युनिस्टों के व्यवहार के कटु अनुभवों ने स्वतंत्रता-प्राप्ति के बाद उनके व्यवहार से और गहरा कर दिया। तेलगंना में कम्युनिस्टों द्वारा संचालित हिंसक आन्दोलन का समाजवादियों ने समर्थन नहीं किया। उनके विचार में नवोदित भारत को एक राज्य के रूप में विकसित एवं सुदृढ़ करना सबसे महत्वपूर्ण काम था। साम्प्रदायिक आधार पर भारत विभाजन के कारण इस दृष्टिकोण को बल मिला।

लोकतांत्रिक समाजवाद के प्रति झुकाव का एक कारण रूसी व्यवस्था के प्रति मोहभंग भी था। सन् 1950 में लिखित 'लोकतांत्रिक समाजवाद' में जयप्रकाश नारायण ने इसी पक्ष पर जोर दिया। उनके अनुसार समाजवादी समाज में राष्ट्रीय अर्थनीति के एक बड़े भाग का संचालक मजदूरों का होना था (अर्थात् औद्योगिक लोकतंत्र) लेकिन इसके बदले रूस में समय-समय पर चुनाव के नाम पर मुट्ठी-भर लोग देश पर ष्टासन और सभी संस्थानों का संचालन करने लगे। वहाँ कुछ लोगों को विशिष्ट स्थान प्राप्त हो गया। इसके अलावा रूस ने न केवल राष्ट्रवाद बल्कि 'सर्व स्लाव' जैसे जातीय आन्दोलन को बढ़ावा दिया।[1]

सन् 1945 में हुए ब्रिटिश चुनाव में लेबर पार्टी की शानदार जीत से भारत के समाजवादियों को लगा कि मार्क्स-एंगेल्स की वह कल्पना कि लोकतांत्रिक तरीके से समाजवाद लाया जा सकता है, प्रतिफलित हो रही है।

मार्क्सवाद पर आधारित लोकतांत्रिक समाजवाद भी भारत के अधिकतर समाजवादियों को संतुष्ट नहीं रख सका। तीसरी दुनिया की विशिष्ट समस्याओं और भारत की पुरानी सभ्यता की दार्शनिक परम्पराओं के संदर्भ में उन्हें नये आधार खोजने की जरूरत महसूस हुई। मार्क्सवाद मुख्यतः पश्चिमी अवधारणा था। पश्चिमी देशों में 'लोकतांत्रिक समाजवादी' सरकारों ने कुछ कल्याणकारी कार्यक्रमों, कुछ क्षेत्रों एवं संस्थाओं के राष्ट्रीयकरण करने के अलावा कुछ नहीं किया। पश्चिमी देशों में पूँजीवाद विकसित हो चुका था, उपनिवेशों की लूट से वहाँ के श्रमिक वर्ग को भी फायदा हुआ था। संगठित और विकसित मजदूर आंदोलन के कारण पूँजीपति वर्ग भी शास्त्रीय मार्क्सवादी अर्थ में मजदूरों का शोषण करने की स्थिति में नहीं था, उनकी समानान्तर शक्ति विकसित हो चुकी थी। लोकतांत्रिक संस्थाएँ जड़ जमा चुकी थीं और पूरा समाज लोकतांत्रिक मूल्यों को स्वीकार कर चुका था। सामन्ती व्यवस्था खत्म हो चुकी थी। संयुक्त पूँजी कम्पनियों के बड़े

आकार और प्रबंध की नयी तकनीक के कारण पूंजीवाद का स्वरूप बदल गया था। वहाँ की समस्या पूँजी की कमी नहीं बल्कि माँग की कमी थी।

तीसरी दुनिया में सामन्ती व्यवस्था बरकरार थी, पूँजी का अभाव था। घोर गरीबी और असमानता व्याप्त थी। उत्पादन का स्तर निम्न था और तकनीक पुरानी थी। जनसंख्या तेजी से बढ़ रही थी। विदेशी गुलामी से मुक्ति के बाद देशी सामन्ती-पूँजीपति वर्ग के विरुद्ध अनिवार्य संघर्ष के लिए उपयुक्त राजनीतिक संस्थाएँ और संगठन विकसित नहीं हुए थे, न लोकतंत्र परिपक्व हुआ था।

आजादी के लड़ाई के दौरान गाँधीजी ने सिविल-नाफरमानी के रूप में संघर्ष का एक नया औजार सृजित किया था और रचनात्मक कार्यक्रमों की एक परम्परा चलायी थी। नये मनुष्य के सृजन की एक नयी तकनीक उभरी। इस विचारधारा में मनुष्य के आर्थिक पक्ष के साथ गैर-आर्थिक पक्ष पर उतना ही जोर दिया गया था। अंतिम लक्ष्यों और तात्कालिक लक्ष्यों में किसी तरह के अलगाव को नकारा गया था। पश्चिमी समाजवादी चिन्तन में 'कम्युनिस्ट घोषणा-पत्र' के मार्क्सवाद से लेकर 'लोकतांत्रिक समाजवादी' मार्क्सवाद तक इनका कोई स्थान नहीं था।

भारत में स्वतंत्र समाजवादी चिन्तन का पूर्ण रूप पार्टी के पचमढ़ी सम्मेलन के अवसर पर राममनोहर लोहिया के अध्यक्षीय भाषण में मिलता है। लोकतांत्रिक समाजवाद से हटते हुए वे कहते हैं–"यूरोप में समाजवाद क्रमिक, संवैधानिक एवं वितरणमुखी रहा है। अब से एवं बाकी दुनिया में समाजवाद को उग्र और जरूरत पड़ने पर असंवैधानिक होना पड़ेगा और उत्पादन पर जोर देना पड़ेगा।"

भारतीय समाजवाद पूँजीवाद, सर्वहारा के अधिनायकवाद, पश्चिमी लोकतांत्रिक समाजवाद आदि के अनुभवों में तीसरी दुनिया की परिस्थितियों में विकसित हुआ। तीसरी दुनिया के पास न इतना समय है कि वह इतिहास के विभिन्न चरणों से गुजरे, सामन्तवाद से पूंजीवाद होते हुए समाजवादी मंजिल पर पहुँचे और न इतना साधन है कि अब तक विकसित प्रौद्योगिकी अपनाकर अपनी गरीबी और असमानता खत्म करे। साथ ही न वह पूंजीवाद के प्रारंभिक काल के अनिवार्य शोषण और न 'सर्वहारा के अधिनायकवाद' के दमन एवं उत्पीड़न के अनुभवों को दुहराना चाहता है। वह पूँजीवाद और साम्यवाद को वैकल्पिक व्यवस्था नहीं बल्कि एक ही सिक्के के दो रूप और आज के लिए अप्रासंगिक मानता है। 'साम्यवाद को उत्पादन तकनीक पूंजीवाद से विरासत में प्राप्त होती है। वह मात्र पूंजीवादी उत्पादन संबंध ध्वस्त करना चाहता है। साम्यवाद दावा करता है कि जब पूंजीवाद अपनी प्रौद्योगिकी को बनायेरखने और विकसित करने में अक्षम हो जाता है तो साम्यवाद उसे बनाये रखता है और विकसित करता है। दो-तिहाई दुनिया के लिए

पूंजीवादी प्रौद्योगिकी के अर्थ को साम्यवादी सिद्धांत पचा नहीं सका है। उनके गुणों और प्रवेगों ने नयी सभ्यता की खोज के लिए उन्हें समान रूप से अप्रासंगिक बना दिया है। यह 'सीमित पूंजीवाद और मिश्रित अर्थव्यवस्था को अटल तरीके से नकारता है।'

भारतीय समाजवाद परम्परागत समाजवाद के कुछ लक्षणों को स्वीकार करता है। एक है निजी सम्पत्ति को खात्मा और दूसरा, वर्ग-संघर्ष की अनिवार्यता, लेकिन इन दोनों ही लक्षणों में अपनाभी कुछ जोड़ता है। एक तो यह कि जिस आर्थिक इकाई में दूसरे व्यक्ति का श्रम खरीदकर न लगाना पड़े, उसे निजी स्वामित्व के अधीन रहने दिया जाय। यह उस सहज तर्क पर आधारित है कि चूँकि ऐसी इकाइयों में 'अतिरेक मूल्य' जैसी कोई चीज उत्पन्न नहीं होती, इसलिए शोषण का सवाल पैदा नहीं होता। इन इकाइयों के अलावा उत्पादन साधनों पर सामूहिक स्वामित्व होना चाहिए लेकिन उसका रूप केन्द्रित नियंत्रण का नहीं बल्कि विकेन्द्रित सहयोग और औद्योगिक लोकतंत्र का होगा।

भारतीय समाजवाद वर्ग-संघर्ष की अनिवार्यता स्वीकार करता है लेकिन यह मानता है कि पूंजीवाद के विरुद्ध अब तक चलाया गया वर्ग-संघर्ष जहाँ पूंजीवाद के कुछ पहलुओं को नाश करने के रूप में अभिव्यक्त हुआ है वहीं उसने कुछ पहलुओं को शक्तिशाली भी बनाया है। 'निजी सम्पत्ति के पहलू का यह नाश करता है, लेकिन प्रौद्योगिकी के पहलू में उसे पुनर्स्थापित करता है।' अतः वर्ग-संघर्ष का वह रूप होना चाहिए जो पूंजीवाद को दोनों पहलुओं में नष्ट करे और इसके लिए उसका तात्कालिकता की कसौटी पर खरा उतरना जरूरी है। सिविल नाफरमानी और रचनात्मक कार्यक्रम नयी सभ्यता के निर्माण के लिए किये जाने वाले वर्ग-संघर्ष का नया रूप है।

नया समाजवादी चिन्तन ऐतिहासिक विकास के विभिन्न चरणों संबंधी मूल मार्क्सवादी एवं लेनिनवादी व्याख्या अस्वीकारता है। तकनीक अर्थात् उत्पादन शक्ति और मानव-मस्तिष्क के रिश्तों की पुनर्व्याख्या करता है। मार्क्सवाद के अनुसार, उत्पादनशक्ति में निरंतर विकास होता है और उसी के अनुरूप उत्पादन सम्बन्ध स्थापित होते हैं। उत्पादन सम्बन्ध कुछ समय के लिए उत्पादन शक्ति के विकास में अवरोधक बन सकते हैं, लेकिन अन्ततोगत्वा उसे उत्पादन शक्ति के अनुरूप होना ही पड़ता है। उत्पादन शक्ति में निरंतर विकास मानव-मस्तिष्क का फल है लेकिन अब तक उसकी दिशा एकमुखी रही है अर्थात् सामान्य तौर पर तकनीक का पैमाना बढ़ता गया है। अब मनुष्य के सामने एक चुनौती यह है कि उत्पादन शक्ति के विकास को वह मनोनुकूल दिशा दे सकता है या नहीं क्योंकि

नयी सभ्यता अर्थात् अपने आदर्शों के अनुरूप नये उत्पादन संबंध हम बना पायेंगे या नहीं, यह इसी पर निर्भर करता है। लोहिया के शब्दों में–"अगर पूँजीवाद और साम्यवाद द्वारा स्वीकृत अभिनवीकरण की पद्धति काम में लायी जाती है और मस्तिष्क अपना तेज और विलक्षणता प्रदर्शित करने से इन्कार करता है तो वास्तव में कोई रास्ता नहीं है।" अभिनवीकरण की एक नयी पद्धति और उसके अनुरूप स्वामित्व की पद्धति का इजाद करना ही होगा। नया समाजवादी चिन्तन इसे संभव मानता है। कुशल छोटी इकाई मशीन उत्पादन शक्ति को मनोनुकूल दिशा देने की ही अभिव्यक्ति है। यहाँ यह मार्क्सवाद से बुनियादी तौर पर अलग हो जाता है। यह उत्पादन शक्ति के विकास को मानव-मस्तिष्क के अधीन मानता है, उत्पादन सम्बन्धों के माध्यम से मस्तिष्क को उत्पादन शक्ति के अधीन नहीं मानता।

एक बार उत्पादन शक्ति को मानव मस्तिष्क के अधीन मान लेने पर यह मान लेना स्वाभाविक है कि मनुष्य के 'आर्थिक लक्ष्य' 'सामान्य लक्ष्यों' के अनुरूप बनाये जाय। अगर व्यक्तित्व के पूर्ण विकास का अवसर है तो सभी तरह की शक्तियों का–राजनीतिक, आर्थिक–विकेन्द्रीकरण आवश्यक है और बड़ी मशीनों द्वारा बड़े पैमाने के उत्पादन वाली व्यवस्था में वास्तविक विकेन्द्रीकरण नहीं हो सकता। इसलिए भारत के समाजवादियों ने छोटी कुशल मशीनों के साथ विकेन्द्रित सत्ता के 'चौखम्भा राज्य' की भी कल्पना की।

गाँधीजी के रचनात्मक कार्यों एवं साध्य-साधन के रिश्ते पर होने वाली बहस का भी भारतीय समाजवादी चिन्तन पर प्रभाव पड़ा। रचनात्मक कार्यों का एक उद्देश्य जहाँ आर्थिक लक्ष्यों को प्राप्त करना था, वहीं सामान्य लक्ष्यों की प्राप्ति के लिए समाज को तैयार करना भी था, अच्छे साध्य के लिए सही साधन भी जरूरी है, को अधिक व्यापक बनाकर लोहिया ने तात्कालिकता की अवधारणा का इजाद किया। इसका मतलब यह कि प्रत्येक कदम लक्ष्य की दिशा की ओर हो। इसमें दो कदम आगे और एक कदम पीछे हटने की कोई गुजाइश नहीं है।

पूंजीवाद और साम्यवाद के कटु अनुभवों से सीखकर भारत के समाजवादियों ने मानव जाति और खासकर तीसरी दुनिया को नये विचार देने की कोशिश की लेकिन उसका परीक्षण नहीं हुआ जिससे कि उसे भी व्यावहारिकता की कसौटी पर कसा जाय। निकट भविष्य में तो भारत में इसकी अधिक संभावना नहीं दिखती है।

संदर्भ

1. ट्राट्स्की सतत् क्रांति की बात करता था।

लेखकों के द्वारा सम्पादित पुस्तक समाजवादी आंदोलन के दस्तावेज, 1934-52 के सौजन्य से साभार।

22

पूँजीवाद एवं साम्यवाद की अप्रासंगिकता (NON-RELEVANCE OF CAPITALISM AND COMMUNISM)

राम मनोहर लोहिया

आधुनिक सभ्यता की तीन विशेषताएँ

पूँजीवाद और समाजवाद की समान पराजय आसानी से समझ में आ जाती है जब हम दोनों को उस एक ही सभ्यता के हिस्से के रूप में देखते हैं जो लगता है कि अपनी यात्रा के समीप आ गयी है। सभी सभ्यताओं का लक्ष्य रहा है आराम, संस्कृति, शांति और आदर्श राज्य। एक सभ्यता को दूसरी सभ्यता से जो चीज अलग करती है वह है उन लक्ष्यों को प्राप्त करने की प्रक्रियाएँ और उनके सूक्ष्म तत्त्व। प्रत्येक सभ्यता जीवन के कुछ उद्देश्यों एवं कुछ विशेष वेगों से संचालित होती है। धार्मिक या इहलोकवादी, अधिनायकवादी या उदार, विवेकपूर्ण या संवेगात्मक, सामन्ती या पूंजीवादी, आध्यात्मिक या भौतिकवादी श्रेणियों के माध्यम से मानवीय उद्देश्यों को समझने की कोशिश समुचित साहसिक कार्य नहीं है। आधुनिक सभ्यता को मात्र लोकतंत्र या अधिनायकवाद, निजी या राजकीय सम्पत्ति की शब्दावली में नहीं समझा जा सकता। आधुनिक सभ्यता के प्रभेदक वेग हैं– अर्थव्यवस्था में विज्ञान का निरन्तर प्रयोग, बढ़ता हुआ जीवन स्तर और बढ़ती सामाजिक समानता। आधुनिक समाज को बढ़ते उत्पादन की प्रेरणा और आधुनिक मनुष्य को बढ़ते जीवन स्तर एवं बेहतर घर की इच्छा गति देती है। किसी पूर्व सभ्यता में यह प्रेरणा नहीं थी क्योंकि उसके पास क्रांतिकारी प्रौद्योगिकी नहीं थी। न ही कोई पूर्व सभ्यता सामाजिक समानता के भावपूर्ण आवेग से इतनी मजबूती

से प्रभावित थी। अब यह भी इस बदलती प्रौद्योगिकी द्वारा सम्भव हो गयी है। अमेरीका में हो या सोवियत रूस में, आधुनिक मनुष्य बड़े पैमाने द्वारा बढ़ते उत्पादन एवं सुन्दर घर के समान लक्ष्यों से प्रेरित होता है और चाहता है कि ये उद्देश्य सभी को, मुख्यतः अपने देश में सभी को, प्राप्त हो सकें। इन लक्ष्यों की प्राप्ति के अन्त में इस पृथ्वी पर स्वर्ग, आदर्श राज्य, समानता, शांति एवं पूर्ण जीवन है।

आधुनिक सभ्यता की तीन विशेषताएँ (क्रांतिकारी प्रौद्योगिकी, बढ़ता जीवन स्तर एवं सामाजिक समानता) संकट में पड़ गयी हैं। क्रांतिकारी प्रौद्योगिकी अपने ही द्वारा सृजित उस राक्षस के सामने खड़ी है जिसे वह मार नहीं सकती। वह राक्षस है–दो-तिहाई दुनिया की भयंकर गरीबी। यह प्रौद्योगिकी अमेरीका या सोवियत रूस में आश्चर्यजनक ऊँचाई तक क्यों न पहुँच रही हो, अपने प्रताप के प्रथम स्थल, यूरोप में फैलने में अक्षम है। वहाँ यह पिछले तीन दशकों से स्थिर रही है। बढ़ते जीवन-स्तर की भूख, स्थिर या घटते उत्पादन रूपी पत्थर पर दांत तोड़ रही है। बढ़ते उत्पादन और जीवन स्तर की कभी खत्म न हो सकने वाली भूख से उत्पन्न चिन्ताएँ तनाव एवं सामान्य खोखलापन असहनीय होता जा रहा है। पूंजीपतियों ने उम्मीद की कि उनका आदर्श राज्य पूर्ण प्रतियोगिता की स्थिति में प्रत्येक व्यक्ति द्वारा स्वहित के लिए काम करने की अवस्था से उत्पन्न होगा। साम्यवादी अभी भी यह उम्मीद करते हैं कि उनका आदर्श राज्य उत्पादन के साधनों पर, सामाजिक स्वामित्व से उत्पन्न होगा। दोनों ही उभय भ्रांतियों से यह स्पष्ट हो गया है कि समाज के सामान्य लक्ष्य अवश्यम्भावी रूप से कुछ आर्थिक लक्ष्यों से नहीं निकलते। मनुष्य की बृद्धि द्वारा दोनों तरह के लक्ष्यों के बीच एक समाकलित सम्बन्ध स्थापित करना होगा। उसी तरह सामाजिक, राजनीतिक एवं आर्थिक समानता इस सभ्यता में उस ऊँचाई तक पहुँच गयी है जितनी किसी पूर्व सभ्यता में नहीं पहुँची थी। इसमें सभ्यता ने राजकुमारी और धोबिन को देखने में करीब-करीब एक-सा बना दिया है। लेकिन यह सभ्यता टूट रही है क्योंकि साथ-साथ आध्यात्मिक समानता की इसने कोशिश नहीं की। अगर पूर्व की सभ्यताएँ, आध्यात्मिक समानता के साथ सामाजिक असमानता होने के भार से टूट गयीं, तो लगता है आधुनिक सभ्यता सामाजिक समानता के साथ आध्यात्मिक असमानता होने के भार से चरमरा रही है। सामूहिक जीवन इतना निर्मम बन गया है कि मनुष्य मात्र प्रयोग का पात्र हो गया है।

आधुनिक सभ्यता का मस्तिष्क कुछ दशक पूर्व अपनी यात्रा के अंतिम छोर पर पहुँचा। वर्तमान शताब्दी ने महात्मा गाँधी के रूप में केवल एक सृजक को

जाना है और अणुबम के रूप में एक अविष्कार की। जिस तरह यह अविष्कार आधुनिक सभ्यता की पराकाष्ठा है, उसी तरह सृजक ऐसे गर्भ से निकलता जिसकी अभी तक स्पष्ट पहचान नहीं है या शक्तिशाली नहीं है। आधुनिक सभ्यता ने 'विचार' को पूर्णत: शक्ति की सेवा में समर्पित कर दिया है और जब तक इसके तीनों प्रवेगों की अनथक परीक्षक नहीं होती, इससे भिन्न हो भी नहीं सकता। पूँजीवाद और साम्यवाद का, अमेरीका और रूस का, एक-दूसरे पर दोषारोपण बढ़ रहा है, लेकिन वे गरीबी और युद्ध के जुड़वे राक्षस को मार सकने में अक्षम हैं। वे जो कहते या करते हैं, वह उनके राक्षसी गुण को मात्र बढ़ाता ही है। उन लोगों ने दुनिया को भय एवं घृणा से ढक दिया है। अब मनुष्य अपने में शांति नहीं है। उसे वर्तमान सभ्यता के दोनों पहलुओं, पूंजीवाद एवं साम्यवाद, से अपने को हटाना होगा। उनके उभय गुणों और प्रवेगों ने उन्हें एक नयी सभ्यता की खोज के लिए समान रूप से अप्रासंगिक बना दिया है। समान अप्रासंगिकता के इस सिद्धांत को समान बुराई या दोनों घरों पर प्लेग (संकट) की तिरस्कारपूर्ण कामना के सिद्धांत के साथ मिलाने की गलती नहीं करनी चाहिए। यह सिद्धांत अपने को उस ऊँचे नैतिक पीठिका (मंच) पर प्रस्थापित नहीं करता जहाँ से यह निर्णय और निन्दा का फतवा दे। यह वर्तमान सभ्यता के अनाशवान गौरव और किसी पूर्व सभ्यता में प्राप्त न होने वाली सामाजिक समानता से पूरी तरह अभिज्ञ है। वर्तमान सभ्यता के विचारों एवं कार्यों से बहुत कुछ सीखना है और इसकी कई विशेषताएँ अवश्यंभावी रूप से मानवीय प्रयास के नये समाकलन में शामिल होंगी। समान अप्रासंगिकता का सिद्धांत नयी सड़क पर के उस यात्री का निर्णय है जो घूम-फिरकर वहीं पहुँचने वाली (गोलाकार) और कहीं न जाने वाली अन्य सड़कों पर चलने के प्रलोभनों को नकारता है। वैसे यात्री के लिए इससे अधिक घातक दूसरी बात नहीं होगी कि वह अन्य दो सड़कों में तुलना करने पर समय खराब करे। उनके लिए दोनों समान रूप से अप्रासंगिक है। अगर जोर से कहने की भाषा का इस्तेमाल जरूरी है तो वे समान रूप से अच्छे या बुरे हैं।

प्रणालियाँ एवं जनता

अतलांतिक एवं सोवियत, दोनों खेमों के मानने वाले समान अप्रासंगिकता के सिद्धांत से एक समान, गहरे रूप में, आघातिक हैं। वे लोग विरोधी के विश्लेषण में सही हैं लेकिन अपने विश्लेषण में पूरी तरह अँधे हैं। साम्यवाद के दमनों एवं अत्याचारों, अर्द्ध-विकसित क्षेत्रों में इसके आर्थिक लक्ष्यों से उत्पन्न बर्बादी और बांझ नृशंसता, जिसका यह प्रतिनिधित्व करता है, पर चुप रहने की कोई जरूरत

नहीं है। उसी तरह ह्रास की ओर से दुनिया की पुलिस एवं प्रशिक्षक बनने, पूरी दुनिया में चारों ओर सख्त व्यवहार एवं सुधार की कमरबंद (पेटी) कसने और आधुनिक सभ्यता की उनकी पागल पराकाष्ठा के लिए अतलांतिक प्रयासों पर भी चुप रहने की जरूरत नहीं है। तथापि, यह कहा जाता है कि लोकतंत्र में परिवर्तन की संभावनाएँ किसी समय इसे तानाशाही की तुलना में बेहतर बनाती हैं। यहाँ तक कि सम्पत्ति-संबंध को बदलना भी बहुत कठिन नहीं है। लेकिन अब तक किसी ऐसी सभ्यता के बारे में लोग नहीं जानते, जो अपने विशेष प्रवेगों एवं उद्देश्यों को बदलने के लिए अपनी चमड़ी (घेरे) से बाहर निकली हो। एक जीवंत सभ्यता या तो उन्नति करती है या पीछे हटती है, यह बदलती नहीं है। मानवीय बुद्धि का यह विरल प्रदर्शन अगर कभी होता है तो इसे प्राप्त करने वाले लोग मानेंगे कि समान अप्रासंगिकता का सिद्धांत सही था। यह सही है कि निर्बंध वार्तालाप एवं वाद-विवाद सभी देशों में सहमना लोगों के बीच सम्पर्क स्थापित करने के योग्य बनाता है। इससे खुशी होती है। इस बीच, साम्यवाद के अंतर्गत एक सशस्त्र पहरेदार, जो प्राप्त करता है वह सामान्यतः लोकतंत्र में घटनाओं के दबाव एवं परम्पराओं द्वारा प्राप्त होता है। इसमें अपधर्मी इनसे घिरे रहते हैं। ऐसा नहीं है कि वर्तमान सभ्यता के ढांचे के अन्दर साम्यवाद में परिवर्तन की संभावनाएँ एकदम नहीं हैं। वे अघोषित रूप में बिना वाद-विवाद के हो जाते हैं। युगोस्लाविया की तरह की घटना विरले ही होती है, लेकिन वह हुई है जरूर, साम्यवाद को नापसंद करनेवाले कुछ समाजवादी युगोस्लाव कम्युनिस्ट पार्टी से अधिक समीपता महसूस करते हें बनिस्बत की कई देशों की सोशलिस्ट पार्टियों के। अंतरराष्ट्रीय साम्यवाद से नाता टूटने के बाद युगोस्लाविया के साम्यवादी समाजवाद की तरफ मुखातिब हैं। उनमें राष्ट्रीय आजादी की शक्तिशाली भावना है, वे दोनों खेमों से अलग एक शक्ति चाहते हैं एवं विकेन्द्रीकरण में उनकी रूचि है।

सभी देशों की जनता में अपने प्रीति का (endearing) गुण हैं। नयी सभ्यता के लिए सभी समान रूप से प्रासंगिक हैं। वर्तमान सभ्यता, पूंजीवाद एवं साम्यवाद, दोनों रूपों में नये सृजन के लिए समान रूप से अप्रासंगिक है, लेकिन उन व्यवस्थाओं में रहने वाली जनता अप्रासंगिक नहीं है। अमरीकियों के नौजवान जीवन शक्ति एवं उनकी सीधी ईमानदारी, जर्मनों के तरीके एवं उनकी सम्पूर्णता, अंग्रेजों के मृदु व्यवहार से कौन मोहित नहीं होगा? जिन कुछ स्लावों एवं चीनियों से लोग मिलते हैं, वे भूख बढ़ाते हैं। स्लाव, कुछ सदी पहले के उभय पुरखों के गृह-विरह की यादें ताजा करते हैं और इस अफसोस के कारण बनते हैं कि कोई व्यक्ति रूस और चीन की महान जनता के साथ अधिक सम्पर्क नहीं बना सकता।

साम्यवादी सरकारों ने अपनी जनता और बाहरी दुनिया के बीच तीन दीवारें खड़ी कर दी हैं। इन देशों में कम्युनिस्टों के अलावा दूसरा कोई रह नहीं सकता जिससे बिना कम्युनिस्ट हुए समान सोच वालों का मिलन असंभव है। यह स्वाभाविक ही है कि भारत का समाजवादी बर्मा या युगोस्लाविया, फ्रांस या अफ्रीका, जर्मनी या अमेरीका के समाजवादियों से रूस या चीन के साम्यवादियों की अपेक्षा अधिक नजदीकीपन महसूस करे। जनता के स्तर पर संबंध अधिक बिगड़ जाता है क्योंकि केवल साम्यवाद के अन्दर ही पूरी जनता और उसकी सरकार सभी देशों की कम्युनिस्ट पाटियों से अपवर्जक मित्रता करती है। स्वभावतः गैर-साम्यवादियों को इससे चिढ़ होती है। अन्त में, निन्दा तर्क की जगह ले लेती है। यद्यपि भारत की सोशलिस्ट पार्टी जितनी अमेरीकी पक्षधर है उतनी ही सोवियत पक्षधर है, लेकिन अन्तरराष्ट्रीय साम्यवाद इसे अमरीकी एजेंट और खुफिया के रूप में बदनाम करने के लिए झूठ-पर-झूठ उगलता रहा है। नयी सभ्यता के निर्माता अपना आत्मविश्वास नहीं छोड़ सकते। वे वहाँ आलोचना करेंगे जहाँ होनी चाहिए। वे अमरीका की प्रत्येक आलोचना के साथ रूस की आलोचना करके प्रति-संतुलन नहीं करेंगे। इसी तरह रूस की प्रत्येक आलोचना का प्रति-संतुलन अमरीका की आलोचना करके नहीं करेंगे। किसी तर्क को अपने रास्ते पर जाना चाहिए और आत्मविश्वास की कमी इसे कमजोर न करे। संगठित अहिंसा को साम्यवाद एवं पूंजीवाद, दोनों के सामने खड़े होने में सक्षम होना चाहिए। उसमें हिचक नहीं हो लेकिन करुणा हो, घृणा न हो लेकिन गुस्सा हो। शत्रुता धुंधली पड़ सकती है।

कुजात वारिस

पूंजीवाद एवं सम्यवाद वर्तमान सभ्यता के एक ही घर के दो हिस्से हैं। इससे पहले अक्सर अपने को पुनर्जीवित करने के बहादुराना प्रयास में एक सभ्यता दो परस्पर-विरोधी भुजाओं में विभाजित होती रही है। उनके आक्रमण की तेज आवाज से पूरी दुनिया के कान बहरे हो जाते हैं और नयी सभ्यता की अब तक धीमी आवाज सुनायी नहीं पड़ती है। मानव सभ्यता पर साम्यवादी सिद्धांत उल्टा है। अगर पहले के आदर्शवाद ने प्रशिया में इतिहास के शिखर पर पहुँचने को मनुष्य का परितोष मान लिया, तो उसी तरह साम्यवादी सिद्धांत पश्चिमी यूरोप में प्राप्त शिखर को पिघलाकर शाश्वत वैभव के रूप में बदलना चाहता है। इतिहास पूरी तरह एक सभ्यता के दायरे में ही नहीं घूमता। अगर ऐसा होता तो कोई सभ्यता कभी नष्ट नहीं होती या पीछे नहीं चली जाती और तब शक्ति का स्थानान्तरण दुनिया के एक हिस्से से दूसरे हिस्से में नहीं होता। जब कोई सभ्यता टिमटिमाने

लगती है, मशाल सामान्यतः कुजातों के हाथ में चली जाती है। वर्तमान सभ्यता का कुजात है–दो-तिहाई अर्द्धविकसित संसार। लेकिन वह मशाल का हकदार तभी हैं जब वह पुराने से अपना संबंध तोड़े और सोचने एवं रहने का अपना स्वरूप तैयार करे। मानव द्वारा इन नये रूपों का निर्माण इस पृथ्वी पर मानव जाति का पहला संयुक्त प्रयास होगा। वह विरलतम बुद्धि का निष्पादन होगा जिसकी हार्दिक आशा करनी चाहिए। इस निरन्तर स्थानांतरण को कौन पसंद करता है? कम-से-कम एशियाई तो नहीं करते जिन्हें याद है कि वे अतीत में इतिहास के शिखर बिन्दुओं पर बैठे थे और उसका भस्मवत् स्वाद कैसा है।

कार्य के स्वरूप

जहाँ यह जरूरी है कि समाजवाद के सिद्धांत को ठोस आधार प्रदान किया जाय, वहीं उतना ही जरूरी है कि कार्य के उपयुक्त स्वरूप की खोज की जाय जिसके माध्यम से सिद्धांत को अमल में लाया जा सके। अबतक कार्य की दो प्रणालियों, चुनावी कार्य एवं विद्रोही कार्य, पर दुर्भाग्यपूर्ण जोर दिया जाता रहा है और इन दोनों के बीच विरोध विकसित होने दिया गया है। असफल होने पर समाजवादी वोट की लोकतांत्रिक प्रक्रिया को रद्द करने, और कम-से-कम भाषणों में विद्रोही कार्यों को अपनाने के अभ्यस्त हो गये हैं। जहाँ तक पार्टी की नीति-वक्तव्य, भले ही उसका वह अर्थ न हो, वोट एवं बंदूक में इस ध्रुवत्व को प्रोत्साहित करता है, वहाँ तक इसे एक स्पष्टीकरण द्वारा पूरा करना जरूरी है।

सभी कार्यों का लक्ष्य जनता की इच्छा एवं संगठन, और जहाँ तक संभव हो, राष्ट्रीय जीवन की पुनर्रचना होना चाहिए। तत्काल भलाई करते हुए, उन्हें समाजवाद के लिए उतनी पर्याप्त शक्ति हासिल करनी चाहिए जिससे वह पूंजीवाद को पराजित कर सके। जनता की इच्छा का संगठन प्राथमिक महत्व का है और वोट या विद्रोह या दूसरे उपयुक्त रूपों में इसकी अभिव्यक्ति आकस्मिक महत्त्व के दोयम नम्बर का सवाल है। समाजवाद की पार्टी को इतनी पर्याप्त शक्ति होनी चाहिए कि वह उनका उपयोग उस काम के लिए कर सके जो उस समय उपयुक्त लगे। वैसी शक्ति और संगठन के निर्णय के लिए समाजवाद की पार्टी को जनता की प्रवक्ता, उसकी इच्छा की संगठनकर्त्री, अन्याय का विरोध करने वाली एवं पुनर्निर्माण की निष्पादिका बनने की निरन्तर कोशिश करनी चाहिए। इसे रचनात्मक कार्यों में हिस्सा लेने, लोकप्रिय निर्णय को प्रबुद्ध करने और उससे प्रबुद्ध बनने, अन्याय का विरोध करने के लिए निरन्तर तैयार रहनी चाहिए। फावड़ा, वोट एवं जेल के रूप में कार्यों की तीन पद्धतियाँ प्रतीक बन चुकी हैं।

सत्ता की पार्टियाँ, जो यथास्थिति बनाये रखने पर निर्भर करती है और जो अपने विकास के लिए घृणा एवं भय का इस्तेमाल करती हैं, रचनात्मक कार्य को सदैव नीरस एवं मन्द काम समझती रही हैं, लेकिन समाजवाद की पार्टी रचनात्मक कार्य को छोड़ दूसरे तरीके से बन नहीं सकती है। विरोध पक्ष में रहने पर भी इसे जनता को, कितने ही छोटे एवं प्रभावहीन नमूने के रूप में क्यों न हो, बताना चाहिए कि वह क्या चाहती है और सरकार में आयेगी तो क्या करेगी। निकट अतीत में सोशलिस्ट पार्टी ने कृषि-पुनर्निमाण को केन्द्र बनाकर रचना-कार्यों के सभी आयामों को दिखलाने की कोशिश की। इसने छोटी नहरों, कुओं, तालाबों को खोदने एवं सड़कों और दूसरी परियोजनाओं के लिए लोगों को तैयार करने की कोशिश की। इस तरह के अन्य रचनात्मक कार्यों को समाजवादी कार्य की प्राथमिक एवं स्वीकृत पद्धति बनना पड़ेगा। हिन्द किसान पंचायत या हिन्द मजदूर सभा जैसे किसानों एवं कामगारों के संगठनों का उतनी तेजी से नहीं बढ़ने का, जितनी तेजी से बढ़ना चाहिए, कारण रचनात्मक कार्यों की उपेक्षा है। किसान पंचायत को जहाँ अन्याय का प्रतिरोध करने के लिए मजबूत करना चाहिए वहीं उसे भोजन, खाने के तरीके, फसल उगाने, खाद बनाने के संबंध में उनकी आदतों को बदलने और उन्हें भंडारण, उपज बेचने एवं अच्छे उपकरण खोजने में सहायता करने के लिए भी बनाना चाहिए।

सत्याग्रह एवं वर्ग-संघर्ष

सत्याग्रह एवं वर्ग-संघर्ष में एक भ्रांतिपूर्ण विरोध बढ़ने दिया गया है। वस्तुतः इस तरह का कोई विरोध है नहीं और एक वास्तविक वर्ग-संघर्ष सिविल नाफरमानी में है। सामान्य तौर पर यह विश्वास किया जाता है कि विरोधी का हृदय-परिवर्तन करना सत्याग्रह का प्रेरणा-प्रवेश है जबकि वर्ग-संघर्ष पूरे वर्ग के इस तरह के किसी परिवर्तन को स्वीकार नहीं करता, इसलिए चालू व्यवस्था को उलट देना जरूरी हो जाता है। यह सही है कि सिविल नाफरमानी विरोधी के हृदय-परिवर्तन की एक पद्धति है लेकिन इसके ऐसा होने का बड़ा कारण यह है कि यह विरोधी की शक्ति कम करने और अच्छे सिद्धांत की शक्ति बढ़ाने का एक प्रयास है। सत्याग्रह एवं वर्ग-संघर्ष शक्ति के लिए एक ही अभ्यास के दो नाम हैं-"बुराई की शक्ति कम करना और अच्छाई की शक्ति बढ़ाना।" हृदय-परिवर्तन होता है, यह तो स्पष्ट है, अच्छे सिद्धांत मानने वालों में तो और भी। जहाँ तक वे कार्य के लिए अधिक निश्चय, संगठन एवं क्षमता प्राप्त करते हैं, ऐसा होता है लेकिन विरोधियों की पंक्तियों में भी हृदय-परिवर्तन होता है। उनमें से कुछ वर्ग-भावना

से मुक्त होना शुरू करते हैं। यह फिर दुहराना जरूरी है कि सत्याग्रह या वर्ग-संघर्ष के किसी कार्य को तात्कालिकता की कसौटी पर खरा उतरना चाहिए और उसे झूठ, धोखा या हिंसा का उपयोग कतई नहीं करना चाहिए। कठोर व्यवहार त्याग देना चाहिए।

किसी समाजवादी बहस में बल का मुद्दा महत्त्वपूर्ण होता है और कुछ समाजवादी विश्वास करते हैं कि वर्तमान व्यवस्था को अंतिम रूप से बिना बल प्रयोग के समाप्त नहीं किया जा सकता। यह बहस समाजवादी सिद्धांत एवं आंदोलन के लिए हानिकर साबित हुई है। बल का प्रयोग होना चाहिए या नहीं, यह दोयम नम्बर का सवाल है। प्रमुख मुद्दा यह है कि जनता की इच्छा को शांतिपूर्ण संघर्ष के आधार पर संगठित किया जाय या दूसरे आधार पर। एक आन्दोलन का प्रभेदक लक्षण यह होना चाहिए कि वह हिंसा की वकालत और उसे संगठित करता है या नहीं। अंततः यह बल का प्रयोग करता है या नहीं, प्रभेदक लक्षण नहीं है। जनता के जीवन में ऐसा क्षण आ सकता है जब चालू व्यवस्था केवल संगीन पर टिकी हो और संगीन लड़खड़ा रही हो और विशाल जनसंख्या में लोग नयी व्यवस्था के लिए दृढ़ निश्चयी हों। इस अल्प क्षण में पुरानी व्यवस्था की प्राण-पीड़ा समाप्त करने और नयी व्यवस्था को जन्म देने के लिए बल के प्रभुत्व का इस्तेमाल करना हम चुन सकते हैं। यह जनता द्वारा की गयी स्वतः स्फूर्त एवं मात्र अल्पक्षण की हिंसा होगी। कोई यह आशा कर सकता है कि यह हिंसा भी अनावश्यक हो। किसी हालत में यह क्षणिक प्रदर्शन संगठन के किसी सिद्धांत का स्थायी आधार नहीं बन सकता।

मनुष्य की गिरावट का एक पैमाना यह है कि वह बल की जनोत्तेजक अपीलें करता या सुनता है। हिंसा की वैसी अपीलें विवेक एवं उस आधार को नकारती हैं जो किसी दिन शालीन जीवन जीने के योग्य बना सके। जो सिद्धांत हिंसा को आदर्श बनाते हैं वे एक वर्गहीन, जातिहीन समाज प्राप्त करने में अक्षम हैं। समाजवाद को हिंसा की वकालत एवं संगठन की सदैव निन्दा करनी होगी और उसे शांतिपूर्ण संघर्षों के ऐसे आधार प्राप्त करने की कोशिश करनी होगी जिससे व्यक्तिगत पहल एवं जिम्मेदारी में वृद्धि हो, शक्ति के केन्द्रीकरण में नहीं। हिंसा के संगठन का अवश्यम्भावी परिणाम होता है–शक्ति का केन्द्रीकरण। आज की दुनिया में हिंसा का इस्तेमाल एक बड़ा मुद्दा है और बड़ी संख्या में लोग महसूस करने लगे हैं कि अच्छे उद्देश्यों तक के लिए भी हिंसा की वकालत और संगठन बुरा है।

विनोद प्र० सिंह, सुनील मिश्र के सम्पादित समाजवादी आंदोलन के दस्तावेज से साभार प्राप्त।

23

THE ISM THAT FAILED

V.M. Tarkunde

Marx himself was a passionate lover of freedom. Yet the philosophy founded by him has led to the negation of freedom in different parts of the world.

Leaving aside religious preachers like Buddha and Jesus Christ, no social thinker has had a greater impact on the shaping of world events than Karl Marx.

The birth of socialism preceded Marx's Communist Manifesto (1848) by merely sixty years. Socialism sprang to life with the great French Revolution of 1789. The early socialists like Saint Simon, Fourier and Robert Owen disputed the laissez-faire theory of the emerging capitalist class and advocated cooperative enterprise. Their schemes, however, remained small and isolated. They were followed by other socialists, such as Louis Blanc in France and the Chartists in England, whose appeal was directed to the working class and who tried to extend the voting franchise. After the unsuccessful revolutions of 1848 and 1849, however, all types of socialism disappeared from Europe for nearly two decades. In 1864, Marx accepted the leadership of the Interantional Workingmen's Association (the First International). From about 1870. Marxism became the dominating ideology of European socialism.

Marx and Engels expected that a proletarian revolution would take place very soon in an industrially developted capitalist country. That, however, did not happen. Although European socialists accepted the Marxian ideal of nationalisation of all the means of production, they did not fully agree with the other Marxian tenet that socialism can be achieved only by revolutionay means. Political democracy was being extended in European countries by the gradual extension of franchise, and socialist leaders could therefore perceive the possibility of improving the workers' lot by recourse to the ballot box. Eventually, Lenin forced a division between workers and socialism. As a consequence of the Bolshevik Revolution in Russia in 1918, the European working class was sharply divided into communists and democratic socialists.

The Bolshevik Revolution of 1918 can hardly be regarded as a proletarian revolution as conceived by Marx. Although the Russian working class took some part in putting an end to the Czarist regime, the revolution was mainly a 'pacifist putsch' by peasant soldiers returning from the First World War. Lenin and the other Bolshevik leaders were well aware that their was not a typically proletarian revolution. They expected that immediately after the Bolshevik Revolution of 1918, a proletarian revolution would take place in industrially advanced capitalist countries, particularly in Germany, No revolution, however, occurred in any other European country and eventually the Russian communists, under the leadership of Stalin, reconciled themselves to "socialism in one country".

The second communist revolution took place in 1949, more than 30 years after the first. Significantly, it took place in an industrially backward country like China. It could not be regarded by any stretch of imagination as a proletarian revolution. The working class was not in picture at all. It was entirely a peasant revolution, brought about by a Communist party consisting of determined revolutionaries who had sprung from the middle class.

After the Chinese Revolution, a few communist revolutions have taken place in some parts of the Third World. They also took place in industrially backward countries and were not proletarian in character. These revolutions, moreover, do not represent the major trend in the Third World. As a result of the Second World War, colonialism came to an end and the countries of the Third World became independent nations. Most of them, after a short period of unstable democracy, came to be dominated by indigenous dictatorships. While a few of these dictatorships are either communist of pro-communist, most of them have emerged from the Right and are definitely against communism.

Reverting to the influence of Marxism on the European continent, two developments are worthy of note. In the first place after the Second World War, most of the socialist parties in Europe have rejected the Marxian tenet that socialism requires the nationalisation of all the means of production. The Socialist International which met at Frankfurt in 1951 declared that "socialist planning does not pre-suppose public ownership of all the means of production". Similar declarations were made by German Social Democrats in 1959 and Swedish Social Democrats in 1960. Nationalisation of Some industries and social control over others, is the objective of most of the socialist parties in Europe.

The second significant development in Europe from the Marxian point of view is the emergence of Euro-communism in western countries. These communists have come to believe that socialism can be established through the ballot box and that a revolution is neither necessary nor inevitable.

Revisionist tendencies are moreover, growing, throughout the communist world. Yugoslavia, Czechoslovakia, Hungary and Poland are obvious instances. But the most impressive revision of orthodox communism is taking place in China. China drifted away from the Russian fold in 1961 and it now regards Russia as its main enemy. Chinese communism is more opposed to the "social imperialism" of Russia than to the capitalist imperialism of the United states. The internal economy of China is also being developed along lines which indicate a departure from orthodox communism.

The thirties of this century saw the apogee of the international communist movement. The wall Street crash of 1929 and the Great Depression which followed appeared to corroborate the Marxian prognosis that capitalism would end in an insoluble economic crisis. Since the beginning of the Second World War in 1939, however, enthusiasm for communism has been continuously on the decline. The Russo German Pact at the commencement of the Second World War shocked the conscience of antifascist supporters of communism. The narrow nationalism resorted to by communist Russia after the Second World War persuaded many communist supporters to look upon Marxism as "the God that failed". The rift between Russia and China in 1961 and their continuing antipathy caused further disillusionment. The main factor, however, which has eroded the legitimacy of communism (and also Marxism) is the indefinite continuation of rigid dictatorships in Russia, China and other communist countries. Experience has proved that a communist state does not wither away but reminas autocratic and authoritarian. Even the economic achievemnts in communist countries are comparatively meagre and unimpressive, and they do not justify the eclipse of civil liberties and human rights. The recent experience of Poland has shown that a communist dictatorship is a dictatorship, not of the proletariat, but over the proletariat. The experience of communism in practice is not such as to invoke enthusiastic supportYoung people are joining the communist rank in large numbers as they used to do in the thirties.

Communism is the political practice of Marxism. Marx himself was a passionat lover of freedom. He declared in the Communist Manifesto that "the free development of each is the condition of the free development of all." He could not possibly have tolerated the prospect of any long-lasting dictatorship. Yet the philosophy founded by him has led to the negation of freedom in different parts of the world.

No scientist, however great, can be claimed to have discovered the final truth. This is true of social sciences as much as of physical sciences. Marx was undoubtedly one of the greatest of all social scientists. Yet the philosophical school founded by him has led to the perversion of its proclaimed ideal.

All the major shortcoming of Marxism can be traced to the theory of economic determinism, the so-called "economic interpretation of history", which is the cornerstone of Marxian philosophy. It is true that man's ideas are influenced to some extent, but only to some extent, by his economic interests. The theory of economic determinism is therefore a half-truth and like all other half-truths is likely to be highly misleading. The economic and political theories of Marxism, which have resulted in the negation of freedom, were deduced from the basic postulate of economic determinism.

Consistently with the theory of economic determinism, Marxism assumed that the wages paid to workers in capitalist countries would always remain at the subsistence level, despite the increasing productivity of labour by the use of advanced machinery. There would consequently be an ever increasing gap between the volume of the goods produced and the ability of society to purchase them. This would lead to a series of industrial crises, each crisis being more severe than the previous one. The limited purchasing power of capitalist society would also lead to the growth of imperialism and to imperialism wars. This brilliant prognosis was apparently borne out by the march of events during Marx's lifetime and for some years thereafter. Eventually, however, events took a different turn. Wages began to rise in capitalist societies. The capitalist class did not act strictly according to the theory of economic determinism. Under the pressure of liberal opinion, and later under the laws of democratic states, there were material improvements in the living conditions of the working class. The expected revolutionary situation did not materialism in industrially developed countries. Capitalism still remains a very defective and unsatisfactory economic system, but this is for reasons other than those visualised by Marx.

The Marxian theory of the state has also not been borne out by the march of history. Guided by the theory of economic determinism. Marx looked upon the state as consisting of a coercive machinery designed to serve the interests of the dominant economic class. A cabinet in a parliamentary democracy, according to Marxism, is in effect an executive committee of the ruling capitalist class. The necessary corollary is that such a state must be ended by a revolution and cannot be mended by reformist action. This theory of the state appeared to be true in Marx's lifetime, but has been falsified by subsequent developments. A modern democratic state in western countries is not just a coercive machinery set up by the capitalist class. A Labour Party cabinet in capitalist England is surely not an executive committee of British capitalism, Capitalist economy in democratic states can be materially altered and even wholly replaced through the ballot box. A violent revolution is not necessary for the purpose.

The main failure of Marxism, however, has been in the region of morality and culture. The theory of economic determinism led Marx to the conclusion that morality and culture are merely an ideological super-structure reared on the basic economic reality and that this super-structure has little independent force of its own. This approach implies that man's ideas and ideals have no role in the shaping of historical events. That is why Marx believed that a proletarian revolution would take place automatically and invitably as a result of the development of the forces of production and that the ideas of human beings will have only a superficial and derivative role in the making of the revolution. History, however, shows that human ideas are not always derived from the economic situation and that these ideas have a progressively powerful role in the making of history in fact, by deprecating morality as a class function, Marxism threw away what should have been its main asset–the moral revulsion which sensitive people feel against exploitation and the glaring economic inequality which it breeds. Moral cynicism has converted communism into a power-oriented political movement which frequently participates in unprincipled power politics.

The Economic And Philosophic Manuscripts, which Marx wrote in 1844 but which were published only recently, shows that Marx had a pronounced aversion to anything which impaired man's liberty. It is difficult to believe that he would have liked to live under any dictatorship, whether of the Right or the Left. The spirit of Marx is represented better by the humanist Sakharov who had to leave Russia for his political opinions than by the communist leader Andropov who occupies the seat of power in Russia.

टाइम्स ऑफ इण्डिया, मार्च 13, 1993 के सौजन्य से साभार प्राप्त।

24

MARXISM GIVES WAY

Kashi Ram Sharma

The Communist leviathan in Eastern Europe has almost crumbled in the last six months or so. The Romanian citadel was the last and the bloodiest. In Poland, Hungary, East Germany and Czechoslovakia, the change was brought about swiftly and without bloodshed. The Soviet Union and China are experiencing far-reaching changes whose accumulated consequences may be climaxed in the not so distant future. No expert on communist affairs could have even anticipated, much less argued, the contents and the contours of changes sought to be ushered therein. To use the word 'change' in this context is a gross under statement. We are witness to a metamorphosis in the communist world. This metamorphosis has reached the climax in Eastern Europe whereas in China and the Soviet Union the contradictions of this metamorphosis are in the process of maturing to their logical conclusions. To many Marxologists, this is a second revolution, while to many die-hard and dogmatic Marxists, it is a kind of restoration. The Marxist maxim that nothing is permanent except change, a half-cliche and a half reality, is applying more to the communist world with its reverse logic.

THE TARGET

What is the target of the change? What is the focus of people's anger and what is the reality which the people are surging forward to change? Among Marxists and non-Marxists, there is a broad consensus that it is Stalinism and its remnants which are the foci of change. The process of de-Stalinisation which was initiated by

Khruschev in the 20th Congress of the CPSU in 1956 is reaching its concluding epoch. The diagnosis is basically correct but grossly inadequate and incomplete. At best it is a half truth. The other half of the truth–and this is important–is that orthodox Leninism and dogmatic Marxism are under attack. Lenin's views on the 'inevitability of war' have already been discarded by the Communist world. This time, it is the quintessence of the Ten Commandments of Marx and Lenin about the 'Dictatorship of the Proletariat' which is being rejected. It is the vanguard role of the Communist Party and its monopoly of political power which is being challenged.

Lenin's supreme contribution was considered to be in the realm of praxis. In 1902 and again in 1905 as the leader of the Bolsheviks, he had propounded the thesis that a Communist Party is the repository of political wisdom and proletarian conscience. It is this aspect of Leninism–the monopoly of political power and political wisdom–sanctified by orthodox Marxism which is being discarded by the masses and intellectuals alike. Lenin's master format of democratic centralism falls flat on the ground. In a word it is not only stalinism which is the caus celebre of people's anger; orthodox Leninism and Marxism are equally the target or ridicule and rejection.

NOT IMMUNE

Marxism-Leninism accords a high priority to praxis. Shorn of its dialectical underpinnings, it could be stated that of all the teachers in life, experience is the most reliable. People in Communist countries have realised through praxis that power is rarely a means to an end. Rather, it is an end in itself. The Communit Parties are as vulnerable, some may say even more, to misuse and abuse power as any 'bourgeois' party. Praxis has taught people that 'dictatorship of the proletariat' in fact means 'dictatorship of the Communist Party' which in turn degenerates into the dictatorship of a charismatic and at times a paranoid leader, be he Stalin, Mao, Pol Pot or Ceausescu. Communist Party members and their near and dear ones by virtue of the fact that they alone monopolise access to power belong to a 'new class'. It is this privileged stratum to which Djilas long back invited our attention.

It has also been demonstrated amply that communist regimes are not immune from the emergence of bureaucracy and bureaucratic corruption. It is an ironic truth that all that revolutions achieve is a change of ruling elites. Gradually the revolutionary elite becomes the power-holder and administrator. Once a commissar becomes a bureaucrat, bureaucratic corruption and bureaucratic manners soon follow. Contrary to the wishes of Marx and Engels, the communist regimes have emerged highly bureaucratic and stratified. No wonder from China to Romania the battle-cry of changers is an immediate end to corruption of the Communist Party. Tens of thousand of protestors at the Tiananmen Square inJune 1989 knew it well that out of 20,000 Chinese students sent to Europe and America for highr studies, about 12,000 were the sons/daughters and close blood relatives of the Communist Party members.

In a word, what is being challenged by protestors in East European countries is not only the left over of Stalinism but people are striking at the very roots of Leninism which favours total state ownership of 'the means of production'. Although European communist countries never adopted Marxian economics in toto, they are thoroughly disenchanted with whatever they had adopted. No wonder, one of the first decress of the new Romanian government is to dismantle collective farming. Romania which was once the granary of entire Eastern Europe had to resort to food imports. The rate of inflation in Poland touched nearly 700 percent per annum in the last several years. It is the Marxian politics with its formula of 'dictatorship of the prolectariat' which is being discarded. Almost in all these European countries which have rejected the vanguard role of the Communist Parties, political pluralism and multiple party system are emerging. Marxism which was perceived once as a liberating and emancipating force has come to be believed as an instrument of new despotism.

ON RETREAT

Consequently, Marxism Leninism which was put on the defensive has been rendered defenceless. It is on retreat. This has come much sooner than expected.

About a year back, one of the top dissident intellectuals of Hungary said that democracy may not be the best form of government, but there is no better form of government than democracy. It is a new awakening in communist countries. It looks like a new dawn. Quite often this argument emanates from people's reaction and anger against communist misrule and abuse of power. Quite often it flows from their social and ethnic pluralism. Whatever may be the source, the fact remains that the sentiments and passions of democracy are sweeping across the entire communist world. In the European part of the communist world these sentiments have acquired the form of a powerful ideological force. These sentiments of democracy and freedom in EasternEurope go much beyond politics. They have pervaded the field of education, culture, arts, literature, painting, cinema and a whole lot of other creative activities. The Gorbachev factor has provided an impetus to this passion. There is a growing realisation in many communist countries that democracy, human rights, civil liberties, right to information are no longer bourgeois values as orthodox Marxism and Leninism perceived them to be.

Another crucial variable propelling change in Eastern Europe is nationalism. Marx was grossly mistaken in assuming that nationalism had already consummated its historical potential and relevance. In Eastern Europe, it is nationalism which is asseting or rather reasserting itself. In the Soviet Union, China, Vietnam and Cuba, nationalism had been successfully blended in their ideological mix of communism. It would be more accurate to argue that in the above mentioned countries, Marxism has been subordinated to the demands and dictatres of nationalism and it is precisely on account of this factor that the Chinese and Cuban citadels of orthodoxy would take somewhat longer to crumple. In Eastern Europe, Stalin and his Red Army in 1945 had succeeded in imposing or rather superimposing communist apparatus on national revolutions. It was a 'revolution' from above; it was a seizure of power.

Most Germans, Poles, Czechs, Romanians perceived the imposition of communist role over them as a fact of alien rule. If Stalin's was an agent of this alien imposition, Gorbachev has facilitated its folding up. One way to put it is that Gorbachev has undone the historic injustice done by Stalin. In all European countries except in Yugoslavia to a certain degree, the communist revolutions were neither historically authentic nor politically legitimate.

ETHNIC CONTRADICTIONS

Most of the social scientists in 1960s and 70s were led to believe that the socialist countries had successfully resolved the ethnic and nationality contradictions. This was just not true. We have been proved completely wrong in our supposition. If you push the problem under the carpet, you do not really solve it. Ethnic contradictions in the Baltic states of the Soviet Union have already exploded. In China, Tibetans, Mongols, Huis, Kazaks, Uigurs, in all about 70 million people, are struggling for equality and dignity. Yugoslavia which has some healthy and strong traditions of moderation has a notorious record on the nationality front. In East Germany, Czechoslovakia and Romania, it is the ethnic search for identity which has contributed to the climate of disaffection against the communist leviathan. In Poland, the Church has made all the difference. In Romania, the Church maintained a strong presence. Hence, it is not only an assertion of nationalism in Eastern Europe but added to this, it is also the assertion of sub-nationalism which has galvanised the mood for change.

हिन्दुस्तान टाइम्स, जून-26, 1990 के सौजन्य से साभार।

25

IS COMMUNISM DYING?

J.D. Sethi

Nearly 100 years of history has been dominatd by Marxism. That history is coming to a close. It is not Bush, Thatcher or Kohl but Gorbachev himself who is closing the unsavoury chapter of Communism, of its repression and historical distortions. Deng Xiaoping is more afraid of Gorbachev than of any Western leader. Indeed Gorbachev has put the entire Communist and non-Communist Left everywhere on the defensive. Communism cannot be saved by painting it as "socialism with a human face". It needs a new paradigm because capitalism is marching into the socialist citadel and is getting warm welcome.

Six recent events that seem to herald the end of Communism are: (a) first the fleeing away of thousands of its citizens from the GDR followed by the pulling down of the Berlin wall; (b) the end of Communist rule and its replacement by a non-Communist Solidarity Government in Poland, (c) the dissolution of the Hungarian Communist party and its choice to be like a European democratic socialist part, under a multi-party system, something which is getting repeated now in Bulgaria and Czecholovakia, (d) the revolt of ethnic, religious, regional groups against the Soviet ideology and its monolithic repressive structure; (e) prolonged civil war in the third world's self-proclaimed Marxist regimes in Angola, Nicaragua, Mozambique, Ethopia, Afghanistan, Campuchia etc. and their willingness to reject Communist system in favour of mixed economy, (f) Vietnam, once the shining example of definance against the biggest imperialism power, has found itself ruined by arrogating for itself an imperialist role.

TYRANNICAL LEADERS

Not only are the people of Poland, Hungary and GDR walking out on Communism, the people of China are also challenging theChinese leaders dare return to red fascism of days of the cultural revolution. Their revolt everywhere is turning into an attack on the Communist Bastille. If Deng is oblivious of the fact that human urge for freedom cannot be suppressed in the name of socialism, which though Marx saw as a system of many freedoms, he will be history's most likely last butcher. If the walls of EasternEurope are being pulled down and if what exists also behind the bamboo curtain is claimed as communism then the people living there know what fraud was perpetrated in the name of communism and the dictatorship of the working people. Stalin, Mao, Polpot and Romanis Ceauscescu, who is called the Polpot of Europe, have contributed significantly to the demise of communism by massacring or forcing out millions and letting them die of famines. Their contribution has been almost as brutally impressive as that of fascist leaders and some third world maniacs and certainly not less brutal than past imperialisms. Another but similar kind of crisis of Communism is that all those third world countries whose leaders prolaimed and imposed Marxism by establishing one party dictatorship are caught in long term civil wars and economic collapse.

DECLINING SUPPORT

The continuous decline of electoral fortunes and working class support for the West European Communist parties pushed Eastern European nations into isolation and paranoia. The latter relied too heavily on building a military power that did put War-saw Pact on par with NATO but the economic cost was so high that it nearly pushed back their economic development by decades. But the political cost was even higher. Every text book Marxist rule or norm was violated as a result of which Communism was discredited all over the world particularly as the Soviet military might galloped on. To get out of the self-inflicted economic crisis, Moscow capitulated on almost every demand Washington made in respect of strategic disputes.

China after the June massacre of the students of pro-democracy movement is totally paralysed. The economy is sliding back even though the West and Japan have refused to put a squeeze on Deng. The power struggle among old men is getting fiercer as people are not cooperating. Though Beijing is promising no turning back on economic reforms, i.e. capitalism, but it is also stoutly refusing political reforms. Rigid Communism and open of controlled capitalism can not be married even by the clever Chinese. There may be no danger of China slipping into the horrors of culture revolution but compulsions of economy, need for external finance and the stubborn refusal of people to yield Deng's butcheries are giving the Chinese leaders one more chance to give up their anachronism or slip into new babarium.

It is the prolonged and unredeemed economic stagnation that has deepened the crisis. The claim or hope and boast that capitalism was inefficient and sooner or later would be taken over by communism proved false, leading to disillusionment and frustration in the entire Left. Chinese Communism will have to collapse either way.

Economic scarcity, violation of economic laws in the name of planning, monopoly of power held by a small elite class of party and state bureaucracy, with professionals force to play a secondary role, accompanied by wide spread corruption required even greatr repression. It is no accident that one of the demands of the pro-democracy movements in GDR and Bulgaria is to put old communist leaders on trial for their corruption and misuse of office. It is corruption and the failure of socialist planning, which once dazzled the whole world, provoked the revolt."

It's bread could not be made available except on ration, communism remains self-condemned. Countries with vast oil resources failed to provide even heating facilities and in Romania, even street-lighting. Needs of the people were ignored as economic growth was artificially maintained at high cost. People's demands were suppressed. In Romania people cannot own a typewriter without registering the type face. They often have to sell their machines in return for food and other needs.

Gorbachev inherited an inefficient and inegalitarian and corrupt economic order. The biggest failure of communist society has been that they failed to provide the basic needs of the people after 70 years of revolution. The slogan "bread tomorrow" in the interest of ideology has not convinced people about the value of communism.

MASSIVE DEBT

The Soviet Union alone has piled up a debt of 40 billion dollar which it cannot pay through exports. Other communist nations are not far behind. Gorbachev knows that without financial support from theWest we cannot accelerate the pace of development nor pay back the loans. He is anxious to enlist the support particularly ofWorld Bank, IMF, GATT etc. But he has to pay a heavy price. He had to invite the Chairman of the federal Reserve of the US for advice. He thus compromised with the uncompromisable. The issue discussed with him was the convertibility of the rouble which is heavily over valued. If the rouble is made convertible it will mean rise in the cost of imports and a fresh push towards domestic inflation. The West wants to extract its pound of flesh. Bush is proving worse than Reagan by rubing Gorbachev's nose in the dust, rather than make the transition smoother for him.

Gorbachev thus has been obliged to give a general thrust of economic policies to turn the Soviet Union into a mixed economy model, mixture of socialism and capitlism which so far has proved a bad mix but may succeed. Ideology apart market principles have to become prime movers of state enterprises. Industry is being opened to multi-nationals and scores if not hundred of joint ventures are planned. The Soviet managers are being instructed to follow the pattern of their western counterparts. Several free zones are beign set up for export promotion. Licenses are being given to Soviet firms to operate abroad. The main emphasis has shifted from target fulfilling to profit and efficiency. All this is tolling the death knell of Communism.

MORAL DECAY

However, even economic prosperity without more political reforms will not do. Gorbachev has opened up the Soviet society. His glasnost is genuine. But his perestroika is not succeeding because without ensuring multi-party system and full economic freedom to enterprises he cannot achieve the objective of high growth rate. The Soviet Union is one communist nation whose success and survival depends upon complete elimination of communist economic planning.

However, Eastern Europe is not a normal case of economic or political crisis only. It faces a crisis of our moral and spiritual degeneration. Economic difficulties were combined with state oppression and moral decay.

In additions to economic crisis, it is the political crisis that is forcing out the communists from power, ironically by their insistence on maintaining the leading role of the party without their people's mandate or legitimacy for such a role. A recent poll in GDR has shown that no more than thriteen percent of the people will vote for the Socialist Unity Party if elections were held now.

No one has been more obliged to expose the ugly face of Soviet Communism than Mikhail Gorbachev. But for him the other countries of EasternEurope would have remained in darkness. He has shown that democracy, responsibility and equality that were what socialism was all about were negated by the Communists. Communist nations failed to achieve even that low standard of living which even the other poorest European countries have achieved. Culturally the Communist societies which were prison houses run by petty dictators and falsehood are now bursting out in revolt. The Communist empire is caught in the kind of crisis that is historically known imperialist powers have faced and disappeared.

हिन्दुस्तान टाइम्स, दिसम्बर, 1989, के सौजन्य से साभार।

26

समाजवादी आन्दोलन और गाँधीवाद
(SOCIALIST MOVEMENT AND GANDHISM)

सच्चिदानंद सिन्हा

महात्मा गाँधी को वास्तव में समाजवादी चिंतकों में इसके साधारण अर्थ में नहीं रखा जा सकता। फिर भी उनके विचारों में गौडविन जैसे व्यक्तिवादी अराजकवादी से कुछ समानता हम पाते हैं। आत्मनिर्भर ग्राम गणतन्त्रों को भारत, चर्खे कर्घे की अर्थ व्यवस्था जिसमें हर व्यक्ति अपनी आवश्यकता की अधिकांश वस्तुओं का स्वयं निर्माण कर लेता है तथा हर केन्द्रित शासन के प्रति अविश्वास उन्हें कुछ हद तक अराजकवादी परम्परा से बाँध देते हैं। लेकिन इस विचार में वे अनीश्वरवादी की जगह (जो अराजकवादी थे) ईश्वरवादी और अध्यात्मवादी थे। उनके विचारों पर स्पष्ट रूप से टॉल्स्टाय के विचारों की छाप पड़ी थी जो आधुनिकता के विरोधी और समता पर आधारित ग्रामीण समाज के समर्थक थे।

लेकिन आज के युग में कोई भी व्यक्ति अब आधुनिक उद्योग धंधों को समाप्त कर पुराने गृह उद्योगों को जीवित करने की बात नहीं सोच सकता। गाँधीजी वास्तविकतावादी थे और उन्होंने इस परिस्थिति का सामना होने पर एक हद तक पूँजीवादी अर्थ व्यवस्था को मान लिया हालाँकि उनके विचारों के अनुसार पूँजीपतियों को अपनी सम्पत्ति को समाज की थाती समझना चाहिये था। लेकिन अगर पूँजीपति अपनी सम्पत्ति को समाज की थाती न समझें? इसका कोई स्पष्ट जबाव गाँधीजी ने नहीं दिया हालाँकि कहीं भी पूँजीपतियों ने अपनी पूँजी को समाज की थाती नहीं समझा है। सच तो यह है कि हर व्यक्ति का विचार वह जैसी समाज व्यवस्था में रहता है उसके अनुरूप बनता है, और जिस हद तक पूँजीपति एक पूँजीवादी अर्थ व्यवस्था और समाज व्यवस्था में रहते हैं उनका

स्वाभाविक रूप से वही विचार होगा जो इस व्यवस्था के अनुरूप होगा। एक दो अपवाद इसके हो सकते हैं लेकिन एक वर्ग के रूप में पूँजीपति वर्ग पूँजीपति ही रहेगा। यह एक साधारण सत्य है। समाजवादी आन्दोलन के सामने इसका जबाव स्पष्ट था। अगर पूँजीपति समाज के हित के लिए अपनी पूँजी का उपयोग नहीं कर सकते तो समाज का कर्त्तव्य है कि वह उनकी पूँजी स्वयं अपने हाथ में लेकर समाज के लिये इसका उपयोग करें। लेकिन गाँधीजी पूर्ण अहिंसावादी थे अत: वे हर तरह के शक्ति प्रयोग के विरोधी थे चाहे वह राज्य या समाज के नाम पर ही किया जाय। इस अर्थ में गाँधीजी के विचार स्पष्ट रूप से समाजवाद विरोधी थे।

लेकिन एक दूसरे अर्थ में गाँधीजी की विचारधारा का सम्बन्ध समाजवादी विचारधारा के साथ हो जाता है वह उनके सविनय अवज्ञा के हथियार का समाजवादी आदर्शों की प्राप्ति के लिए उपयोग। यह आन्दोलन का तरीका बिल्कुल नया नहीं था। यह एक पुरानी परम्परा से सम्बन्धित थे जो एथेन्स में सुकरात ने शुरू किया था और आधुनिक युग में अमेरिका में थोरो ने सरकारी अन्याय के विरुद्ध इसका उपयोग किया था। लेकिन गाँधीजी ने इसे एक नया रूप दिया। उन्होंने इसे व्यक्तिगत अवज्ञा के स्तर से उठाकर सामूहिक अवज्ञा के स्तर पर ला दिया। इसके इस रूप में समाजवादी आन्दोलन को, जो सिर्फ किसी एक वर्ग की मुक्ति का आन्दोलन नहीं बल्कि सारे मानव समाज की मुक्ति का आन्दोलन है, इसकी आवश्यकता न सिर्फ इसके प्रारम्भिक काल में बल्कि इसके हर स्तर पर होगी।

समाजवादी आन्दोलन उन समस्याओं का समाधान सशस्त्र जन विद्रोह या पार्लियामेन्टरी पद्धति से कर सकता है जिसके पीछे जनता के बहुमत का समर्थन इसे प्राप्त है। लेकिन हमारा समाज अनेक तरह के तत्वों से बना हुआ है जिनमें बहुत से अल्प संख्यक स्वार्थ हैं। उन लोगों की मुक्ति के लिए कौन-सा मार्ग होगा? खास तौर से उस हालत में जब उनके स्वार्थ बहुमत वाले लोगों के निहित स्वार्थों से विपरीत पड़ते हों? एक अल्पमत न तो सतारूढ़ बहुमत के विरुद्ध शस्त्र लेने की क्षमता रखता है न पार्लियामेन्टरी पद्धति से बहुमत को अपनी बातों को मानने के लिये मजबूर कर सकता है। ऐसी स्थिति में सविनय अवज्ञा का ही एकमात्र उपयुक्त मार्ग रह जाता है जिससे अल्पमत बहुमत पर ज्यादती से अपनी बात थोपने के खतरे के बिना अपनी न्यायसंगत बातों को उनसे मनवा सकता है। आज अमेरिका में समता के लिये नीग्रो लोगों का व्यापक सविनय अवज्ञा, यूरोप के देशों में आणविक शस्त्रों के विरुद्ध वहाँ के शांतिवादी लोगों के संघर्ष का सविनय अवज्ञा का रूप लेना इस दिशा में इसकी सार्थकता के प्रबल प्रमाण हैं।

अगर धर्म तथा नस्लों के आधार पर समाज का विभाज समाप्त भी हो जाय तब भी अल्प संख्यकों की समस्या समाज में हमेशा रहेगी। पेशे के आधार पर समाज का विभाजन दिनों दिन बढ़ने की ही सम्भावना है। अलग-अलग पेशे में काम करने वाले लोग पूरे समाज की दृष्टि से हमेशे अल्पसंख्या में होंगे। उनकी अपनी विशेष समस्यायें होंगी और उनके न्यायपूर्ण समाधान के लिये, अगर समाज के अन्य स्वार्थों से उनका स्वार्थ विपरीत पड़ता हो तो, सविनय अवज्ञा का मार्ग ही उपयुक्त होगा अगर आपसी बातचीत से मामला नहीं सुलझ जाता। राज्य के हाथ में आर्थिक शक्ति के पूर्ण रूप से आ जाने के बाद व्यक्ति तथा अनेक अल्पसंख्यक समूहों की हित रक्षा की समस्या सर्वाधिक महत्व की बन जायेगी। इस समस्या के सम्बन्ध में बर्टरैन्ड रसेल ने लिखा है:

> "यथेष्ट मात्रा में स्वतन्त्रता को बचाने का एकमात्र उपाय (और यह भी बहुत छोटे अल्प संख्यकों के लिये काफी नहीं होगा) विशेष स्वार्थ वाले नागरिकों का छोटे समूहों में संगठन होगा जो अपने आन्तरिक मामलों में अपनी स्वतन्त्रता बनाये रखने के लिए कटिबद्ध होंगे, आवश्यकता होने पर हड़ताल के द्वारा हस्तक्षेप को रोकने के लिये कटिबद्ध होंगे, आवश्यकता होने पर हड़ताल के द्वारा हस्तक्षेप को रोकने को इच्छुक होंगे, और वैसी स्थिति में जब उनका उद्देश्य ऐसा है जिसे अधिकांश लोग उचित समझते हैं, सरकारी शक्ति का मुकाबला (स्वयं या जनता की सहानुभूति को अपील करने की अपनी शक्ति से) सफलता के साथ करने में समर्थ होंगे। अगर इस उपाय को सफल होना है तो हमें न सिर्फ आवश्यकता के अनुसार संगठन चाहिये बल्कि स्वतन्त्रता के प्रति व्याप्त प्रतिष्ठा तथा सिद्धान्त और कर्त्तव्य में सरकार के सामने न झुकने की भावना चाहिए।"
>
> **(रोड्स टु फ्रीडम-बर्टरैन्ड रसेल)**

सरकार के सामने न झुकने की भावना तथा स्वतन्त्रता की भावना को समाज में आगे बढ़ाने में सविनय अवज्ञा से अच्छा कोई दूसरा उपाय नहीं हो सकता। साधारणतः अल्प संख्यकों को हिंसात्मक प्रतिरोध आतंक के रूप में व्यक्त होता है। लेकिन जहाँ इस तरह के आतंक से एक विशेष समूह की स्वार्थ रक्षा हो जाती है वहाँ इस बात की गारंटी नहीं रहती कि अल्प संख्यकों के स्वार्थ न्यायोचित होंगे या दूसरे अल्प संख्यकों या बहुसंख्यकों की स्वतन्त्रता पर ये आघात नहीं पहुँचायेंगे। इसके विपरीत सविनय अवज्ञा का मुख्य आधार बहुमत की सहानुभूति से अपील करना है, स्वयं, अपने विश्वास के लिए, कष्ट उठाने की तैयारी से। ऐसी स्थिति में अगर माँग न्यायोचित न होगी तो सविनय अवज्ञा करनेवाले का कष्ट निरर्थक होगा पर दूसरों पर किसी अल्पमत का विचार इस तरह नहीं लादा जा सकेगा।

लेकिन सविनय अवज्ञा का जो स्वरूप है इससे यह स्पष्ट है कि इसकी सफलता सिर्फ एक ऐसे समाज में सम्भव है जहाँ एक हद तक विचारों तक प्रचार की स्वाधीनता है। चूँकि सविनय अवज्ञा बहुमत के न्याय की भावना को अपील करने के आधार पर खड़ा है, वैसे समाज में, जहाँ लोग स्वतन्त्र रूप से कोई समाचार या विचार नहीं जान सकते, इस तरह के आन्दोलन का कोई प्रभाव नहीं पड़ेगा। जहाँ तानाशाही शासन है वहाँ तो अवज्ञा के विचार को अँकुरते ही कुचल दिया जायेगा और फिर शाँतिमय तथा खुले ढंग से इस तरह का आन्दोलन नहीं चलाया जा सकेगा।

इस तरह गाँधीजी के विचारों का सम्बन्ध भविष्य के समाजवादी समाज रचना से तथा दुनियाँ भर के लोगों की (जिसमें अल्पमतों का सवाल प्रमुख है) बराबरी के समाजवादी लक्ष्य की पूर्ति के लिये भरपूर रूप से है, भले ही समाजवाद के मूल आर्थिक लक्ष्यों से उनका मेल न खाता हो।

गाँधीजी के विचारों का असर भारतीय समाजवादी आन्दोलन पर बहुत अधिक पड़ा। कुछ लोगों पर तो चुनावों की हार के बाद की निराशा में गाँधीजी के आध्यात्मिक विचारों में ही एकमात्र प्रकाश की रेखा दिखाई पड़ी और वे समाजवादी आन्दोलन और राजनीति से सन्यास लेकर अलग हो गये। लेकिन दूसरे लोगों ने, जिसमें डा० राम मनोहर लोहिया प्रमुख हैं, सविनय अवज्ञा को समाजवादी आन्दोलन का एक स्थायी हथियार बनाने का प्रयत्न किया। उन्होंने किसानों के कई महत्वपूर्ण सवालों पर, जैसे उत्तर प्रदेश में नहर रेट बढ़ती के विरुद्ध, इसका सफल प्रयोग किया है। औद्योगिक क्षेत्रों में मजदूरों के परम्परा गत हथियार हड़ताल का ही उपयोग उनकी माँगों के सम्बन्ध में होता आया है। फिर भी जहाँ सरकार हड़ताल के अधिकार पर कानूनी रोक लगाती रही है वहाँ हड़ताल का स्वरूप राजनीतिक बन जाता है। कहीं कहीं इन क्षेत्रों में सरकारी हस्तक्षेप के मुकाबले में हड़तालों के साथ-साथ सविनय अवज्ञा को भी जोड़ कर इसे अधिक बल प्रदान करने का प्रयास हुआ है।

शुरू में यह विश्वास यहाँ के समाजवादियों में घर करने लगा था कि सविनय अवज्ञा का सफल उपयोग हर तरह के राष्ट्रीय या अन्तर्राष्ट्रीय संघर्षों में हो सकता है। अगर बहुसंख्य लोगों की कष्ट बर्दाश्त करने की शक्ति और साहस को असीम मान लिया जाय तो सैद्धान्तिक रूप में इसे सम्भव न मान भी लिया जा सकता है। लेकिन वस्तु स्थिति कुछ इससे भिन्न है। समाज में आमूल परविर्तन के लिये शक्ति प्रयोग के अलावे अभी कोई दूसरा उपाय सामने नहीं आया है। यह बात अलग है कि शक्ति प्रयोग सशस्त्र उठाव के रूप में न होकर राज्य शक्ति के प्रयोग के रूप

में हो। यह बात और भी स्पष्ट हो गयी जब चीनी आक्रमण के समय गाँधीजी के सबसे नजदीक रहने वाले लोगों ने भी सीमा रक्षा के लिये सविनय अवज्ञा के हथियार का उपयोग करने की दिशा में कोई सक्रिय कदम नहीं उठाया बल्कि सबों ने सैनिक तैयारी पर ही जोर दिया।

लेखक की पुस्तक 'समाजवाद के बढ़ते चरण' से साभार प्राप्त।

27

समाजवाद और गाँधीवाद
(SOCIALISM AND GANDHISM)

अशोक मेहता

सभी अनर्थकारी परिवर्तन की अवधियों में दो तरह की प्रतिक्रियाएँ होती है। उसी तरह औद्योगिक शोषण के प्रति भी दो प्रतिक्रियाएँ हुई। अनर्थकारी परिवर्तन के समय लोग अपने स्वभाव के अनुसार भिन्न-भिन्न प्रतिक्रिया व्यक्त करते हैं। जो लोग परिवर्तन की शक्तियों को समझते हैं, वे इसे बुद्धिमानी से निर्देशित करना चाहते हैं। वे प्रगति की गति को तेज कर दुख की अवधि छोटी करना चाहते हैं। दूसरी ओर सम्भवतः अधिक मानवीय या कम बुद्धिमान लोग होते हैं, जो परिवर्तन में निहित मानवीय दुखों से भयभीत हो जाते हैं। उनका भय समझ में आ सकता है, उचित भी हो सकता है, लेकिन वे जो नतीजे निकालते हैं वे सही नहीं है। वे फिर पुरानी अवस्था में चले जाना चाहते हैं। वे यह भूल जाते हैं कि वर्तमान दुर्व्यवस्था पुराने तरीके की तार्किक परिणति है। मुड़कर पीछे जाने की कोई भी कोशिश सम्भव तो नहीं ही है, इससे समस्या का समाधान भी नहीं होता है। पूँजीवाद के रूप में प्रकट औद्योगिक क्रान्ति के प्रति भी दोनों तरह की प्रतिक्रियाएँ हुईं।

रॉबर्ट ओवेन और उससे भी अधिक सेंट साइमन को परितवर्तन की शक्तियों का कुछ आभास हुआ। अतः उन लोगों ने उसका स्वागत किया। लेकिन उन लोगों की समझदारी मात्र अनुमान पर आधारित थी। मार्क्स ने पूँजीवादी उत्पादन के मूलभूत नियमों को सुलझाया और परिवर्तन की प्रक्रिया को समझा। उसके सिद्धान्त से वैज्ञानिक समाजवाद का जन्म हुआ। समाजवाद अब अस्पष्ट नहीं रहा, वह वैज्ञानिक और क्रान्तिकारी बन गया।

इसके साथ-साथ दूसरी प्रतिक्रिया भी हुई। यह स्वछंदता वाद के रूप में हुई। इन लोगों ने अर्थशास्त्र के विज्ञान को मनहूस विज्ञान का नाम दिया क्योंकि यह अमानवीय शोषण को मान्यता देता था।

अधिकतर पश्चिमी देशों में समाजवाद एक उग्रवादी आन्दोलन के रूप में शुरू हुआ। लेकिन कुछ ही दिनों के बाद इसने अपना संघर्षशील चरित्र खो दिया। बहादुरी से समाजवादी शब्दावली दोहराते हुए यह संवैधानिक विपक्ष के रूप में बदल गया। अक्सर इस अधःपतन को सर्वव्यापी मान लिया जाता है और विश्वास के साथ भविष्यवाणी की जाती है कि सभी नई मार्क्सवादी पार्टियाँ कल सोशल डेमोक्रेटिक पार्टियाँ बन जायेंगी। यह तो जानबूझकर पैदा की गई विकृति है या पूर्ण अज्ञानता।

पूँजीवाद के विकास का एक परिणाम उपनिवेशवाद हुआ। उपनिवेशों की लूट का एक हिस्सा वहाँ के पूँजीपतियों ने मजदूरों को दे दिया। इससे उनकी हालत में भी सुधार हुआ। लेकिन परिणामस्वरूप वहाँ का मजदूर वर्ग राजनीतिक रूप से लड़ाकू नहीं रह गया और अवसरवादी नेतृत्व पनपा।

समाजवाद में अवसरवादिता उत्पन्न होने के दो कारण थे। एक, जनसंख्या में तेजी से वृद्धि और दूसरा, उद्योगीकरण। उद्योगीकरण के कारण बढ़ती जनसंख्या का उच्च स्तर पर निर्वाह दुनिया के प्रमुख पूँजीवादी राष्ट्रों में संभव हो गया। इन नये विकासों के फलस्वरूप स्वच्छंदता वादी प्रतिक्रिया मर गई। पीछे जाने का नारा अर्थहीन हो गया। कारण कि इसमें निहित विचार अव्यावहारिक था। अतः मास्को का रास्ता अवश्यंभावी है।

निजी मुनाफा पूंजीवादी का आधार है। स्वभावतः पूँजीपति लागत कम करना और कीमत बढ़ाना चाहता है जिससे कि उसका मुनाफा बढ़ सके। अतः वह अपने मजदूरों की मजदूरी कम करने की प्रत्येक कोशिश करता है। मजदूरों का जीवन स्तर जहाँ तक संभव हो, वह नीचे रखना चाहता है। लेकिन मुनाफा कमाने के लिए जरूरी है कि प्रचलित कीमत पर सामान के खरीदार तैयार हों। खरीददार कौन हैं? जो उत्पादक हैं वे ही उपभोक्ता हैं। लेकिन कामगारों के जीवन स्तर में गिरावट के कारण उनके पास सामान खरीदने के लिए रुपये नहीं होते। वे वस्तुएँ तो चाहते हैं पर उनके पास प्राप्त करने का साधन नहीं होता अर्थात् उनकी माँग प्रभावी माँग नहीं बन पाती।

बुर्जुआ अर्थव्यवस्था का सम्बन्ध मात्र प्रभावी मांग से है। इससे पूँजीपति उलझन में फँस जाता है, जिससे निकलने के दो रास्ते हैं। एक, राष्ट्रीय आय में मजदूरों का हिस्सा बढ़ाना, जिसमें वह उत्पादित वस्तुओं का उपयोग कर सकें।

दूसरा, विदेशी व्यापार का फायदा उठाकर अपनी वस्तुओं का निर्यात करना। वह पहला विकल्प स्वीकार नहीं कर सकता, क्योंकि इससे उसका मुनाफा खत्म हो जायेगा और पूँजीवाद का ही खात्मा हो जाएगा। अत: वह दूसरा तरीका उत्साह के साथ अपनाता है।

जब तक औद्योगिक पूँजीवादी देश कम हैं और शोषण करने के लिए उपनिवेशी बाजार उपलब्ध हैं, यह नीति बहुत हद तक सफल होती है। यह मुनाफे का उच्च स्तर बरकरार रखती है और अपने अन्तर्विरोधों से पूँजीवाद का नाश रोकती है। वस्तुओं के निर्यात के साथ-साथ पूँजी का निर्यात भी होता रहता है। पूँजी और तकनीकी ज्ञान का निर्यात उपनिवेशों को अपने यहाँ देशी पूँजीवाद विकसित करने में सक्षम बनाता है। लेकिन पूँजीवादी देशों और इन उपनिवेशों के बीच प्रतियोगिता होती है, जो घातक सिद्ध होती है। इसका कारण यह है कि उपनिवेशी देशों में मजदूरों का जीवनस्तर पुराने औद्योगिक देशों से नीचा होता है; और दूसरे यह कि इन देशों में मजदूरों के असंगठित होने के कारण उनका अधिक शोषण होता है। उपनिवेशी पूँजीवादी के पूर्ण विकास के कारण दूसरे विकल्प का समय भी अब खत्म हो गया है।

पूँजीवाद की आधुनिक समाजवादी आलोचना में आया परिवर्तन महत्वपूर्ण है। अब पूँजीवाद पर हमला केवल नैतिक दृष्टि से नहीं किया जाता। अब इसमें निहित अन्याय ही हमारी आलोचना का आधार नहीं है। अब इसके साथ कुशलता के आधार पर भी पूंजीवाद की आलोचना की जाती है। हमारी आलोचना के आधार में परितर्वन का बुनियादी महत्व है। अकुशलता के कारण पूँजीवादी अन्याय कुई गुणा बढ़ जाता है। आलोचनाओं के दोनों पक्षों को मिला देने पर तो वह लाजबाव बन जाती है। स्टेफोर्ड क्रिप्स ने लिखा है, "अगर इस व्यवस्था को अमल में लाना है तो यह आवश्यक है कि उत्पादन की सभी बड़ी इकाइयाँ राज्य के हाथ में सौंप दी जायँ। यह किसी भावना या मात्र न्याय के तर्क के आधार पर नहीं कहा जा रहा बल्कि इसलिए कि पर्याप्त उत्पादन और वितरण के लिए कोई दूसरा तरीका नहीं है।"

अत: आज दुनिया के लिए एकमात्र लक्ष्य समाजवाद ही उपलब्ध है। देर-सबेर दुनिया के राष्ट्रों को मास्कों के रास्ते पर जाना पड़ेगा।

स्वच्छंदतावाद पर समाजवाद की विजय

भारत में स्वच्छंदतावादी प्रतिक्रिया प्रमुख रही है। लेकिन गाँधीजी के कारण यह प्रतिक्रिया अर्थहीन और मात्र भावनात्मक नहीं रही। अन्य देशों में लघु बुर्जुआ लोगों

की प्रतिक्रिया के साथ गाँधीवाद को मिला देना अन्याय होगा। दोनों में समानता है, लेकिन गाँधीवाद की विशिष्ठता भी उतनी ही महत्वपूर्ण है।

यहाँ भारत में, अगर बुद्धिवादी दृष्टि से नहीं तो संवेदनात्मक दृष्टि से गाँधीवादी प्रतिक्रिया प्रमुख रही है। यह देश और अतीत के प्रति भक्ति दर्शाती है और स्वदेशी की अवधारणा में प्रकट होती है।

हमारे देश में यह प्रतिक्रिया इतनी प्रमुख क्यों बनी? इसका मुख्य कारण ऐतिहासिक है। भारत में मशीनी अर्थव्यवस्था का प्रादुर्भाव विदेशी विजय की लहर के साथ हुआ। साम्राज्यवादी मालिकों द्वारा मशीनों से बनाई गई सस्ती वस्तुओं के लिए बाजार हासिल करने के सिलसिले में यहाँ के हस्त एवं कुटीर उद्योगों का जंगली नृशंसता और अमानवीय शोषण के द्वारा नाश कर दिया गया। हमारे लिए इसका भयंकर परिणाम हुआ। बेरोजगारी, गरीबी और दरिद्रता अभूतपूर्व पैमाने पर फैल गई। अत: ऐसी परिस्थिति में स्वाभाविक था कि हम अपने शोषकों के उस बुनियादी साधन पर प्रहार करते जिसके द्वारा हम गरीब बनाये गये, और वह साधन मशीन थी। इतिहास इसका गवाह है कि विश्व अर्थव्यवस्था में भारत की स्थिति अभेद्य थी। उस उज्जवल अतीत से हम अब मात्र कच्चे माल का उत्पादन और आपूर्ति करने वाला, एक उपनिवेशी देश बन गये। इस कारण चेतन या अचेतन रूप में हमने मान लिया कि हस्तशिल्प अर्थव्यवस्था की ओर लौटने पर हम अपनी पहली जगह प्राप्त कर लेंगे। हमारा धर्म और हमारी संस्कृति हमें शिल्प-सभ्यता स्वीकार करने का पाठ पढ़ाती है।

समाजवाद से हमारा सम्पर्क इसके अँग्रेजी रूप के माध्यम से हुआ है। यह सर्वाधिक प्रतिक्रियावादी रूप है। भारत के प्रति इसके सौतेले दृष्टिकोण ने न केवल इसकी पार्टी को बदनाम कर दिया बल्कि इसका दर्शन भी बदनाम हो गया। युद्ध के दौरान और उसके बाद समाजवादी अभियान की समाप्ति, युद्धोत्तर विश्व-व्यापी अव्यवस्था आदि ने समाजवादी विकल्प की निरर्थकता के प्रति हममें विश्वास पैदा कर दिया। लेकिन दो शक्तिशाली कारणों ने हमें अधिक प्रभावित किया-(1) यह विश्वास कि प्राचीन हस्तशिल्प अर्थव्यवस्था में जनता खुश थी और इसके द्वारा अब भी खुशहाली लाई जा सकती है। (2) जिस मशीन युग से हम परिचित हैं वह अपनी गिरती अवस्था में है। इसकी कुरूपता और अमानवीयता स्वभावत: हमें इससे अलग करती है। तकनीक के दूसरे चरणों को जानने के कारण हमने मशीन को रद्द करने का और हस्तशिल्प की खुशियों और सुन्दरताओं की ओर लौटने का फैसला किया।

शिल्प अर्थव्यवस्था के अन्दर लोगों की हालत

यह सही नहीं है कि अतीत में आम लोगों की आर्थिक समस्याओं का समाधान हो गया था। जितनी जल्दी यह भ्रम टूटे उतना ही सभी सम्बन्धित लोगों के लिए अच्छा है। यह सही कि कुछ शिल्पकार धनी थे। उन्हें स्वामित्व और सृजन का आनन्द था लेकिन किसानों और मजदूरों का समूह दयनीय जीवन बिताता था। लिविस ममफोर्ड ने लिखा है, "पाषाण युग से लेकर आज तक के मानव-इतिहास की अधिकतर अवधि में कला, दर्शन, साहित्य, तकनीक, विज्ञान और धर्म की सर्वोच्च उपलब्धियों लोगों की बहुत छोटी जाति में सिकुड़ी रही है।"

भारत इस सामान्य नियम का अपवाद नहीं था। जवाहरलाल नेहरू ने कहा है: "हमें यह ध्यान में रखना चाहिए कि आर्यों में अपने बीच लोगों को बहुत स्वतंत्रता थी लेकिन उन लोगों ने श्रमिक वर्ग को नीचे दबाकर रखा था और अपने लोकतंत्र में हिस्सा नहीं लेने दिया था।"

शिल्प अर्थव्यवस्था की बुनियादी लक्षण

क्या आर्थिक दृष्टि से हमारे लिए शिल्प अर्थव्यवस्था की ओर लौटना या उस पर निर्भर रहना सम्भव है? क्या हम इसके द्वारा इतनी बड़ी जनसंख्या के जीवन की आवश्यकताओं को पूरा कर सकते हैं? यह सोचा जा सकता है, बशर्तें कि उसकी तीन शर्तें पूरी हों: (1) हम अपनी आवश्यकताओं में कटौती कर, उसे न्यूनतम स्तर तक ले जाएँ। (2) हम खूब मेहनत करें और कोई आराम न करें। (3) जनसंख्या में कमी आए या कम से कम उसमें वृद्धि न हो।

इनमें से पहले दो गाँधीवादी विश्वास के सिद्धान्त हैं। भौतिक आवश्यकताओं और आराम की जरूरत को, जहाँ तक सम्भव हो, कम करना वांछनीय है। काका कालेलकर ने लिखा, "मानव हाथ और पैर को कृषि और उद्योग में जहाँ तक सम्भव हो, काम करने देना वांछनीय है।

न्यूनतम आवश्यकताओं का सिद्धान्त

आवश्यकताओं को कम करने के सिद्धान्त को दो स्रोतों में खोजा जा सकता है। एक, हमारा धर्म और हमारी संस्कृति भौतिक सम्पत्ति के प्रति न केवल उदासीन होना बल्कि उसका तिरस्कार करना भी सिखलाती है। दूसरे, बढ़ती आवश्यकताओं की बेवकूफी भरे पूँजीवादी सिद्धान्त के प्रतिक्रिया स्वरूप में भी।

जो लोग वर्तमान औद्योगिक सभ्यता में विकास करते हैं उन लोगों ने बढ़ती आवश्यकताओं के सिद्धान्त को बहुत हद तक स्वीकृत मान लिया है। काका

कलेलकर ने अपनी पुस्तक में एक सर्वेक्षण के आधार पर लिखा है: ''सर्वेक्षण से निर्णायक तौर पर यह साबित हो गया है कि आवश्यकताओं की पूरी तरह सन्तुष्टि नहीं हो सकती। एक आवश्यकता के बाद दूसरी आवश्यकता उत्पन्न होती जायेगी। निष्कर्ष यह है कि आर्थिक रूप से मैदान असीमित है। जितनी तेजी से पुरानी आवश्यकताएँ पूरी होती जायेंगी, नई आवश्यकताएँ पैदा होती जायेंगी।' गाँधीवाद ऐसे ही अनर्गल सिद्धान्त को रद्द करता है और यह सही भी है। लेकिन ऐसा करते हुए, वह दूसरे छोर पर चला जाता है, जो उतना ही अनर्गल है। यह मशीनी अर्थव्यवस्था को रद्द करने और आवश्यकताओं को त्यागने के दर्शन के सिलसिले में बहुत दूर तक चला जाता है। जनता इतनी गरीब और दरिद्र है कि उत्पादन और उपभोग के विस्तार के लिए अथक प्रयास करने की जरूरत है। वर्तमान स्थिति में आवश्यकताओं को सीमित करने की बात करना करोड़ों भूखे लोगों के प्रति मजाक है। कोई भी ऐसी चीज जो इन करोड़ों लोगों के भोजन, वस्त्र, आवास और शिक्षा उपलब्ध कराने में मदद करती है, उसका हमें स्वागत और उपयोग करना चाहिए। जब तक हम अपनी पुरानी छिाल्प अर्थव्यवस्था के बदले अधिक उत्पादक अर्थव्यवस्था नहीं अपनाते, तब तक हमारी इतनी बड़ी जनसंख्या को जीवनोपयोगी वस्तुएँ, उपयुक्त मात्रा में, सही तरह से, उपलब्ध नहीं कराई जा सकतीं। यही मशीन अर्थव्यवस्था का महत्त्व है।

लोगों को आराम और करने योग्य काम चाहिए। हम जिन सांस्कृतिक लक्ष्यों को पूरा करना चाहते हैं उसके लिए आराम जरूरी है और मात्र मशीन ही आराम प्रदान कर सकती है। हम जिस आधारभूत साम्यवाद की कल्पना करते हैं, मशीनी अर्थव्यवस्था उसका आवश्यक आधार है।

काम और आराम

कुछ हद तक काम करना जरूरी है, बल्कि स्वाभाविक भी है। लेकिन ऐसा कहने का मतलब यह नहीं कि कालेलकर की अधिकतम मेहनत की बात हम मान लें। लोग अपने आराम के समय का सही उपयोग करेंगे, इसके बारे में गाँधीवाद निराश हैं। गाँधीजी विश्वास करते हैं कि अपने जीवन-निर्वाह के लिए प्रतिदिन आठ घंटे काम करना अत्यन्त आवश्यक और सर्वाधिक वांछनीय है।

इनके अनुसार लोग कुछ घंटों से अधिक का आराम सही ढंग से उपयोग नहीं कर सकते। वे मजदूरी से विश्वास करते हैं कि अगर शोषण समाप्त करना है तो कोई भी व्यक्ति अपनी जीविका आठ घंटे से कम काम करने पर अर्जित कर ले, यह असम्भव है। अगर यह असम्भव भी हो तो वांछनीय नहीं है। अत: वे विश्वास

करते हैं कि प्रकृति चाहती है कि हम आठ घंटा काम करें। मैं इन तर्कों को समझ नहीं सकता। किसी एक अच्छी तरह से विनियमित समाज में आराम का इस तरह उपभोग किया जा सकता है कि वह मनुष्य की सांस्कृतिक और नैतिक प्रगति में सहायक है।

दुनिया अधिकतर मन लायक काम और आराम के रास्ते पर जा रही है। क्या यह सम्भव है कि हम लोगों को दूसरे रास्ते पर ले जायँ? मुझे लगता है कि समाजवादी सभ्यता का आकर्षण हम पर छा जायेगा। हम जनसंख्या की समस्या का समाधान कैसे करने जा रहे हैं? पश्चिमी देशों में इसका समाधान इसलिए हुआ कि (1) आम लोगों के जीवन स्तर में वृद्धि के साथ-साथ जनसंख्या दर में कमी आई, (2) बड़े पैमाने पर कृत्रिम तरीकों से जन्मदर नियन्त्रित की गई।

गाँधीवाद दूसरे तरीके को नकारता है और पहले तरीके में अवरोध पैदा करता है। इसके बदले में यह नैतिक आत्म नियन्त्रण का तरीका प्रदान करता है वर्तमान परिस्थितियों में जनसंख्या में इससे वृद्धि कहाँ तक रोकी जा सकती है, यह मैं पाठकों के निर्णय पर ही छोड़ देता हूँ। अन्ततोगत्वा मालथस का प्राकृतिक नियन्त्रण काम करने लगेगा।

मशीनी अर्थव्यवस्था का विरोध: लोग मशीन के खिलाफ क्यों हैं? क्या मशीन बुरी है? हम यह स्वीकार करते हैं कि यह दो कारणों से हुआ है। एक पूँजीवाद के कारण और दूसरा हमारे तकनीक का अविकसित और निम्न स्तर होने के कारण। उद्योगवाद के खिलाफ निम्नलिखित मुख्य आलोचनाएँ हैं:

(1) मशीन बेरोजगारी पैदा करती है। (2) मशीन मनुष्यों को यन्त्रवत् बनाती है। (3) मशीनी सभ्यता कुरूप और घटिया है और यन्त्र पर जोर देने के कारण मानव गुण का नाश करती है।

क्या मशीन बेरोजगारी का कारण है

बेरोजगारी पूँजीवाद के कारण है। पूँजीवाद के अन्तर्गत उद्योगवाद का मतलब बेरोजगारी हैं यह इसलिए कि पूँजीवाद के लिए बेरोजगारों की आरक्षित फौज जरूरी है और वह इसे खत्म नहीं करेगा। लेकिन यह स्थिति समाजवाद में नहीं होगी क्योंकि उसमें ऐसी नियोजित अर्थव्यवस्था होगी जिसमें काम का समाजिक वितरण होगा और सबको काम ओर आराम का अपना हिस्सा मिलेगा। पूँजीवाद के खात्मे के साथ बेरोजगारी स्वत: समाप्त हो जायगी।

नयी तकनीक और स्वतन्त्र समाज—हम उद्योगवाद को नकारकर एक लोकतांत्रिक स्वतन्त्र और संघीय समाज निर्माण करने की उम्मीद नहीं कर सकते।

इसका मतलब होगा—प्राचीन तकनीकी सभ्यता की हानियों की ओर लौटना। जनसंख्या में वृद्धि के कारण ये हानियाँ पहले से अधिक हो गई हैं। इसके बदले हम आधुनिक तकनीक से भी आगे जाना चाहते हैं। हम ऐसी तकनीक का आविष्कार करना चाहते हैं जिसमें बड़े पैमाने के उद्योग बुनियादी साम्यवाद का आधार प्रदान करते हैं और साथ ही जिसमें शिल्प-जीवन एवं छोटे कारखानों को भी उचित स्थान मिलता है। ये हमारी अर्थव्यवस्था के आधार नहीं बनाये जा सकते। उनका उचित स्थान ऊपरी ढांचे (सुपरस्ट्रक्चर) में है। वे कला और मनुष्य के व्यक्तित्व को अभिव्यक्त करने का अवसर देते हैं। क्षेत्रीय विकेन्द्रीकरण और कार्यात्मक विभाजन तिमिंगल (लेवियाथन) का सृजन नहीं करेगा (इसे गाँधीवादी ठीक ही रद्द करते हैं), बल्कि एक पूर्ण स्वतंत्र और संघीय समाज का निर्माण करेगा। तब बिना गरीबी और दरिद्रता के और आज की तरह जनसंख्या के सर्वहाराकरण के बिना हम ग्रामीण जीवन की खुशियाँ प्राप्त करेंगे। अगर सही दृष्टि हो तो कोई कारण नहीं कि विज्ञान और मूल्यों में द्वन्द्व हो ही। आज विज्ञान हमें इस द्वन्द्व को समाप्त करने का आश्वासन देता है बशर्त्ते कि हम जानते हों कि विज्ञान का मानव जीवन के लिए कैसे उपयोग किया जाय।

उद्योगवाद का खौफ तकनीक के पिछड़ेपन और पूँजीवाद की नृशंसता के कारण है। अब तकनीक विकसित हो गई है और कोई कारण नहीं कि पूँजीवाद खत्म नहीं किया जा सके। अगर भारत में सही उद्योगवाद स्थापित करना है तो इसे खत्म करना ही होगा।

नया जीवनः मशीनी अर्थव्यवस्था के विरुद्ध हमारा आरोप उसी क्षण शक्तिहीन हो जाता है जब हम निम्न बदली परिस्थितियों पर विचार करते हैं:

(1) पूँजीवाद का खात्मा; (2) उद्योगवाद में नवतकनीक का चरण; (3) सहज उपभोग के साथ क्षेत्रवाद और संतुलित अर्थव्यवस्था; (4) प्रशासन में शक्ति का विभाजन और विकेन्द्रीकरण; (5) समाजवादी समाज को आधार प्रदान करने के लिए मशीनी अर्थव्यवस्था। इसके द्वारा प्रदत्त आराम का अन्य चीजों के अलावा कला और विशिष्टता अभिव्यक्ति में उपयोग और इस तरह हस्तशिल्प के लिए उचित स्थान की पुनः प्राप्ति।

क्या ये अवस्थाएँ हमारी सभी आकांक्षाओं को सन्तुष्ट नहीं करतीं? उद्योगवाद एवं समाजवाद से सम्बन्धित हमारी शंकाओं को शान्त नहीं करतीं? हम लोग कोई विशाल तिमिंगल (लेवियाथन) का निर्माण नहीं कर रहे बल्कि हम एक ऐसी आर्थिक और सामाजिक व्यवस्था के लिए काम कर रहे हैं जिसमें व्यक्ति के अन्दर जो सर्वोतम है वह उसका सही उपयोग करेगा। स्टालिन कहता है; "केवल

समाजवादी समाज ही व्यक्तिगत हितों को सर्वोत्तम तरीके से पूरा कर सकता है। इससे भी अधिक, केवल समाजवादी समाज ही व्यक्ति के हित की मजबूती से रक्षा कर सकता है।'' इससे अधिक सत्य बात कभी नहीं कही गयी।

स्वच्छंदतावाद ने अपनी ऐतिहासिक और मूल्यवान भूमिका अदा की है, लेकिन अब इसका समय पूरा हो गया है। उद्योगवाद ने इसकी आलोचना के अनुरूप अपने को सुधार लिया है। अब इसे एक समानता और स्वतन्त्रता वाले समाज के निर्माण के लिए क्रांतिकारी समाजवादी शक्तियों के साथ सहयोग करना चाहिए। हमें उन शक्तियों का समझना है जो औद्योगिक महल को नया रूप दे रही हैं। हमें पूँजीवाद के पुरानेपन और उसके प्रति कठोर प्रतिक्रिया को महसूस करना है। हम उस सही लोकतन्त्र के लिए जियें और काम करें जिसका सपना युगों से हम देखते आये हैं। अब सोशलिस्ट का विरोधी होना मात्र दकियानूसी है। क्या उसने स्वच्छंदतावाद की सभी सही एवं जीवन्त आलोचनाओं को स्वीकार और पचा नहीं लिया है? क्या स्वच्छंदतावादी अब सूखी हड्डी के लिए लड़ेंगे? थोड़ा अध्ययन, थोड़ी सहानुभूति दोनो ग्रुपों को नजदीक लायेगी। क्या अपील बेकार जायेगी?1

संदर्भ

1. अशोक मेहता ने 1935 में समाजवाद और गाँधीताद के नाम से एक पुस्तिका लिखी थी। इससे गाँधीवाद के प्रति समाजवादियों के दृष्टिकोण का पता चलता है। इसमें एक ओर मार्क्सवादी तर्कों का सहारा लिया गया है, रूस की सोवियत व्यवस्था, उद्योगीकरण की अनिवार्यता आदि को स्वीकारा गया है तो दूसरी ओर गृह एवं शिल्प उद्योग को उचित स्थान देने की बात की गयी है। अशोक मेहता गाँधीवाद को बहुत हद तक स्वच्छंतावाद (रोमान्टिसिज्म) मानते हैं और इसके एवं समाजवाद के बीच समन्वय की अपील करते हैं। उस पुस्तिका का संक्षिप्त हिन्दी रूपांतरण यहाँ दिया गया है।
2. कांग्रेस सोशलिस्ट पब्लिकेशन लि., सोशलिस्ट रिसर्च इन्स्टीच्यूट, टैक्ट नं.-4, 1935-

28

NEHRU'S FABIANISM AND GANDHI
(नेहरू का फेबियन समाजवाद एवं गाँधी)

Pravir Krishna

Nehru found Gandhian variety of socialism utopian, his trusteeship, doubtful and its development content slow and therefore while heralding a planning era in India just after the death of Gandhi, he was trying to be more pragmatic in spelling socialism. The system was actually not socialist but socialistic. It was less radical than Gandhi (Myrdal) and was prompted by the idea that 'the cart must move and move fast'. As Gandhi said, 'he likes to fly, I don't.

Gandhi had village uplift and distributive justice in his mind. Nehru was for heavy industrialisation for which villages would not work as the base. The difference was fundamental and Gandhi wanted that people should know it. (Gandhi's letter dated 5 oct. 1945) Nehru visualised an active role of the state via planning and public sector was given the pride place. Gandhi treated society as distinct from state. Naturally people's socialism was to be different from state socialism. Nehru's plan (Mahalonobis's second plan) was a marxist model but assumed a parallel system of private sector. Though Nehru was not opposed to small industries but he maintained that such industries could not be sufficient to meet the growing needs of the nation.

Socialism under the leadership of Nehru came more as a grand idea than a strategy for social change. (Ashok Mehta). Gandhi was for change without 'class war' in a decentralised set up of government but Nehru treated state planning, cooperativisation of land and parliamentary democracy as vanguard of change. Nehru had started as an ardent socialist but after the death of Gandhi he grew into a Fabian. Fabianism grew in Britain just after the death of Marx in 1883. Nehru's choice for a less radical system was due to existence of a private sector which could work and passivity of the rural poor. Even the labour leaders who won elections preferred shifting to liberal groups.

Nehru's socialism is therefore moderately socialistic to be realised through practical reforms on ordinary parliamentary lines. It thus assumes a continuous prgress to socialism and an irrestible progress of democracy.' Both Gandhi and Nehru favoured a classless society as did Marx but the former were not in favour of a ruthless abolition of private property. Gandhi gave out the concept ofTrusteeship which meant a change of heart for transfering possessions from the top to the lower class, a spirit of non-possession (Aparigrah). Nehru gave another variant cooperativisation at the village end and state control on the industrial end. Can we say here that both presuppose a harmonious cooperation of labour, capital and land and that both would fail?

In Gandhian system agriculture and cottage industry held the key. The swadeshi spirit implied autonomy, self reliance and non-exploitation. This is a grass root approach stressing redistribution. In Nehruvian system big industries hold the key with a lot of planning. The country adopted the Nehru concept. Though India has made good progress, the strategy is not without serious lacunae. There has been concentration of wealth and economic power. The islands of growth are surrounded by vast seas of poverty. Lately the recent thinking is to evolve an optimum mix between the two diverse strategies. This does open up possibilities of holding Gandhi and Nehru working in tandem, though this may be a difficult task.

Nehru found Gandhian variety of socialism utopian, his trusteeship, doubtful and the development content, slow and therefore while heralding a planning era in India just after the death of Gandhi, he was trying to be more pragmatie in spelling socialism. The plans were actually not socialist but socialistic. The system was thus less radical than Gandhi (Myrdal) but was prompted by the idea that the cart must move and move fast.' 'He likes to fly' as Gandhi said.

The cause for a less radical choice may be the same as that which made British variety (Fabian) of socialism so. The Indian attitutde too was individualistic, while the poor working millions are less radically dissastisfied with existing order. The effect of Marx on Nehru is quite easily disceraible and so every body's right to work and earn was accepted as the equaliterian norm. But the 'class' element was discarded and parliamentry democracy was accepted as a vanguard of change.

The failure of the more rabid Marxian varieties in India was another cause of the choice. Even the labour leaders who won elections preferred shifting to liberal groups. It is a strange coineidence that as Fabianism developed in Britain just after the death of Marx (1883), Nehru's Fabian outlook grew just after the death of Gandhi. The main socialist content here was some order of cooperativisation of 'land' and state participation and state competition in every department of production. Gandhi always thought of 'society' as distinguished from 'state'. This was a view closer to Marx. Nehru thought of a state socialism to reconstruct India according to plan' (socialims under Nehru was more a grand idea than a strategy of social change. (Ashok Mehta).

Nehru's socialism is therefore more 'developmental' although not averse to 'moderately socialistic programmes to be realised through practical reform on ordinary parliamentary lines. It thus assumes a continuous progress to socialism' and an 'irrestible progress of democracy.'

It is to be examined however, if Nehru's Fabian belief could click in India conditions, as it did in England with partial extension of governmental ownership and regulation of industry, the latter beig more prominant. Individualism was slowly dying in British capitalism due to managerial revolution but it is not so in India. Further, land was not a big problem of ownership change in England and so a gradual socialisation of land ownership through 'single taxes' could be worked out. The task is not that easy in Indian conditions. The village poor do represent a class whose woes cannot be remedied just by top planning and government legislations, or fiscal reforms. Gandhi's letter, Oct. 5, 1945 told of his difference as fundamental, people must know it. People will have to live in villages. Nehru's reply was why a village should necessarily embody truth.

Under such conditions the state may not be an effective representative and trustee of the people nor is able enough to appropriate the economic rent (unearned incomes) from both land and capital. A Gandhian bias for redistribution of land and production on land may modify the Nehruvian bias on capital development and state control. The real problem remains how to develop people's socialism and people's power at the gras roots in place of state socialism and state power.

29

MOVING AWAY FROM MARX

Nikhil Chakravarty

In the midst of the excitement over the dramatic development taking place before our eyes in the Soviet Union, we lend to miss their historic signficance. In the presence of History, one is apt to miss its majesty.

Perhaps no other single event since the Second World War can match the current revolution in the Soviet Union in its far reaching dimensions. Never before the crack-up of such a powerful state has taken place with so little of violence. Barring the Indian and Chinese revolutions, no other even in the contemporary world has seen such a vast nmber of people spread over such a far-flung country been stirred to protracted political action as one witnesses in the Soviet Union today. Compared to what has been taking place in the entire Soviet Union now, the start of the Bolshevik Revolution in 1917 was a relatively small affair though its cost in terms of human losses was far greater. And all this has been happening without conforming to text-book forecasts, and that's the reason why its unpredictability has baffled both the Communists and anti-Communists all over the world. It's not the End of History as some very learned scholars predicted in the United States, but the Beginning of a new period in the mankind's march to freedom.

The highroads of history are never straight and smooth, but invariably tortuous, with its ups and downs. It is precisely in this context that one has to realise the untenability of the tenacious belief that Marxism is immutable as also of the equally aggressive ideology that Market decides the fate of mankind. It is worth nothing that

Karl Marx himself, though downright emphatic to the point of being aggressive in stating his views, never tried to stamp them with a sense of finality. In course of his turbulent career, he changed his views over and over again. And yet the socio-political theory associated with his name has merged as the most hidebound in modern times, invested with the authority of an oracle. Those who, in some form or other, have taken Marxism as a doctrine, a dogma, an article of faith are honestly baffld by the convulsions that are now taking place in the Soviet Union.

How and why has this happned? This can be understood only by referring to the history of socialist thought in the last two centuries, even if we leave out the early stirrings for social justice which in one form or other have been inscribed in human history. More specifically in the European traditions, from Spartacus to Thomas More with his Utopia, on to the Levellers, it is a remarkable saga of human urge for social justice. During the French Revolution with its banner proclaiming Liberty, Equality and Fraternity, there were thinkers who aspired to the vision of socialism. For instance, Babeuf's Conspiracy of the Equals wanted to carry forward the principle of political equality to the sphere of private property. The stirrings for social equality that Babeuf represented, failed because of "the absence of material conditions" at the time as Marx analysed. In fact Babeuf was the pecursor of Blanquism, and his ideas cropped up again and again in the revolutionary upheavals of the nineteenth century France. In contemporary England, Godwin in his Enquiry Concerning Political Justice propagated what can be considered as *ethical communism,* with an overdose of anarchist thinking.

With the Industrial Revolution bringing in unprecedented turbulence in social, economic and political arena, one finds on one hand the phenomenon of the Luddites spontaneously breaking the new machines, followed by a programme of political action as exemplified by the Chartists. On the other hand, in the world of thought and social enquiry, one comes across the early pioneers like Robert Owen, and then came up a whole galaxy of thinkers who were absorbed in studying the unfolding of the industrial revolution and its social impact. Bentham, Hall, Thompson and Ricardo were all groping for some form of social justice in the new revolutionary context. In France appeared Saint-Simon, Fourier, Proudhon and Louis Blanc to name only a few, while in Germany appeared thinkers from Kant to Fichte to Feurbach and Rodbertus.

It is in this background of the remarkable intellectual churning up that Marx and Engels tried to assimilate different streams of thought from Hegel to Godwin, Fourier to Bakunin and Duhring. While Marx and Engels made assertive claims, they constantly tried to add up or revise their views. Engels, for instance, claimed: "Just as Darwin discovered the law of evolution in organic nature, so Marx discovered the law of evolution of human history". At the same time, he acknowledged on another occasion the relative independence of spiritual forces in history. When the Paris Commune rose in 1871, Marx was ecstatic over this storming of heavens and hailed it as "the glorious harbinger of a new society". At the same time when it was suppressed with ruthless ferocity he and Engels did not hesitate to dissect it with clinical objectivity.

Throughout the nineteenth century, one notices this remarkable feature of constant rethinking on the part of the leaders of socialist thought. As the naked violence of the early phase of industrial revolution gave place to a stable capitalist development, Marxist thinking also correspondingly moved. The strident call in the Communist Manifesto in 1848, reflecting the aggressive tone of the First International was considerably modified when the Second International was formed in 1889. By this time, internationalism itself was tempered by the shift in the focus to the growth of socialist movements in different countries under different conditions.

In the camp of the German Socialist who were then in the forefront with their Erfurt programme, the Marxists found themselves to be a minority force. In England, the movement concentrated in the building of trade unionism, while the Fabian society with a pragmatic outlook, worked as a sort of a bridge between trade unionists and socialists and helped in the formation of the Labour Party by the turn of the century.

It is worth nothing that just about this time, Bernstein came out with outspoken criticism of Marxism, pointing to the need for Marxists to take into account the changing realities of life, and demanded a critical revision of the entire Marxian system of thought and action. In a sense, he pressed for a radical democratisation of the Marxist movement. The attack on Bernstein came from Karl Kautsky who represented the orthodox revolutionary school. Out of Bernstein's demand for revision of Marxist thinking came the term. Revisionism, which continued to be a dirty word in Marxist vocabulary until Gorbachev.

The militant tenor of Russian Marxism is to be traced to the prevailing objective situation in the country where the ideology under the leadership fo Plekhanov faced conditions of extreme underground functioning having to fight the black repression of Tsarism. The first battle of the new Marxist trend was against the Narodnik revolutionaries who believed in the cult of individual terrorism as the principal means of overthrowing the Tsarist regime. The focus of activity was among working class and revolutionary youth, into which Lenin came. Within the newly formed Russian Social Democratic Labour Party, the effort was to build an iron-clad under ground revolutionary party under conditions of total repression.

The origin of the rigid tradition of the Communist movement is to be traced to those early days in Russia when objective conditions kept no other opening. It was precisely on this point that the split in the party came in the 1903, when the majority insisted on a highly centralised organisation with a militant programme, while the minority favoured a more cautious programme and a cooperative approach towards other revolutionary groups. The majority, the Bolsheviks took over the party and threw out the minority, the Mensheviks and thereby was established the principle that dissent could have no plae in a Marxist party.

The Parting of company within the Second International came with the outbreak of the war, when the leadership of socialists in most countries supported the war as a patriotic duty while the Bolsheviks under Lenin branded it as an imperialist war in which the working class has no interest in victory. There were intrepid revolutionaries in other countries taking the same position such as Rosa Luxemburg in Germany and even individuals in Britain and France.

The war brought disaster for Tsarism and that led to its over throw in February 1917. In that revolution, the Bolsheviks had no role to play and the new government under Kerensky was a democratic government. When Lenin promptly returned from exile, he gave a call for strengthening democracy in what came to be known as his April Thesis, and he regrouped the party under conditions of semilegality. When the conservative pro-Tsarist elements under General Kornilov tried to over throw the much-harassed Kerensky Government in July 1917, Lenin gave the call for the defeat of the Kornilov rising and thereby moved into the centre-stage of Petrograd politics at the time. Then as the war brought more misery, and mass discontent welled up with the government proving to be impotent, Lenin gave the call to strike, and the Winter palace was captured and power came to the Bolsheviks. It was by no means a mass upsurge but a determined band of revolutionaries rousing the entire people that succeeded.

An outstanding feature of this November revolution was that it was led by a whole cluster of outstanding political figures of whom Lenin was the leader–Trotsky, Bukharin, Zinoniev, Radek, Sverdlov and Stalin to name only the more well-known. It was no doubt a party of iron discipline, but all these leaders exchanged views freely and sometimes in the open–with angry polemics but no intimidation. There was extraordinary political ferment and intellectual exchanges in the early days of the revolution. That was how Lenin managed to switch from one set of policy-strategy to another very different without any difficulty. From War Communism to New Economic Policy was the most unorthodox switch over and it emerged out of intense debate.

A steak of intolerance towards other parties is generally the feature of a revolutionary situation, but within the Bolshevik leadership under Lenin, there was uninhibited exchange of views, side by side, in the newly-formed Communist International, free and intense divergence of views were expressed as could be seen in the famous exchange between Lenin and M.N. Roy in assessing national liberation movements.

All this was put down once Stalin managd to get control of the party leadership. He was unsparing in hounding out political opponents. Starting with Trotsky, his liquidation drive physially eliminated all the noted Bolsheviks. The bloody purge spread to the armed forces with the liquidation ofTukachevsky and Blucher among others. No doubt Stalin displayed tremendous dirve in changing the face of the Soviet Union by his planned programme of industrialisation. But the cost in terms of human losses was enormous as could be seen in the forced collectivisation of agriculture which took a ghastly toll of millions of peasant lives and their livestock. Even today the Soviet Union has to pay for this crippling of agriculture.

While it would be absurd to hold Stalin responsible for all the faults and shortcomings in the Soviet system, there is no doubt that Stalin behaved in the ruthless tradition of Peter the Great–a character emerging out of the Russian history than a leader of an international movement. This could be seen most forcefully during the Second World war when the heroic feat of the Red Army was invoked in the name of Mother Russia, and it was called the Great Patriotic War– not the war in defence of the only socialist state, as the Communists the world over wanted to believe. This stamp of totalitarian authority was asserted with utmost ferocity within the party and the Soviet security when the slightest dissent led to banishment and the terror, the labour camp and total subservience became part of Soviet life.

The Communist International was frankly turned into an extended arm of Stalin's foreign policy. No dissent or difference was possible–that was why Mao kept the Chinese Communist Party away from the Comintern, while Thaelman's independent approach in Germany was frowned upon and Ulbricht became Stalin's favourite. Rosa Luxemburg's independent views within the framework of Marxism was banned and so were the reminiscences of Lenin's widow, Krupskaya. Even Lenin's will was suppresssed.

Stalin's approach towards the great powers–his negotiations with Nazi Germany leading to Molotov-Ribbentrop pact of 1939, and later with Churchill and Roosevelt–were all permeated with blatant cynical power-politics without any streak of ideological considerations, or susceptibilities towards smaller States.

It was therefore nothing unusual that the change in the leadership of the Soviet Communist Party after Stalin was pulled off by a virtual coup–first by Malenkov and then by Khruschev, ousting, Malenkov and killing Beria in the Central Committee itself. Khruschev's exposure of Stalin's misdeeds shook the Communist world. While many of the fellow-travellers left, the Communist monolith itself was shaken. The Hungarian uprising of 1956 was its direct result, while most of the Communist parties in Europe were left in disarray. Within the world Communist movement, conformity was broken. From peking to Rome to Prague to Warsaw, there were ample signs of the Moscow authoritarianism becoming a total misfit.

But Khruschev while exposing Stalin did not question the system itself. This is where Gorbachev, preceded by Andropov, made the qualitative difference. Its impact is felt not merely in the Soviet Union but the whole world. The perestroika-glasnost revolution has literally changed the face of the world. There is a tendency nowadays to say that Gorbachev's intervention in international affairs was beneficial, but he messed up at home. In a sense, this sounds true. Gorbachev has brought about the end of the Cold War and has made striking progress towards disarmament both nuclear and conventional, so much so that the threat of instant nuclear annihilation has to a large measure disappeared.

Within the Soviet Union, the economic mishandling when shifting from the outworn command structure has resulted in dislocation and shortages. Glasnost has stirred demands for independence by the constituent republics. There is little doubt that despite Gorbachev's efforts at accommodating the conservative elements in the party and correspondingly earning the annoyance of the radicals, the hardcore within the Soviet Communist Party thought that they would take advantage of the prevailing discontent and thereby oust Gorbachev. It was this which led to the putsch of August 1922.

Why did the coup fail? The miscalculation of the hardliners was that they thought they would be able to cash in on popular discontent to takeover power. They little realised the new temper of the people whose disaffection was with the half-hearted nature of the reforms and not with the reforms themselves. Even the armed forces could not be summoned by the coup leaders to put down public resistance. How did these conservative leaders make such miscalculations?

The fact of the matter is that in the new world that has opened up with technological advance, the consciousness of the common man has also undergone considerable change. This could be seen in Eastern Europe where the all-powerful party establishments with police and armed forces at their command, fell like a house of cards. The glasnost has changed the political climate in the Soviet world, And this enabled even a hastily set up popular resistance under Yeltsin to defeat the coup and bring back Gorbachev from detention. The amzing absence of violence in such a lightning political operation also testifies to the strength of the people's consciousness.

Unless this point is understood in all its dimension, the Soviet developments are not possible to explain. The ignominious crumbling down of the mighty Soviet Communist Party has to be ascribed to the fact that such a huge organisation has been totally divorced from the new trend represented by the perestroika. Rather it tried to act as a brake upon the reforms, while the winds of change initiated by Gorbachev's New Thinking did not appear to have entered its musty corridors. No doubt there are individual Communists who are attuned to the new developments–Gorbachev himself is one–but the Leviathan that the CPSU had become, is found to be out of :ouch with the new realities.

From this overview of the Communist movement, what emerges is that the movement started by Marx was born out of exciting discussions, highpitched debates in which conformism was never imposed. The Bolshevik contingent having to move in conditions of repression developed its own rigidities, on which was imposed the qualities of Russian tradition. Since it became successful in capturing power under extraordinary circumstances–rather defying Marx's calculation that the revolution would come first in an industrially advanced country–that revolution was held aloft as a model, making it almost impossible for the entire Communist movement to move in cooperation and collaboration with other Socialist forces. This very weakness of the movement has so long been tom-tomed as its strong point. The result was that it failed to absorb new ideas, new approaches. It is not just an accident that the Communist movement did not throw up a counterpart of John Maynard Keynes. Perhaps there were quite a few who might have been, but liquidated or spent their lives in Stalin's labour camps.

Now that the mighty flood has swept off the old, outworn edifice, it is time for all Socialist thinkers–in the Soviet Union as also all the world over–*to invest the concept of Socialism with new qualities*–not only of democracy but other concepts of social developments as well. Human kind has reached a new crossroad–transiting from the industrial revolution to the technological revolution, demanding new and more adequate guarantees of social justice. The pioneers of socialist thought in the past were pathfinders to a new world of advanced productive forces. It is for their descendants today to discard old mores and *move on to new horizons–to strive, to seek, to build a brave new world of freedom, justice and equity.*

By Courtesy Hindustan Times, Sept. 15, 1991.

30

COLLAPSE OF MAOISM–SOME LESSONS
(माओवाद का पतन–कुछ सबक)

K.K. Sinha

The past history of the Maoist system in China was no doubt pro-poor and pro peasant, which turned China into people's republic in October 1949. But Mao Tse-Tung was a guerrilla leader, defying the leadership of Russia, (Khrushchev) and reaffirming revolution as an act of violence whereby one class overthrows the other. In fact it became a war between two factions, Kuomintang and communists, who had worked jointy in overthrowing the Manchu Kings. Mao representing the Communist International under Stalin, was helped by troops under Chu The and supported by peasants. Chinese leadership was again of the nature of war leadership and the success of change solely depended on one man. The infighting between the two factions went on even after the revolt of 1949. This was an eye opener to violent changes, which tended to perpetuate as a Cultural Revolution and fighting the 'renegades' within the political group. It was actually a battle for succession but in garb, it was a massive mobilisation of people for political rather than social struggle. Those who came in power in 1949 fought feudalism internally and imperialism (both American and Russian) externaly, but not capitalism so much as the bureaucrats.

The apparent theme of the cultural revolution, which was declared in 1967 a civil war by Lin Piao, a Mao loyalist, was the struggle against bureaucracy, elimination of differences between mental and manual labour, and town and country, its hostility to technocratic consumerism, the soviet model of socialism and parasitic over-industrialisation.8 The real fear in all this was of a leadership vacuam with the side lining of the proletarian culture. For that the guerilla spirit had to be restored and pushed forth indefinitely.

The greatest flaw in communist dialectics (China or Russia) related to poverty, was that the final stage of an ideal system of decentralised governance could not actually come up and so it could not involve people at the grass root. It created a strong state power in the name of people's power. The rise of a strong bureaucratic class was more despotic than in capitalism. A clumsy system of shadow pricing in public management, public ownership and decision taking in order to replace markets, could not work and both China and Russia had eventually to abandon it. It appears that the whole dialectical process went on extending even after the class struggle phase. At this juncture the cold war covering the two world blocks started diluting when the experiments of the communist block in evolving an economic system of their own started succumbing to the market system. The Russian system was actually collapsing in the 1980's giving way to market economy fully during the regime of Gorbachev, while China after Mao, used markets with private lease system and collective ownership with individual use rights, and took to pro-market reforms almost by the same time.

Could these developments now declare the virtual win of the market economics with the difference that markets in communist countries run in a redistributive framework while markets in the capitalist economy, may have such goals and state keeps away from intervening with markets even where redistributive justice demands the state to intervene. What was a positive gain for such change nevertheless was the creation of a better groundwork for a redistributive society in which the markets could perform better. This again vindicates the Indian norms of justice infused in land ownership under JP's leadership, which could allow other market reforms with a redistributive framework, which the post-Mao reformers are now trying to accommodate.

MAOISM AND CULTURAL REVOLUTION

Chinese communism takes its birth in 1949, embarks upon the commune model with all round collectivisation by 1957 and fearing the bourgeous restoration (at the leadership end) declares a civil war in 1967, known as the cultural revolution. Thus it is thought that class struggle, as a part of communism has to continue indefinitely in a guerilla spirit, externally against imperialism and internally against the nonchangers. The fear of opportunism and revisionism, thus becomes an accepted part of the theory of dialectical materialism, which Lenin also conceded. Mao declared a civil war to cheek the going back from the path of struggle and make compromises. This is what the Indian Maoists (Naxalites) took as an all-time tenet of social change.

In China cultural revolution was forced upon the people on account of a fear of losing state power at the center. Even those belonging to anti-feudal liberation army seemed to detract. The first such class was the new managerial and administrative elite in large state farms who had elevated their cooperatives to a large-scale wholesale business. The second class was the petty bourgeois revolutionaries who "loved dragons but when a live dragon came down the road they ran away as fast as they could.' They went against feudal power but were engaged in capitalism. The third were the conscious revisionists and believers in Khruschev's theory of peaceful coexistence, peaceful competition and peaceful transition, (i.e. the Shao Chi group) More rebellious were the vanquished landlords and the expropriated compradors and the underworld gangs and lumpen elements under them, who were supported from abroad, the imperial powers.

This development created a cultural crisis between experts versus revolutionaires. Thus "technique in command" challenged "politics in command", that is, a fight between those who preferred production and those who wanted self-reliance and driving the imperialists. A development-prone system actually created capitalism within the socialist frame in China after 1978, when the Shao Chi group argued that "whether the cat is white or black makes no difference so long as it can catch mice." But the regimented group with strong party caderes was not ready to compromise. "The tree would prefer calm, but the wind refuses to subside–was what Mao preached to help the upsurge in the Third World and also within China against the Russian and American imperialists. The Chinese Cultural Revolution thus went to mobilise the left, win the middle and isolate the diahard, which meant uniting almost 95 percent of the masses. This was the theory behind the movement–"from the masses to the masses."

The way it was carried may have some lessons for Indian politics because the political changeover in China later by 1978 gave a blow to the whole procss of cultural revolution and to the effort of dictatorial leadership of brain washing through education and hero worship of the leader, when the successor of Mao snatched the mantle of leadership through a coup, and initiated liberalisation in 1979. (The pro-market new dawn was quite a different event from what the Naxalites dreamed about in their grim struggle in India).

Nevertheless, but for denial of democratic openness and freedom and excesses of cultural revolution in terms of human rights and one-child rule, the Chinese dialecties had prepared a redistributive ground work which gave great strength to the market system which followed. Further, the stress of the revolution on village comunes and "building on the worst" brought in the masses in the decision-making, and industries, and education in rural areas became oriented to the disadvantaged. To quote.

"In many ways, Maoist ideology rejects the capitalist principle of building on the best... While capitalism strives one-sidedly for efficiency in producing goods; Maoism in numerous ways builds on the worst. Experts are pushed aside in favour of decision-making by the masses; new industries are established in rural areas; expertise or work proficiency, in the narrow sense, is discouraged, new products are domestically produced rather than imported "more efficiently"; the growth of cities as centres of industrial and cultural life is discouraged; steel, for a time, is made by every one instead of by only the much more efficient steel industry." (John G. Gurely, 1971, Capitalist and Maoist Economic Development, Monthly Review, Feb. pp. 23-24).

This was a village fetish, which partially resembles Gandhism. The rural education was made basic to the needs of rural production what the "Buniadi Talim" of Gandhi signified. The natural distaste for such education was however checked in China by promoting a cadre of workers with socialist consciousnes and culture. Students were selected from among workers and peasants and should return to production after a few years of study. This was a way of Chinese resistance to imperialism. This again looks like the Swadeshi (use of home goods) movement of Gandhi and JP, when separate cadres were to come up as committed groups. But in absence of a cadre of young workers in India, the structural and proletarian changes in villages could not occur and thus the building from below could not become the engine of growth on its own.

The real aim of all such movements, socialist or democratic, have been to remove poverty and exploitation, not governments as such. But surely the reconstructional part of all these movements, which follow the struggle, was never complete, and tended to deviate from the pre-conceived goals, the former due to state capture of local communes and the latter due to state distaste against local panchayats. State power thus ruins the whole process of reconstruction and change, whether it is socialist or democratic.

The Russian Anarchists wanted therefore the state to go just after the struggle was over, the Gandhians wanted to decentralise state power to villages and minimise governance. The communists too wanted the small communes to be the new system of a withering State, but their norms of a non-market system went up adding more power to the State to contain 'outside threat to the state', while the democratic ones went power-corrupt.

WHAT CHECKED THE COLLAPSE OF MAOISM IN CHINA?

In China, the Maoist rule was checked from collapsing with a more cautious change over to market socialism than it happened in Russia or, in some sense, India. Deng Xiaoping who replaced Mao in 1979 took up villages as the first organizations of change when power was seized. The real and important of the radical reforms came from a completely unexpected quarter, what is known as the Township and Village enterprise (TVE) sector. Of course the movement-borne governments in India too put up several anti-poverty schemes for the village poor, but they were nothing but 'bribes' to the poor for facing poverty and the status quo. There was no structural change in the village economy as the first task, what Mao in China ruthlessly did. This emphasis paid fully when Deng in 1979 took over. The village communes were decollectivisd with redistribution of land according to the size of households, and a contract responsibility was put on the new cultivators.

But a much faster response was from the TVEs, which got market incentives without much further help from the government. They bought and sold their product in the market at market prices and they were out of the central planning process. The plan sector withdrew where they came in. If they competed so well, but if not, they were out of business. This grew out of the rural communes which were not so successful in cultivation but quite so in local industries and related service enterprises. The local governments supported them and founded infrastructure (inputs and electric power) as their share. Most were former collectives but thrived with local governments as joint partners. Some were even owned by local governments while others were registered as private firms.

The rural small scale industry programme had technicians from towns and had learning cadres of the communes with them. But as government officers, these were not regulators but promoters. Though the commune system as a regulatory organ of the state was abolished in 1987, the cadres assumed a positive role of promotion and not just taxers and controllers.

But in India, in spite of an apt experiment taken by JP to reshape the local panchayats the process remained vitiated by a highly indifferent governance for power at the centre. Of course India introduced local elections as mandatory under the 73rd Constitutional reforms in 1993 but for lack of development on the economic front, the village panchayats so created had nothing to do. The panchayats in Bihar which were elected late in 2001 started languishing for want of work while the poor people remained outsiders to gram sabhas and had no expectations from the government. In China the government left all decision taking in the hands of elected villages. But in Indian villages, development was a subject of the Centre.

INDIAN CASE

A Musahari like situation thus reappeared again in the 90s, twenty years after JP's experiment, when India embarked on New Reforms of a global market. The norms of a village reconstruction were neither enforced nor even created in India, when China under Deng not only introduced market reforms of the global form, but also explored it first at the agricultural and rural industry front. The distribution of retail sales by ownership in 1995, China shows a relative percentage of 39% from individual non-farm sector, 18% from individual farm and 11% from collective farms, while 32% from state owned non-farm sectors. Similarly the industrial output from local collectives increased to 43%, private to 13%, foreign to 13% and state to 31 only. This shows an increasing share of local enterprises and downsizing of the state sector.

What kept the system still socialist was that democracy was being introduced incrementally, first from local governments and slowly to wider areas. The nostalgia for a powerful Nation-State or a Party-State always remained, which got lost in Gorbachev Russia as a 'shock therapy' for a market system. The motto of the Deng regime in 1998, was "development first and democracy later."

J.P.'s idea behind a Total Revolution after the 1978 general elections was more reconstructional, once a government was dismantled, because only then could people keep the centralised governance under control. This made development subsidiary to decentralisation of government. In China in the post Mao phase, egalitarian and democratisation policies were backed by universal drive to make money at all costs. J.P.'s total revolution was retaining the rigour of struggle even after governments were changed, more like the Anarchists, than the communists.

Commune democracy had failed the Anarchists. What J.P. was looking to was a socialist society at the base and a State deriving its powers from the base and not vice-versa. J.P.'s struggle wanted bread and liberty at the same time. It was neither an over-ambitious bread system, (which in China is being termed as over-heating) nor a Party-State as a ruler. This made the political and economic system pyramidal or resting on the base, the villages, when the Chinese system developed fast as an inverted pyramid.

Gramdan panchayats were of course not to have the same metal as the Maoists had. J.P. here conceived of a resistant class struggle joined by the poor and doubly by another pressure group of youth and intellectuals. This could create a change of the rural order and the ownership structure of land in villages and an urge for helping the poor for rural uplift. Empowerment of the gram sabhas against its inbuilt feudal content, and suppression by the higher governments in their own political interests, remain still the crux of reconstruction.

What became the advantage in post-Mao China was actually the ruthless restructuring of the small communes in rural areas. The Party cadres were more more tutored and committed than social volunteers generally are. This helped Deng when he introduced market reforms more at the national levels than local, but the TVEs flourished in less time because they were made more independent than the national sector where State-control was losing space only very slowly.

J.P's system seems to be graudalistic and slow so far economic growth is concerned. China's Party socialism meant a political Nation-State but its democratisation from the bottom. This has helped it in having a faster growth. But the adoption of economic reforms and an open global system in India may boost growth, but will tend to keep its base at the bottom poor and backwashed. A gramdan orientation of the village panchayats is therefore imminent to strengthen dualistic development in tune with both sectors.

CONFUCIUS VERSUS GANDHI

It is interesting to see that Deng tried to make his system a democracy of his own requirements and a value derived from the Chinese roots from Confucius. This made a cultural basis of fast development in China. But the religious tenets in India which guided the movement for change were against stocking and self-consumption, thus the rich donating the poor for equality (Danam samvibhagah) Any revolution conceived here had to be more social and less monetary. It is why the systemic changes claim to obtain basic equality at the need level shunned monetary growth for over-consumption. People in India have therefore greater urge for organizing themselves in neighbourhoods for a better life, but proper education is necessary even for this.

China and India may move to a meeting ground, one away from the land socialism while the other, towards land socialism, till a balance is reached between efficiency in governance and Party rule, on the one hand and between democracy and development, on the other. China now talks about democracy "of its own style" with village elections, strengthening local people's congrss and allowing more freedom to non-governmental organisations (NGOs) and the media. But the "threat to China" keeps it tied to a strong Nation-State, or a strong Party-State. Local elections were introduced in 1987 and villages came up, not as regimented communes but as freer units under a contract responsibility system to take up production. This actually is the point where J.P.'s Gramdan villages would become worth while in India.

China preferred development and a single party-run democracy to what prevails in India, i.e., representative democracy ad centralised development. Such preference has however pushed China towards a Rule of Law with diminished governmental controls and more social space for individual expression. India too stepped up economic reforms and open door policy for a market development but its decentralisation and social content at the village level remained much behind China. Further the party freedom in India seems to create more "tiananment Square" like tragedies here than what happened in China in 1989 in the wake of liberalisation of Party controls. The

East Asian model of "economic development first, democratisation later" thus oriented plural societies to development, when it still lacks in India case. The success of Post-Mao China is thus attributed to democratisation at local levels for development and not to Democracy as such.

Extract from author's Book-Poverty of Economics, 2005.

31

FABIANISM AND FABIAN SOCIALISM

Khalid Mirza

The doctrine of socialism took a different form in England known as Fabian socialism. Fabianism is an English version of evolutionary socialism. It is socialism redefined in harmony with new conditions and developments that came over in Englnd in the last quarter of the nineteenth century. George Bernard Shaw, Sydney Webb, Sydney Oliver and Graham Wallas were its pre-eminent exponents.

The main object of the Fabians was to spread the socialist doctrine as they understood it throughout the educated middle class and to persuade the national and local governments of Great Britain to put the doctrine in practical operation. The Fabian Society was established in January 1884 by a band of such reformers for the study and discussion of current problems of social ethics. The ultimate aim of this association was the "reconstruction of society in accordance with the highest moral possibilities."

Primarily, Fabianism was a method of propoganda relying on the method of evoking consciousness in a community for a piecemeal growth. The Fabians asserted: "The competitive system assures the happiness and comfort of the few at the expense of the suffering of the many, and that society must be one constituted in such a manner as to secure the general welfare and happiness." The original Fabians pledged themselves to this general basis of agreement. In course of time, however, they began to believe in the social ownership as the logical consequence of socialism. This by implication meant the largest possible extension of State activities for the control of community created values.

Sydney Webb propounded the historical basis of Fabian socialism. He observed, "It may now fairly be claimed that the socialist philosophy of the day is conscious and explicit assertion of the principle of social organisation which have been already in great part unconsiously adopted. The economic history is an almost continuous reward of the progress of socialism."

According to Sydney Webb, "history constantly demonstrates both the irresistable progress of democracy and the almost continuous progress of socialism." The growth of unrestrained capitalism has put an end to economic individualism. Society has progressively adopted the principle of control of economically ncessary concentration by a gradual extension of Government ownership of regulation of industry.

There is no room inWebb's theory of increasing misery or of regulation as suggested by the Marxists. Important changes can only be democratic, gradual, moral and constitutional. The purity of the means is the most important consideration for him. Here we find similarity with Gandhi for whom the means determined the ends. According to Webb, People's control of production and organised co-operation can gradually bring about socialism. To him, economic side of democracy itself is socialism; a friendly attitude towards the State ownership and increased public regulation can only be foundations of democratic socialism.

George Bernad Shaw formulated the economic basis of socialism. He repudiated Marxism and was very much influenced by Recardian Theory of Rent. He saw injustice in private appropriation of land. He went on to say that "with one law alone-the law of rent-they destroyed the whole series of assumptions upon which private property is based." As such, argued Shaw, there should be a convenient transfer of land and also of industrial capital to society at large. He further observed that purchasing power which commands luxury in the hands of the rich would command true wealth in the hands of all.

Shaw put forth the idea of socialisation in rent from land as well as from ability, but their uses must be made for public purposes. He repudiated Marxian labour Theory of value. To him, value lies not in labour but in utility. Although, Shaw agrees with Marx in denying investment as the title of value, he differs from him in admitting the conflict not between the employers and the employees but between the community and the rich. He wanted to transfer ownership of land and capital to the community by making it fully representative.

The industrial basis of Fabianism was prepared by Clark. He observes, "as regards the great combination of capital, State action may take one of the three courses; It may prohibit and dissolve them, it may tax and control them or it may absorb and administer them." In either case, says Clark, the socialist theory is inspired towards a collective control over industry.

Syndney Oliver presented the moral basis of Fabian socialism. He criticised the present system as immoral and said that there was a need for education and industrial cooperation. The morality of socialism is the expression of external passion of like-seeking in satisfaction through the striving of each individual for the free and fullest activities.

In describing the socialist idea Graham Wallas makes a forecast for socialist society in which there shall be no room for private property. He declared that in substance the socialists work for the ownership of the means of production and consumption not by the individuals. Thus, under Fabianism there is to be a transfer to the community of the administration of such industrial capital as can conveniently be managed by society.

For the fulfilment of this ideal, Wallas held that representative democracy and State control of production were the two inter connected fields of Fabianism. In his book The Great Society Wallas says that such ideas do not mean occupation as charged by some of the critics of socialism.

Annie Beasant, another Fabian socialist, made it amply clear that "there shall be nonprofit incentives under socialism." Such a theory demands of a State which is neither selfish nor incompetent. It demands gradual extension of the franchise and the transfer of rent and interest to the State. It considers State as the representative and trustee of the people. Annie Beasant puts the point concisely : "There will never be a point at which a society crosses from individualism to socialism. The change is ever growing forward, and our society is well on the way to socialism."

The essence of Fabian socialism lies in the fact that there is a continuous progress and continuity in the process of absorption of the State. "Slice after slice" and "step by step" the process goes on gradually and peacefully, and to a large extent unconsciously.

The Fabian method of attack on capitalism and its technique has been the object of severe criticisms. Barker says : "The Fabian society is the least open and least straight forward socialist organisation." Some critics allege that Fabianism has an alliance with bureaucracy. But Prof. Ernest Barker has come to the rescue of the Fabian socialists at this point when he says: "What is demanded was partly indeed a more efficient and expert Central Government but primarily an expert local civil service in close touch with and under the control of a really democractic municipal Government. It is difficult to say that this is buraucracy or that it is not desirable."

Fabianism almost became a doctrine of municipal socialism. Sydney Webb announced a programme of unlimited municipalisation of public services and a wide extension of corporate activity. The most practicable step for community control over essential things was for electors to "capture the councils." Accordingly, as the Fabians believed, the private producers will gradually disappear not because of any law against them but because ease, freedom and community service will overcome the worries, harassments and anxieties of individual struggling for livelihood.

The new Fabians brought about certain changes in the theory of Fabianism. It was charged by some for neglecting the working class movement. But it must be noted that the Fabians were collectivists and they never took class point of view but held to bring community control into being.

It is also criticised for underestimating co-operative movement. Its solution for unemployment are said to be inadequate. It failed to think in terms of internationalism. It neglected the importance of independent political solution. It was simply faced with scientific reconstruction of society. It is because of some of these defects that the new Fabians suggested some new policies:

- *The continued extension of free social service.*
- *More and more nationalisation of industries.*
- *The continued proliferation of industries.*
- *Further redistribution of income by direct taxes.*

The Fabian ideas, however, have immensely affected the labour movement, so much so that the identification of Fabianism with Labour Party of Great Britain ended the career of the Fabian society as a definite school of socialist thought. The Fabian literature and its ideas influencd the man in the street and moulded the thoughts of the readers to some extent.

By courtesy H.T. 29 May, 1999

32

जनतांत्रिक समाजवाद और भ्रष्टाचार

प्रियम कृष्ण

पिछले पचास वर्षों से जनतंत्र की गाड़ी भ्रष्टाचार के पहिए पर चल रही है। नोबेल अर्थशास्त्री मिर्डल ने भारतीय राजनीति की चर्चा करते हुए कहा है कि आजादी के बाद भ्रष्टाचार ने राजनीति और व्यापार की जटिल मशीन को चलाने में तेल का काम किया। सबसे बड़ी बात थी कि सभी ने इसे स्वीकार कर लिया; अगर सभी भ्रष्टाचार कर रहे हैं तो हम क्यों न करें? ऐसी स्वीकृति की मानसिकता आज भी गई नहीं है। शायद सदियों से गुलाम रहने के बाद राजा और प्रजा का भेद कभी भी मिटा नहीं। अपना भी हो तो शासक ही था, आजादी का अर्थ केवल विदेशी शासक को हटाना था।

आजादी मिलने के समय देशी सत्ता अंग्रेजों की शैली में ही ढल जाएगी—ऐसा अनुमान न था। आजाद देश का राष्ट्रपति अंग्रेज गवर्नर के आलीशान बंगले में छः घोड़ों की सवारी करता हुआ ही गया तथा प्रधानमंत्री अंग्रेज सेनाध्यक्ष के सुसज्जित भवन में दाखिल हुआ। गाँधी के अभाव में ऐसा लगा कि आजादी गरीब देश को नहीं मिली थी बल्कि राजनेताओं को मिली जिसके पीछे एक तथाकथित मध्यम वर्ग था जो सम्पन्नता के रहते हुए भी मध्यम ही बना रहा। आजादी के कारण राजनेताओं को इतना महत्व मिला कि उसने गरीब देश के लिए भी शासन का एक इतना खर्चीला रूप रचा जो अब तक बढ़ता जा रहा है और एक भ्रष्टतंत्र के बोझ से गरीबों को दबोचे जा रहा है।

आजादी के लड़ाई में गाँधी ने सदा गरीबी से मुक्ति को ही आजादी का मुद्दा रखा था। यद्यपि नेहरू गाँधी की ही रचना थे पर गाँधी और उनकी विचारशैली में इतना फर्क होता गया कि जब भारत के आर्थिक विकास की योजना बनने लगी

तो यह राज्य के प्रभुत्व तथा खर्चीले शासनतंत्र की चेरी बन कर रह गई। विकास का रूप निर्माण भी राजनैतिक भ्रष्टाचार से जुड़ गया जहाँ राज्य की भूमिका एक समाजवाद जैसी व्यवस्था की बढ़ती हुई ऊँचाईयों से जोड़ी गई। यहाँ राजनैतिक भ्रष्टाचार का एक दूसरा गढ़ तैयार हो गया, जब तेज आर्थिक विकास के लिए एक सामाजिक दण्ड, भ्रष्टाचार के रूप में दिया जाने लगा।

भ्रष्टाचार के बदलते आयाम

जिस संसदीय जनतंत्र की रचना हुई उसमें केन्द्र शासन तथा राज्यों के बढ़ते हुए शासन क्षेत्र से शासकों में सत्ता का महोबोध करा दिया। ऐसी स्थिति में गणतंत्र एक मंत्रीतंत्र में बदल गया जहाँ मंत्रियों के निजी स्वार्थ, दल तथा देश सबके ऊपर होते गए। व्यक्तिगत सत्ता के बढ़ने से भ्रष्टाचार को बल मिला। सत्ता का स्वरूप अंग्रेजों के अधिकारों और सुविधाओं में बदलता गया। प्रसिद्ध गाँधीवादी कृपालानी ने इस तथ्य को अपनी पुस्तक 'पौम्प एण्ड पोवर्टी (1957) में उजागर किया। राजनेताओं के दिखाने की भर्त्सना करते हुए उन्होंने कहा कि यह अंग्रेज शासकों की देन थी जिसका खर्च इतना अधिक था जो देश की गरीब जनता के सहन के बाहर था।

राजनेताओं की सत्ता नौकरशाहों के गठबंधन से और प्रशस्त हो गया। अंग्रेजों ने एक कुशल शासनतंत्र दिया था लेकिन उनके हटते ही इसका भी राजनीतिकरण हो गया तथा नौकरशाह राजनेताओं के 'प्रोटोकाल' के अलावे अन्यत्र कोई माने नहीं रखते थे। इस गठबंधन में उद्योगपतियों तथा व्यापारियों ने हाथ मिला लिया और इस तरह से तीनों ने सुविधाभोगी वर्ग का स्थान पा लिया जो पूर्ण सत्ता-सम्पन्न हो गया। ऐसी स्थिति में संसदीय जनतंत्र के चुनाव भ्रष्ट हो गए और इन्हें किसी जन संघर्ष का संकेत नहीं माना जा सकता था, जैसा कि फ्रांस के समाजवादी अर्थशास्त्री पियरे प्रूढ़ों का सोचना था। इसमें किसी बदलाव की प्रक्रिया नहीं हुई बल्कि विरोध और असहमति की आवाज दलों की सत्ता की लड़ाई में दब गई। जहाँ व्यक्ति की महिमा बढ़ती है वहाँ दल भी व्यक्तियों के साथ जुड़ जाते हैं; वे किसी समुदाय का बोध नहीं करते।

इन स्थितियों में भ्रष्टाचार आकाश छूता हुआ नजर आता है जैसा कि 1964 में संथानम कमिटी में प्रकाशित किया। संसद में कई दल थे पर वे सभी अपने नेता के नाम से जाने जाते थे। इसमें भी प्रभुता केवल एक दल की थी जिसके नेता नेहरू स्वयं थे। सत्ता के इस तरह से केन्द्रित होना सभी भ्रष्टाचारों की जड़ साबित हुआ। संथानम कमिटी की रिपोर्ट भ्रष्टाचार पर पहला लिखित दस्तावेज है। आश्चर्य है कि यह नेहरू काल में तब की है जब संसदीय जनतंत्र का स्वर्णकाल

कहा जा सकता है। रिपोर्ट में स्पष्ट रूप से भ्रष्टाचार का कारण राजकीय दफतरों तथा प्रभावशाली नेताओं का दुराचरण तथा घूस था। यह भी कहा गया कि यह जनता में भी व्याप्त था और शासन में जल्दी काम करा लेने का 'स्पीड मनी' था। मूल कारण अर्थतंत्र में फैसला लेने का अधिकार था जो कुछ ही लोगों के हाथ में सीमित था। संथानम कमिटी ने भ्रष्टाचार का पर्दाफाश तो किया लेकिन केवल कुछ शासकीय सुधार, वेतन वृद्धि तथा दण्ड विधान की चर्चा की। पर उसने मंत्रियों के सोलह वर्ष के कार्यकाल पर स्वर्थपरता, परिवारवाद तथा धन संचय का आरोप लगाते हुए यह भी कहा कि केन्द्र तथा राज्यों में मंत्रियों की ईमानदारी भ्रष्टाचार को हटाने की पहली शर्त है।

1970 के पहुँचते ही एक ओर गरीबी की स्थिति विस्फोटक हो गई, मूल्यों में बहुत बड़ी तेजी आई तथा योजना का राज्य क्षेत्र अकुशलता तथा घाटे का व्यापार बन गया, दूसरी ओर काला धन जो 1956 में ब्रिटिश अर्थशास्त्री काल्डर के अनुसार 400 करोड़ रुपये था वह दस वर्षों में, वंचू कमिटी के अनुसार 1200 करोड़ रुपये आंका गया। जनता का आक्रोश शासकों पर उभरने लगा जो परिवारवाद तथा निरंकुशता तथा जन विरोधी फैसलों से ग्रस्त थे। जे.पी. ने गाँधी की दिशा में अवज्ञा आंदोलन शुरू किया और चार वर्षों के आंदोलन को आजादी की दूसरी लड़ाई का नाम मिला। शासक तथा सत्ता परिवर्तन हुआ, भरमार दल दो मूल दलों में संगठित हुए तथा बुद्धिजीवी वर्ग कई प्रकार के सुधारों को लेकर आगे आया।

काला धन जो विलासिता, दहेज, मुकदमेवाजी, सट्टेवाजी और सरकारी विज्ञापनों और तड़क-भड़क के रूप में मूर्त्त हो रहा था वह शिक्षा तथा सार्वजनिक संस्थाओं में भी सरकारी नियंत्रण के नाम पर फलने फूलने लगा था। चुनाव के खर्च को तो काला धन की गंगोतरी कहा जाता था। जे.पी. ने सत्ता के विकेन्द्रीकरण तथा पंचायतों में भूदान के द्वारा एक समता मूलक समाज की नींव डालनी चाही लेकिन सत्ताधारी जिन्होंने गाँधी की समाधि पर स्वच्छ प्रशासन देने का शपथ लिया, वे फिर सत्ता के उसी खेल में फंस गए जो राजनीति ने अपना ली थी। सत्ता से बाहर रह कर न गाँधी ही कुछ कर पाए थे और न जे.पी. ही और भ्रष्टाचार का एक नया चरण 1980 से शुरू हुआ जब राज सत्ता तथा दलों की महिमा फिर बढ़ने लगी और व्यक्तियों के नाम से फिर दलों ने अपना उल्लू सीधा करना शुरू कर दिया। नतीजा यह हुआ कि कालाधन की राशि 1200 करोड़ से बढ़कर 1980 तक राष्ट्रीय आय का 48 प्रतिशत आंकी गई। इस तरह अब यह 48 हजार करोड़ रुपये थी। स्पष्ट है कि हर 100 रुपया कमाने के लिए भ्रष्टाचार का खर्च 50

रुपया था। जनतंत्र में पुनः राजा 'राज करे, गरीब भूखों मरे' की स्थिति आ गई। राजनेताओं के ठाट-बाट तो बढ़ते ही गए।

अपराध का विस्फोटक चरण

1993 में एन.एन. वोहरा कमिटी ने भ्रष्टाचार के एक विस्फोटक स्थिति को प्रकाशित किया। इसके अनुसार राजनेताओं का संबंध अब अपराधी गिरोहों (माफियों) से होने लगा है और इस तरह सत्ता का गठबंधन अपराधी तत्वों के हाथ में चला गया है। इससे राजकीय हिंसा तथा आतंक का माहौल खड़ा हुआ है। स्वाभाविक है कि राजनेताओं की रक्षा के लिए अंगरक्षकों की व्यवस्था है जो अत्यंत खर्चीले हैं। विधायकों के लिए मोटर में चलना जरूरी हो गया है। उनके आगे पीछे बचाव करने वालों की भी संख्या बढ़ी है। दूसरी ओर जनता के सम्पर्क टूट जाने से सरकार को विज्ञापनों और अपीलों द्वारा चलाया जाता है। कैसी विडम्बना है कि जनता से चुना हुआ नेता स्वयं अंग रक्षकों तथा बन्दूकों के बीच रहता है तथा जन कार्यों को खर्चीले विज्ञापनों से सिद्ध करना चाहता है।

अब सत्ता को कायम रखने के लिए अपराधी गिरोहों में आपसी शीत युद्ध होते रहना भी जरूरी हो गया है। जनता के उभरते हुए आक्रोश को दबाने की एकमात्र राजनैतिक दवा यही रह गई है। राज्य हिंसा का यह फेज 'जातीय कम्युनिज्म' का रूप ले रहा है पर इसमें जातियों का हित न होकर व्यक्त्यिों का ही हित हो रहा है। इसे सामाजिक न्याय की लड़ाई न मान कर सत्ता हथियाने की लड़ाई कहना ठीक होगा। राजा कोई हो सत्ता का स्वरूप वहीं रह जाता है-वही काला धन, अंगरक्षक, वही शान शौकत तथा वही विज्ञापनों की चकाचौंक। नोबेल अर्थशास्त्री मिर्डल ने इसे 'साफ्ट स्टेट' (दुर्बल राज्य) का नाम दिया है, जो हो सकता है, हिंसक राज्य का भी नाम ले ले। मिर्डल ने दुर्बल राज्य को बिखरते हुए समाज तथा टूटते हुए अनुशासन का रूप माना है। ऐसे राज्य में परिवार बनते हैं, समुदाय तथा संगठन टूटते हैं। इसमें न राज्य ही मजबूत होता है और न संगठन ही। जे.पी. ने साम्यवाद की जगह समुदायवाद का नारा लगाया ताकि हमारे गाँव, जहाँ भारत की अधिकांश गरीब जनता रहती है, पड़ोस की भावना में बँधे और संगठित होकर ऊपर की सरकारों को भी आंदोलित करे। पर जहाँ सत्ता का केन्द्र ऊपर ही है वहाँ की राजनीति नीचे से खड़ी करना बहुत ही कठिन होता जा रहा है।

भ्रष्टाचार के इस चरण में एक राष्ट्र-प्रबल राज्य (नेशन स्टेट) का निर्माण सम्भव नहीं तथा राज्य क्षेत्रीय स्वार्थों में ग्रस्त होने लगा है। जब बड़े देश

राष्ट्र-प्रबल होकर एक कल्याणवादी समाज को समुदाय तथा अनुशासन की भावनाओं में बाँध रहे हैं, भारत जातियों, सम्प्रदायों तथा क्षेत्रीय स्वार्थों में टूटता जा रहा है। इसे राजनैतिक भ्रष्टाचार की परिणति कहा जा सकता है। यहाँ तमिल, कन्नड़, बंगाली, पंजाबी, हिन्दू, मुसलमान, ब्राह्मण, शुद्र तो मिलते हैं पर एक हिन्दुस्तानी कहीं नजर नहीं आता।

क्षेत्रीय गुटों को मिलाकर जिस संयुक्त सरकार की रचना 2004 में हुई है वह इसी 'साफ्ट स्टेट' का स्वरूप है। दुनिया में कहीं भी परस्पर विरोधी दलों को मिला कर तथा क्षेत्रीयता का जामा पहनकर देश की सरकारें नहीं बनी है। पिंजड़ों में कई प्रकार के जानवर किसी चिड़ियाघर में तो एक साथ रह जाएँगें पर इससे कई फूलों से सुगंधित कोई बगीचा तो नहीं बन सकता। विडम्बना यह है कि संयुक्त सरकार की रचना इस बात पर हुई है कि उसमें कुछ दलें अपने को बहुत पाक साफ समझते हैं तथा दूसरे को सम्प्रदायवादी। इस राजनैतिक समझदारी का नाम सेक्युलरिज्म देते हैं पर यह रचना तो अंग्रेजों की दी हुई है, जो हिन्दू-मुसलमान को लड़ाते रहने तथा विभाजित रखने का यंत्रमात्र है। इसके पीछे सत्ता को हथियाने के लोभ के अलावे कुछ नहीं लगता। यह एक बहुरूपी (प्लूरल) समाज का नमूना नहीं, यह क्षेत्रीय तथा बहुभँजित टूटे हुए राष्ट्र का संकेत देता है।

राजनीति से गाँधी के मूल्यों का आजादी के साथ ही लुप्त हो जाना देश के लिए बहुत मँहगा पड़ा है। 100 रुपये का जीवन बिताने के लिए अगर सरकारी भ्रष्टाचार के लिए 50 रुपए देना पड़े तो यह कैसा जनतंत्र है? जब तक राजनेताओं में वैचारिक परिवर्त्तन न हो तथा गरीब जनता में दबी हुई आकांक्षाओं को प्राप्त करने का एक सामाजिक उभार न आवे, तब तक इस भयावह स्थिति से मुक्ति के आसार नहीं नजर आते। नोबेल अर्थशास्त्री जैन टिनबर्जन ने ऐसे नए जागरण को एक आंदोलन ही माना है जो गाँधी की सादगी और कमखर्ची के सिद्धांतों पर आधारित होगा। शायद टिनबर्जन का संकेत 'तेन त्यक्तेन, भुज्जीथा' के आदर्श से है। क्या आज के शासक इससे समझौता कर पावेंगे?

इसके लिए जनता की निर्भयता की भी जरूरत है और विरोध करने की शक्ति की भी। ये दोनों ऐसे गुण है जो बिना खर्च के एक नए आंदोलन का जन्म दे सकते हैं जिसे कुछ गैर-मार्क्सवादी चिंतकों ने "उभरती हुई आकांक्षाओं का आंदोलन" कहा है। इसमें बुद्धिजीवियों की तथा जन-संगठनों की बहुत बड़ी भूमिका है। पर ये स्वयं भ्रष्टाचार की हवा में बहते जा रहे हैं, यद्यपि उससे लड़ने की ताकत भी अगर है तो इन्हीं की।

धर्म और राजनीति

यह भी तय है, राजनेताओं का स्वार्थ सत्ता और उसके सुख-सुविधा से जुड़ गया है। इनका देवता और धर्म सबकुछ इसी में फंसे रहेंगे। धर्म वहीं है जो उन्हें सत्ता की कुर्सी पर बिठाए रहे। चुनाव-का खर्चीला रास्ता भ्रष्टाचारण से मुक्त नहीं हो सकेगा और न नैतिक मूल्यों की ओर मुड़ेगा। राजा राज करेगा और गरीब भूखों मरेगा। धर्म संगठनों की दिशा अगर गरीबों की ओर न मुड़े तो उनका कोई प्रयोजन सिद्ध नहीं होता। विवेकानंद भारत के पहले ऐसे संन्यासी थे जिन्होंने गरीबों को 'जाग्रत देवता' का रूप दिया और उनकी सेवा के व्रत को ही ईश्वर की सेवा का रास्ता बताया। ईश्वर का मानवीकरण करके उन्होंने बीसवीं सदी के भारत में एक समाजवादी धर्म का स्वरूप खींचा है। पर क्या राजनीति राजसुख को छोड़ने के लिए तैयार है और क्या धर्म धर्मान्धता से मुक्त होना चाहता है?

इस समस्या की निष्पत्ति में ही समाज के सामने एक समाधान मिलेगा, जिसे दृढ़ता से तय करना है और उन विकल्पों को चुनना है जिससे एक सुदृढ़ सामाजिक व्यवस्था की दिशा मिल जाए। क्या भारत को अब एक आध्यात्मिक विकल्प की आवश्यकता नहीं है जो मनुष्य को धर्मों के ऊपर रख कर एक नैतिक मानववाद से जोड़ दे?

33

PERESTROIKA AND GLASNOST

Prabhavati Sinha

'Perestraika' and 'Glasnost': The meaning of these two expressions was, till a couple of years ago, intelligible only to the Russians or a few outsiders knowing Russian.

Today these expressions are being understood, discussed, debated and analysed throughout the world. "Perestroika" means restructuring. 'Glasnost' means openness. Taken together they imply the 'ongoing process of pervasive renewal, covering eonomic, political, social, legal, constitutional, cultural and ideological spheres of life in the Soviet Union.'

The present movement was pioneered by Mikhail Gorbachev who appears to be more a philosopher-statesman in search of a solution to national and international problems than a political prophet with a readymade blueprint for our current problems. There is no longer any doubt that Gorbachev's crusade is going to introduce profound changes in the old order, particularly with respect to state ownership, central planning and the one-party domination which have so far ben essential features of the Soviet socialist system. Vital aspects of these institutions and their concepts are being openly questioned today in the Soviet system.

Gorbachev has made it clear that 'perestroika' is not just' a whim on the part of some individuals or a group of leaders. 'It is a movement which is urgent due to the necessity arising out of the development in the Soviet Society.'

He also cautions that delay in implementing Perestroika would lead to serious social, economic and political crises. The radiations from perestroika are no longer confined to the Soviet Union. They have already had a profound impact on a number of other socialist countries in Europe and Asia where the drive for democratisation has gained momentum.

Even in the western countries of the capitalist and free enterprise system perestroika has set in a new thinking on the socialist system the Soviet Union is no longer considered 'an evil empire'.

Perestroika is a process through which the Communist Party of the Soviet Union under Gorvachev's leadership is endeavouring 'to find a path towards socialist construction, liberation of man and creation of a new society, a path which, under the new evoluation was lost in the maze of authoritarianism, command, coercion, coterie dictatorship, primitive personality cult and even slaughter of the genuine revolutionary soul of the society right since the death of Lenin.'

Perestroka is also described as 'a negation of negation' since it is negating the negatives perpetrated by Stalinism on Leninism. It is, thus, obvious that Perestroika is essentially directed against the 'administrative command system' of Stalin.

Gorbachev also states that Perestroika is a continuation of the arrested Leninist New Economic Policy (NEP) in the changed circumstance of the Soviet Union. He and the present leadership are not discarding Marxism-Leninism. What they are discarding are the distortions in the present Soviet setup. They aim at a qualitative change with a view to bring changes in the economy and lifestyle of the Soviet People.

It is generally presumed that the pre-Gorbachev period was barren of any urge for reform. However, a close look at the history and developments during the period after Stalin's death and prior to the ascendency of Gorbachev shows that Perestroika and Glaznost didnot drop down on the Soviet Scene suddenly.

On the contrary, there were intermittant flashes of these concepts during this period, even though these may have been weak, partial or short-lived. The subdued voices of opposition were heard even during Stalin's lifetime but they were silenced and annihiliated brutally.

During the post-Stalin years we have traces of it in the powerful impetus given to the drive for renewal by Y.V. Andropov in 1982, who stressed the need to bring the activities of the party and the state bodies closer to the interest of the people through publicity, i.e. glosnost.

Earlier, Khrushchev's secret speech on Stalin is itself an example of a critical examination of the serious distortions during the Stalinist period and as a corollary, an attempt to make a break with the ugly past and restore greater democracy in the Soviet party, state and social life.

This trend of greater liberalisation has been reflected in a number of dissenting voices and works of the intelligentia in the field of arts, literature and science. All these however, do not and must not belittle the unique significance of Gorbachev's initiative and role in this regard. Gorbachev conceived the idea of Perestroika and Glasnost with their deep implications and as being organically interrelated, with their consequent ramifications extending into all aspect of 'Soviet life, constitutional, political, social and intellecutal.

Explaining the need for change in Soviet society Gorbachev elucidated in his speech at the plenary meeting of the Communist Party of the Soviet Union on February 18, 1988.

"It is certainly, above all, the desire to solve the most urgent problem caused by stagnation of the previous period that made us aware of the need for Perestroika'.

The need for a new special order was felt in order to get rid of 'crustation' and deformation of everything that shockled the society and prevented it from using the potentials of socialism in full measure.'

Gorbachev and his supporters believe that lack of initiative, inertia and absence of democratic functioning in economic, social, cultural and political fields are stumbling bloks in the path of growth and progress of the Soviet economy and society. In order to get rid of the administrative command method of functioning of the Communist Party and state authorities, Perestroika and Glasnost are essential.

Perestroika and Glasnost offer to the society ideas and opportunities that are capable of uniting and rallying people, not by regimenttion and dictates, but on the basis of a variety of human potentials, aspirations, interests and capabilities. As such it opens up the maximum opportunity for educating people by life and by their personal experiences of participating in social transformation.

They also create conditions under which these vast opportunities may really be exploited in practise. In its spiritual dimension

Perestroika is also a decisive attempt to restore in the eyes of everyone the superior importance of socialist values by removing the rust of bureaucratisation' from the values and ideals of socialism.

Perestroika is based on democratisation through which alone the human factor can be given full play in the profound transformation of all aspects of life in society, in real process of management and self management. The new leadership is fully conscious that the party can ensure its guiding role of the vanguard and lead the masses to effect far-reaching changes only by adopting democratic methods of work so that grass-root initiative, endeavour and independence may completely be unshackled. Basing itself on this understanding and assessment, the new leadership has also charted out the path for economic and political reforms and has taken concrete steps to effect suitable changes.

Perestroika, in its economic aspect, has the objective of ensuring a rapid rise in the production of material goods and provision of better and more efficient services, and achieving all these on the basis of cost effectiveness. This is to be realised through (a) decentralisation of management accompanied by (b) opportunities for private gains.

In its practical aspects this means (a) transition (departure) from the existing centralised management, (b) operational autonomy and a changeover from work collectives to self-management; (c) to serve the personal interest of every person through material incentive (d) in the field of agriculture to achieve these objectives by means of promotion of cooperatives and lease contract arrangements with individual families; (e) price reforms based on assessment of cost, and results of production and equivalent exchange of goods and services and (f) introduction of real competition between factories and organisations including competition between governments and cooperatives.

In the political arena Perestroika implies:

(a) almost unlimited freedom of expression;

(b) separation of party from State and Public organisations;

(c) thorough going legal and constitutional reforms with a view to establish socialist rule of low state.

(d) restrictions limiting the terms of office for elective posts in the party leading organs which has been fixed at two consecutive terms.

(e) an overall thrust to provide maximum scope to the process of self regulation and self government of society and creation of condition for the full development of initiative of citizens, representative bodies of government, party and public organisations and work collectives.

Projections of Perestroika are also evident in the field of foreign policy where Gorbachev is consistently giving a new orientation to the relations of the Soviet Union with countries of the West and the third block and for major global problems faced by the human race currently. Addressing the 19th conference of the CPSU Gorbachev said:

> *"We have begun to base our contacts in relations between state on dialogue; in the sphere of disarmament a readiness to accept for reaching reciprocal verification we, thereby, discovered a considerable potential of mutual understanding and of acceptance of coexistence and coopertion even in influential quarters far removed from us ideologically."*

This aspect of Perestroika has had a tremendous impact on the international situation since it made possible a major breakthrough in the world political affairs and above all in the field of disarmament as reflected in Geneva and Reykjavek which laid the basis for real progress in the process of negotiations and pre-determined the success of summit meetings later on.

As a result of these developments the entire international situation is changing. Besides, there are already clear signs of the axis of international affairs shifting away from confrontation towards cooperation, mutual understanding and negotiations.'

Improvement in Soviet-American relations, the conclusion of a treaty on scrapping of a portion of nuclear armaments, withdrawal of Soviet troops from Afganistan, etc, are clear proofs of the shift.

GLASNOST

Soviet leadership has been energetically promoting the spirit of Glasnost which is both an end and a means to achieve success in different directions. Now Soviet newspapers and other publications and media are publishing all kinds of news and materials which are critical and may be unpalatable to the establishment and various authorities. The wind of Glasnost is also blowing in institutions like schools, universities, institutes and other intellectual circles.

It is interesting to note that whereas Gorbachev's Perestorika and Glasnost reforms have received almost unanimous appreciation and support in the western capitalist circles there is unequivocal endrosement or acceptance of these reforms among socialist allies of the Soviet Union. A cursary review of the East European response to Gorbavhev's Glasmost and Perestroika in the Soviet Union and other communist counries indicates an extremely varied picture ranging from guarded suppport and vacillation to determined hostility and outright rejection.

Albania has not welcomed these reforms. It's party daily Zori Popullit described Perestroika as nothing less than a 'frontal attack against Marxism-Leninism' aimed at reestablishment of capitalism in the USSR, and Glasnost as no more than a pretext to carry out an 'unbridled atack on Joseph Stalin'.

Rumania has refused to fall in line with these reforms and is totally opposed to the process. On the other hand, Hungary and Poland have welcomed these reforms which are progressing there with spectacular speed and astonishing results from the traditional Marxist standpoint.

The implmentation of the reforms in the Soviet Union itself has not been smooth sailing. There is division of opinion over the pace of reforms to be adopted. The Conservative group led by Legachev is in favour of a cautious approach. On the other hand the extremist group led by Boris Yeltsin, the Moscow Maverick is advocating swift and revolutionary changes in Soviet society. His dissenting voice has been heard from the very beginning. His move to form an opposition group and his utterances in other countries of the world are providing to be an embrarrassment for Gorbachev.

Further, the ethnic outbursts in the Baltics and other republics have proved to be a serious challenge to the reforms and their practical implementation. Gorbachev's reforms have come under fire on several grounds. Dr. Paul Gregorious, the president of the World Council of Churches, Geneva, who spent a month in the Soviet Union recently and had the chance to meet people belonging to various sections of the Soviet society observes that the Soviet people's hopes from the reforms are not being realised. Their grievancs are that Perestroika has not produced any positive results for the ordinary consumer-prices have gone up, quality of goods have deteriorated, cooperatives have also failed as they are producing lower quality of goods at higher prices. The bureaucracy and party are still inefficient and corrupt.

Many others in the Soviet Union feel that Gorbachevism is confined to the top. Only a small party of the people have learnt to cast off the habits of indifference to public needs, false courtesy or hyprocracy, slavish and unquestioning obedience to higher authorities and the like. It has also been observed that the privileges and prerogatives of the party and state have not yet been taken away.

The role of the Congress of people's Deputies is also not satisfactory for many. There is the feeling in some quarters that the present leadership is not doing anything to prevent the disintegration of the socialist system. Poland's opting out of the socialist system and the clamour by some Soviet republics for secession from the USSR are viewed with alarm and serious apprehensions.

The present assessments of Perestroika and Glasnost and their roles and results are bound to be of a tentative nature.It is too early to come to a definite conclusion regarding the ultimate results of Perestroika and Glosnost in the Soviet society and the world at large.

Soviet society is at the moment in the midst of a serious struggle for making a break with the past and for creating an altogether new socialist life and environment. Naturally, the din and bustle and the floating dust of conflicting opinions and actions make the entire picture rather hazy. Only time will show the ultimate picture in its proper focus and perspective.

There are however, some questions which crop up in one's mind, like whether Perestroika and Glasnost are, like the NEP, merely a tactical retreat from the hitherto accepted Marxian or Socialist concepts of state, economy and society or are they a strategic defeat and collapse of the Marxian Socialist edifice that the USSR has been claiming itself for more than 70 years?

Again, a reflection on the possible extraordinary future results of Perestroika and Glasnost on Soviet life and economy raises another question–whether the current gleeful rejoicings in the western capitalist ruling circles will not end up in discovering their own waterloo in war against the communists. The point to ponder over is: if the Soviet Union could emerge from a backward state to a super power even under a totalitarian and regimented set up and could throw serious challenge to the entire western world, what will happen if this socialist,state is, under the new reforms, endowed with the additional and hitherto unknown advantages of initiative, unfettered exercise of talents and competition based on merit.

These results of Perestroika and Glasnost will certainly give a new thrust to the Soviet economy, industry, services and its scientific and defence capabilities enabling it to surpass decisively the combined strength of the entire western world.

By courtesy H.T., Dec. 12, 1989

34

WELFARE DILEMMA AND GANDHISM
(कल्याणवाद का संकट तथा गाँधी)

K.K. Sinha

Amartya Sen's great contribution lies in extending ethics to welfare economics. A general welfare in Gandhian concept of Sarvodaya meant welfare of the meanest in society. This is actually what Sen has made a premise of welfare economics. Such a pro-poor choice was not forthcoming in economics firstly because economists in the west had only market welfare through factory production in their mind, where poverty was casual and its intensity, very low, and secondly because a market supply and demand was value-neutral and took market rationality as a fool proof system of general welfare.

RATIONALITY VERSUS VALUE JUDGEMENT

What prevented economics from being pro-poor was the absence of value judgement in a system where market profit and self-interest gave a rational choice for social production and justified rich growing richer even if poverty existed. The early utilitarians like Bentham (1825) tried to measure additions to utility with every increase in production. Marshall (1890) however discussed lower utility surplus of the poor consumers but compromised with the situation if production was high and prices, low because in that case both rich and poor could maximise their satisfaction by equalising their marginal utilities. He however expected lags in such system and suggested subsidies to boost under-production and taxes to discourage over-production. This could secure a welfare equilibrium in the long run?

Pigou, (1912) another utlitarian made still wider provisions for subsidies and taxes by introducing social costs (e.g. pollution) and social gains (e.g. infrastructure) for which the private producers paid nothing. This included tax on Ricardo's rent also which was an unearned surplus. But all this could only condition production to some social norms assuming at the same time that incomes would flow to poor pockets as water covers its levels. Thus utilitarian doctrine remained tagged to market surpluses under a universalised social morality, which did not touch the poor.

There was a retreat to pure rationalism again after Pareto (1906) and in this new welfare economics, reasoned self-interest and all time consistent social choices for production could add to general welfare if some on was better off without any body else being worse off. Such a consistent social choice made income distribution in favour of the poor quite redundant. It was a choice for rich becoming richer without making the poor poorer. If however the poor became poorer, Hicks (1939) introduced a compensation criteria and justified such a state, if the richer could 'bribe' the poor to accept the change, e.g. constructing a railway line and compensating the losers whose lands were acquired. But such a state, though rational, would become unacceptable because such compensation at a wide scale could be only 'potential' and not actual. It could not be a pro-poor scheme at any rate.

It may be noted here that in the above scheme welfare was only additive looking at the poverty issue as if something was added without considering existing poverty at its original state.

The system of social choice for the poor was shifted to 'voting' in a democratic process by Bergson (1937) and Samuelson (1956), thus taking no risk of ethical judgement. A unique point of bliss or social welfare was visualised assuming that[1] social welfare function exists and[2] continuous redistribution was possible.[4] But leaving the final choice on political concensus could not do the trick. As I.M.D. little found, it could be a choice only of a superman,[5] particularly if it was going to be pro-poor. Arrow (1970) argued that social choice by this process could not be possible due to plurality of choices. Thus welfare of the poor could not be obtained without being dictatorial or regimented. At this point welfare economics ended in a fiasco and economics was left with some weaker choices or the second best to be more pro-poor, or alternatively it had to surrender to central planning.[6]

TILT TO ETHICAL VALUE JUDGEMENT

At this juncture market economics was faced with a dilemma of poverty and it had to evolve some value judgement which was more ethical though not inconsistent or unreasoned. Thus newer welfare economics after 1970's seems to have a Gandhian tilt to ethical value judgement so that the meanest or the poorest of the poor became the main unit of welfare and development. Gandhi had no regard for market rationality unless it was decentralised in smaller units. He also felt that rationality was in no way averse to ethics. Quoting Ruskin's book–Unto This Last (1860) and renaming it as Sarvodaya, Gandhi says that 'there is no wealth but life' and that 'the richest having perfected their own lives had also to help by this possession the lives of others.[7] The implication here was not any religious charity but a social trust or contract and 'the state will be there to carry out the will of the people.' This was invoking Rousseau's general will which was sacrosant, and such an ethical system in Gandhian frame might thwart mass production but could produce for the masses and secure general welfare.

But this line was not forthcoming in economics due to its moral overtone and succumbling to any second best alternative. Sen and some others however made a case for impersonal and just choice where self-interest and subjective preference was only one of the alternatives. Market rationalism provided a necessary but not sufficient condition for general welfare unless it secured a priority to the interest of the poor over the interests of the rich.[8] Such norms could not be set either under cardinal comparison of utilities (Marshall, Pigou) or under Pareto's general equilibrium or under any voting process, which were scared of ethical preferences.

SEN'S ETHICS

Though quite resembling Gandhi's, Sen's ethics is less moralised but quite critical to the egoistic, self-interested revealed preference and its numerical manifestations in economics. Sen terms it as a 'robust piece of evasion',[9] as personal interest is only one among a variety of other non-utility preferences which are expressed 'through a sense of commitment to some particular group, or say, to the neighbourhood.'[10] Here commitment does not exclude reasoning, and in so far as its consequences on others are to be more clearly understood, it only expanded the scope of reasoning.[11] Community interest was only another extension of self-interest and an intermediate between a universalised moral system of utilitarians and self-interest of general equilibrium. Thus it lies between oneself and all.[12] More over commitments give concrete and ordinally comparable situations for the market calculus.

J.P., a Gandhian talks of communitarian society in almost the same sense as Sen discusses commitment to neighbours.[13] It is not a totalled up self interest but a general will which motivates men to action in society. As Sen explains, 'two selfish strategies may produce worse outcome than two unselfish strategies' even if the game is repeated many times.'[14]

Sen refers to Harsanyi (1967) and Rawls (1971) who explain how individual choices, to beome a social choice, take an ethical route instead of a personal self-interest route. The ethical social choice, according to Harsanyi, is what is more utilitarian to the group. For Rawls the social choice is what is more just to the worst off in the group. Preferring the latter, Sen observes that the inadequacy of welfare economics lies in rejecting the non-utility informations and its relevance to welfare.'[15] Impersonal or non-utility chocies would cover access to primary social goods, basic liberties in terms of rights and opportunities, income and wealth and the social bases of self-respect; 'which every rational man is presumad to want.' These are non-utilities but are comparable ordinally, being different with different groups. On the basis of Rawlsian Difference Principle the welfare of the worst off would mainly depend on this equality on the non-utility front.

BASIC EQUALITY

The concept of equality distinguishes the utilitarian equality with Rawlsian which is based on the norms of justice. The utilitarian objective is to maximise the sum total of utility irrespective of distribution. This requires the equality of marginal utility of every one, as if every one had equally urgent needs. But Rawlsian equality indicates a situation in the original position and under the veils of ignorance, where personal biases or contingencies disappear and one gives a choice of welfare of the worst off as if he was in that position.[16]

Basic goods equality visualised under the above state would remove the difference and would be furthering the interest and efficiency of the worst off people while basic liberties would promote capabilities. Sen therefore makes Rawlsian basic needs expanded to urgency and to equality of capabilities; not only goods but what goods do to meet health, educational, shelter rquirements, and not only basic liberties but how they promote participation in the social life of the community. Thus non-exploitation and non-discrimination would cover such hard cases and widespread real differences within the poor groups.[17]

Here Gandhian concept of basic equality is quite comparable. When Gandhi talks about levelling down of the few rich and the levelling up of the semi-starved naked millions he has a utilitarian moral system but when he talks about equality of needs, he feels that the essential needs of the poor must be satisfied first, i.e., a balanced diet, a decent house to live in, facilities for education for one's children and adequate medical relief.[18] He also talks of land ownership patterns, social stratification, untouchability and women up-lift as areas of basic liberties. Gandhi had a Vedantic equality of power and privileges in his mind which would patch up the diferences between the strong and the weak, ruler and the ruled, rich and the poor and knowledgeable and the illiterate.[19] Many of such differences or deprivations are ordinally measurable.

It is true that the indexing of privileged equality as above, or of capabilities equality of Sen or of primary goods equality of Rawls may have many difficulties in varying degrees as Sen foresees, but these are technical issues which are solved by measuring intesity of poverty and the differences or inequalities involved therein. Sen measures the welfare index by income index alongwith intensity of inequality, and the poverty index by share of population in income below a poverty line and the intensity of inequality within the poverty group. This tells that giving a boost to the income of the poor does not by itself remove poverty unless it reaches the worst off and tells who is the worse off than whom. This is what Gandhi wanted to bring in light and what welfare economics was evading for long.

When sen prefers to be more like Kautilya and Adam Smith than Kant and Krishna[20] he wants only to avoid too much of virtuousness and morality from his calculus, but by advocating political protest and opposition[21] he only gives a welfarist direction to Gandhi's satyagrah.

NOTES AND REFERENCES

1. Sinha K.K. & Uma (1993), Socialism, Market and some Moral Issues, in Das D.K. (ed) Economics of Markets, Deep & Deep, Delhi.

2. Sinha K.K. (1990), Marshallian Economics and the Poverty Issue, IEJ, Conf. Issue.
3. For Acceptability as a Norm see, Pattanaik P. (1974), Some Aspects of Welfare Economics, IEJ, Conf. Issue.
4. Koutsoyiannis A. (1982), Modern Microeconomics, Macmillan, p. 540.
5. Little I.M.D. (1970), A Critique of Welfare Economics, Oxf. Univ. p. 85.
6. Blaug M. (1978), Economic Theory in Retrospect, p. 639.
7. Gandhi M.K. (1956), Ruskin-Unto This Last, Navajivan, Ahmedabad, pp. 34, 36, 40.
8. Sen Amartya (1982), Choice Welfare and Measurement, Blackwell, p. 335.
9. Ibid. p. 89.
10. Ibid. p. 100.
11. Ibid. p. 105.
12. Ibid. p. 106.
13. Narain J.P. (1964), Communitarian Society and Panchayati Raj.
14. Sen, op. cit., p. 103.
15. Ibid. p. 340.
16. For an Exposition see, Uma Devi (1974), Reent Trends in Welfare Economics, IEJ, Conf. Issue, Bombay.
17. Sen, op. cit., pp. 366-7.
18. Gandhi M.K. (1960), Trusteeship, Navajivan, Ahmedabad, p. 17.
19. This is Implicit in Gandhi's Concept of Ram Rajya. See, Sinha K.K. (1985): Had Gandhi a theory of Planning, IEJ.
20. Sen A (1998), in Econ. Times, 15 Oct., Also see, Vinay Bharat Ram, (1998), Economics and Ethics, in The Times of India, 21 Oct.
21. Sen A. & Jean Drese (1995), India Economic Development & Social Opportunity.

35

विश्वीकरण—एक भ्रामक विकास प्रक्रिया (GLOBALISATION–A DUBIOUS PARADIGM)

के.के. सिन्हा

पिछड़े देशों के बाजार को खुला रखने तथा बड़े देशों से होड़ लेने की प्रक्रिया को विश्वीकरण कह सकते हैं। समान धनी देश तो ऐसा कर व्यापार से लाभ उठा सकते हैं, क्योंकि वे अपनी सस्ती चीजें बेचेंगे तथा दूसरे की सस्ती चीजें खरीदेंगे और सौदा बराबरी का रह सकता है। अगर व्यापार संतुलन बिगड़ने लगे तो वे द्विपक्षी समझौता कर सकते हैं तथा कर्ज अथवा सोना देकर तुरन्त घाटे को खत्म कर लेंगे।

परन्तु पूंजीवाद अर्थशास्त्री रिकार्डों (1820) ने गरीब और धनी देशों के बीच भी खुला व्यापार कर लाभ कमाने की बात कही। गरीब देश भी कच्चा माल सस्ता बेच सकते हैं, तथा उसकी जगह धनी देशों से मशीन तथा पूँजी के समान ले सकते हैं, जिन्हें वे स्वयं आसानी से नहीं बना सकते। ब्रिटेन और भारत के बीच इस तरह का खुला बाजार 1850 के बाद लाभदायक सिद्ध हुआ, क्योंकि इसके कच्चा माल के लिए काफी दाम मिलता रहा तथा इसे भी मशीन और पूँजी मिली जिससे इसके सड़क, रेल मार्ग, बिजली तथा बुनियादी उद्योगों का विकास हुआ।

नए तर्क—इसी अर्थ मे 1980 के बाद भारत ने पुनः विश्वीकरण और खुले बाजार की नीति पर जोर दिया क्योंकि संरक्षण से सरकारी उद्योग घाटे में होने लगे थे तथा निजी उद्योग देश के भीतर ही बेच कर काफी लाभ कमाने लगे। उधर व्यापार का घाटा बढ़ने लगा तथा विश्व व्यापार में भारत काफी पिछड़ गया। स्वतंत्र होने के बाद भारत ने जिस योजना के द्वारा विकास का मार्ग चुना वह काफी घाटे का सिद्ध हुआ। इसलिए निजीकरण द्वारा विश्व बाजार में एक प्रतियोगी और

कुशल विकास की धारा बहाने की जरूरत थी और एक चुनौती से भरा हुआ मार्ग अपनाया गया। उदाहरण के लिए एशिया के कुछ छोटे देशों (कोरिया, जापान, मलेशिया, ताइवान आदि) को रखा गया जो निजीकरण और विश्वीकरण द्वारा काफी धन कमा रहे थे तथा विश्व के उन्नत और बड़े देशों से होड़ ले रहे थे।

इस प्रकार भारत का नया तर्क केवल कच्चे माल का निर्यात करना नहीं था, बल्कि उद्योगों का विकास कर अपने विदेशी घाटे को कम करना था।

नेशन स्टेट बनाम कम्पनी राज्य—पर रिकार्डों के व्यापारिक बहुमुखी लाभ की धारणा को बड़े देशों के वाणिज्यवादी नीति ने प्रारम्भ से ही भ्रामक सिद्ध किया। खुले व्यापार ने भले ही पश्चिम के देशों में औद्योगिक क्रांति को स्थाई बना दिया पर पिछड़े देशों की सौदेबाजी की श्ाक्ति क्षीण होती गई और बड़े देशों में अल्पाधिकारी फर्म तथा बहुदेशी उद्योग बलशाली होते गए। कच्चे माल के कई विकल्प होने से तथा पूँजी-प्रधान तकनीक के कारण श्रम का महत्व गिरने से पिछड़े देश खुले व्यापार का कोई लाभ नहीं ले पा रहे थे, उधर अल्पाधिकारी फर्म तथा बहुदेशी उद्योग अपने राष्ट्र की सीमा से फैल कर अन्य देशों की राष्ट्रवादी शक्ति को क्षीण करने लगे। फर्म अपने ही अन्य फर्मों को जो दूसरे देशों में स्थित थे, खरीदने-बेचने में जीते रहे तथा बहुदेशी उद्योग एक जैसी वस्तुओं को ही विज्ञापनों के आधार पर दूर देशों में बेचने के लिए होड़ करने लगे। इससे राष्ट्रवादी राज्य (नेशन स्टेट) की धारणा ध्वस्त होने लगी तथा व्यापार में बहुदेशी उद्योगों का पूर्ण वर्चस्व हो गया। अब व्यापार देशों के बीच नहीं फर्मों और बड़े उद्योगों के बीच हो गया जो देश के हितों के लिए नहीं उद्योग के मुनाफा और एकाधिकार के हितों का संवर्द्धन करने लगा। ये एक जैसे उद्योगों के फैलाव में भी बाधक हुए, और पूँजीवाद देश के हितों से मुक्त हो, वाणिज्यवादी हो रहे थे।

खुले व्यापार का ध्वंस तथा संकट—1900 ई० के बाद ही जब पिछड़े हुए देश, जो बड़े देशों के उपनिवेश थे, आर्थिक दृष्टि से कुछ संभलने लगे थे, अपने आयातों पर निर्भर हो गए तथा निर्यात को बढ़ाने में विफल हो गए। इससे उनका व्यापारिक घाटा बढ़ने लगा तथा वे बड़े देशों पर निर्भर हो गये। उधर बड़े देश अन्य धनी देशों से द्वि-पक्षी समझौते तथा व्यापार पर जोर देकर अपने उद्योगों को बढ़ाते रहे तथा पिछड़े देशों को बहिष्कार कर अपने व्यापार की सुरक्षा (प्रोटेक्शन) में लग गए। पर रूस ने अपने देश को बड़े देशों के व्यापार से बंद कर लिया तथा धीमी गति से बढ़ती जनसंख्या के लाभ को योजना द्वारा संसाधनों के विकास द्वारा औद्योगिक विकास में बदल दिया। यह विकास विदेशी व्यापार से मुक्त था।

विश्वीकरण नीति का विस्फोट: 1980 के बाद धनी देशों की निर्यात वृद्धि की नीति तथा गरीब देशों की आयात प्रतिस्थापन की नीति बिल्कुल टकराव की स्थिति में आने लगी। वास्तव में धनी-देशों ने इतनी पूँजी और उपभोग की वस्तुएँ तैयार कर ली कि उनकी खपत होना कठिन था और इसलिए उनकी विकास दर 3 प्रतिशत तक घट गई जो गरीब देशों के आयात प्रतिस्थापन के कारण हुई विकास दर के बराबर ही थी। गरीब देशों में मूल्य तेजी की दर 10 प्रतिशत हो रही थी तथा धनी देशों में बेरोजगारी की दर भी उतनी ही थी।

ऐसी स्थिति में धनी देश अपने निर्यात को बढ़ाने तथा आयात को घटाने के लिए संरक्षण की नीति पर उतर आए न कि खुले बाजार की। उधर पिछड़े देशों का विदेशी घाटा इतना बढ़ गया कि जब तक उनके ऋण के बोझ को बड़े ऋणदाता-संगठन अथवा बड़ी कम्पनियाँ छूट न दें तब तक इन्हें बड़े देशों से व्यापार करना बहुत कठिन हो गया। पड़ोसियों से व्यापार कर ये देश कोई विशेष लाभ नहीं कमा सकते। बहुदेशी कम्पनी इनके 75% व्यापार को अपने प्रभाव में रखते हैं।

पिछड़े देशों को सबसे बड़ा संकट आयात के बढ़ने तथा निर्यात के घटने से होगा। साथ-साथ ऐसे देशों के पूँजी का प्रवाह भी कम है क्योंकि प्रत्यक्ष पूँजी निवेश बड़े देश बड़े देशों में ही करने लगे हैं तथा कुछ, जो पिछड़े देशों के मुद्रा बाजार द्वारा अप्रत्यक्ष निवेश होते हैं, वे बड़े देश अपने पेटेन्ट के लगान वसूलने के ख्याल से, अंश के रूप में देते हैं; वे पेटेन्ट को बेचना नहीं चाहते।

पर बड़े देशों का सबसे ज्यादा वित्त प्रवाह सट्टा बजार में होता है जो व्यापार प्रवाह से 90:1 के अनुपात में हो रहा है। यह प्रवाह वास्तविक निवेश नहीं बल्कि सट्टा से अल्पकालिक लाभ उठाने के लिए ही होता है। यह पूरे वित्त को अस्थाई तथा जुए जैसी अटकलबाजी में फँसाए रखता है। इस तरह पूरे विदेशी मुद्रा में ऐसे वित्तीय प्रवाह का नब्बे गुना ज्यादा होना पिछड़े देशों के विकास के लिए खतरे की घंटी है।

कुछ निष्कर्ष: विश्वीकरण छोटे और बड़े देशों के बीच विषमता को बढ़ाएगा क्योंकि व्यापारिक समझौते (GATT के अधीन) जो अब विश्व व्यापार संगठन (W.T.O.) के नाम से जाना जाता है, अमेरिका द्वारा निर्मित संगठन है और अमेकिरा व्यापार में अपना वर्चस्त खोने लगा है। स्वाभाविक है कि बड़ी मछली छोटी मछलियों के अनुकूल समझौते नहीं कर सकती।

दूसरा दोष यह होगा कि पिछड़े देश संगठित और असंगठित क्षेत्रों में तेजी से बढ़ते जायेंगे जहां असंगठित क्षेत्र संगठित क्षेत्रों की तुलना में पिछड़ता जाएगा जिसे

मिर्डल ने 'अविकास का प्रभाव' (बैकवाश इफेक्ट) कहा। पिछड़े देशों को हवाई जहाज की तेजी में उड़ा कर ले जाना और उड़ाते जाना "यहां की जीवन शैली तथा कार्य विधि" से मेल नहीं खाता, न यह पश्चिम की तरह मुनाफा कमाने की अथक दौड़ का आदी है। ऐसा आर्थिक विकास इसकी गरीबी की समस्या को बढ़ाता जाएगा और एक छोटे धनी टापू के चारों ओर गरीबी का महासमुद्र उमड़ता रहेगा। इसे नव-उपनिवेशवाद के रूप में देखा जाने लगा है।

जब तक देश के भीतर गरीबी के महासमुद्र का मंथन नहीं होगा तथा स्वदेशी संरचना को गठित नहीं किया जाएगा, खुले व्यापार अथवा निजीकरण की प्रतियोगी व्यवस्था देश के 20 प्रतिशत हिस्से से अधिक तक कभी नहीं पहुंच सकती। 20 प्रतिशत का विकास क्या विकास की एक भ्रामक प्रक्रिया नहीं होगी?

लेखक के प्रकाशित अंग्रेजी लेख का हिन्दी अनुवाद।

36

पूंजीवाद का संकट

Pravir Krishna

पूंजीवाद इस बात पर टिका हुआ है कि अगर उत्पादन होगा तो उसकी मांग आप से आप होगी क्योंकि उत्पादन से लोगों को आय मिलती है जिसे बाजार में वह मांग के रूप में लगाता है। इस तरह उत्पादन बढ़ता जाएगा तथा मांग भी और सभी लोगों को रोजी मिलती जाएगी।[1]

लेकिन 1930 में पूरे विश्व बाजार में मंदी हुई और उत्पादन की मांग गिर गई और बाजार में सामान की खपत नहीं होता देख उत्पादक उत्पादन में तेजी से कटौती करने लगे तथा लोगों के रोजगार में भी कटौती होने लगी। उत्पादक मूल्य में थोड़ी कमी करके भी बेचने में असमर्थ था क्योंकि लोगों की मांग एक हद तक आमदनी के बढ़ जाने पर, बढ़ती नहीं और इस तरह उत्पादक को उत्पादन बढ़ाने में भय हो जाता है कि अब बाजार में बिक्री बढ़ाना संभव नहीं होगा। केन्स (अर्थशास्त्री) ने इसे पूंजीवाद का संकट बताया। अब न मूल्य कम करने से ही, न मजदूरी में कटौती करने से ही बाजार में मांग बढ़ाई जा सकती थी।

पूंजीवाद का यह संकट हल हो सकता था अगर उत्पादन न बढ़ाकर लोगों की मांग को ही सरकारी खर्च बढ़ाकर कोई-कोई सरकारी कार्यों के जरिए लोगों के हाथ में रुपया दिया जाता जिसे वे बाजार में जाकर खर्च करते और जिसे देख उत्पादकों को फिर उत्पादन करने की संभावना दिखाई पड़ने लगती। इस तरह केन्स ने पूंजीवादी संकट का एक सरकारी समाधान खोज निकाला जब पूंजीवादी बाजारों में पुनः लाभ की आशा का जन्म हो जाता और फिर उत्पादन और रोजगारी बढ़ने लगती।

समाजवादी अर्थशास्त्र में मार्क्स ने पूंजीवादी मंदी को इसका ध्वंस मान लिया था जो किसी भी तरह बचाया नहीं जा सकता था तथा राज्य को पूरे बाजार को अपने हाथ में लिए बिना बेरोजगारी को हटाना संभव नहीं था। केन्स ने पूंजीवाद को बचाने की एक नई राह दिखला दी जिससे मांगपक्षी अर्थशास्त्र पुनः पूर्ति पक्षी हो जाता क्योंकि कृत्रिम तरह से भी सरकार के मांग बढ़ा देने पर लाभ खोजने वाले उत्पादक फिर बाजार को खड़ा कर लेते तथा पूरी रोजगारी की स्थिति फिर खड़ी हो जाती।

लेकिन केन्स की यह अल्पकालीन तकनीक पूंजीवादी संकट को लम्बें समय तक कायम कर सकती थी या नहीं इस पर भी शंकाएँ उठने लगी। 1930 से 1950 तक जो पूंजीवादी विकास हुआ अवश्य पर 1960 से दशक में यह विकास मूल्य वृद्धि और तेजी में बदलने लगा,[2] जब उत्पादन तो बढ़ा लेकिन मूल्य भी बढ़ने लगे और लोगों की खरीदने की शक्ति कम होने लगी। लेकिन इससे बाजार का कोई संकट खड़ा नहीं हुआ क्योंकि मूल्य के साथ मजदूरी भी बढ़ी और पूंजीवादी देशों में क्रय शक्ति घटी नहीं और न उत्पादक ने डर कर उत्पादन या रोजगारी में कटौती करना ही जरूरी समझा। मजदूरी के बढ़ने से तेजी और मूल्य में वृद्धि तो हुई लेकिन उत्पादन और रोजगारी में कटौती नहीं हुई। बेरोजगारी 4% से ज्यादा नहीं हुई।[3]

1970 के लगभग बेरोजगारी 10% हो गई लेकिन मजदूरी को 2% बढ़ा देने से भी उत्पादन और रोजगारी बढ़ गई। सरकार ने उत्पादकों पर टैक्स बढ़ाकर अपनी झोली भर ली और अपने भी खर्च बढ़ाकर तेजी के बाजार में मांग को कम नहीं होने दिया।[4]

लेकिन 1970 के दशक में तेजी और रोजगारी दोनों के बढ़ने की प्रक्रिया खत्म होने लगी और मूल्य की तेजी के कारण मांग घटने लगी और उत्पादन में ठहराव आने लगा जिससे बेकारी भी 10 प्रतिशत से ज्यादा हो गई।[5]

पूंजीवाद के संकट का यह दूसरा काल हुआ जो 1930 की मंदी के लगभग 40 साल बाद फिर उठ खड़ा हुआ। एक तरफ मूल्य और मजदूरी में तेजी आने लगी, दूसरी तरफ उत्पादन में ठहराव तथा बेकारी में 20% से भी अधिक वृद्धि हो गई। सरकार करों द्वारा अपने क्षेत्र में उत्पादन और रोजी दे सकती थी लेकिन निजी उत्पादक अपनी उम्मीदें खोने लगे तथा सरकार अब संकट को बचाने में विफल हो गई। यह केन्सीय तरीकों का भी संकट कहा गया।[6]

पूंजीवादी देश (अमेरिका तथा ब्रिटेन) इस संकट में, जिसे तेजीयुक्त ठहराव (स्टैग ल्फेसन) कहा गया, घबरा गए तथा कोई दूसरा उपाय खोजने लगे[7] केन्स

ने बताया था कि पूर्ण रोजगारी की स्थिति के बाद ही मूल्य बढ़ते हैं और तेजी और मँहगाई होती है, पर कुछ दिनों तक मूल्य बढ़ना और रोजी बढ़ना तो दोनों साथ-साथ हुए जिसे फिलिप ने इंग्लैण्ड के आंकड़ों से बतलाया, लेकिन 1970 के बाद तो मूल्य बढ़ते गए और रोजगारी तथा उत्पादन घटने लगे।

इस संकट को अमेरिका के अर्थशास्त्रियों ने स्वाभाविक माना जो तेजी की उम्मीद के बढ़ने के कारण उत्पादन को रोकने लगता है लेकिन थोड़े समय के बाद वह आप से आप सही गति पकड़ कर अपने को ठीक कर लेता है। ये अर्थशास्त्री 'मुद्रावादी' कहे गए जिनके अनुसार मुद्रा की पूर्ति को संयमित दर (4%) पर बढ़ाते रहना चाहिए जिससे उत्पादन में कोई गतिरोध न हो और न बहुत ज्यादा मुद्रा बढ़ाया जाय जिससे तेजी की गति बढ़े।[8]

दूसरे मत के अर्थशास्त्री केन्स की धारणा के अनुसार ही सरकार के बजट को बढ़ाने और खर्च करने की नीति को ही संकट टालने के लिए जरूरी समझते रहे। लैफर ने केन्सवादियों के इस तर्क को यह कह कर काट दिया कि सरकार के खर्च बढ़ाने से उत्पादन में जो थोड़ी बहुत वृद्धि होगी भी वह निजी उत्पादकों के पलायन करने के कारण घुमिल पड़ जाएगी।[9]

अब एक तीसरा मत यह हुआ कि पूंजीवादी व्यवस्था को निजी पूर्ति को बढ़ाते जाना चाहिए और इसके लिए सरकार को अपने करों को कम रखना चाहिए ताकि निजी उत्पादकों पर कर का दबाव न पड़े। इस तरह 1980 के बाद पूर्ति पक्षी अर्थशास्त्र फिर उठ खड़ा हुआ जिसका पुराना विश्वास जाग्रत हुआ कि पूर्ति बढ़ाने से मांग खुदबखुद बढ़ती जाएगी।[10]

इस नये पूंजीवादी अर्थशास्त्र में निजी उत्पादकों को मूल्य बढ़ाने का एकाधिकार हो जाता है, उधर व्यापार संघों को मजदूरी बढ़ाने की छूट भी मिल जाती है जब मुद्रा स्फीति की स्थिति में भी उत्पादन को बढ़ाना संभव रह जाता है। ऐसे पूंजीवाद में सरकार के सामने केन्सीय मार्ग खुले नहीं रह जाते। साथ ही साथ फ्रिडमैन की मुक्त मुद्रावादी नीति में भी, केन्स और फ्रीडमैन की मुद्रा से मांग बढ़ाने की नीति नहीं मानी गयी।[11] केन्स और फ्रीडमैन इन दोनों को सैमुएल्सन ने मांगवादी समग्र अर्थशास्त्र का ही नव पूंजीवादी समन्वय कहा।[12]

पूंजीवाद के संकट को टालने के लिए किए गये नया तीसरे विकल्प-पूर्ति पक्षी अर्थशास्त्र का जन्म हुआ है वह पहले की तरह व्यक्तिवाची (माइक्रो) नही हो कर समग्र बाजार (मैक्रो) को सामने रखता है। स्वभावत: यह मजदूरों की मजदूरी को बढ़ाए जाने के विरोध में है तथा सरकार के कर बढ़ाकर खर्च बढ़ाने के भी विरोध में[13] नया मैक्रो पूर्तिपक्षी अर्थशास्त्र सरकार के बजट बढ़ाने की नीति

का तो विरोध करता ही है, वह फ्रीडमैन के मुद्रा बढ़ाने की मुक्त नीति को भी गलत मानता है।

इस तरह यह मुद्रावादियों के मुद्रा की पूर्ति को बढ़ाए जाने का भी विरोध करता है तथा सूद की दर को बढ़ाकर साख पर नियंत्रण तथा मांग पर नियंत्रण कर तेजी की स्थिति पर रोक लगाना भी जरूरी समझता है।[14] पर नया पूंजीवाद कई अन्तर्विरोधों से ग्रस्त होता जा रहा है।[15] यह केन्स के मांग पक्ष को सामाजिक सुरक्षा के रूप में रखना भी चाहता है लेकिन केन्स को कुछ लोक सेवाओं के अलावे अन्य सरकारी उत्पादन के क्षेत्र के बढ़ाने से अलग रखना चाहता है। उत्पादन तो निजी हाथों में ही रहना चाहिए जो अतिशय-बजट वाद के विरोध में है। पीटर एफ-ड्रकर के अनुसार नया पूंजीवाद केन्स को मानते हुए भी उससे बहुत अलग हो जाता है। केन्स का नया रूपांतर केन्स को बढ़ाकर नहीं बल्कि उसको उसीके घेरे के अंदर ही रखना है ताकि वह समाजवाद का स्वांग नहीं बन जाए।[16]

शूम्पीटर ने केन्स के सामाजिक खर्च को एक उदार प्रजातंत्र में बांधने के लिए तीन शर्तें रखी है:

1. राजनैतिक निर्णयों पर प्रभावी सीमा
2. एक पूर्ण दक्ष नौकरशाही
3. राजनैतिक सत्ता पर स्व-स्थापित दबाव।[17]

वास्तव में केन्स के अत्यधिक प्रयोग से एक तरफ रोजगारी के नाम पर मजदूरी को बढ़ाने की मांग भी बढ़ती गई है तथा दूसरी तरफ बड़े उद्योगपति अल्पाधिकारी की तरह मूल्यों को बढ़ाते गए। इसके अलावे सरकार के द्वारा कुछ समय तक बाजार में मांग सृजित करने का प्रयास नए रोजी पाने वालों में बेईमानी भी पैदा कर सकती थी जो उपभोग को बढ़ाता है पर उत्पादन को नहीं।[18]

पिछड़े हुए देशों का पूंजीवादी संकट

विकसित पश्चिमी देश तेजी और बढ़ते हुए मूल्यों के साथ भी उत्पादन बढ़ाकर बेकारी को रोक सकते हैं पर पिछड़े देश तेजी की समस्या से बच नहीं सकते और मूल्यों के बढ़ने के भय से उत्पादक बिक्री के गिरने की आशंका से ग्रस्त हो जाता है। ऐसी स्थिति में गरीबों की मांग को बढ़ाने के लिए उत्पादन बढ़ाने के साथ-साथ गरीबों में आपको समुचित रूप से वितरण करने की समस्या भी प्रबल हो जाती है। पूंजीवादी व्यवस्था में वितरण का सवाल सदा बहुत कमजोर रहता है।[19] बड़ी कम्पनियों को बाजार चाहिए पर आवश्यक वस्तुओं का नहीं बल्कि

आराम की वस्तुओं का। ऐसी वस्तुओं के आयात से बचने के लिए गरीब देशों में खाद्यान्न की उपज बढ़ाकर आराम की वस्तुओं के आयात से बचना होगा। इसके अलावे ऐसी लोक सेवाओं का बढ़ना भी जरूर है, जिससे गरीब वर्गों को अधिक लाभ पहुँचे, जैसे स्वास्थ्य, शिक्षा, परिवहन, अस्पताल आवास आदि।[20]

इन सेवा क्षेत्रों के बढ़ने से निजी उत्पादकों को कोई क्षति नहीं पहुँच सकती है जैसा धनी देशों में देखा गया। बल्कि गरीबों की आय के बढ़ने से उनकी मांग भी बढ़ती जाती है और रोजगारी की वृद्धि भी होती जाती है। इस तरह केन्स का मांग-पक्षी सिद्धांत जो धनी देशों में उत्पादकों में पलायन करने की स्थिति पैदा करता है, वही गरीब देशों में आवश्यक उत्पादन विस्तार कर गरीबों के मांग की सृष्टि करता है।[21] स्पष्ट है कि पूंजीवाद का पूर्तिपक्षी सिद्धांत जो अब आर्थिक सुधार के नाम से निजी कम्पनियों के पक्ष में जा रहा है, गरीब देशों में गरीबों के संकट का सिद्धांत बन जाए।

उचित विकल्प के प्रश्नः

पिछड़े हुए देशों की गरीबी की दृष्टि से पूंजीवाद के पूर्ति-पक्षी तर्क बड़ी कम्पनियों के पक्ष में जाता है। वहीं केन्स के उदारवादी प्रजातंत्र के नियम, सरकार के बजट और उसके खर्च को समाजवाद से कहीं अच्छा विकल्प देता है पर इसमें भी बजट के विस्तार से मांगपक्षी तेजी की सृष्टि होती है जो गरीब देशों के लिए घातक है। मुद्रा की पूर्ति के बढ़ने से तथा मजदूरी की मांग बढ़ने से भी तेजी की संभावनाएँ बढ़ती जाती है और उत्पादन की संभावनाएँ कम।

पर यहाँ हम कह सकते हैं कि गरीबी के हटाने के लिए केवल पूर्ति या केवल मांग को पुष्ट करने का सवाल नहीं महत्व रखता क्योंकि यहाँ पूर्ति का बढ़ना काले बाजार का निर्माण करने लगता है तथा मांग का बढ़ना केवल मुद्रा-आय को बढ़ाता है जो भ्रष्ट आय में और भ्रष्ट मांग में बदल जाता है।

इसलिए विकसित पूंजीवाद में जहाँ पूर्ति-पक्ष पर ही जोर दिया जाता है तथा मांग-पक्ष को सरकार की असमर्थता तथा पूर्ति पक्ष को कमजोर बनाने वाली शक्ति माना जाता है--इसे गरीब देशों के लिए कोई उपयोगी दृष्टिकोण नहीं माना जा सकता। इसलिए कुछ भारतीय अर्थशास्त्री वैसी पूर्ति का पक्ष लेते हैं जो गरीब मजदूरों की जरूरतों की पूर्ति करें तथा सरकार को ऐसे क्षेत्रों में खर्च नहीं करना होगा जो तेजी में बदल कर रह जाए।[22]

इसीलिए पिछड़े देशों की गरीबी और बेकारी के समाधान के लिए वर्त्तमान समग्र (मैक्रो) बाजार के पूर्त्ति-मांग के सिद्धांत अत्यन्त बेकार सिद्ध होंगे। पर[23]

बाजार को अंशों तथा क्षेत्रों में बांट कर बाजार के नियम बनाए जा सकते हैं[24] जो व्यक्ति के व्यवहार से जुड़ कर समूह अथवा समुदायों से जुड़ता हो। इस तरह यह अर्थशास्त्र मार्शल की तरह मांग-पूर्ति को कैंची के दोनों धारों का बराबर महत्व का मानता है तथा गाँधी के अर्थशास्त्र की तरह व्यक्ति के विवेक पर नहीं बल्कि छोटे समूहों की भलाई की धारणा पर आधारित करता है। लिप्सी ने इसे बाजारों का विकेन्द्रीकरण कहा है जो पूँजीवाद के केन्द्रित दृष्टिकोण को नकारता है।[25]

NOTES

1. K.K. Sinha, Economic equilibrium and capital in development theories. Ind. Econ. Jour., Conf. issue, 1980.
2. R.G. Lipsey, Positive Economica, 1976, P. 799.
3. A.W. Phillips, The relation between unemployment and the rate of change in money wages in the U.K., 1862-1957, Economics, 1958.
4. W. Beveridge, Quoted, K.K. Sinha, Regional frictions and unemployment, Ind. Econ. Jour., Dec. 1969.
5. Stonier & Hague, Textbook of Econ. Theory, 1977, p. 571.
6. J.D. Sethi, Crises of International capitalism, Mainstream, July 18, 1981.
7. Name given to the Neo-Keynesians (particularly Joan Robinson) by Schumpeter, (see, H.G. Johnson, Cambridge in the 1950's, Encounter, June, 1974)
8. Inflation before full employment could be bad as it redistributed incomes in haphazard way especially when it was un-anticipated. But if on the average GNP grew by 3% with 5 to 15% rise in prices, the average house wife was not so much affected as housewives of particular class. (Lipsey, op. cit., p. 784).
9. J. Tobin, The New Economics One Decade Older, 1972, p. 50.
10. Friedman finds that natural rate depends on worker's choice between work and liesure and not on any 'money illusion'.
11. Proceedings of American Econ. Review, May, 1972.
12. Tobin, op. cit., p. 97.
13. Lipsey, op. cit., pp. 557, 768.
14. For a disoussion see, American Econ. Review, March, 1972.
15. The development of a bourgeois intellectual new left movement was foreseen by schumpeter in his 1942 classic. (Tobin,op.cit.)
16. Peter F. Drucker, Towards new economics, Public Interest, Special Issue, 1980.
17. Quoted, S. Britain, Can Democracy manage an economy, in Skidelsky (ed), The End of Keynesian Era.

18. Fred Hirsh, Social Limits to Growth, 1977, p. 134.
19. Ibid., p. 132.
20. A.K.N. Reddy, Quoted Ibid.
21. An All India Survey of Demand and Supply Position establishes recession in India in spite of increase in production. This is due to increase of supply in some fields but shortage in other leading to inventory stocks and under-utills on at the same time. (Econ. Times, 26 July, 1982). Also P. on India reession, times of India, 16.8.02
22. P.R. Brahmanand, IMF Loan and India's Economic future, 1982, p. 77.
23. The Dutta Commission (1969) rightly suggested a tilt of public sector to consumption fields to complete out bit luxury producers, and induction private suppliers for middle scale capital sector. (Report of the Industrial Licensing Policy Inquiry Committee, Govt. of India, 1969).
24. See Lispey, op. cit., pp. 782-83, 789, 797, 809, 810 Also K.K. Sinha, Regional Frictions, Ibid.
25. Macro and Micro economics are only higher or lower levels of aggregation and shades into one another (Ibid. p. 810).

लेखक के इन्डियन इकोनौमिक जर्नल 1986 में छपे 'पूंजीवादी मंदी और पूर्ति-पक्षी अर्थशास्त्र (अंग्रेजी में) का भावानुवाद।

37

YOU'VE NOTHING TO LOSE BUT MARX

Abu Abraham

Millions of people around the world must have been amazed and shocked as they saw on their television screens the frenzied scenes of youthful mobs pulling down or desecrating statues of Marx and Lenin in various parts of Soviet Russia. And, it could not have been only the Marxists who were shocked; others must have been, too.

But history is unlikely to take into account the current turbulence in the Soviet Union and its stormy effect when it gives its final judgement on Marx and the influence his ideas have had on society in the last hundred years. There may be differences of opinion in the assessment of Marx, but no serious historian can belittle the role he had to play in our contemporary world.

I have been reading an old classic (that is, 30 years old), The Future of Socialism by Anthony Crossland, one of the leading ideologues of the British Labour Party. He was not a Marxist, and he belonged to the liberal centre in the Labour Party spectrum. The Left generally labelled him Right. He believed that Marx had little or nothing to offer the contemporary democratic socialist, either in respect of practical policy, or in the correct analysis of modern society. 'His prophesies have been almost without exception falsified and his conceptual tools are now quite inappropriate."

Crossland went on to say (and I shall let him speak for me, too): 'But this is no reason for adopting the current fashion (he was writing in 1961), and sneering either at the man or his achievement. Intellectually he remains a towering giant amongst socialist thinkers, a man of the stature, in other fields, of Freud and Keynes, and very few others over the last hundred years. His analytical insight into the essential, dynamic nature of nineteenth-century capitalism, the range and sweep of his interests, his grasp of the crude reality underlying the surface parliamentary struggles, his passionate conviction, the wit and compelling power of his language–all these, even now, have an electric effect on the reader, and make the work of his countemporaries amongst the classical economists seem by comparision flat, pedestrian and narrowly circumscribed.

"And his astonishing output was the work of a man in constant pain, who was often underfed, always poor, living usually in conditions of squalor and privation... the man was a dedicated genius; and only moral dwarfs, or people devoid of imagination, sneer at men like that."

Precisely, there are many who are seemingly going through a kind of spurious euphoria at the sight of the Soviet Communist system collapsing and Communist and socialist ideology being stood on its head.

However, what is important, and also very essential, is that socialists everywhere must constantly review their ideas and revise their aims. This is where Soviet Communist failed. They simply accepted their dogmas as immutable and permanent. They never tolerated dissidence or even intellectual argument. True Marxists always claimed that such differences were a consequence of class divisions and conflict of economic interests. This intolerance was a fatal flaw in the Communist system.

In Britain, on the other hand, socialist ideas developed in a variety of ways, starting as a movement of ways. Starting as a movement to assert the rights of the ordinary industry worker, British socialism, with the intellectual support of the educated middle classes, took many forms, absorbed different doctrines. Owenism, Chartism, Marxism, Christian Socialism, Fabianism and Guild Socialsm, all were supported at the same time. In every decade and with every new generation, British socialists discussed with diligence and vehemence the social and political trends in their society and accordingly revised their views on the means and the ends of socialism.

Many traditional views had to change, because capitalism itself was changing, largely because of the impact of socialist action. The old dogmatism about individualism and competition, the unconditional right to private property and the unfettered exercise of private rights, all this had mellowed a great deal.

In the United States, anything that remotely resembles egalitarianism is frowned upon as 'creeping socialism'. On the other hand, unlike in Britain, American society is not classbound and therefore social mobility is greater. Thus equality, at least in principle, is open to all to attain.

The relevance of socialism in the sense of a struggle for equality and equal oportunities, is greater, in my view, in India than anywhere else. Centuries of caste oppression and oligarchical rule have made the task of acheiving this formidable. But I see no other way of bringing about a just society than by the State intervening on a massive scale on the side of the poor and the oppressed.

Neither private enterprise nor State enterprise have a monopoly of virtue but the general aim must be to narrow the gap between the excessively rich and the abysmally poor. We will then understand what a waste of human resources our brand of feudalism and capitalist enterprise has been throughout our history.

In India, in the last two decades, there has been no serious debate on what form an Indian model of socialism should take. There has been no cohesive thinking on these matters even at our party conferences. Our intellectuals, many of the leading ones, have spent their mental energies on denigrating political personalities, on character assassination. We have indulged in intellectual bitchliness and strife rather than constructive and cooperative thinking. Many have already declared communism dead, prematurely, in my view. (After all there is still China–a quarter of the world's population–to reckon with).

Not only that, some are now prepairing to preside over the demise of democratic socialism. 'Public sector should be consigned to the dustbin of history' recommends a Gandhian and former member of the planning Comission. Such sloganisd thinking is part of the current mood. America, having shown its power in Iraq, is being seen as the leader of the world and as a role model.

But the United States with all its power and seeming prosperity, built over some centuries on its own as well as other people's resources, still has open sores on its body. Its level of unemployment, its slums and its homeless, are no recommendation for a new capitalist world order.

In contrast, Sweden, despite some of its recent difficulties in the management of its economy, still stands as a proud nation, conscious of its role as a model socialist state. Others in the West have praised it as the 'conscience of the world'. It is free of slums, has bountiful social benefits and enlightened employers and unions. It is on the whole a rational and humane country and almost free of violence.

A recent study on Swedish socialism done by an American professor at Harvard Univeristy, Steven Kelman, has noted that the Social Democrats have been lately modifying their policies to take into account the changes in the world economy. But they still have a fast rate of growth and they spend 60 percent of the GN'P on welfare –health insurance, housing subsidies, child allowances, sickness pay, disability pensions, government paid parental leave, now 18 months for each child, and day-care subsidies.

Such humanitarian values are the core of socialism. They spring from a belief in social equality which is the ethical inspiration of every socialist doctrine and is certainly not the stuff of which the dustbins of history should be full.

By Courtesy Hindustan Times, Sept. 15, 1991.

खण्ड-3

जन समाजवाद

(The Third Path)

38

विकल्प की खोज में 'वर्ल्ड सोशल फोरम' (QUEST FOR ALTERNATIVE)

प्रकाश लुईस

1990 के दशक से विश्व स्तर पर एक विशेष आर्थिक प्रक्रिया दिखती है जिसे 'नया वर्ल्ड इकोनॉमिक ऑर्डर' कहा जा रहा है। इसके आधारभूत तत्व हैं–उदारीकरण, निजीकरण व भूमंडलीकरण।

कुछ हद तक यह प्रक्रिया स्वतः स्फूर्त हो रही है पर हाल के वर्षों में इसे वांछित दिशा देने के लिए कुछ सांगठनिक प्रयास भी हुए हैं। 'वर्ल्ड इकोनॉमिक फोरम' एक ऐसा ही मंच है जो मूलतः पश्चिम के विकसित देशों की आर्थिक नीतियों को नियमन देता है। हर वर्ष जनवरी में इसकी बैठक स्वीट्जरलैंड के दावोस नामक नगर में होती है।

ठीक इस प्रक्रिया के समानान्तर एक और प्रयास हाल के वर्षों में आरम्भ हुआ है। एक तरह से यह नये वर्ल्ड इकोनॉमिक ऑर्डर के शिकार हो रहे सामान्य जनों, मजदूरों व सभी अभिवंचित समूहों के लिए एक वैचारिक व सांगठनिक मंच प्रदान करना है। 'वर्ल्ड सोशल फोरम' जिसको प्रथमतः ब्राजील के कुछ राजनीतिक–सामाजिक्र कार्यकर्ताओं ने आरम्भ किया आज एक विश्व स्तरीय मंच बन चुका है। मूलतः वैश्वीकरण की आर्थिक प्रक्रिया के विरोध में तमाम सामाजिक ष्टाक्तियों को मुखरित करनेवाला एक केन्द्र। विकेन्द्रीकरण एवं फेडरलिज्म को मान्यता देते हुए इसकी चुनौतियाँ समानता के आदर्शों को मानने वाली एक राजनीतिक–आर्थिक विश्व संरचना का भी निर्माण है। चूँकि 'समाजवाद' या कम्युनिस्ट राज्य व्यवस्थायें वैचारिक तौर पर पटाक्षेप में चली गयी हैं एक नई बौद्धिक एवं वैचारिक परिकल्पना भी वैकल्पिक व्यवस्था की मांग है और इसमें

भी ढेरों अन्तर्द्वन्द मौजूद हैं। हाल ही में सम्पन्न हुए 'वर्ल्ड सोशल फोरम' के मुम्बई सम्मेलन पर प्रस्तुत है यह रिपोर्ट–अपेक्षाओं और सम्भावनाओं को लेकर समालोचनात्मक दृष्टि देता हुआ।

इस वर्ष की शुरूआत दो प्रमुख मुद्दों की चर्चा पर केन्द्रित रही। पहला, अप्रैल महीने में होने वाला आम चुनाव। लोक लुभावन घोषणायें, फीलगुड' और 'शाईनिंग इन्डिया' की चर्चाएँ। एक तरह से देश को आश्वस्त करता हुआ कि उदारीकरण-वैश्वीकरण की नीतियाँ कितनी कारगर हुई हैं। दूसरा मुद्दा रहा, मुम्बई में आयोजित 'वर्ल्ड सोशल फोरम' के सम्मेलन की जो जनवरी माह में ही सम्पन्न हुआ। हॉलाकि प्रिंट एवं इलेक्ट्रॉनिक मीडिया में यह मुख्य खबर नहीं बन पाया फिर भी सम्मेलन के आयोजन के पूर्व जो अपेक्षायें बनीं और इसके आयोजन के दौरान उठाये गये सवालों को उजागर करने की दिशा में मीडिया ने जो काम किया उसे वर्ल्ड सोशल फोरम और भी चर्चा का विषय बना रहा।

भारत की औद्योगिक राजधानी मुम्बई में 16 से 21 जनवरी, 2004 तक यह सम्मेलन चला। भारत एवं अन्य दक्षिण एशियाई सहित विश्व के करीबन 100 देशों से आये लोगों ने अपनी बातों को रखा, विचारों का आदान-प्रदान किया, स्थानीय एवं राष्ट्रीय तथा अन्तरर्राष्ट्रीय मुद्दों पर बहस की और एक बेहतरीन दुनिया के निर्माण के लिए विकल्प की संभावनाओं पर केन्द्रित रहे। वैश्वीकरण के विरूद्ध विकल्प को तलाशने को निकले करीबन 1 लाख लोगों के बीच एक अजीब सा उत्साह दिखा। विविधता में एकता के एक से एक मिसाल भी यहाँ दिखे। भारत के विभिन्न क्षेत्रों की पारम्परिक वेशभूषा, अनगिनत नृत्य-नाटक, अपने विचारों एवं वेदनाओं को हजारों लोगों के सामने रखने में कारगर हुये भारत के कोने-कोने से आये लोग एवं अनेक समूह मंडलियाँ। इसलिए यह स्वभाविक था कि कुछ लोगों ने इसे महामेला की संज्ञा दी।

गोरेगाँव के नेस्को मैदान में इकट्ठे सामाजिक कार्यकर्ताओं, स्वयंसेवी संगठनों, बुद्धिजीवियों, युवा एवं महिला संगठनों का यह एक बड़ा जनसैलाब दिखायी पड़ा जिससे नेस्कों मैदान गूंज उठा–'सम्भव है एक बेहतर दुनिया, आइए हम सब मिलकर इसका निर्माण करें।' कुल 6 दिनों तक चले इस सामाजिक कुंभ में 12 सम्मेलनों, 36 संगोष्ठियाँ एवं 1,200 कार्यशालाओं का आयोजन हुआ जिनमें पूरे 1 लाख प्रतिनिधियों ने अपनी पूरी भागीदारी निभायी। सम्भवतः इन सारे लोगों के मन में एक ही बुनियादी बात थी–हमारे समाज, देश और विश्व भर में जो कुछ भी हो रहा है, क्या वह सही है? कम से कम गरीब-भूखों के संदर्भ में यह विचार स्पष्ट रूप से रखा गया कि इस वैश्वीकरणकी प्रक्रिया के लाभ पुनः एक बार

साधन-सम्पन्न और शक्तिशाली, मात्र 20% उच्च वर्ग तक ही सीमित होकर रह गए हैं। भूमंडलीकरण की प्रक्रिया में एक बार फिर मेहनतकश आवाम और गरीब महिलायें वंचित रह जायेगें, बल्कि शोषित किये जायेंगे। वे इस बात को बार-बार दुहरा रहे थे कि भूमंडलीकरण की प्रक्रिया को बनाये रखने के लिए उन्हें ही अभूतपूर्व कुर्बानियाँ चुकानी होंगी। शोषण, उत्पीड़न और दमन के कुचक्र के फँसे इस आम आवाम को इस कारण भी विकल्प के लिए वचनबद्ध होना होगा।

इससे पहले कि भूमंडलीकरण के विरूद्ध उभरे हुए अन्तरराष्ट्रीय संगठन के विषय में हम चर्चा करें, वैश्वीकरण से जुड़ी अनेक बातों पर चर्चा आवश्यक है। आये दिन राष्ट्रीय एवं अन्तरराष्ट्रीय स्तर पर देखने को मिलता है कि कुछ लोग वैश्वीकरण के पक्षधर हैं तो कुछ लोग पूरी तरह इसके विरोध में। इसी तरह कुछ लोग वैश्वीकरण को सभी देशों को आर्थिक संकट से उबरने के एक नये आयाम के रूप में देखते हैं, यह तर्क देते हुए कि इसके परिणामस्वरूप आज पहले से कहीं ज्यादा नई तकनीकी एवं नये-नये अविष्कार एक देश से दूसरे देश में बिना किसी रूकावट के पहुँच रहे हैं, और इसके कारण ही आर्थिक आयाम में विकास आया है। इन नये आविष्कारों की बदौलत ही गम्भीर बीमारों एवं अनवरत भुखमरी पर काबू पाने की उम्मीद जगी है। इतना ही नहीं, नयी तकनीक के विकास से सूचना एवं संचार में बेइंतहाँ परिवर्तन आया है। इसका एक बुनियादी प्रभाव मानवाधिकारों के क्षेत्र में भी दिखता है, यानी कि मानवाधिकारों के उल्लंघन का विरोध आज इससे जुड़े संगठन न केवल स्थानीय स्तर पर बल्कि राष्ट्रीय एवं अन्तरराष्ट्रीय स्तर पर भी उठा पाने में सक्षम हुए हैं। यह भी दावा किया जाता है कि इस नई प्रक्रिया से न केवल औद्योगिक क्षेत्र में बल्कि कृषि क्षेत्र में भी अभूतपूर्व विकास आया है। साथ ही मुद्रास्फीति में गिरावट आयी है और रोजगार बढ़ने के आसार जगे हैं। भूमण्डलीकरण ने एक तरह से पूरे आर्थिक आयाम में राष्ट्रीय सीमाओं को तोड़ने का काम किया है। इसके दो पक्ष तो साफ दिख रहे हैं। एक तो यह कि वैश्वीकरण के कारण ही आज लाभ दूर-दूर तक आव्रजन कर पाते हैं, न केवल उच्च शिक्षा प्राप्त विशेषज्ञ बल्कि तकनीकी शिक्षा प्राप्त लोगों का भी एक बड़ा समूह एक देश से दूसरे देश जाकर रोजी-रोटी प्राप्त कर रहे हैं। दूसरा, भूमण्डलीकरण का एक और नारा है संपूर्ण विश्व को एक सूत्र में बाँधना', जिसका आपेक्षित परिणाम है कि इंसान जाति, वर्ग, क्षेत्र, धर्म इत्यादि जैसे सामाजिक प्रकोष्ठों से ऊपर उठकर विश्व नागरिक बन जाना।

दूसरी ओर वैश्वीकरण का विरोध करने वालों का मानना है कि यह प्रक्रिया विकसित देशों के उच्च वर्गीय समूहों को भले ही कुछ लाभ दे पाया हो, आम

जनता के लिए, खास कर निम्न-मध्यमवर्गीय परिवारों एवं गरीब मजदूरों, महिलाओं, दलितों एवं आदिवासियों के लिए यह हानिकारक सिद्ध हुआ है। इसके प्रभाव से राष्ट्र की सम्प्रभुता खतरे में पड़ जाने की सम्भावनायें दिख रही हैं–अब राष्ट्रीय सरकारें शासन के लिए संपूर्णतः जिम्मेदार नहीं, बल्कि विश्व बाजार की शक्तियाँ या कॉरपोरेट कम्पनियाँ, किसी भी देश की तकदीर तय करेंगी। एक भरोसा यह भी दिया जाता है कि जहाँ पर राष्ट्रीय शासनतंत्र मजबूत हैं उन देशों में ज्यादा घबड़ाने की जरूरत नहीं, परन्तु पहले से संकटग्रस्त एवं समस्याओं से घिरे देशों में यह निश्चित तौर पर अस्थिरता उत्पन्न कर सकती है। इतना ही नहीं, वैश्वीकरण से जुड़ी उदारीकरण की नीतियों के बदौलत जो विशेष प्रावधान कमजोर वर्गों को उपलब्ध होता था वे भी समाप्त किये जायेंगे। इससे इन वंचित वर्गों को जीवन बद से बदतर होता चला जायेगा।

इस तरह खगोलीकरण की प्रक्रिया के पक्ष और विपक्ष में उठती आवाजें अंततः स्थानीय एवं राष्ट्रीय सीमाओं को पार कर अब अंतरराष्ट्रीय मंच प्राप्त कर चुका है। गौरतलब है कि वैश्वीकरण की वकालत करने वालों का यह भी मानना है कि भूमंडलीकरण की प्रक्रिया उच्च स्तरीय विकास के दौर में स्वाभाविक है और इसका कोई विकल्प नहीं। इनका नारा है 'देयर इज नो ऑल्टर्नेटिव' (टीना), यानी वैश्वीकरण का कोई विकल्प नहीं है। इसके ठीक विपरीत, विरोधी पक्ष का मानना है कि वैश्वीकरण का विकल्प न होना एक मिथ्या है। इनके अनुसार बाजार की ताकतें इस मिथ्या भ्रम के प्रचार-प्रसार से ही अपना वर्चस्व बनाये रखना चाहती है। इस खेमें का यह भी मानना है कि 'देयर आर मेनी ऑल्टर्नेटिव्स' (टामा), यानी वैश्वीकरण के कई विकल्प है। इनके बीच जभी कुछ लोगों का कहना है कि 'सोसलिज्म इज द अॅल्टर्नेटिव' (सीता), यानी वैश्वीकरण का एक निश्चित विकल्प समाजवाद है। इससे जुड़ा नारा है 'दूसरी दुनिया संभव है, आइये हम सब मिलकर इसका निर्माण करें।'

इस तरह वैश्वीकरण की प्रक्रिया एवं उनके परिणामों के विरोध में विकल्प ढूँढने की जो यह मुहिम विश्वस्तर पर प्रारम्भ हुई है उसी ने एक दौर में विश्व-सामाजिक मंच (वर्ल्ड सोशल फोरम) का रूप ले लिया। पूरे विश्वस्तर पर जोभी व्यक्ति, संगठन, संस्था, समुदाय या सरकार वैश्वीकरण के विकल्प की खोज में थे वे सभी सर्वप्रथम ब्राजील के एक शहर पोतों एलेग्रो में इकट्ठे हुए जब यह मंच उभर कर सामने आया। 2001 में आयोजित इस सम्मेलन में करीब 20,000 लोग शामिल हुए थे। यहाँ कुल मिलाकर 458 गोष्ठियाँ व विचार-विमर्श के कार्यक्रम हुए थे। 2002 में पुनः दूसरा सम्मेलन वहीं ब्राजील में ही हुआ और

करीब 40,000 लोग शरीक हुए यहाँ करीबन 745 कार्यक्रम तथा विचार-चिन्तन आयोजित हुए। फिर 2003 में तीसरा सम्मेलन सम्पन्न हुआ (ब्राजील में ही) जिसमें 80,000 लोग शामिल हुए और यहाँ 1,358 कार्यक्रम आयोजित हुए। इसी प्रक्रिया को जारी रखते हुए यह चौथा सम्मेलन मुम्बई में सम्पन्न हुआ जो ब्राजील से बाहर किसी भी दूसरे देश में आयोजित इस मंच का पहला सम्मेलन था।

'वर्ल्ड इकोनॉमिक फोरम' बनाम 'वर्ल्ड सोशल फोरम'

'वर्ल्ड सोशल फोरम' के बारे में लोगों की एक और जिज्ञासा है कि यह हर बार जनवरी महीने में ही क्यों आयोजित होता है? दरअसल यह वर्ल्ड इकोनॉमिक फोरम' के विरोध में जबाव स्वरूप खड़ा किया गया संगठन है और चूँकि उसका आयोजन दावोस (स्वीट्जरलैंड) में हर वर्ष जनवरी महीने में होता रहा है, जाहिर है कि इस मंच के सम्मेलनों के लिए भी यही समय तय किया गया। दावोस में उदारीकरण की प्रक्रिया एवं बाजार-उन्मुख शासन प्रणाली पर नीतियाँ बनायी जाती है।

इस सम्मेलन में जुड़ा दूसरा सवाल यह है कि ब्राजील से सीधे भारत में ही इसका आयोजन क्यों तय हुआ और वह भी मुम्बई में? यह सवाल भी उतना ही स्वाभाविक है। विश्व स्तर पर जो भी लोग या समूह भूमण्डलीकरण के विकल्प ढूँढने में लगे हैं उनक सोच में ब्राजील ने अपनी अग्रणी भूमिका निभायी। अतः इस मंच का पहला, दूसरा एवं तीसरा सम्मेलन वहीं हुआ। परन्तु शुरू से ही यह सोच बनी रही कि यदि विश्व स्तर पर आर्थिक, सामाजिक, राजनैतिक एवं सांस्कृतिक आयामों का विकल्प ढूँढना है तो इस मंच को भी किसी एक देश में स्थाई रूप से नियंत्रित नहीं रहना चाहिए, बल्कि इसके सम्मेलनों का आयोजन हर वर्ष भिन्न-भिन्न देशों में होना चाहिए। बात जब आगे बढ़ी तो यह भी सवाल उठने लगे कि अगर हम वैश्वीकरण के विकल्प को ढूँढने में लगे हैं तो इसके महानायक अमेरिका एवं यूरोपीय महाद्वीपों में इस मंच के सम्मेलनों का आयोजन विडम्बनाओं से भरा होगा। यद्यपि ये महाद्वीप आर्थिक रूप से ऐसे आयोजनों के लिये अधिक समृद्ध हैं, फिर भी यह विकल्प ढूँढने की प्रक्रिया में शायद आत्मघाती होगा। इसी विचार के तहत् इसके आयोजन में दक्षिण अमेरिका, अफ्रीका एवं एशियाई देशों को प्राथमिकता देने का फैसला किया गया। दूसरे, भारत विकासशील देशों में एक अग्रणी देश है जहाँ दलित, आदिवासी, मजदूर, महिलायें, पर्यावरण, भूमि आन्दोलनों के साथ-साथ साम्प्रदायिक और फासीवादी ताकतों के विरूद्ध अनगिनत और महत्वपूर्ण आन्दोलन खड़े होते रहे हैं। पिछले एक दशक में भारतीय शासकों की

उदारीकरण नीति के विरूद्ध अनेकों जनसंगठन एवं जनान्दोलन मुखरित हुए हैं। जिस प्रकार यह देश विविधता में एकता के लिए बहुचर्चित है उसी प्रकार यहाँ जातिवाद, सामंतवाद, पुरुष प्रधानता, साम्प्रदायिकता और निजीकरण के विविध विकल्प भी ढूँढे जा रहे हैं।

वर्ल्ड सोशल फोरम, 2004 का आयोजन भारत में करने के पीछे एक और भी कारण है। ठीक एक वर्ष पहले यहाँ एशियन सोशल फोरम का आयोजन सफलतापूर्वक किया जा चुका था। 2 से 7 जनवरी, 2003 तक हैदराबाद के निजाम कॉलेज मैदान में सम्पन्न इस सम्मेलन में (जो एशियाई स्तरपर उभरे इस फोरम का पहला सम्मेलन था) विश्व के विभिन्न भागों से 15,000 से ज्यादा सामाजिक एवं राजनैतिक कार्यकर्ता, स्वयंसेवी संगठनों के सदस्य, बुद्धिजीवी, युवा मंचों के कार्यकर्त्ता, दलित, आदिवासी तथा नारी संगठनों के प्रतिनिधि जमा हुए थे। वैश्वीकरण के कुप्रभावों के साथ-साथ शान्ति एवं सुरक्षा, विकास, व्यापार, कर्ज एवं पूंजीनिवेश का उभरता स्वरूप, राष्ट्र, प्रजातंत्र एवं बहिष्कृत आवाम, सामाजिक संरचना व मूलभुत सुविधायें, पर्यावरण, संस्कृति एवं सामाजिक ज्ञान इत्यादि विविध विषयों पर चर्चाएँ हुई थीं। इसी तजुर्बे को मन में रखते हुए देश की स्वयंसेवी संस्थायें, कुछ डोनर संस्थायें, बुद्धिजीवी समाज एवं सामाजिक कार्यकर्ताओं ने मिलकर वर्ल्ड सोशल फोरम का आयोजन भारत में करने की जिम्मेदारी ली। मुंबई में इसके आयोजन के पीछे एक महानगर की सुविधाओं की उपलब्धता के साथ श्रम संगठनों से मिलने वाली सक्रिय कार्यकर्त्ताओं की बड़ी संख्या भी एक महत्वपूर्ण कारण बनी। साथ में यहाँ साम्प्रदायिक ताकतों, स्वयंसेवक संघ एवं शिवसेना का बोलबाला या फिर वंचित वर्ग के दो अग्रदूत–महात्मा ज्योतिराव फूले एवं डा० भीमराव अम्बेडकर की मजबूत राजनीतिक धारा का होना भी एक महत्वपूर्ण बात थी। अगला सम्मेलन अफ्रीका के किसी देश में आयोजित करने की बात तय हुई है।

गोरेगाँव के मैदान में आयोजित इस महामेले में जिन चार प्रमुख मुद्दों पर विचार-विमर्श हुआ वे हैं–

- सैन्यवाद, युद्ध और अमन
- मीडिया, सूचना एवं ज्ञान
- प्रजातंत्र, पर्यावरण एवं आर्थिक सुरक्षा
- सामाजिक बहिष्कार, आत्मसम्मान और मानवाधिकार

भारत के कोने-कोने में आये करीब एक लाख लोगों ने अपनी उपस्थिति का एहसास अपने मोर्चे के प्रदर्शन, नाच-गानों, नुक्कड़-नाटकों, संगोष्ठी व कार्यशालाओं के जरिये कराया। इनमें भी दलित, आदिवासी, महिलाएँ एवं अल्पसंख्यक समुदायों ने अपनी मुद्दों को सफलतापूर्वक रखा। इनके कार्यक्रमों में एक तुलनात्मक संदर्भ भी था। साधारणतया गणतंत्र या स्वतंत्रता दिवस के अवसरों पर आयोजित दिखावे वाले आदिवासी नृत्यों से बहुत भिन्न यहाँ जुटे आदिवासी समुहों ने अपना जमीन-स्तरीय प्रदर्शन के माध्यम से अपनी व्यथा एवं संकल्प को कहीं अधिक परिपक्वता के साथ रख पाने में सफलता हासिल की। इसी प्रकार हमेशा ऊँची जातियों एवं उच्च वर्गों के शादी-श्राद्ध समारोहों में बाजा बजाने वाले दलित समूहों ने भी न केवल अपने विचारो को रखा बल्कि ढोल-नगाड़े बजाकर एक वैकल्पिक समाज की परिकल्पना भी रखी।

एम. आर. सम्मेलन-एक सामानान्तर धारा

गौरतलब है कि गोरेगाँव के नेस्को मैदान के ठीक सामने मुम्बई रेजिस्टेंस, 2004 नामक एक सामानान्तर आयोजन भी इन्हीं दिनों सम्पन्न हुआ जिसका नारा था 'जनसंघर्ष को तेज करो' भूमण्डलीकरण का प्रतिरोध करो, साम्राज्यवाद को ध्वस्त करो और जनता के संसार का निर्माण करो।'

इस सामानान्तर सम्मेलन का मानना था कि अगर वर्ल्ड सोशल फोरम वैश्वीकरण का विरोध करने का एक मंच है तो इसके आयोजन में साम्राज्यवादी ताकतों से आर्थिक मदद लेकर उनका विरोध करने की बात करना एक ढोंग है। इनका यह भी आरोप था कि दूसरी दुनिया का निर्माण, बहस एवं घोषणाओं से नहीं बल्कि आम जनता के बुनियादी मुद्दों के लिए संघर्षरत होने से होगा और यह जनान्दोलन को तेज करने से ही संभव है। इससे भी बढ़कर उनका मानना था कि साम्राज्यवाद को सुधारा नहीं जा सकता, उसे ध्वस्त करना होगा। उनका यह भी मानना था कि अगर दूसरी दुनिया पूंजीवादी व्यवस्था के बाहर बनानी है और यह जनता की दुनिया होगी-**तो यह अनिवार्यतः समाजवादी व्यवस्था की ओर ही अग्रसर होगी।**

वर्ल्ड सोशल फोरम की मुम्बई सम्मेलन की समाप्ति पर जो सवाल इसके इर्द-गिर्द उठ रहे हैं उन्हें दो भागों में बाँटा जा सकता है। एक खेमा जो इसके आयोजन से जुड़ा था और काफी सक्रिय रहा उसका मानना है कि इस आयोजन को अदभुत सफलता मिली। परन्तु उन्हें यह नहीं भूलना चाहिए कि जो आम जनता अनेकों मुसीबतों का सामना करके इस बड़े आयोजन में शामिल हुई, उसकी

अपेक्षायें क्या हैं? आलोचकों का यह कहना कि यह विचारों के आदान-प्रदान का एक केन्द्र भर है और इतना कुछ से ही कोई वैकल्पिक संसार के निर्माण की बात नहीं सोची जा सकती–कुछ हद तक सही भी है। परन्तु इस कारण ऐसे प्रयासों को इस नजरिये से पूरी तरह से नकारा भी नहीं जा सकता। आज जो भी सचेत व्यक्ति वर्ल्ड सोशल फोरम के हर पहलू से वाकिफ है वह यह जानता है कि इसका एक निश्चित उद्देश्य और अपनी कार्ययोजना है। इसके अनुयायी भी हैं और इसकी अपनी एक ऐतिहासिक पृष्ठभूमि भी। अतएव मुम्बई सम्मेलन का मूल्यांकन इन्हीं तथ्यों के इर्द-गर्द किया जाना उचित होगा और लाभप्रद भी। यह जरूरी है कि प्रतिवर्ष सिर्फ सम्मेलन कर लेने से बेहतर दुनिया के निर्माण में कोई प्रगति नहीं होती। किन्तु यह निश्चित तौर पर एक बेहतर दुनिया के सृजन हेतु विचार-विमर्श करने का मंच प्रदान करता है। ऐसे सम्मेलनों में न सिर्फ स्थानीय एवं राष्ट्रीय विकल्पों की चर्चाएँ होती हैं बल्कि विश्व स्तर पर लोगों द्वारा प्रयोग में लाये गये वैकल्पिक तौर-तरीकों का भी आदान-प्रदान होता है। आम जनता की भागीदारी में जो उत्साह देखने को मिला वह भी काफी आश्वस्त करता है। हालाँकि एक बेहतर और वैकल्पिक दुनिया के निर्माण की बातें बहुत दूर की लगती हैं, साथ ही उसकी परिकल्पना भी कोई अभी ठोस आकार नहीं ले सका है, फिर भी आमलोगों का विश्वास एक बड़ी चीज होती है। अगर एक ठोस परिकल्पना उभर सकी और उसे विश्व के करोड़ों लोगों तक पहुँचाया जा सकता तो वैकल्पिक दुनिया संभव है। वर्ल्ड सोशल फोरम अभी इन्हीं आरम्भिक तैयारियों में संलग्न है, इसलिए इसे खारिज नहीं किया जा सकता।

एक तीखी आलोचना यह भी है कि इस मंच के इन सम्मेलनों, विशेष कर मुम्बई जैसे महामेले से, न तो कोई प्रस्ताव पारित हुआ न ही कोई कार्ययोजना या रणनीति घोषित हुई। ऐसे आयोजनों पर करोड़ों रुपये खर्च कर कोई कार्यक्रम एवं भविष्य योजना या कोई निश्चित रणनीति का सामने न आना सम्मेलन के आम सहभागियों एवं इस आयोजन के आलोचकों–दोनों के ही समझ से परे हैं। लेकिन इस मंच के प्रायोजित घोषणा-पत्र के अध्ययन से यह साफ होता है कि इस बैनर से न तो कोई प्रस्ताव पारित होने का प्रावधान है और न ही किसी कार्ययोजना की तैयारी की गुंजाइश। बल्कि वर्तमान स्थितियों में मुखरित होते मुद्दों को मात्र उजागर करने का एवं उचित विकल्पों को ढूँढ़ने के लिए यह एक व्यापक और खुला मंच है–किसी भी बदलाव के लिए सम्भवतः पहली एवं मौलिक शर्त की तरह।

मुम्बई सम्मेलन में एक और महत्वपूर्ण बात सामने आयी। वह यह कि यहाँ दलितों, आदिवासियों, महिलाओं एवं असंगठित क्षेत्र के मजदूरों के मुद्दे काफी

चर्चा के विषय बने। याद रहे 2001 में दक्षिण अफ्रीका के डरबन शहर में नस्लवाद के विरूद्ध जो अन्तरराष्ट्रीय सम्मेलन हुआ था उसमें पहली बार भारत के दलित समूहों ने अपने मुद्दों को अन्तरराष्ट्रीय समुदाय के समक्ष रखने में सफलता पायी थी। इस बार भी दलितों एवं आदिवासियों ने अपने जीवन संघर्षों को तमाम माध्यमों से व्यक्त किया। चूँकि इन समूहों के कलाकार काफी मात्रा में उपस्थित थे इसलिए इनकी पहचान कि सफलतापूर्वक उजागर हुई। इतना ही नहीं कई संगोष्ठियों एवं कार्यशालाओं में वे खुद ही वक्ता बने। यद्यपि भारतीय मीडिया ने ऐसी अनेकों सच्चाईयों को नजरअंदाज किया, फिर भी वहाँ उपस्थित अन्तरराष्ट्रीय मीडिया के लोगों ने इसे बखूबी महसूस किया।

शायद एक और मुद्दे को उभारने की जरूरत है। पूरे विश्व में सीविल सोसाइटी के सामाजिक-राजनैतिक एवं सांस्कृतिक मुद्दों की अभिव्यक्ति के लिए मीडिया में जो गुंजाइश थी वह धीरे-धीरे सिकुड़ती जा रही है। लोकतांत्रिक देशों में जो सरकारें प्रजातंत्र के नाम पर शासन कर रही हैं धीरे-धीरे फासीवादी, तानाशाही और एकलवादी विचारों तथा व्यवहारों से आप्लावित होती जा रही दिखती हैं। ऐसे में सिविल सोसाइटी के बुनियादी मुद्दों को सत्ताधारियों के समक्ष रखने के लिए लगभग सभी देशों में समय, जगह और गुंजाइश की कटौती होती जा रही है। ऐसी परिस्थिति में सामाजिक-राजनैतिक-सांस्कृतिक कार्यकर्त्ताओं, युवा-महिला संगठनों, दलित-आदिवासी जनसंगठनों एवं तमाम वंचित समुदायों को अपने मुद्दो को उजागर करने के लिए कम से कम एक बेहतरीन अवसर यह फोरम जरूर प्रदान करता है।

फिर इससे ही जुड़ा एक और तथ्य है जिस पर चर्चा होनी चाहिए। वर्ल्ड सोशल फोरम नागरिक समूहों के स्थानीय मुद्दों को राष्ट्रीय, क्षेत्रीय एवं अन्तरराष्ट्रीय मंचों पर चर्चा का विषय बनाने के साथ ही विकल्प की तलाश के लिए एक साझा मंच है। मगर ऐसे आयोजन अगर मात्र विचार-विमर्श या अनुभवों के आदान-प्रदान या फिर व्यथा सुनने-सुनाने तक सीमित रह जाती है तो इसका क्या कोई औचित्य है? इस प्रकार की प्रक्रियाएँ तो ऐसे मंचों के बगैर भी जारी हैं। चूँकि यह एक खुला मंच है और इसमें जो भागीदारी करते हैं वे अपने बल-बूते पर ही, इसलिए यह और भी जरूरी है कि वे पहले से ही तय कर लें कि इस मंच से उनकी अपेक्षायें क्या हैं और बाद में अपनी कार्ययोजना एवं मुद्दों के चयन में या फिर साझा मंच के गठन में उन्हें क्या कुछ करना चाहिए–इसकी स्पष्टता भी कर लें। इसके विपरीत अगर आयोजक कोई बहुत बड़ा करिश्मा कर देने की बात करें और इनके आलोचक केवल खामियों को ही उजागर करने में लगे रहें तो विश्व के

तमाम नागरिक समूहों के सामने जो भी गुंजाइश बन रही है वह समाप्ति हो जायेगी।

तमाम बहसों के बाद, कुछ सवाल फिर भी अनुत्तरित रह जाते हैं। क्या वर्ल्ड सोशल फोरम के सम्मेलन हर वर्ष आयोजित होने चाहिए? इसके आयोजन में जो विशाल राशि खर्च होती हैं वह कहाँ से आयेगी? यह किन-किन स्रोतों से लिया जाये और किन किन से नहीं?

इन सवालों के जबाव जल्द तलाशने चाहिए। अन्यथा यह भी पहले से संचालित कई अन्य मंचों की तरह ही कुछ खास कार्यकर्त्ताओं, बुद्धिजीवियों एवं डोनर संस्थाओं पर निर्भर होकर रह जायेगा ओर फिर इन्हीं की नई दुकान भर ही होगा जो अन्तत: एक बड़ी निराशा को जन्म देगा। यूँ एक बेहतर दुनिया की खोज और वह भी मेहनतकश आवाम के लिये, शायद अब भी स्वप्नलोक के किसी दूर देश की कथा जैसी है। परन्तु यह भी सच है कि मजदूर वर्ग जब भी एकजुट हुआ है तो कुछ खास उभर कर आया है, और यह आगे भी संभव है।

सहयात्री, त्रैमासिक पत्रिका, राँची के सौजन्य से साभार।

39

आधुनिक बनाम पाश्चात्य–तृतीय विकल्प

दत्तोपंत बाबूराव ठेंगड़ी

पहले से ही विचार था कि आधुनिकता माने पश्चिम नहीं है किन्तु वैचारिक दृष्टि से इस विचार को एक आह्वान के रूप में सर्वप्रथम क्लौड अल्वारेज ने अपनी किताब में रखा और प्रश्न किया कि "Western Paradigm is the universal model of progress and development" ऐसा मानना ठीक है क्या? पश्चिम की जो विकास की कल्पना है वही सब देशों की होनी चाहिए यह ठीक है क्या? और उन्होंने यह बताया कि हरेक देश का एक कल्चर है। अपने-अपने कल्चर के मुताबिक विकास का मॉडल होना चाहिए। तो क्लौड अल्वारेज और उनके साथ धर्मपाल जैसे कुछ लोग थे जिन्होंने यह प्रश्न पहले ही उठाया। विकास की कल्पना के बारे में 35 साल पहले मैक्सिको के समाज-सुधारक इवान इलिच इन्होंने आह्वानात्मक प्रश्न quote किया कि विकास की जो तुम्हारी कल्पना है पश्चिम की वह ठीक है क्या? आज 35 साल बाद संयुक्त राष्ट्र की एक कमिटी यू.एन.डी.पी. ने इसी बात का उत्तर दिया कि अभी तक विकास की जो धारणा थी उसमें आमूल परिवर्तन की आवश्यकता है और क्या होना चाहिए–यह यू.एन. डी.पी. कहती है कि अभी तक Man used to revolve round development. Now we should see that development revolves round man. विकास को केन्द्र समझना और इसके इर्द-गिर्द मनुष्य का घूमना–यह आज तक विकास की कल्पना थी, किन्तु मनुष्य को केन्द्र समझकर और विकास का उसके इर्द-गिर्द घूमना यह होना आवश्यक है–ऐसा कहा गया। ये अलग-अलग बातें हैं, इनका अलग-अलग संदर्भ है किन्तु पुस्तक की पृष्ठभूमि समझने के लिए यह आवश्यक है।

अब ऐसा है कि अभी तक हमारे अँग्रेजीदाँ लोगों के मन पर पाश्चात्य विचारों का प्रभाव है। वे संभ्रात लोग हैं। उनके ऊपर तो इन विचारों का ही प्रभाव होगा, लेकिन उनके मन पर पाश्चात्य विचारों का प्रभाव होने के कारण पाश्चात्य कल्चर का भी प्रभाव होना शुरू हो गया है। और ऐसा बताया गया है कि मानसिक गुलामी भी आ रही है। यहाँ तक कि एक श्रेष्ठ संस्कृति वाला यह देश उसमें अमेरिका का जो माइकेल जैक्सन जिनका नाम आप जानते हैं, वह माइकेल जैक्सन कल्चर हमारे देश में भी लोकप्रिय होने लगा है। इसकी मानसिक गुलामी भी अपने यहाँ फैल गयी है।

विचारधारा के नाते अभी तक यह माना जाता था कि साम्यवाद और पूँजीवाद ये दो ही विचारधाराएँ हैं। वैसे तीसरी विचारधारा भी यहाँ थी किन्तु किसी ने उसे गंभीरता से लिया नहीं जिसका नाम समाजवाद था। वैसे सी.एम. जोग ने कहा कि समाजवाद एक ऐसी टोपी है जो किसी भी सर पर ठीक बैठ जाती है। जैसा सिर का का आकार होगा वैसा आकार वह टोपी धारण कर सकती है। पर किसी ने इसको गंभीरता से लिया नहीं। परन्तु जिसको वैज्ञानिक समाजवाद कहा गया जो कम्युनिज्म है, उसको और पूंजीवाद को गंभीरता से लिया गया। अब यह Communism ध्वस्त हुआ है। बीच में एक-दो समाचार जो समाचार पत्रों में आए हैं, उनके कारण भ्रम पैदा हो सकता था। ये जो समाचार पत्रों में समाचार आते हैं वे ऊपरी खतरे हैं और इसके कारण तह में जाने की आवश्यकता है। बीच में ये आया था कि एक दो देशों में कम्युनिस्ट पार्टी फिर से ऊपर आ रही है। कम्युनिस्ट पार्टी न कि कम्युनिज्म ऊपर आ रही है। क्या हो रहा है कि वहाँ जो कम्युनिस्टों को वोट मिला है वह communism को नहीं मिला है, communist party के साइनबोर्ड को मिला है, लेकिन वो नकारात्मक वोट मिला है। कम्युनिज्म जाने के बाद जो प्रस्थापित सरकारें बनी, उन्होंने अपना काम ठीक ढंग से नहीं किया, जनता में असंतोष निर्माण हुआ, और असंतोष के कारण प्रतिस्थापित सरकार को हटाना चाहिए यह विचार आया। यद्यपि किसको लाना यह महत्व की बात नहीं थी और नकारे जानेवाले दल में Communist Party भी एक पार्टी थी, इसके कारण कुछ वोट उसे भी मिला। इतना नहीं मिला, इसमें 25% के करीब, किन्तु वह नकारात्मक वोट था। बहुमत नहीं मिली वह अलग बात थी। 25% भी जो मिला वो नकारात्मक वोट था। केवल उदाहरण देना हो तो आपातकाल के कारण श्रीमती इंदिरा गाँधी बहुत अलोकप्रिय हो गयी थीं। तो इंदिरा गाँधी को हटाना यह विचार जनमानस में था। उन्होंने जनता पार्टी को वोट दिया। जिस समय जनता पार्टी को वोट दिया उस समय जनता पार्टी का ठीक से गठन भी नहीं हुआ

था। उसके सिद्धांत क्या हैं–किसी को पता नहीं था। यह भी निगेटिभ वोट था। लोकनायक जयप्रकाश बाबू को एक व्यक्ति के नाते वह वोट था। जनता पार्टी क्या चीज है किसी को पता नहीं था। और जब जनता पार्टी का शासन कुछ दिन चलने के बाद उससे जब जनता ऊब गयी तो फिर से नकारात्मक वोट के नाते श्रीमती इंदिरा गाँधी को लाया। दोनों नकारात्मक वोट थे। पार्टी का तख्ता और पार्टी का सिद्धांत–इनमें अंतर करना चाहिए। 1947 से आजतक दिल्ली में केन्द्र सरकार हमेशा गाँधीवादी रहीं। दिल्ली में गाँधीवाद है ऐसा कोई कह सकता है क्या? आज कलकत्ता में जो मार्क्सवादी कम्युनिस्ट पार्टी का शासन है, कोई कम्युनिस्ट हिम्मत के साथ कह सकता है कि वह मार्क्सवाद के आधार पर या कम्युनवाद के आधार पर चल रहा है। वो तो स्पष्ट ही पूँजीवाद के और बहुद्देशीय कम्युनियों के सामने गिड़गिड़ा रहे हैं ज्योति बाबू। तो केवल नाम देखने से नहीं होता है। कम्युनिज्म का सिद्धान्त पहले ही पूरा खत्म हुआ है। कम्युनिज्म खत्म होने के बाद पूँजीवाद के समर्थकों ने ये कहना शुरू किया कि अब कम्युनिज्म मानने वाले लोग पूंजीवाद की ओर आ रहे हैं। ये भी बात गलत थी। वे पूंजीवाद की ओर नहीं जा रहे थे, वे उपभोगवाद की ओर जा रहे थे। पूंजीवाद की ओर नहीं और फिर आज दिखता है कि पूंजीवाद भी नीचे जा रहा है। अब ये दोनों सिद्धांत नीचे जा रहे हैं, क्या कारण हैं?

ऐसा है कि ये दोनों सिद्धांत और समाजवाद का सिद्धांत भी इनका निर्माण पिछली शताब्दी के उत्तरार्द्ध में हुआ। उस समय यूरोप में एक हर्षोन्माद था, विज्ञान प्रगति पर था और प्रगति नई होने के कारण लोग उससे इतने प्रभावित थे कि हर्षोन्माद का, यूफोरिया का उन्माद इतना था कि अबतक ईसाइयत ने जो कुछ कहा यह सब गलत है। ईश्वर नाम की कोई चीज नहीं है। अब ईश्वर हमारे कोई टेलिस्कोप में आयेगा तभी हम उसका अस्तित्व मानेंगे नहीं तो हम मानेंगे नहीं। सारे विषयों पर हम विजय प्राप्त करेंगे। प्रकृति पर हम विजय प्राप्त करेंगे। इस तरह और विज्ञान ने उस समय बताया था कि सारे अस्तित्व का मूल तत्व कुछ होगा तो वह वस्तु है। इसके कारण वस्तुवाद में वस्तु यही प्रधान है। Mind is only a super structure of matter और इसके कारण विचार की अलग से चिन्ता करने की आवश्यकता नहीं है। वस्तु ही सब कुछ है। मेरे यहाँ चर्चा चली उन सारी चर्चाओं को बताने की यहाँ आवश्यकता नहीं। ईसाइयत के समर्थकों ने कहा कि विचार प्रधान है। विज्ञान के समर्थकों ने कहा कि वस्तु प्रधान है। तो वस्तु प्रधान है या विचार प्रधान यह चर्चा समाचार पत्रों में इतना चला कि लोग ऊब गये और ये कहा कि चलो अब बन्द करो] What is mind does not matter and what is matter need not mind. ऐसा लोगों ने कहा। लेकिन इस समय मूल बात यह थी कि विज्ञान ने घोषित किया था कि Matter is material (प्रमुख बात वस्तु ही है,) सारा अस्तित्व वस्तु से भरा हुआ है वस्तु छोड़कर वो कुछ नहीं है। ऐसा उन्होंने कहा। उस समय की ये बात है। इसी हर्षोन्माद की अवस्था में ये तीनों सिद्धान्त निर्मित हुए–पूंजीवाद, साम्यवाद और समाजवाद। अब क्या हुआ तो विज्ञान ने तो प्रगति की है। हमारा जो हिन्दू वैश्विक दर्शन है उसके नजदीक विज्ञान आ रहा है। किन्तु 19वी सदी के विज्ञान के आधार पर ये तीनों विचार पद्धतियाँ जो शुरू हुई वे वहीं रही मानो Socialism, communism, capitalism ये तीनों विचार पद्धतियाँ पिछली शताब्दी में रहीं। विज्ञान ने प्रगति की और प्रगति करके पिछली स्थितियाँ उसने छोड़ दी। हिन्दू वैश्विक दर्शन के नजदीक विज्ञान आ रहा है। और इसके कारण विरोधाभास जैसा वहाँ निर्माण हुआ। तो ये सारा वस्तुवाद के आधार पर है। तीनों परस्पर विरोधी हो सकते हैं पर तीनों का गोत्र एक ही है–वस्तुवाद जैसे मेरा गोत्र है गौतम 'त्रिप्रवरा नित्य: गौतम, अंगिरषाय चित:' किन्तु गोत्र है गौतम। वैसे ही त्रिप्रवरा नित्य है– Socialism, capitalism, communism ये हैं भिन्न-भिन्न किन्तु तीनों का गोत्र है–वस्तुवाद और वस्तुवाद धर्म के दायरे से बाहर है।

जिसको हम सनातन धर्म कहते हैं वह दोनों पक्षों की चिन्ता करता है– आध्यात्मिकता और भौतिकता। (Materialism and Spiritualism) These are the two faces of the same coin—ये मानता है। दोनों दो अलग-अलग बातें हैं यह नहीं मानता है। आध्यात्मिक प्रगति और भौतिक प्रगति एक ही सिक्के के दो पहलू हैं ऐसा सनातन धर्म मानता है। इस दृष्टि से सनातन धर्म की सारी रचना है। केवल भौतिकता को लेना सनातन धर्म के दायरे के बाहर है और हमारे शास्त्रों ने कहा है कि जो भी विचार पद्धति या समाज व्यवस्था सनातन धर्म के दायरे के अंतर्गत रहेगी उसके भीतर कभी भी अंतर्विरोध (Internal Self Contradictions) पैदा हो नहीं सकती और जो विचार पद्धति अथवा समाज-व्यवस्था सनातन धर्म के दायरे से बाहर है उसमें अंतर्विरोध (Internal Self Contradiction) अवश्यमेव पैदा होगी। किसी तरह का अंतर्विरोध होने में समय लगता है, हर चीज को, पर अवश्य ही अंतर्विरोध पैदा होगा और ये पद्धतियाँ, ये व्यवस्थाएँ अपने ही अंतर्विरोध के बोझ के नीचे दबकर खत्म होंगी–बाहर से कोई आक्रमण हो या न हो। ऐसा हमारे शास्त्रों में कहा है। यही हश्र हम कम्युनिज्म का देखते हैं। पूँजीवाद की भी यही बात है और हमारे देश में भी पूँजीवाद से भी प्रभावित बहुत लोग हैं। द्वितीय विश्व युद्ध के पश्चात् अमेरिका विश्व का नेता माना गया। उसकी स्थिति

भी अच्छी थी क्योंकि युद्ध-क्षेत्र से दूर होने के कारण उसका नुकसान कम हुआ था। अत: विश्व का नेता माना गया। उनकी व्यवस्था वस्तुवाद के आधार पर चली रही है। सनातन धर्म के आधार पर चलने वाले लोगों का कहना है कि अमेरिका भी ज्यादा देर तक अपने नम्बर एक के स्थिति पर नहीं रह सकता और पूंजीवाद भी वैसे ही जायेगा जैसे कम्युनिज्म गया है। क्योंकि ये सब सनातन धर्म के दायरे से बाहर है। अब जब ये बात कही गयी उस समय पूंजीवाद अमेरिका में अपने चरम उत्कर्ष पर होने के कारण सबने कहा कि यह दिवास्वप्न (Wishful thinkng) है किन्तु आज हम इससे भिन्न स्थिति देखते हैं। यह कहा गया था इस शताब्दी के अंत तक अमेरिका अपना स्थान खो देगा। किन्तु आपको मालूम होगा चार महीना पहले विश्व बैंक ने राष्ट्रीय धन का आकलन किया और इसके आधार पर घोषित किया कि नम्बर एक का स्थान जो अमेरिका का था वह अब आस्ट्रेलिया का है। हमारे देश का स्थान जैसा कि हमारे राज्यकर्ता कहते हैं हमेशा पिछड़ा है, किन्तु अमेरिका का स्थान बारहवाँ हैं ऐसा विश्व बैंक ने घोषित किया। ऐसा सोचा गया था कि अमेरिका 2000 साल तक अपना नम्बर खो बैठेगा पर पिछले साल ही उन्होंने अपना नम्बर खो दिया। अब पूंजीवाद की बात है तो पूंजीवाद नीचे जा रहा है। आज पूंजीवाद के प्रवक्ता भी यह बोल रहे हैं। दुनिया में पूंजीवाद के सबसे बड़े प्रवक्ता सैमुएल्सन माने जाते हैं। उसने कहा कि यह Capitalism नीचे जा रहा है। अब उसका नीचे जाना रोका नहीं जा सकता। इसके कारण अब तीसरे रास्ते की तलाश की आवश्यकता है। ये कहा कि तीसरा रास्ता यदि खोजना है, तो पूंजीवाद समाप्त होने के बाद वह काम हम अमेरिका वाले ही कर सकते हैं। क्योंकि हमारी बौद्धिक प्रगति जितनी दुनिया में किसी के पास नहीं है। तो पूंजीवाद नष्ट होगा तो तीसरा रास्ता दिखाने का काम भी हम ही करेंगे ऐसा उन्होंने कहा।

अपने यहाँ सनातन धर्म मानने वालों ने ऐसा कहा था कि पूंजीवाद इतनी तेजी से नीचे जा रहा है कि दो हजार दसवें साल तक "capitalism will have completely collapsed" यह समाप्त हो गया रहेगा। प्रबंधन शास्त्र के अमेरिका के प्रमुख प्रवक्ता पीटर ड्रकर ने कहा कि पूंजीवाद नष्ट होगा तो कब होगा यह मुहूर्त्त भी बताया जो 2010-2020 के बीच का नौ-दस साल होगा। तो 2010 और 2020 में बहुत ज्यादा का अंतर नहीं है। लेकिन नीचे जा रहा है यह बात वहाँ भी कही है। इसी कारण पश्चिम में भी What is the third way यह चर्चा शुरू हो गयी है। 6-7 साल पहले ही शुरू हो गयी है कि तीसरा मार्ग दुनिया के लिए क्या है? इस पृष्ठभूमि पर एक किताब The third way लिखी

गई है। इसमें जो विचार है वह अद्भुत है, नवीन है ऐसा नहीं है। किन्तु अभी तक ये विचार नहीं प्रकट हो रहे थे, आज प्रकट हो रहे हैं, इसका मूल कारण यह है कि अब तक इन विचारों का ग्रहण करने की क्षमता जनता में नहीं थी। वह साम्यवाद नष्ट हुआ, पूंजीवाद नष्ट हो रहा है यह दिख रहा है, इसके कारण यह मान्यता लोगों के मन में तैयार हो रही है। अत: इस समय यह किताब आयी है।

आज प्रमुख विचार है कि नई व्यवस्था यदि देनी हो तो वो कैसी हो। अब इसके विषय में भी हमारे देश में एक मानसिकता बनी है जो कम्युनिस्टों के कारण बनी है। यहाँ के कम्युनिस्टों ने सबको गुमराह करने के लिए ये प्रचार शुरू किया कि बाकी लोगों के पास कौन-सा नक्शा है–आनेवाले समाज का । जैसे उनके पास नक्शा पहले से है। असल में उनके पास भी कोई नक्शा पहले से नहीं है। वो तो ऐसे ठाठ से बात करते थे जैसे कि सारी दुनिया का क्या होगा वो उनकी जेब में है। अब ये जो मनोवृत्ति है वह लोगों को गुमराह करने वाली जरूर है लेकिन यह सत्य पर आधारित नहीं हैं ऐसा नक्शा हो नहीं सकता, और ऐसा होना भी नहीं चाहिए। होना यह बुद्धिमानी का लक्षण नहीं है, लड़कपन का लक्षण है। कार्ल मार्क्स को उनके फ्रांसिसी कम्युनिस्ट पार्टी के जवानों ने एक प्रार्थना की थी चूँकि मार्क्स को पत्र लिखना कठिन था इसलिए एंगल्स को पत्र लिखा कि हमारी प्रार्थना मार्क्स को बताइये। दो प्रार्थनाएँ बतायीं। पहली प्रार्थना थी कि हम अपने को कम्युनिस्ट कहते हुए प्रसन्न नहीं हैं। हम अपने को मार्क्सवादी कहना चाहते हैं। इसकी इजाजत देनी चाहिए और दूसरी प्रार्थना कहा कि अब समय आ गया है कि हमें कम्युनिस्ट समाज का मूल रूप स्पष्ट करना चाहिए। तो इन प्रश्नों के बारे में मार्क्स ने कहा कि ये फ्रांसिसी कम्युनिस्ट पार्टी के जवान लोग बहुत भावुक दिखते हैं। मार्क्सवादी जो अपने को कहने के विचार में उन्होंने कहा कि what I know is that I am not a marxist यहीं छोड़ दिया। और मूल तथ्य के बारे में उन्होंने कहा कि वो क्या ऐसा समझते हैं कि जब किसी भी देश में कम्युनिज्म के मुताबिक समाज रचना करने का समय आ जायेगा तो समाज रचना करने वाले लोग एक हाथ में हम आज जो लिख रहे हैं वह Text book लेंगे और दूसरे हाथ से रचना करेंगे-ऐसा मानते हैं क्या? वो तो उस समय की परिस्थितियाँ, उस समय की आवश्यकताएँ, उस समय की मानसिकता–इसके आधार पर समाज रचना करेंगे। हाँ, मार्गदर्शक सिद्धांत उसके प्रकाश में रचना होगी। ये मार्गदर्शक सिद्धांत हमारे दिये गये हैं लेकिन कैसे समाज का चित्र होगा यह आज जो हमने लिखा तो यह देखकर कोई समाज रचना करेगा क्या? यह मार्क्स का वाक्य है कि They will care a lack for what we write today; आज हम लिखते हैं उसकी वो फिक्र भी नहीं करेंगे।

एम.एन. राय ने साम्यवाद को लाँघकर रैडिकल मानववाद के सिद्धांत का प्रतिपादन बहुत अच्छे ढंग से किया। लेकिन उसके मुताबिक जो समाज रहेगा उसका Final Ideal Structure क्या रहेगा-ये बताने का समय भी आया तो राय ने यूटोपीया का मतलब समझाया। अंतिम और आदर्श रूप प्राप्त कर लेने के बाद आगे प्रगति अखण्ड होनी चाहिए। राय ने कहा कि प्रगति यदि अखण्ड होनी चाहिए तो कोई भी Social Picture–ये Final and binding नहीं माना जा सकता है।

हाँ आज की इस अवस्था से अगली अवस्था तक, अगली अवस्था से उससे अगली अवस्था तक यह बात अलग है लेकिन अंतिम स्थिति ऐसा चित्र देना इसका मतलब है वहाँ तक पहुँच जाने के बाद फिर प्रगति की आवश्यकता समाप्त होती है। तो फिर गतिरोध ही आना चाहिए। यथा स्थिति रहना चाहिए ठहराव आना चाहिए–Do you want stgnation? उन्होंने कहा stagnation नहीं। इसलिए ऐसा चित्र नहीं देना चाहिए यह राय ने कहा। उन्होंने ऐसा कहा कि धारणा देना गलत है। जो भविष्य तक हम सोचते हैं वह क्षितिज के समान होना चाहिए ऐसा उन्होंने कहा। क्षितिज हमसे उतना दूर है। हम दो मील यदि क्षितिज की ओर जाते हैं तो क्षितिज हमसे उतना ही आगे खिसकता जाता है। तो हमेशा प्रगति की स्थिति ही समाज में रहे, ऐसा हम मानते हैं। हमेशा Ideal and Final स्थिति नहीं दिया जा सकता। तो दिशा-निर्देश देनी चाहिए। ब्लू प्रिंट की बात करना, जो कम्युनिस्टों ने लोगों को बतायी गुमराह करने के लिए (क्योंकि उनके पास भी ब्लू प्रिन्ट नहीं था केवल दिशा-निर्देश थे) तो आगे यदि प्रगति करनी है तो दिशा-निर्देश चाहिए और हमारे यहाँ दिशा-निर्देश धर्म है। उनके यहाँ भी एक बार प्रयास हुआ दिशा-निर्देश देने का। वह सफल नहीं हुआ हम जानते हैं। पहली बार मैग्नाकार्टा 1215 में जो आया उस समय लोकतंत्र के कुछ अधिकार माँगे गये लेकिन सिद्धांत में एक बार फ्रांसिसी क्रांति के पहले आयी स्वतंत्रता, समता, बन्धुता लेकिन डा० बाबा साहेब अम्बेदकर ने कहा कि मैं भी स्वतंत्रता-समता और बन्धुत्व को मानता हूँ लेकिन फ्रांसिसी क्रांति और इसके पश्चात यूरोप में ये तीनों सिद्धांत/प्रस्थापित नहीं हो सके। बाबा साहेब ने कहा कि स्वतंत्रता सिद्ध हुई तो समता बिगड़ गई समता को लाने का प्रयास हुआ तो स्वतंत्रता समाप्त हो गयी; स्वतंत्रता और समता दोनों एक साथ नहीं आ सके और इसका कारण उन्होंने बताया कि तीसरा जो महत्वपूर्ण सिद्धांत था बंधुत्व, फ्रेटरनीटी वह आयी ही नहीं और बंधुत्व जब तक

नहीं आता तो स्वतंत्र ओर समानता साथ-साथ आ नहीं सकते और बंधुत्व जो है उसी को डा० बाबा साहेब अम्बेदकर ने कहा कि उसी को हमारे यहाँ धर्म कहा गया है।

धर्म की भूमिका

धर्म इसके आधार पर जो होगा उसे सामान्य दिशा-निर्देश हम कहते हैं वह धर्म है, और धर्म के आधार पर जो रचना होगी वही चिरस्थायी हो सकती है क्योंकि धर्म का मतलब ही है धारणा करने वाला। अब धर्म शब्द के विषय में, हिन्दू शब्द के विषय में पर्याप्त गलतफहमियाँ हैं। इसका विरोध करनेवालों में हैं ऐसा नहीं इसका समर्थन करनेवालों में भी हैं। ये बड़ी दुखद बात है। धर्म और हिन्दू शब्दों का समर्थन करनेवालों में भी दोनों धारणाओं के बारे में मतभेद हैं यह बड़ी दुखद बात है, थोड़े शब्दों में मैं ये स्पष्ट करना चाहता हूँ। धर्म का अर्थ है धारणा करनेवाला-जीवन की धारणा करनेवाला। व्यक्ति-जीवन की धारणा करनेवाला व्यक्ति धर्म, समाज जीवन की धारणा करनेवाला समाज धर्म, मानव जीवन की धारण करनेवाला मानव धर्म, विश्व जीवन की धारणा करनेवाला विश्वधर्म। हर स्तर पर जीवन की धारणा करनेवाला जो तत्व है, वह उस स्तर पर धर्म है। ऐसा अपने यहाँ माना गया और इस दृष्टि से धर्म का अर्थ रेलिजन नहीं है, पूजा विधि नहीं है। इसी कारण हिन्दू जो सनातन धर्म कोलेकर चलते हैं वो किसी एक रीलीजन को लेकर नहीं चल रहे हैं। हिन्दुओं के कई रिलीजन हैं। लोगों में पहले अंग्रेजीदाँ लोग जो अपने बारे में कुछ नहीं जानते थे उन्होंने धर्म का भाषान्तर किया। रेलिजन याने पंथ यानि कि उपासना पद्धति। एक मत हिन्दुओं की कौन-सी उपासना की एक पद्धति है? कोई वेदों को मानता है कोई नहीं मानता है। कोई आस्तिक है, कोई नास्तिक है। कोई एक देवता को मानता है कोई दूसरे देवता को मानता है। वो भी कहने वाले कोई हिन्दु ही थे जो कहते थे "त्रयोदस्य कर्त्तार: धूर्त भण्ड निशाचर:" अर्थात् वेदों का निर्माण करनेवाले धूर्त थे, ढोंगी थे, भण्ड यानि निशाचर यानि राक्षस थे। ऐसा कहने वाले व्यक्ति भी हिन्दू थे। सब तरह के लोग हिन्दू हैं।

अत: हिन्दू एक रेलिजन नहीं है, सभी रेलीजन इसमें हैं। हाँ रेलीजन की तरफ देखने का हिन्दू दृष्टिकोण है। इसी कारण गाँधीजी ने कहा कि इस्लाम और ईसाई भी हिन्दू दृष्टिकोण के अंतर्गत आ सकता है। यह दृष्टिकोण क्या है? संक्षेप में ये कहा तो You can have salvation through Mohammed the Prophet only आप Mohammed the Prophet के मार्ग से ही मोक्ष प्राप्त कर सकते

हैं– ऐसा यदि कहा तो Non Hindu बात हो गई, किन्तु ऐसा यदि आपने कहा कि You can have salvation through Mohammed the Prophet also मोहम्मद the Prophet के द्वारा भी आपको मोक्ष प्राप्त हो सकता है–पूर्णत: हिन्दू। आप यदि कहते हैं कि Through Jesus Christ only–Non Hindu है। Through Jesus Christ also पूर्णत: हिन्दू। तो हिन्दू दृष्टिकोण कौन है–वह सर्वसमावेशक है।

हमने कहा कि सोचिए–एक हिन्दू शब्द को प्राचीनत्व नहीं; वेदों में नहीं, रामायण में नहीं, महाभारत में नहीं, उपनिषद में नहीं, कहीं पुराणों में भी नहीं है। किन्तु यह Minus Point है या Plus Point है? ऐसा था कि प्राचीन काल में इस देश में संस्कृति का उदय हुआ, इस देश के लोग सुसंस्कृत थे, और सम्पूर्ण मानव जाति के साथ अपने को एकात्म मानते थे। वे सम्पूर्ण मानव जाति के बारे में ही अपना विचार करते थे। उन्होंने कहा–बाकी मानवों से हमारी कोई अलग पहचान है हम अलग हैं, ऐसा विचार ही कोई नहीं था इसलिए वेदों में आप जब प्रार्थना देखते हैं तो ऐसी प्रार्थना नहीं है कि हम कोई अलग हैं, बाकी मानव जाति से। सभी मानवों के लिए प्रार्थना है।

Let man protect man from all sides हाँ मनुष्य में यह भेद जरूर किया कि दुष्ट लोगों से हमारी रक्षा करो, दुष्ट लोगों का नाश करो। सज्जन और दुर्जन केवल इतना ही भेद है। सभी मानव के साथ हम एकात्म है, यही भावना सब में थी। इसके कारण मानव जाति से अलग ऐसी पहचान हमारे यहाँ नहीं है। इसलिए पहचान का कोई नाम भी नहीं है किन्तु हजारों-साल के बाद इस धरती के पृष्ठ पर कहीं कुछ ऐसे लोग निर्मित हुए जो अपने को सम्पूर्ण मानवता के साथ एकात्म करने को तैयार नहीं थे। पृथक अपनी अस्मिता अपनी पहचान रखना चाहते थे और बाकी मानव से अलग अपनी पहचान रखना चाहते थे। सिर्फ इतनी ही बात नहीं कि वह अस्मिता या पहचान तलवार के भरोसे पर लोगों पर थोपना चाहते थे।

और ऐसे लोग जब हिन्दुस्तान में आये तब सवाल आया कि हम वो नहीं है, हम वो नहीं है। ये दिखाने के लिए कुछ अलग नाम हमको लगा जो पश्चिमात्य लोग आये उनको भी लगा कि उनकी पहचान अलग होनी चाहिए क्योंकि वे ऐसे नहीं है। जो लोग आये वे सम्पूर्ण मानव जाति के साथ एकात्म होने को तैयार नहीं थे–हमारी अलग कोई पहचान नहीं थी। हम सबके साथ एकात्म थे। लेकिन हम उनके समान नहीं थे इसीलिए अलग से नाम की आवश्यकता हुई। हमने खुद नहीं निकाला। पहले से चल रहा था यूरोप, अरब में सिन्धु तो हिन्दु पहले से चला आ

रहा था। यही नाम दिया गया। हिन्दू नाम अलग से निकाला नहीं है। सिद्धान्त ये है कि जो समाज की धारणा करने के लिये उपयुक्त है, क्योंकि एक समय समाज की धारणा करने के लिये एक ही नियम बनाये जाते है। समय जैसे बीतता है परिस्थिति में परिवर्तन होता है। पुरानी समस्यायें कालबाह्य होती हैं। नई समस्यायें निर्माण होती हैं और पुरानी जो नियम हैं वे नई समस्याओं का समाधान करने में असमर्थ होती है और इसके कारण यह आवश्यकता होती है कि कालबाह्य नियमों को छोड़ दिया जाये, नया नियम बनाया जाये जो इन नई स्थितियों का मुकाबला कर सकते हैं। जैसे Lord Tennyson ने कहा Old order changeth giving way to the new and the God fulfils himself in many ways, lest one good custom should corrupt the world. उन्होंने यह नहीं कहा है कि Lest one bad custom, उन्होंने कहा है Lest one good custom should currupt the world. यानि कि custom good है। इसका आज लाभ है किन्तु कालान्तर से इसके परिस्थिति में परिर्वन होने के पश्चात वही समाज के लिए घातक हो सकती है। इसलिये अपने यहाँ स्मृतियाँ-अलग-अलग स्मृतियाँ हुई हैं। एक बार जो नियम बनाए गए वही कयामत के दिन तक चलेगी ऐसी परिकल्पना हमारे यहाँ नहीं। इसलिए स्मृति है, वृहस्पति स्मृति है, मनुस्मृति है, ऐसी कई स्मृतियाँ हमारे यहाँ हैं। कौटिल्य आये-तो हमेशा परिवर्तन रहा है। अपरिवर्तनीय वैश्विक नियमों के प्रकाश में अखण्ड परिवर्तनशील समाज रचना-यह धर्म की विशेषता रही। किन्तु हमेशा हमारे यहाँ परिवर्तन होता रहा है क्योंकि सनातन धर्म के वैश्विक नियमों के प्रकाश में यह सारा परितर्वन होता रहा है। अब यह जो 'थर्ड वे' किताब हैं इसे यह दावा नहीं किया गया है कि हम तीसरी समाज रचना का चित्र पेश कर रहे हैं—गलत बात है। ब्लू प्रिन्ट देना ये लड़कपन की बात है। मार्गदर्शक सिद्धान्तों की चर्चा है और हमारे यहाँ मार्ग दर्शक सिद्धान्त हमेशा धर्म रहा है।

मैंने आपको बताया कि विज्ञान ने एक शताब्दी में इतनी प्रगति की है कि it is coming very near to Hindu cosmology आपको मैने ये भी बताया कि Socialism, Capitalism Communism वो विज्ञान के साथ प्रगति नहीं कर गये—ये अभी पिछले शताब्दी में है और जिस समय Matter is material यह कहा गया था कि जो कुछ भी है वह Material है। Materialsim यह Dominating Principle था, और इसके कारण विचार था कि सब Matter ही है तो मेरे जीवन का उद्देश्य क्या है। मेरा सुख Man is the measure of every thing. Man is the centre of universe. यानि I am the centre of Universe.

मैं विश्व का केन्द्र हूँ ऐसा विचार था। और यदि मैं विश्व का केन्द्र हूँ तो मेरा सुख यह अंतिम ध्येय है। हमारे यहाँ भी माना गया है कि सुख ही ध्येय है। हमारे यहाँ भी माना गया है कि सुख ही ध्येय है। लेकिन हमारी परिभाषा अलग है, यह विषय मैं यहाँ नहीं लेना चाहता हूँ। वो मेरा सुख यही अंतिम लक्ष्य है। और मुझे ज्यादा सुख प्राप्त करने के लिए बाकी लोगों का यदि शोषण करना पड़ता है, बाकी लोगों को दुखी करना पड़ता है, शोषण करने में और उनको कष्ट देने में आपत्ति क्या हो सकती है? क्योंकि जीवन का ध्येय ही ये है कि केवल मुझे अपने को सुखी करना चाहिए और मैं सुखी होना चाहता हूँ और मैं Materialist हूँ, भौतिकवादी हूँ इसका मतलब मैं Consumerist हूँ, उपभोगवादी हूँ तो मैं ज्यादा-से-ज्यादा उपभोग कर सकूँ यही मेरे जीवन का ध्येय है। ज्यादा से ज्यादा उपभोग लेना तो उपभोग के साधन ज्यादा से ज्यादा उपलब्ध होना चाहिए। उपभोग के साधन ज्यादा से ज्यादा उपलब्ध करना है तो ज्यादा से ज्यादा पैसा चाहिये तो इसके लिये जो कुछ मैं काम करता हूँ उसमें ज्यादा से ज्यादा मुनाफा चाहिए। Profit motive is the supreme motive आखिर Profit motive कैसा होता है? केवल उदाहरण के लिए ये बताया जाये कि एक कारखाना है। कच्चा माल इसलिए किसानों का शोषण, सस्ते में उत्पादन प्रक्रिया इसके लिए मजदूरों का शोषण और ग्राहकों से ज्यादा पैसे लेने के लिए ज्यादा कीमतों से ग्राहक का शोषण इसके आधार पर कारखाने का अधिक लाभ होता है। Capitalism के बारे में Broadly यही बात है। तो अन्य लोगों का शोषण करने में कोई आपत्ति नहीं यह तय हुआ।

हमारा वैश्विक दर्शन भिन्न है। हमारे ऋषियों ने मुनियों ने यह बताया नहीं –थ्योरी नहीं बिठाई–साक्षात्कार किया महसूस किया। क्या अनुभव था? ब्रह्माण्ड क्या है? उन्होंने महसूस किया कि यह सारा विश्व ब्रह्माण्ड एक अस्तित्व है। अलग-अलग नहीं। सर्वखल्विदं ब्रह्मं किसी ने कहा ये संस्कृत मेरे समझ में नहीं आता है तो मैंने कहा, मैं अँग्रेजी बताता हूँ All is one. All are one नहीं All are one का मतलब होता है, चीजें तो अलग-अलग हैं, उसमें कुछ सहयोग है। एकात्मा है यही All is one सब मिलकर एक ही अस्तित्व है, फिर वो चीजे कैसे हम देखते हैं प्राणी है पक्षी है, पत्थर है, वनस्पति है ये क्या है? ये नाम रूपात्मक जो विविधता है वह एक ही अस्तित्व के विभिन्न आविष्कार है। जैसे सोना एक ही तत्व है, लेकिन सोना के विविध अलंकार बनते हैं–विविध आकार के विविध अलंकार बनते हैं। अलंकार विविध होंगे, तत्व एक है। आटा एक ही है। लेकिन उससे विविध प्रकार के विविध पदार्थ बन सकते हैं। उससे ब्रेड बनेगा, उससे रोटी बनेगी, उससे हलवा बनेगा और कुछ बनेगा, आविष्कार अलग-अलग है मूल तत्व

एक ही है। वैसे मूल तत्व एक ही है आप उसे ब्रह्म कहिये, ईश्वर कहिये, अल्ला कहिये और कुछ कहिये मूल तत्व एक है लेकिन उसके आविष्कार ये नाम रूपात्मक है–यह हमारा आधार है। यह हमारा जीवन मूल्य है। All is one. इसके कारण तथाकथित निर्जीव और तथाकथित सजीव सृष्टि भी हम एक ही मानते हैं। इसमें एक धरती पर जो कुछ भी दिखता है, वह सारा अस्तित्व एक मानते हैं।

सम्पूर्ण समाज एक ही इकाई है, इसके अंदर के अवयवों के रूप में हम सब अलग-अलग व्यक्ति हैं, उसके कारण सम्पूर्ण समाज का सुख सभी व्यक्तियों का सुख है, सम्पूर्ण समाज का दुख सभी व्यक्तियों का दुःख है। ऐसा नहीं है शरीर में कि मसूढ़े में रात में यदि दर्द होगा तो दाँत के अवयव कहेंगे–अरे दर्द तो मसूढ़े में है, हमें क्या करना है–हम तो सो जायेंगे, ऐसा नहीं होता, सारा शरीर जागरण करता है। मेरे सर पर प्रहार करने के लिये कोई दंड लेकर आता है तो हाथ उसका प्रतिकार करने खुद चले जाते हैं इसलिए नहीं कि धर्मशास्त्र में कहा गया है इसलिये नहीं। स्वाभाविक रूप से-हाथ समझते हैं कि ये मेरा शरीर है। ये मेरा ही सर है, इसका बचाव करना चाहिए। यह जो अंगांगीभाव है, अंग याने अवयव, अंग माने शरीर-अंगांगीभाव, यह हमारे वैश्विक दर्शन से निकलने वाला Deduction है। और यह जो मेम्बर है इसका Relationship Social Contract theory से निकलने वाली बात है। अर्थशास्त्र पर इसका असर क्या होता है। व्यक्ति केन्द्र है, उसका सुख, उसके लिए लाभ उसके लिए कृत्रिम अभाव हेतु यह है कि कीमतें बढ़ती जायें। इसके लिए पश्चिम के अर्थशास्त्र स्पष्ट बताता है, कि गये कई शताब्दियों में It is an economy of rising Prices वैदिक Economy is an economy of falling prices. कीमतें कम होती जायें ये हमारी विशेषता है। ताकि कीमतें कम होंगी, ज्यादा से ज्यादा लोगों को वस्तुएँ प्राप्त होंगी। ज्यादा-से-ज्यादा लोग सुखी होंगे, सर्वान् सुखिनः सन्तु। मैं ज्यादा कमाऊँ ऐसी बात नहीं, सब सुखी हों।

चिति प्रकाशन माला, पटना के द्वितीय अंक, 2004 सं. के सौजन्य से, साभार।

40

GANDHI AND VIVEKANAND
(गाँधी तथा विवेकानन्द)

B.R. Nanda

For nearly a hundred years, Vivekananda has occupied a unique position in the history of this country as the prophet of a resurgent Hinduism. He had shot into fame with his address at the Chicago Parliament of Religions in September 1893. His exposition of classical Hinduism thrilled his countrymen, as it satisfied a deep and long-felt psychological need of the Hindu intelligentsia.

Thoughout the 19th century, Hinduism had been on the defensive, believing itself to be beleaguered by erosion from within and assaults from without. The problem, as the founders of a new religious society, the Tatbabodhini Sabha had posed as far back as 1839, was : "How to propagate an ancient, dignified and intellectual form of Hinduism.... to put a ban to the spread of atheism and Christianity." Experienced British observes openly said that Enlgish education, railways and modern communications would undermine Hinduism. A senior British civilian, Sir Alfred Lyall, predicted in 1872 that "the old gods of Hinduism will die in these elements of intellectual light and die as a net full of fish, lifted up out of water."

The Hindu response to this challenge was two-fold: efforts at internal reform and a reassertion of religious identity. In the mid-1890s there were signs of a religious revival. "A dozen yeas ago," the Amrit Bazar Patrika wrote on October 4, 1895, "when educated men sat together they talked of politics; now, generally speaking, they talk of religion."

REVITALISE HINDUISM

It was against this background that we should appraise the role of Vivekananda. He sought to purify and revitalise Hinduism so as to fit the 20th century. As his ardent disciple sister Nivedita said, he was the first to formulate the basic character of Hinduism as a system of thought and way of life in the modern age. He expounded the Vedanta of the Upanishads not as a life-negating and other-worldly philosophy, but as "a universal and practical creed which was to be carried into everyday life, city life, the country life and home life of every nation." His Vedanta was based on eternal principles and did not depend on any particular book; it embraced all the scriptures of the world; going beyond toleration and brotherhood, it recognised God in every soul and God immanent in nature.

He looked forward to universal religion which would be "infinite like the God it would preach and whose sun would shine upon the followers of Krishna and of Christ, on saints and sinners alike, which would not be Brahmanic, Buddhist, Christian or Mohammedan, but the sun total of all these and still have infinite place for development." There would be no conversions and upon the banner of every religion would be inscribed: "Help and not fight" "Assimilation, not destruction" and "Harmony and peace and not dissension."

MORAL REVOLUTION

To the Hindus, Vivekananda presented Vedanta as an instrument of a spiritual and moral revolution in which reason was to be an active agent of change. He felt that India had a strong rationalist tradition, but over the centuries rationalism had been pushed to the background. He ridiculed the mumbo-jumbo of ritual and superstition in which an ignorant and selfish priestly class had entangled the Hindu masses. "Think of the last six hundred or seven hundred years of degradation" he said, "when grown-up men have been discussing for years whether they should drink a glass of water with a right hand or the left, gargle five or six times... Our religion is in the kitchen. Our God is in the cooking pot." He blamed the priests for "doling out ditch water, overlooking the eternal fount of amrit (nectar) that lies behind us." He denounced the degeneration of the caste system and the curse of untouchability. What sense did it make, he asked in preaching Advaitism, after reducing bhangis and pariahs to their degraded condition? He condemned child marriages and called the opponents of the Age of Consent Bill "religious hypocrities as if religion consists in making a girl a mother at the age of twelve or thirteen."

Vivekananda had the courage to clash head-on with Hindu orthodoxy. Once, while he was explaining at a meeting in Madras the nuances of Vedanta, somebody from the audience interjected: "Why if this was so, it had never before been mentioned by any of the old masters." "Because", Vivekananda shot back, "I was born for this and it was left for me to do so." When the code of Manu was invoked, Vivekananda declared that all social rules which stood in the way of unfolding freedom must be destroyed. He wanted to raise the status of women in Indian society; the level of a civilisation, he said, was judged by the way it treated its women; "With 500 motivated men it will take me 50 years to transform India, with 50 motivated women it may take me only a year."

He considered "the great national sin" was the neglect of the masses. Priestly power and foreign conquest had trodden down the poor of India for centuries. No amount of politics would be of any avail, until the masses were "welleducated, well-fed and well-cared for, if we want to regenerate India, we must work for them... I do not believe in a God who cannot give us bread here, giving eternal bliss in heaven."

As for relations between adherents of different religions, Vivekananda was not for tolerance but for acceptance of other forms of worship. "If you are born a Christian," he said, "be a good Christian," If you are born a Muslim be a good Muslim." Mankind had to realise that religions were but the varied expressions of The Religion which is Oneness so that each may choose the path that suits him best. He especially commended the spirit of equality in Islam and in a letter dated June 10, 1898 to a Muslim correspondent, even envisaged "a junction of the two great systems, Hinduism and Islam," into "a Vedantic brain and an Islamic body."

RELIGIOUS HARMONY

Vivekananda's pleas for religious harmony did not mean that he agreed with or commended every thing that had been said or done in India or elsewhere in the name of any religion, whether Hinduism, Buddhism, Islam or Christianity. As we have already seen, he did not spare his own co-religionists. He had a knack of applying a sort of shock-therapy to jolt the orthodox, the complacent, the arrogant, and the bigoted. Some of his critics in the Paliament of Religions had argued that since the Hindus had never been conquerors of other lands, and were also poor, he had no business to preach his religion in western countries. Vivekananda told them that he admired the life and teachings of Jesus Christ, but wondered whether they understood the religion they professed. "All this prosperity," he said, "all this from Christ! Those who call upon Christ care for nothng but to amass riches! Christ would not find a stone on which to lay his head among you..."

Vivekananda pooh-poohed the idea that the adoption of western ideas, western language, western food and western manner would make Indians as strong and powerful as the western nations. "Does the ass in lion's skin" he asked, "become a lion?" At the same time he rebuked those of his co-religionists who advocated a revival or restoration of India's past. What he wanted was "the strength of old India finding new applications and undreamt of expression in the new age." He longed to see Hinduism imbibe something of "the masculine vigour and dynamism" which had so fascinated him in the European nations.

(II-GANDHI'S RELIGIOUS QUEST)

Gandhi was the most charismatic Indian leader of the 20th century as Vivekananda was of the 19th. They were contemporaries though they never met, nor had any interaction while they lived. Their public life started about the same time. Gandhi's South African odyssey began in 1893, the year of Vivekananda's triumph at the Chicago Parliament of Religions. The two men vastly differed in their family background and the educational and social milieu in which they grew up. Vivekananda was a religious leader, the proclaimed heir of the great saint of Bengal, Sri Ramakrishna. Gandhi plunged into the political arena at the age of 24 and for the next 50 years led struggles against recialism and imperialism. Vivekananda was only six years older than Gandhi, but died young in 1902 at the age of 39. Despite these obvious differences, it is possible to detect remarkable similarities between their thought patterns and teachings so much so that it seems as if it was Gandhi's historic role to carry forward the work for reform and revitalisation of Hinduism, which Vivekananda left unfinished.

Unlike Vivekananda, Gandhi's life was not suddenly transformed by contact with a great saint. His religious quest really began soon after his arrival in South Africa when some missionaries tried to convert him to Christianity. He had a sceptical streak in him and decied to study not only Christianity, but other religions, including the religion of his birth. A decisive influence on him during this formative period was that of Rajchandra, young jeweller, poet and savant of Bombay, who was (in Gandhi's words) one of the "three moderns" who had influenced him most, the others being Tolstoy and Ruskin. Rajchandra gave a sense of direction to Gandhi's religious quest; he stressed the importance of accord between belief and action; it was the way a man lived, not the recital of a verse or the form of prayer which made him a good Hindu, a good Muslim or a good Christian. Himself a Jain, Rajchandra restored Gandhi's faith in Hinduism.

LIMITLESS VISTAS

The book which became Gandhi's strongest bond with Hinduism was the Bhagavad Gita. Two words in the Gita Gita opened to him limitless vistas. Aparigraha (non-possession) implied that he had to jettison the material goods which cramped the spirit; Sambhava (equabilty) required that he must remain unruffled by pain and pleasure, victory or defeat, and work without hope of success or failure. After pondering day after day on the Gita, he came to believe that what could not be followed in day-to-day life could not be called religion. Meditation and worship "were not exclusive things to be kept like jewellery in a strong box." they had to be seen in every act of the religious aspirant.

Gandhi's religious quest triggered off his metamorphosis from an upper middle class barrister into Churchill's 'half-naked faqir', a sanyasin, all but in name. Religion transformed Gandhi, but he also transformed religion.

MONSTROUS PROGENY

Like Vivekananda Gandhi threw down a gauntlet to Hindu orthodoxy, and questioned the validity of some centuries-old dogmas and practices. He condemned animal sacrifices, child marriages, the dowry system, the greed of the priests and dirt around the temples His severest strictures were reserved for the aberrations of the caste system and its monstrous progeny, untouchability.

When an eminent Hindu Mahasabha leader, Dr. Moore cited verses to prove that untouhability was part of Hinduism, Gandhi told him: "I do not accept everything written in Sanskrit as gospel truth." No book, he said, could be limited to a single interpretation, irrespective of time and place, and every formula of every religion must be subject to "the acid test of reason". He reinterpreted both in theory and practice several Hindu concepts to suit the changing times. For example, fasting was not merely a necessary ritual for the pious; it could be used a tool of social action. An ashram was not merely a place for prayer and meditation, but for training workers for service of the country.

Gandhi worked ceaselessly for the breaking of barriers between various castes, communities and religions and even nations. Like Vivekananda, he called for a new deal for women, and for the "naked hungry mass" in the villages. It is curious that the word, daridranarayan, which Gandhi often used, was coined by Vivekananda'; it wa not meant to idealise poverty, but to bring out both the cruel predicament and essential nobility of the poor of India. Like Vivekananda, Gandhi also attempted to shift Hinduism from its predominantly individualistic and other-worldly moorings. "The way to find God," he said, "is to see him in his creation and be with it."

Vivekananda had taken his lessons in religious tolerance from his master, Sri Ramakrishna. Gandhi delved into the scriptures of major religions and discovered an underlying unity in their teachings. "God's grace and revelation," he said, "is not the monopoly of any race or nation; they descent equally upon all who wait upon God." No religion was absolutely perfect, but every religion was to be judged not by its worst specimens, but by the best it produced. "If you read the Koran," Gandhi wrote, "you must read with the eye of the Muslim; if you read the Bible, you must read with the eye of the Christian' if you read the Gita, you must read it with the eye of the Hindu. What is the use of scanning details and then holding up a religion to ridicule?

For Gandhi communal harmony was not an academic issue; it was vital for success of his struggle against the imperial power which claimed that it was the discord between the religious communities which barred India's progress towards self-government. Like Vivekananda, Gandhi, while deriving sustenance from the unsullied fount of ancient Indian spirituality, responded to western influences with judicious discrimination, accepting what was life-giving and rejecting what was deleterious.

SPIRITUAL REVOLUTION

In one important respect, Gandhi differed with Vivekananda, and it was fortunate that he did so. Vivekananda had rejected politics. "The Greeks had sought political liberty," he had noted in one of his lecture notes, "the Hindu had sought spiritual liberty". Vivekananda called for a spiritual and moral revolution to precede a political revolution. He neither used the word nationality, nor proclaimed an era of nation-making. "Man-making", he said, was his task.

Gandhi's political mission and religious quest began simultaneously when he was in his twenties; his religious convictions gave him the strength and the stamina for a half-century of a crowded political career. He was accused fo introducing religion into politics, but it was not the organised religion of dogmas, rituals, superstition and bigotry. In the very passage where he said that politics could not be separatd from religion, he had made it clear that religion in this context was synonymous with ethics: "Here religion does not mean sectarianism. It means belief in the ordered moral government of the universe. This religion transcends Hinduism, Islam and Christianity."

In a recent book, Creating Minds, Howard Gardner, has profiled seven genuises of the modern era–Einstein, Freud, Gandhi, T.S. Eliot, Stravinsky, Martha Graham and Picasso–who, among other things, not merely solved existing problems but identified new ones. Looking back from the vantage point of the 1990s, it seems remarkable that, in the first decade of this century, Gandhi should have launched his crusades against recialism, colonialism, run way indusrialism, religious fundamentalism and violence. A Good deal of Gandhi's agenda is likely to spill into the next century.

टाइम्स ऑफ इण्डिया, सित. 30, 1993 के सौजन्य से साभार।

41

PRACTICAL GANDHISM
(व्यवहारी गाँधी-दर्शन)

Vijay Kumar

[Vijay Kumar argues why Gandhian philosophy is the only hope for the future in a world which has lost direction and is engulfed in free-market competition].

No study of the fundamental problems of Gandhian philosophy can be fruitful without the awareness that it is intimately related to the basic issues of general philosophy and way of life. His theory of State and society, and of the position of the individual of them derives more often unconsciously than consciously ... from a more comprehensive conception of the world and man's place in it. His philosophical systems are always reflected in exactly corresponding types of political outlook and action, a remarkable parallelism exists between his basic philosophical and political conceptions, a parallelism which is partly logical, partly psychological and partly historical based more on "voice of conscience" than on scientific pretentions.

The word 'philosophy' is one of which the meaning is by no means fixed. Like the word 'religion' it has one sense when used to describe certain features of historical cultures, and another when used to denote a study or an attitude of mind which is considered desirable. However, philosophy, as pursued in the universities everywhere, is at least in intention, part of the pursuit of knowledge, aiming at the same kind of detachment as is sought in science, and not required to bring about desirable changes in the way of the life of the student and his environment. Many teachers of philosophy, including Gandhian philosophy, would repudiate, not only the intention to influence their pupil's politics, but also the view that philosophy should inculcate virtue. Knowledge, according to them, is the sole purpose of university teaching.

Gandhian philosophy has resulted from an attempt to produce a synthesis of science and religion, or, perhaps more exactly, to combine a doctrine as to the nature of the society and man's place in it with a practical ethic inculcating ment and failure of the followers of Gandhi to throw up a true leader to carry, forward his ideas with dedication.

Gandhian Community Living Centres could be started for practical courses on non-violent living techniques. Such ashrams could be located in lush green villages where the inmates could come in contact with Indian masses. Retired men and women could join these centres and work for the uplift of the villagers-running schools for children, organising prayer meetings, heading adult education centres, popularising cottage industries and doing socially useful works. These community centres could also act as racial and religious harmony centres.

The Gandhian universities and departments could offer consultancy and also provide resource personnel for the peace centres, conflict resolution centres, environment management centres and community living centres. The department can offer short term courses for Government officials in Gandhian philosophy because even mere awarenss of Gandhian philosophy may reorient their living pattern and way of thinking. Infusion of Gandhian morality through such courses would go a long way in eradicating corruption, inculcating moral values, creating work-culture, and promoting a life of frugality and harmony with nature.

In a world which has lost direction and is engulfed in free market competition and has gone berserk in the absence of a viable ideology, Gandhism seems to be the only hope for the future. In 1992, Orlando Fals Borda, the influential Colombian educator and politician described the world condition thus : "The contradictions, abuses and conflicts of rampant capitalism and its social system are more obvious today and are becoming progressively more intolerable in the 21st century but have failed to synchronise our courses and curriculum to match the needs of the coming century. When violence rocks the country and the world we talk of the relevance of Gandhi but what attempts have been made to establish conflict management centres based on Gandhian principles? How many universities include even a chapter on this area in their curriculum? When not even a chapter is taught on this topic how can the students obtain practical lessons in this field?

Gandhian philosophy of persuation needs special attention in our courses and action programmes. Gandhi spent much of his life bringing other people round to his view be it the Government of South Africa, the indigo planters of Champaran, the mill owners of Ahmedabad, the Government of Great Britain and even the leaders of independent India when they failed to pay back the five million rupees to Pakistan from the Consolidated Fund of India after partition. Gandhi's art of persuation could be used in social conflict management, socio-political tension management, terrorism and violence management. Today, when the villages of India have become battlegrounds of caste and class conflict panchayatiraj institutions (PRIs) could be entrusted with these responsibilities and their functionaries trained in these skills. The Gandhian thought departments could run these programmes and involve their students in action oriented courses.

The concept of sustainable development emerged as an important theme in 1987 on the recommendations of the Brundtland Commission onEnvironment and Development which pointed out in its report, Our Common Future:

> *"In order for development to be sustainable, it must meet the needs of the present without compromising the ability of the future generations to meet their own needs."*

After the report, many Indians including Gandhian thinkers began to quote passages from Hind Swaraj, first published in 1909, which had predicted long back what Brundtland said nearly 80 years after. This book published long before the negative consequences of industrial civilizations were exposed to the common experience, must have appeared to the generation of his times a book of reaction and retreat from modernity and civilization.

The modern younger generation which wears American jeans and hears pop music, wondered at the weired ideas of the Mahatma when he read it as a classbook text. But suddenly there was a revival of interest in Gandhi's ideas on sustainable development. It has taken nearly 80 years for the Indians to realise the significance of this idea regarding industrialisation, cottage industries, environment protection, etc. No wonder, there is no teaching and research in Gandhian Environmental Management Techniques. Naturally when there is neither teaching nor research, there are no action programmes as well, People like Bahuguna, Medha Patkar and a few others have to fight lone battles for their people.

Gandhi is looked upon as a guide to mankind in the development of the deeper moral sense and a path-finder in the integral upward and onward evolutionary march and progress of mankind. From very early in his political life he came to appreciate the life of community living in the ashram. He established many in this South African days and always lived in an Ashram in India too. Gandhi Ashrams fell in disuse after Gandhi, because of the gross neglect of the Government.

Structural reforms continue to be necessary and urgent because the worldwide triumph of capitalism has not solved the problems of war, ignorance and poverty, nor the exploitation of the majorities, much less the abuses of nature and the environment."

The disaster of neoliberalism is confronting the developing countries with the threat of social revolt. The economic system imposed by the International Monetary Fund (IMF) and World Bank on our countries has made the poor much poorer and they are becoming progressively worse off while the wealthy are wealthier and are becoming increasingly better off. This kind of a system cannot last long.

An article written by P. Xabier Gorostiaga, SJ., contains data on the wealth of the world according to percentages in terms of how it is distributed and utilized. It divides the world's population into five groups of 20 per cent each. The 20 per cent who are most affluent represent 82 per cent of the world's wealth. Eleven per cent of the world's riches belong to the next group, 2.3 per cent of the riches is held by the third group, 1.9 per cent belong to the fourth group, and 1.4 per cent to the fifth group. The graph is designed in the form of a champagne glass. It is wide at the top. The rest is very thin. Things always break at their weakest point, and the point in question here is the portion of the population excluded from the world's wealth, a figure of 60 per cent. With such an unequal distribution of riches and resources, it is only a matter of time that the world would be in the danger of losing its social stability. The hour has come to abandon alien models of development and to seek our own. There may be many alternatives but Gandhism provides a lab-tested technique for our socio-economic development. Could we not reuse his techniques with required modifications? What was the best way of life according to him. An essential part of his philosophy was to tell men how to live. He tried to solve the fundamental problem of ethics and politics by reconciling the needs of social life with the urgency to curb individual desires in the right directions.

Economic exploitation and political dominance by the British and European traders, the advent of the Western industrial civilisation fed by mechanization and technology, continued exhaustion of natural resources and raw materials for urban centres, wide prevalence of rural unemployment and part employment, large measure of mass poverty and starvation coupled with feeling of misery and helplessness, provided the grist to the mill of Gandhian philosophy. The village condition was the truth for him. He saw it and resolved to take steps to attack it. He, therefore, in actual life identified himself with the lowliest of the rural, illiterate, hungry, homeless peasant of India and worked for his deliverance.

Gandhi's philosophy of political goals, political programmes, political methods, his view of the State and nature of political obligation are not speculative and divorced from the realities of public life. He was not a politician first and a theoretician later. His philosophy has deep and intimate connection between theory and practice. His whole approach was pragmatic and empirical rather than scholastic and systematic. Gandhi was not only the philosopher of politics but also the philosopher of life and civilization. Unlike most arm-chair, ivory tower philosopher who lead a closeted life, Gandhi, was primarily a man of action, a supreme karmayogi. He did nothing and spoke nothing without intimately relating it to his own life. Hid idealism consisted in putting his ideas into practice at even great hardship and expense to himself.

The uniqueness of Gandhian philosophy is its wideranging scope and its sheer brilliance. The collected works of Gandhi span more than 100 sizeable volumes and the work of collection has still not ceased. Naturally, Gandhian philosophy has many facets. To the rural masses he was a saint, to the politically minded he was a seasoned, hardbail politician and social reformer, to academicians he was an educationist beyond compare, to a few intellectuals he was a brillianct economist, to the environmentalists he was a great conservationist and naturalist, and to his friends and followers he was an advisor in matters of health, simple medicine and naturopathy. He was all these and much more in totality. He was a seeker after truth and came to realise that the highest truth for him was that the supreme being was present in all beings. Probably it was this fact which tempted Romain Rolland to subtitle his book Mahatma Gandhi: The Man Who Became One with the Universal Being.

Without a trace of fanaticism or doctrinairism, narrow sectarianism or superstitious obscurantism Gandhi was able to balance all forces of his time to provide an alternative to the Western society—its way of life, its philosophy, its economy, its polity based on indigenous values of the Indian culture.Calling 'my life is my meassage', Gandhi used the mass media, mass symbols and mass idioms living the life of karmyogi full of action to awaken the people of this country and through them people of the world. His epigramatic sentences make him resemble Confucius.

He put in a nutshell what political pundits failed to express successfully in long essays. To quote some examples, "Good Government is no substitute for self-Government, Truth is God", "Violence is better than cowardice but non-violence is better than violence." characterised Cripps proposals as "post-dated cheque drawn on a crashing bank, etc. His action-oriented philosophy made him the "quintessence of the conscious and subconscious will" of the people of India, to use the phrase of Nehru. To be detached from the fruits of action and at the same time to be involved in an intense direction can be essentially a philosophy of a very superior man of action who can convert the "pursuit of happiness into—the happiness of pursuit."

Gandhian philosophy cannot be understood in the class-room. The society is the laboratory and Gandhian philosophy its practical lesson. One can understand Gandhism in action more readily than from the text book and class book lessons. Gandhian philosophy provides us an approach and methodology in search of truth, for solving the emergent and emerging problems, for humanizing the social order, ensuring universal peace and security and harmonizing man-nature relationship.

Gandhian philosophy is directly related to our real life problems and problems of the society-poverty, unemployment, environmental crisis, violence, communal tension, over-population, loss of morality and values.

This is not to contest the relevance of the traditional courses in the university and teaching institutions of the Gandhian institutes and departments, but only a plea to make the courses action oriented and socially useful. The study has also to be made job oriented and employment-friendly otherwise there would be no students pursuing a university level course without an employment value in the open market system.

हिन्दुस्तान टाइम्स अप्रैल 19, 1997 के सौजन्य से।

42

MARKET VERSUS MORALITY
(बाजार और नैतिकता)

Uma Sinha

Theory of markets and of socialism, both developed around the philosophical ideas of the time. It was either religion or natural law or metaphysics as a proxy for religion, which guided the market or production norms. The causal relation between supply, demand and price of modern economics, for example, was first started by the ethical question of a fair price, so that the natural price could be controlled for the salvation of man and for his eternal life. Thomas Aquinas (1270) tried a reasonable compromise between doctrine and reality, but the case for a just price was never abandoned.[1]

With growth of mercantilism (early 17th century) however the market problem was analysed from the point of view of national welfare and state intervention and not of religion and ethics. They aimed at the good of the state, inspite of self-interest. With growth of capitalism, the national norm for a price system was lost and Adam Smith (1776) brought in normative foundations in an abstract frame of natural laws.[2] Like the other philosophers of the Enlightenment, Smith assumed that the economic systtem of natural liberty would operate within a framework of reason and moral law and it required no conscious regulation by state. Thus prices, costs, wages, rents and profits were believed to be all closely interrelated, forming part of a natural order, as planets were of a solar system. Thus the good of the state could be achieved without social control.[3]

The restraining part of reason, moral sentiments and competition oriented the individualist ego of the economic man to fairness and social good.[4] The French physiocrats wanted to put a seal on natural economic laws by 'legal despotism' of the state[5] but the Smithian system was too free to doubt the validity of the three conditions above.

A dismal science of self-interest becoming utilitarian was supported by Bentham (1825) who explained how egoistic hedonism of individuals led to an universal happiness. Though individuals are active in promoting their self-happiness, they are passive if all are doing it. Thus utility became additive in a free individualistic system, and in an abstract model of market of the classical, a subjective element in terms of 'happiness' was firmly placed.

There were reasons to be sceptical about such a market model which J.B. Say (1803) summarised as 'supply creating demand' leading to full employment, what Ricardo (1817) and Mill (1848) termed as a stationary state or economic Nirvan. The dangers of disproportionate development of population and capital (Ricardo) and of over-savings (Malthus, 1820) has plagued the 'law of markets' ever since the classicals who raised doubts but eluded the issues by abstractions (Ricardo) or by over-moralising (Mill). Mill shifted to idealism from materialism to mystic utilitarianism from hedonism. An asceptic devotion to altruism & benevolence and practical state action could achieve a greater good.[6] It was the beginning of dilution of the freedom of markets in economic theory, though the belief stayed that there will be harmony at last with profit falling and working class restricting their number in relation to capital. The system was therefore better than socialism as the natural equilibrum of the market system led to a stationary state, the Nirvan of the economy or a stabilisation at a blissful point.

But the uncritical acceptance of Say's law of market appears to have delayed the study of business cycles for many decades? Under-developed economies could have supply creating demand for a long time with expansion of world market but the developed markets could be destablished in the short run, remaining exposed to a trial and error of the market. The utilitarian optimism of the classicals by-passed this aspects of the market theory.

Further private property, private profit and free prices were prone to alienate the labour class, the human factor of production, and lead to exploitation and unemployment. Thus what was a stationary state of a market economy would be actually, a 'breakdown' point of it.

This change in economic thinking can be discerned in the change of philosophical ideas from Kant (1724-1804) to Hegel (1770-1831). Where as Kant stressed at the 'unsocial sociability' of man and man's power of moral self-determination, Hegel made man a historical product in a process of dialectical change.[8] Man had to assert and deny. Man was alienated by the need to adapt to the requirements of market. Property was individualistic and as individuals were unequal, property should be unequal. It was however history which brought about an optimistic synthesis between the opposites. Thus where Kant's morality requires the belief in God, freedom and immortality,[9] Hegel's dialectical logic finds that God is a product of only a free mind. The Marxian faith in socialism was thus the product of the deterministic theory of change by Hegel, which implied class struggle.

TOWARDS A NON-MARKET SYSTEM

By 1920 the market theory of the classical was riddled with the phenomena of increasing monopolies and fading competition on the one hand, and with short run fluctuations, and poverty on the other. The basic aversion to a free market system however demanded a shift to some non-market technique to impute human values to the productive system. A pro-labour stance in Marx (1856) gave rise to planned production where capital and land were to be publicly owned and profit and prices were to be eliminated. Whether class struggle was a necessary adjunct to it or not, a non-market socialism was in the offing. The economic Nirvan in this system would be achieved after the 'whithering away of the state' as visualised by Marx.

After 1871, market was defended by the neo-classicals, alongwith property, individualism and moral ideas. There was yet another group fo economists who wanted to reunite property and labour with a pro-labour stance. This retained markets but the socialism visualised here was termed utopian or bourgeois by Marx. What was common in the socialists was disengagement of ethics from religion and opposition to the utilitarian harmony of Kant and Bentham. Thus Proudhon was against all types of religion and mysticism while Carlyle decried Benthamite ethics as 'pig philosophy.[10]

The revival of the market philosophy of the Marginalist however, is based on a synthesis of utilitarianism & romanticism, what can be ascribed to Compte's positivism. Thus the metaphysical or speculative abstraction of economic theory had to be ascertained by historical investigation. Thus a theory of natural progress and equilibrating order of society would be explained. The stress was on social duty and moral ideas. But a science-based moral order could not be a substitute for religion as it made humanity an abstract idea.[11]

It may be noted here that the market theory of the classicals of its negation by Marx, was all based on philosophical assumption about the economic man and so the production systems in both the worlds were an abstraction and half truths. After 1840's, the Historical School in Germany highlighted this fact. Though philosophy gave aproximation about human nature, the economic reasoning based on these remained axiomatic and so market laws could not be true to all times and all countries on that account.

It was therefore stressed that religion was not an outcome of a system rather it could be cause of the system. Here Weber (1904) was talking of a 'genuine religion'. Such norms and ideals become connected with the practical affairs of life, and empirical situations, which other wise would have remained confused. Capitalism as a rationally conducted system for profit could be analysed under the effect of such religious norms. Weber (1885-1920) felt that development of western capitalism was the effect of the protestant work-ethics, other than the market laws.

German romanticism was thus dominated by the super-sensual, the divine and the infinite and became a cultural movement, treating man as a part of universe and not as an isolated individual, and adhering to an idealistic point of view. In England, Carlyle, as a romantic, is also sometimes placed among the Christian socialists, who in 1840's encouraged the trade unions and Church to cooperate against capitalism. They also felt that socialism had ignored the spiritual needs of mankind. This tradition was carried by Fabian socialists too.[12]

Thus a market system protected by local factors and under an idealistic condition had a nationalist fervour and sought state intervention for reforming the system.[13]

WELFARE CAPITALISM VERSUS MARKET SOCIALISM

The neo-classicals in late 19th century were market theorists but had certain social philosophy. It cuts across classical class concept and makes economic theory 'an engine of Social Progress',

(Marshall). They shunned the mechanistic and static view of economic life and extended it to the realm of welfare and reforms.

Religion was accepted to have strong effect on ordinary life and there was utopian optimism, while hard work was taken as a religious duty. A free market stood for maximum welfare with a policy of transfer of wealth from the rich to the poor, if such a transfer does not diminish national income.[14]

Marshall regards 'moral character' a firm basis for the growth of welfare, thus supporting a glorified utilitarianism. IMD Little finds Pigou's welfare as a sceintific ethics, and Joan Robinson calls Marshall a 'Moralizer'. Marshall was a humanitarian with religious feelings but no creed. He loved to preach the gospel of noble life and wished to serve his nation. Marshall defined the problem of economics as how to open up to all 'the material means of a refined and noble life. He believed that morality led to material welfare and spiritual welfare. Marshall devoted many years to the study of the problem of poverty.[15]

Thus market theory could turn to welfare but socialism has remained in flux for want of a workable basis of its productive system. In Russia 'from each according to his ability and to each according to his work' was the dictum to replace the market system, with an overall planning by a central body but the former was difficult to apply while the latter remained arbitrary and fallible. The stalinist dictatorship made 'the whithering away of state' a remote dream, while most of the Hegelian systems have fallen back on some sort of market mechanism.[16]

It is strange that in the Soviet system labour was alienated in production with a bureaucratised set up, while capital investment was artificially cheap and consumer goods, artificially costly, thus distorting production, what a market system won't have allowed.

MARKET SOCIALISM

Yugoslavia however tried to introduce market socialism in a Marxian system to save it from collapse. Oscar Lange has tried to introduce a trial and error princing by the Managers under a broad frame of a national plan. But such 'shadow pricing' has to be based on innumerable data and by the time such data are collected, the basic data might have changed. Jan Drawnowski's system however introduces consumer's perferences side by side with state perferences, and market prices in a dual order are allowed to grow step by step.

In the first degree market consumer have individual choices but productions centrally planned; in the second degree market, even commodities are decided by individual preferences but quantities and investments are centrally planned; but in the third degree market, both consumption and investments are according to consumer's demand but the aggregate is decided by the state. The state prices are used for national accounting but the consumer prices for sale.

Yugoslavia switched over to market socialism in 1948. Russia has switched over to this in Gorbachev regime recently. This means a privatisation of agriculture and small industry sector generally and a worker's management (including white Collar) in the rest of the sectors.

THE INDIAN EXPERIENCE

The Indian market system has its own problem. With a hybrid of both private and public prices, the system has been marked by inefficiency and corruption. The prices in the free system are inevitably influenced by administered prices and monopoly power in one, and political power in the other have led to a corruption multiplier with which the India inflation can be easily indexed.[17]

V.K.R.V. Rao[18] has recently talked about spiritual socialism for India. This is naturally neither a religion-dry socialism nor the hedonistic utilitarianism of the west. This has to be based on the national heritage and would be closer to the welfare-capitalism with faith in individual virtues and potential divinity of man.

Gandhian socialism leaned a lot on this concept, Gandhi was not a planner nor was Marx.[19] Whether capitalism or socialism, what was more important is to force in the market system true humanist values with glow of divinity in each individual. Such individualism was a work-ethics, which glows with a sense of service to others with no greed but love and respect. If you plan some sectors, it is again the character of the people which would matter and not the monolithic state power behind it.

Swami Vivekanand owes the concept of spiritual socialism, and calls it practical vedant. Here individual rationality is divinished and is not hedonistic. God here is nothing but a sum total of all souls, and religion here is not any dogma or belief but a realisation of 'oneness' or 'sameness' of all souls. Practical vedant entails four things-knowledge (Gyan), devotion (Bhakti), action (Karam) and self-searching (Sadhana).

Spiritual socialism rests on patriotism and fellow-feeling. It is a positive movement and not dialectical. 'Say no one harsh word against the society'; 'Reform, yes but destroy, never' are the dictums or Vivekanand, 'castes are simply an outgrowth of political institutions, hereditary trade guilds.Religion concerns with soul, not social systems. If social individuality is restored, castes will go. Thus class and caste have no real meaning. What was to be broken was privileges so that 'sameness' is established. Thus socialism here is not a political concept but a true religion where there is a feeling of oneness. To quote Vivekandanda, 'Before flooding India with socialist and political ideas, deluge the land with spiritual ideas."20 Vivekanand replying to the question-could it remove proverty, said, yes, because it meant service to the poor.

It is clear that oneness is a better word than equality in a socialist order. In a people's movement in 1974 in India, the people demanded total change which meant that the market system needed an orientation from economic, political, educational, social and spiritual sides. This is how the market would grow to a stationary state and the Indian point of bliss, with a world view of religion and God.

NOTES AND REFERENCES

1. Kapp and Kapp, ed. History of Econ. Thought, 1956, pp. 3, 33, 64.
2. J. Oser, the Evolution of Econ. Though, 1970, p. 115.
3. J. Robinson & Eatwel, An Introduction of Modern Economics, 1974.
4. The Principle of Self-Interest of which Smith's "Wealth of Nations", speakes must be read in Conjunction with his 'Theory of Moral Sentiments' whcih Smith nevr abandoned (Kapp and Kapp, Op. Cit., p. 64.)
5. Ibid., p. 63.
6. J.S. Mill, Utilitarianism, 1863, quoted K.N. Prasad, Development of Philosophical Thought in Economics, 1985, p. 175. (Mill talks about 'Philosophical radicalism', which is a Combination of Bentham's Utilitarianism and Hartley's Metaphysics.
7. Oser, Op. Cit., p. 116.
8. Schumpeter, History of Economy Analysis, 1954.
9. Kant, Critique of Practical Reason, quoted, Prasad, Ibid, 192.
10. R. Lekachman, A. History of Econ. Ideas, 1967.
11. K.N. Prasad, Op. Cit., p. 230.
12. Prasad, Op. Cit., 226 n.

13. Oser, p. 183.
14. Economic Theory in Retrospect, 3rd ed. p. 636.
15. P.T. Homan, Contemporary Economic Thought, 1928.
16. The cause of building socialism was extemely distorted by the establishment of a totalitarian system. The Creative energy of people who had been freed was suppressed by state property, the political power of party-state bureaucracy, the monopoly power of a vulgarised Marxist ideology and intolerance towards democracy and glasnost. (Tony Barber, quoted Hindustan Times, 31 July, 91.)
17. K.K. Sinha, Corruption Multiplier, I.E.J. Conf. Issue, 1985.
18. V.K.R.V. Rao, Swami Vivekanand, Prophet ofVedantic Socialism, Pub. Div., Ministry of Information, Govt. of India, Also spiritual socialism of Swami Vivekanand, Kanyakumari, 1991.
19. K.K. Sinha, Had Gandhi a plan, I.E.J. Conf. Issue, 1988.
20. Quoted, V.K.R.V. Rao, Ibid.

By Courtesy, D.K. Das ed. Economics of Markets, Deep & Deep, 1993.

43

CASE FOR SERVICE SOCIALISM

P.R. Brahmanand

(A movement from free society to state controlled society was followed by a reaction back to free world. But how welfare to all is to be guaranteed?

By protecting the disintegrating non-competing groups (poor men, castes and regions), this is possible. How to secure better distribution so that everybody has equal chance to join the welfare game?

Rawlsian rule of inequclity is subject to minimum for all. The author wants here a normative choice, a cooperative federation where the large fish has to give up a great deal in order to welcome the small fish.

The author suggests a normative state where economic space is only one among many spaces, which have to be balanced by philosophy, the Indian concept of Dharm. This may require utilitarianism plus service socialism—editors).

The 18th century witnessed in economics the overthrow of the Mercantilist system. (the carly precursor of the modern planning state), and the emergence of the Quesnay- Turgot-Smith-Ricardo-Malthus system, or the Physiocratic-cum-Classical system. The touchstone, the sole reference point, of the above system was the well being of the masses of ordinary people. Consumption is the sole end of production, declared Adam Smith. The establishment of a competitive framework, maximisation of gross produce, the enlargement of trade, stable prices, highest feasible real wage-rate through limitation of population growth because of diminishing returns-all these became the desiderata for the macro-appraisal of the economy. The long term concern with the labouring poor became the dominant passion of economists. The system of natural liberty, of Laissez-faire at home and aborad, austere governmental tax and expenditure rules, the promotion of thrift and the regulation through moral restraint of number became cornerstones of the new political economy. James Mill and Jermy Bentham spoke of the material good of the largest number as the key goal of the economy.

However, the 19th century brought forth the ideology of socialism, based on class dichotomy, the nation-state, and general protectionism. These three ideas could be termed as a reaction against the ideas of the 18th century. In a sense the 19th century was concelling out the 18th century. The pursuit of International Communism through a network of communist states displaced international relations through free trade with the gold standard under individualistic motivations. Hegel, Marx, List, were the great names of the 19th century. Economists like Keynes later argued the faith of the classical system in the invisible hand of the market in achieving full employment and in avoiding depressions was misplaced. The gold standard was displaced by managed paper currency standards. Keynes even wrote that laissez-faire had seen the end.

In a sense the first half of this century saw the continuation of the 19th century's ideas which an in the case of such ideas started taking a practical shape. A significant portion of the world went under communist planning. Developing countries under the leadership of Prebisch, Nehru, Mahalanobis etc., starting aping the Soviet Union's economics. Rostow's stages theory was disrupted by the concept of forced industrialism and Gereshenkorn rightly saw that agricultural fundamentalism and consumer welfare had little appeal to the developing countries.

But the second half of the present century is witnessing as its closing stages, the birth of practice of an entirely new set of movements in ideas. We are witnessing the end of the nation state in Western Europe and the birth of a new macro-economic monetary, fiscal and trade union. In Eastern, Central and Southern Europe we are witnessing disintegration of multi-ethnic political entities, which previously had strong central plans. We are witnessing the collapse both of socialism and of the Soviet Union. The second and the third worlds as ideologically knit blocks have disappeared. Even in the first world only the U.S.A. has emerged as the single most dominant world power.

Certainly the great idea of the 19th century are getting evaporated with the abolition of war. With the surge towards free markets, and the end of socialism and of central planning, it seems that the dominant ideas of the 18th century, are reappearing in a new form and with greater vitality. Marx and his disciples had tried to separate workers from others and had sought to forge unity of workers under the rubirc of an eventual socialist state. In the process, they sought to undermine the individualistic utilitarian foundations of economic activity and substituted in its place a collectivist power-centered ideology with socialist state as the goal. The issue of why socialism was required for the vast masses of the poor did not came much into discussion at all. If the end of the economic activity is the fulfilment of wants involving productions of consumer goods or wage-goods, obviously the socialist movement had to ground itself on its efficiency for achieving this goal and on a continuous dynamic basis as against a competitive market-governed and politically free system.

It is to the great credit of Schumpeter that he showed that a competitive free market system was dynamically efficient in carrying out innovations. He also stated that progress consists in making available to orginary people goods which were accessible only to those in the top brackets. Once again the utility basis of economic activity, thought now, through productivity growth and materialist equality in terms of a consumption levelling up and the breaking of the link between hierachical status and consumption accessibility started getting analytical attention.

What really are the causes that are responsible for the catalysic movement and changes in economic and related ideas? Why has socialism collapsed? Why has Central Planning become unpopular? Why are people craving for improved materialist states?

II

Alfred Marshall had stated that the unifying link in economics is the money measure to appraise the sacrifices disutilities, and satisfactions. He throught that Adam Smith was the originator of the concept of the money measure. But whether Marshall is right in this or not is not important. What is important is his idea that the maximisation of the money measure of net satisfaction in the key goal of the human beings in economic activities. Obviously net satisfaction relates to net consumption satisfaction including of special advantages from satisfactory jobs as such. Now these ideas go back is essence to Bentham. Maximisationof net utilities is the key goal and a society's goal is the greatest good of the greatest number. If a course has support from 50 percent only and 50 percent do not favour it, we need a cardinalization of the utility concept to make choices. That is where the 'greatest good' is necessary for Bentham. Forgetting about the greatest good for the present this notion boils to the maximisation of the net utilities of the majority of this population. If the majority happen to be low income workers, the unemployed and the poor, obviously the net utilities of these groups have to be increased and we may interpret the greatest good as the conscious policy of promoting continuously the net wellbeing states of the majority as above.

One difficulty with Bentham's rule is that he does not provide for the case where the majority may consist of the same continuously. If this goes on it is probable that the excluded portion of the population would be not at all participating in the gains of improvement. We have to amend the Bentham rule by the proviso that every individual in the society must have the equal chance of being in the majority. This would mean that under Bentham's rule with this proviso every individual has an equal chance of getting the improvement.

Let us take the case where the majority improves its status but some portion may get its status absolutely lowered and suppose this lowering effects the same people. Obviously from the society's angle this may not be desirable. Through we may say that the concept of the majority may be interpreted in a net sense, there is still a problem. So we have to introduce a second proviso that every individual must have an equal chance of falling into the net majority, further there should be no room for the same individuals to go down and down.

Let us now turn our attention to a community in which there are several non-competing groups like sociological castes, religions and economic classes, regions etc. The term 'non-competing' would include the cases wheein non-competition may be for some aspects and not for all. In this case the Bentham rule and the proviso (s) need further amendments. Every non-competing class, region, must have an equal chance of being in the majority or in the net majority in all or relevant respects. It would also follow that no non-competing class, region, should get its position continusouly.

We have now laid down a reasonable number of provisions to the general rule. The issue now is whether these rules are being observed more or less continuously in different economic systems etc. If the rule and its provisos are not observed, under free political choices and full information,the scope for disintergrations emerges. Such disintegrations may emerge partly because one non-competing group, region etc., may get such a phase of continuous improvement that it may like to opt out of a union in order to obviate any probable future possibility of having to share its prosperity with other classes, regions etc. Any scheme which leads to skewed benefits where a sustained period to a particular region or a non-competing group or such group-dominated region may throw up the possibility of that class, region seeking to opt out and to reduce its responsibilities to the collectivity go down.

If the deteriortion continuously occurs with respect to a region, or a non-competing class-dominated area etc., again disintegrations may occur.

III

The lesson from the above is that where non-competing groups, region, castes etc., exist, there is a natural probability of the distribution becoming skewed. This would mean that the bond of unity would be loosened both ways. Either there must be scope for full mobility in all respects thus removing non-competition or the introduction of the provisos or schemes of redistribution must be built in overall growth programmes at each stage.

My submission is that the simple Rawlsian rule of inequalities subject to minimum for all will not work unless the community is on the whole homogenous and the provisos are not required.

The main reason why socialism has failed is because it did not accept the utilitarian concept at all. The good of the greatest number is the maximisation of net consumers satisfaction of masses. Secondly the disintegrations are occuring because in the conglomerates the provisos have not been applied.

Thus these two problems are affecting the Soviet Union. First there is no Smithian or Classical reference point. Secondly, from a regional angle, distributions are getting skewed not simply from economic but from also political angles. In Yugoslovia the regional inequalities have worked both ways. The better offs want to go out, the worse offs also want to go out.

Whatever is happening in Europe has lesson for India. We seem to be suffering from both the Soviet as well as Yugoslavian maladies and we do not have even reasonable mobility in labour, let alone full mobility. How do we tackle the distribution issue? We cannot also afford to be content with low growth rates; we must increase mobility in all respects but we must have also the higher growth rate and reduce the spread among the classes and regions. Most important of all, we must pay attention to the poorer and the unemployed portions of the population and we should not accentuate the inequalities.

There is no reason to believe that the concept of the good of the greatest number applies only to a whole nation but it must also apply within each unit and classes and regions.

IV

In the above I have tried to grope towards an understanding of the earth-shaking events that are taking place in the world today. Ideologies and conglomorate states are collapsing like nine pins. I have sought to explain why these events are occuring. The unitary state as a mixture of different ethnic groups bound by a strong centre is out. The sole exception is the U.S. where the concept of non-competing groups has faded over time. The basis for Myrdal's dichotomy between the whites and the blacks has become amorphous. Besides, the U.S.A. has tremendous internal mobility and competition is so fierce that individuals and groups move up and town. Further, the U.S. has a federal basis. It is only under an emergency that the President can exercise great powers. The U.K. is an entity where conventions are strong. In Africa, states are finding it difficult to come together because of fierce tribal loyalities. If loose federations are to be formed, for separate units growth and equity rules mentioned carlier have to be brought in. Every unit joining a federation must face a strong probability of its status getting improved. In any Federation the largest unit has a great responsibility, for if it allows its own aspirations to dominate, the federation will not be formed. *The large fish has to give up a great deal in order to welcome the small fish.* Such federations cannot be formed without strong rules and the confidence that such a rules will be enforced must imbibe each unit. Let us watch what happens in the new Germany?

I now turn to the philosophical base for my observations. Economic space is only one of the several spaces in which man's social relations are grooved. Economic goods are not the sole sources of happiness. But they provide a foundation on which other components can be pursued. Pigou's dichotomy between economic welfare and other aspects of welfare did not appeal to Marshall. It was also challenged by Robertson. Selfare is a component of several types of satisfactions and the proportion will go on changing. As Kahn recently remarked, the separability postulate underlying welfare economics cannot be supported as a plausible picture of reality.

Human beings also seek normative states. Economics seeks maximum efficiency from human beings in the economic space. In the process, it assumes neutrality of its effects in economic space on other spaces. Other spaces are concerned with outside of each of the spaces. This means that criteria must be evolved from philosophy in order to establish the basis of a balance. The philosophy here must be dynamic because the components go on changing.

I may refer here to a common prescription in India's ancient texts of Brihaspathi, Chanakya, Kamanduka, Somadeva Suri etc., All seem to hold that of the three ends of human activity like Dharma, or thepursuit of righteousness, Artha or the pursuit of wealth, and Kama or the pursuit of sensual pleasures, Artha is superior to Kama when there is a conflict; Dharma is superior to Artha,, and to Artha and Kama when there are conflicts among them. There is therefore an implicit hierarchy embedded in these texts. If we pursue this idea further we notice why the neglect of Dharma of right cousness is probably responsible for the collapse of socialist and the collapse of conglomerates like Soviet Union, Yugoslavia etc. I refer to Dharma in a secular sense, a sense in which it has been applied by some of the great seers. A state or an ideology not founded on Dharma, has to face the probability of collapsing or disintegrating.

The late John Hicks came to the conclusion Welfare Economics is a critique of economics. He identified economics with Plutonomy, the space dealing with the pursuit of wealth. Welfare economics in its wider sense must have a philosophical basis and ground itself on permanent values. The economic race has no finish line for individuals, groups, classes or regions. The concept of a trickle effect across or vertically is not a sound basis for holding regions together. Equity in the relevant sense is not a once and for all concept. Rawlsian minimal or Sen's entitlements by themselves cannot sustain for all time the integrity of a community. There is an optimum measure of inequality which can hold a state. But this optimum is dynamic.

Socialism in the usual sense is dead but that socialism is the socialism of power but the concept of service socialism, an idea which inspired Sismondi, Proudhon and in our own day Gandhi, Roy to some extent, and others, lives. If we neglect the ideas of these thinkers, even India may disintegrate. There is no divine rule that India will hold together. Patriotism is very necessary but patriortism must be supported by pursuit of Right and Right here involves all individuals, classes and regions. A policy grounded on inequity, corruption, inequality and force cannot endure. Rules utilitarianism plus servie-socialism may have a chance of keeping India together. But alas; these are mundane, earthy ideas.

Special Lecture delivered at the Anantpur, Indian Economic Association, 1991.

44

हमारा देशीय समाजवाद

OUR INDIGENOUS SOCIALISM

जयप्रकाश नारायण

आजकल समाजवाद का काफी बोलबाला है। इसकी काफी चर्चा होती रहती है। हर कोई एक-से-एक ऊँचा समाजवादी होने का दावा कर रहा है। बिड़लाजी भी कहते हैं कि काँग्रेस समाजवाद स्थापित करना चाहती है, तो वह जरूर स्थापित होना चाहिए। जनसंघ भी भारतीय समाजवाद की बात करता है। इसलिए आज कौन समाजवादी नहीं है? शायद राजाजी को छोड़कर दूसरे सब समाजवादी है। बस, प्रस्ताव कर देते हैं कि बैंकों का, कारखानों का, खनिज सम्पत्ति का राष्ट्रीयकरण होना चाहिए। ठीक है। जरूर हो। ऐसा करने से हमारे आर्थिक, सामाजिक प्रश्नों का कोई हल निकलता हो तो जरूर राष्ट्रीयकरण हो।

किन्तु मैं यह पूछता हूँ कि इस कृषिप्रधान देश में आपका यह समाजवाद गाँवों में कैसे आयेगा, इस सम्बन्ध में क्या कभी आपने विचार किया है? आप लोग समाजवाद-समाजवाद की बातें करते हैं, किन्तु इस देश में 82 प्रतिशत लोग तो गाँवों में रहते हैं। उनके लिए समाजवाद का क्या चित्र है? इन गाँवों को आपका यह समाजवाद कहाँ स्पर्श करता है? गाँवों के लिए आप क्या करते हैं?

मात्र नारे लगाने से समाजवाद नहीं आ जायेगा। दूसरे देशों की नकल करने से भी समाजवाद नहीं लाया जा सकेगा। खासकर यूरोप के देशों के अनुभव पर से हमें विशेष मार्गदर्शन नहीं मिल सकेगा। क्योंकि एशियाई देशों की जनता अधिकांश ग्रामीण ओर खेतिहर है। यूरोप के समाजवादी इस प्रकार के वातावरण में समाजवाद कैसे कायम किया जाय, इससे परिचित नहीं है। इसलिए हमारे यहाँ समाजवाद लाने के लिए जो कुछ चिन्तन, प्रयोग आदि करने पड़ेंगे, उनका बहुत बड़ा हिस्सा तो हमें खुद ही करना पड़ेगा।

कृषिप्रधान देश में समाजवाद यानी क्या?

सवाल यह है कि हमारे कृषिप्रधान देश के लिए समाजवाद का अर्थ क्या है? जो कुछ थोड़ा-सा मुझे समाजवाद का ज्ञान है, उस पर से मुझे तो केवल एक ही उत्तर सूझता है। वह यह कि जमींदारी-उन्मूलन या भूमि की सीमा का निर्धारण या काश्तकारों को अपनी काश्त की जमीन पर संरक्षण, या भूमि या एकीकरण, या खेती का बीमा, या इस तरह की अन्य भूमि-सुधार की बातें जिनके लिए कानून बने हैं अथवा बनाने की चर्चा की जाती है, दरअसल समाजवाद नहीं है। इस देश में कृषि-विषयक समाजवाद का केवल एक अर्थ है: भूमि का समुदायिक स्वामित्त्व और उसकी व्यवस्था। (इस व्यवस्था का मतलब सामूहिक खेती से नहीं है, जो कि व्यवस्था ऐसी भी हेा सकती है।)

जमींदारी-उन्मूलन से क्या हुआ? यह कोई समाजवाद का कार्यक्रम नहीं है। अमेरिका में तो कोई जमींदारी नहीं थी। आजभी वहाँ न तो जमींदारी है, न रैयतवारी है। किन्तु इतने से वहाँ कोई समाजवाद नहीं आ पाता। और, हमारे यहाँ हदबन्दी भी की गयी, तो किस हद की? अरे, वहाँ जापान में मैकार्थर जैसे ने तीन एकड़ की हदबन्दी की थी। हमारे यहाँ तो उसकी कोई कल्पना भी नहीं कर सकता। नम्बूदरीपाद ने केरल में 15 एकड़ सिंचित भूमि की हदबन्दी की थी। अब आप ही कहें, मैकार्थर तो नम्बूदरीपाद की अपेक्षा अधिक क्रान्तिकारी ठहरा न? समाजवादी भी अधिक-से-अधिक क्या माँग रखते हैं? छोटे किसानों से लगान मत लो। लेकिन इसमें कौन-सी क्रान्ति है?

व्यक्तिगत स्वामित्व-विसर्जन

मैं कहना चाहता हूँ कि भारत जैसे कृषिप्रधान देश में समाजवाद का स्वरूप कैसा हो, उसका जवाब ग्रामदान देता है। **मेरा यह दृढ़ विश्वास है कि जिस समाजवाद का या नये समाज का सपना हम देखते हैं, वह ग्रामदान के आधार पर ही खड़ा हो सकेगा।** ग्रामदान में व्यक्तिगत स्वामित्व के विसर्जन द्वारा एक बड़ा क्रान्तिकारी कदम उठाया जाता है। इसके अलावा, भूमिहीनों के लिए भूमि का बीसवाँ हिस्सा मिलता है। प्रतिवर्ष पैदावार में से चालीसवाँ हिस्सा ग्रामकोष में मिलता है। गाँव का कामकाज सर्वानुमति से चलाने का निर्णय होता है। इन सबसे ग्रामीण समाजवाद की एक तस्वीर खड़ी होती है। देश के लाखों गाँव ग्रामदान द्वारा इस नये मार्ग पर चलने को तैयार हो जायँ, तो उसका असर शहरों पर भी पड़े बिना नहीं रहेगा। यह कितना बड़ा काम है।

जो भी उत्पादन के साधन हैं, उन पर समाज की मालिकी होनी चाहिए, यह समाजवाद का बुनियादी सिद्धान्त है। और जो सम्पत्ति पैदा हो, वह समाज के हित में खर्च हो। लेकिन जबतक लोकमत तैयार न हो, तब तक यह चीज कानून से नहीं हो सकती। कानून से न किसी को ट्रस्टी बनाया जा सकता है, न जमीन की मालिकी समाज की बनायी जा सकती है, न किसी मालिक को समाज के हित में खेती करने के लिए कहा जा सकता है। किन्तु समझाने से ग्रामदान द्वारा यह हो सकता है।

कोई भी दल यह कहने की हिम्मत नहीं कर सकता!

मैं देश के सभी दलों के घोषणा-पत्र देखता रहा हूँ। उसमें कोई दल यह लिखने की हिम्मत नहीं कर पाता कि हमारे हाथ में राज्य आयेगा तो हम जमीन की व्यक्तिगत मालिकी समाप्त कर देंगे। अरे, साम्यवादी तक ऐसा नहीं कहते। और दल तो क्या कहेंगे! उन्हें वोट की चिन्ता होती है न? जबकि ग्रामदान द्वारा स्वेच्छा से जमीन की व्यक्तिगत मालिकी का विसर्जन होता है। भूमि-क्रान्ति, कृषि-क्रान्ति की दिशा में यह एक बहुत बड़ा कदम है। राजनीतिक दल तो इसका विचार तक नहीं कर सकते।

यद्यपि आज समाज में जिस प्रकार का मानस काम कर रहा है, जो वृत्ति है, वह व्यक्तिगत मालिकी के विचार को मान्य करता है। व्यक्तिगत मालिकी को एक मूलभूत अधिकार माना जाता है। उससे व्यक्ति की स्वतन्त्रता सुरक्षित रहती है और अभिक्रम कायम रहता है ऐसा दावा किया जाता है। इसलिए इस सम्बन्ध में कुछ गहरी छानबीन की जरूरत है।

मालिकी व्यक्ति की है, यह विचार हमें जड़मूल से ही बदलना है। और मात्र जमीन के लिए ही नहीं, बल्कि हर प्रकार की सम्पत्ति के लिए भी यह उतनी ही सही बात है, खासकर उत्पादन के साधनों के लिए। उपभोग की वस्तुओं के लिए भी यह बात थोड़ी-बहुत लागू होती ही है। अन्यथा राशनिंग का कोई अर्थ न रहता। राशनिंग किस औचित्य पर चलता है? **उपभोग की वस्तुओं में भी सबका हिस्सा है** यह तथ्य उसमें निहित होता है।

मालिकी मानव-स्वभाव का मूलभूत गुण नहीं

आज मनोविज्ञान का जो कुछ विकास हुआ है, उस पर से भी यह फलित नहीं होता कि मानव-स्वभाव में मालिकी की बात रूढ़ है। व्यक्तिगत मालिकी मानव-स्वभाव का मूलभूत गुण है, ऐसा नहीं माना जा सकता। उलटे मनोविज्ञान

ने तो यह प्रकट कर दिया है कि कुम्हार के हाथ की मिट्टी से घड़ा भी बन सकता है और कृष्ण की मूर्ति भी बन सकती है, उसी तरह मानव-स्वभाव भी बहुत परिवर्तनशील है, उसे भिन्न-भिन्न आकार दिया जा सकता है, बदला जा सकता है। दुनिया में इस विश्वास के साथ ही सबलोग काम करते हैं कि मनुष्य के स्वभाव को 'एजुकेट' किया जा सकता है, शिक्षित किया जा सकता है और उसकी वष्टत्तियों को बदला जा सकता है, जातीय वष्टत्ति को भी मोड़ा जा सकता है।

मनुष्य कभी अकेला नहीं रह सकता

व्यक्तिगत मालिकी का इतिहास भी देखिये। यह बात समाज में कब से आयी? मनुष्य कभी अकेला नहीं रह सकता। वह सामाजिक प्राणी है। पहले के जमाने में मनुष्य 'कबीले' बनाकर रहता था। उनके पास जो भी सम्पत्ति होती थी, वह उस छोटे समूह की होती थी। व्यक्तिगत मालिकी का विचार तो बाद में आया। कोई यह कहे कि यह तो एक सांस्कृतिक मूल्य है, मानव'-संस्कृति आगे बढ़ी है उसकी निशानी है, तो भले कहे। बाकी, शरीर में जैसे विविध कोषाणु एक दूसरे से गुँथे हुए हैं, उसी प्रकार मानव-समाज भी गूँथा हुआ है।

मनुष्य का स्वतंत्र व्यक्तित्व और पृथक् व्यक्तित्व, ये दो अलग-अलग चीजें हैं। आज मानव-स्वभाव वहाँ पहुँचा है, जहाँ मानव बालू के कणों की तरह एक inorganic mass (निर्जीव समुदाय) बनकर जी रहा है। उसमें से पुनः हमें Organic community (जीवन्त मानव-समुदाय) बनाना है। आज तो जीवन का टुकड़ीकरण हो गया है, छिन्न-भिन्न हो गया है। आज लोग साथ रहते हैं, किन्तु लोक-जीवन साथ नहीं चलता। पाश्चात्य देशों में भी इस बारे में पुनः विचार हो रहा। वे लोग भी पुनः ऐसा समाज स्थापित करने का प्रयत्न कर रहे हैं, जिसमें लोग एक-दूसरे की चिन्ता करते हों, परस्पर मदद करते हों, एक-दूसरे के लिए जहाँ त्याग और सहयोग की भावना हो। और यह लोक-कल्याणकारी राज्य द्वारा नहीं, बल्कि आदमी की हैसियत से एक-दूसरे को मदद करे, ऐसी स्थिति वे लाना चाहते हैं। लोक-कल्याणकारी राज्य द्वारा उन्होंने सामाजिक सुरक्षा की व्यवस्था की, एक तन्त्र खड़ा किया। किन्तु उससे पारस्परिक सहयोग का मूल्य मानव-हृदय में प्रवेश नहीं कर पाया। उन लोगों ने समाज-व्यवस्था को स्पर्धात्मक ही रहने दिया। उसमें व्यक्तिगत मालिकी को एक बहुत बड़ा मूल्य माना गया। क्या हम भी इस तरह अपने समाज को छिन्न-भिन्न हो जाने देना चाहते हैं? यह तो गलत होगा, खतरनाक सिद्ध होगा।

मालिकी की बात बाद में आयी है

यह व्यक्तिगत मालिकी की बात कोई विज्ञान-सिद्ध बात नहीं है। न तो यह मानव-स्वभाव में रूढ़ हुई बात है। पहले जमाने में तो जमीन समूचे समाज की थी। व्यक्तिगत मालिकी की बात बाद में आयी। उसके कारण समाज में भेद की दीवारें खड़ी हुई हैं। एक तरफ मजदूर, दूसरी तरफ मालिक, ऐसी दो दुनिया खड़ी हो गयी है। मालिक-मजदूर का यह भेद नहीं रहना चाहिए, ऐसा हम मानते हैं। सर्वोदय, समाजवाद, साम्यवाद, ये सब विचारधाराएँ इस विषय में एकमत हैं। इन भेदों से शोषण की व्यवस्था कायम रहती है, विशेषताओं के लिए रास्ते खुले रहते हैं और संघर्ष चलते रहते हैं। मालिकी समाज की हो जाने पर अशान्ति का एक बड़ा कारण दूर होगा।

मालिकी की इस प्रथा से समाज का नैतिक पतन हो रहा है। जो मालिक नहीं, वह मालिक बनना चाहता है और जो है वह अधिक-से-अधिक सम्पत्ति इकट्ठी करना चाहता है। लाठी से, घूसखोरी से, बेईमानी से और ऐसे ही दूसरे गलत साधनों से वह दूसरों की मालिकी हड़पने की कोशिश करता है। देश और दुनिया में जो नैतिक पतन दिखाई देता है, जो लड़ाइयाँ होती हैं, जो अशान्ति है, उन सबके मूल को हम काटना चाहते हैं।

मालिकी कोई सनातन सत्य नहीं

कोई समाजशास्त्र या धर्मशास्त्र यह नहीं कहता कि व्यक्ति मालिक है। व्यक्तिगत मालिकी की बात कोई सनातन सत्य नहीं है। इस पृथ्वी पर जो कुछ है, वह सबका है, भगवान् का है। यह कुदरत की देन है। भगवान् के यहाँ से काई यह लिखाकर नहीं आता कि यह 500 बीघा जमीन मेरी है। यह सब तो मनुष्यों ने—भगवान् की संतानों ने—स्वयं खड़ा किया है।

उत्पादन की प्रक्रिया एक सामाजिक प्रक्रिया

जमीन भगवान् की देन है। किन्तु प्रकृति के गर्भ में जो कुछ है, उसका उपभोग मनुष्य ज्यों-का-त्यों नहीं करता। मनुष्य सीधे मिट्टी तो नहीं खाता, वह जमीन में से अन्न पैदा करके खाता है। जो कुछ धरती के अन्दर-बाहर और हवा में है, उन सबमें से मनुष्य अपना श्रम और अपनी बुद्धि लगाकर कुछ नया पैदा करता है। और इसके लिए सारे समाज की सहायता की जरूरत पड़ती है। फिर भी कोई कहे कि इसका मालिक मैं हूँ, तो यह बात शत्-प्रतिशत गलत है, असत्य है। **उत्पादन की प्रक्रिया एक सामूहिक प्रक्रिया है, सामाजिक प्रक्रिया है, एक Social**

process है। उसमें प्रत्यक्ष, अप्रत्यक्ष रूप से अनेक लोग मदद करते हैं। मेहनत, पूँजी, बुद्धि, सब एक साथ लगती है, तब उत्पादन होता है। इसलिए उसमें सारे समाज का हिस्सा है। एक कहे कि बुद्धि मैंने लगायी, इसलिए मैं मालिक हूँ। दूसरा कहे कि पूँजी मैंने लगायी, इसलिए मैं मालिक हूँ तो यह बात एकदम गलत है। पूँजी लगाने से आप मालिक हो गये और जिसने मेहनत की, उसका कोई हिस्सा ही नहीं? बैंक का ब्याज चुका दिया, मेहनत की मजदूरी चुका दी; इसलिए बाकी का सारा मुनाफा आपका हरगिज नहीं। उस मुनाफे में भी पूरे समाज का हिस्सा है।

किसी ने कच्चा माल पैदा किया, किसी ने मेहनत कर उसे पक्का माल बनाया, किसी ने रेलगाड़ी चलायी .... इस प्रकार उसमें इन सबका हिस्सा है। इस तरह समाज में जो कुछ उत्पन्न होता है, उसका उचित वितरण हो, यह जरूरी है। सम्पत्ति पूरे समाज की और उपभोग कुछ थोड़े से व्यक्ति करें, यह उचित नहीं। कोई सम्पत्ति व्यक्ति की नहीं। उसका न्यायोचित बँटवारा होना चाहिए।

दायित्वपूर्ण सहयोगी मानव-समाज स्थापित करना है

एक दायित्वपूर्ण समाज–responsible society बने, ऐसा क्रान्तिकारी विचार इस ग्रामदान में है। मात्र गरीबों पर दया नहीं कर रहे हैं, बल्कि व्यक्तिगत मालिकी का विसर्जन भी कर रहे हैं। पहले गाँवों में सहयोग तथा सहजीवन का जो मूल्य था, वह हमें पुनः स्थापित करना है। ग्रामदान सहयोगी मानव-समाज स्थापित करने की दिशा में पहला कदम है। उसमें व्यक्तिगत मालिकी का विसर्जन एक बुनियादी विचार है। समाज में जो भी सम्पत्ति है, उस पर व्यक्तिगत मालिकी हो ही नहीं सकती। वह सारी सम्पति पूरे समाज का है। ग्रामदान-आन्दोलन के पीछे यह एक मूलभूत विचार है। किन्तु यह विचार हमें तलवार, बन्दूक अथवा कानून द्वारा अमल में नहीं लाना है, बल्कि लोग समझ-बूझकर अपनी मालिकी समाज की समर्पित करें और मालिक तो समाज है, भगवान है, ऐसा मानें, यही हमें करना है। ग्रामदान-आन्दोलन द्वारा हम ऐसा करने का प्रयत्न कर रहे हैं।

सात्त्विक समाजवाद यानी सर्वोदय

सर्वोदय की अपनी एक खास पद्धति है। समाजवाद और सर्वोदय में जो महत्वपूर्ण अन्तर है; वह है कार्यपद्धति और साधन का। समाजवाद की स्थापना सभी देशों में सामान्य रूप से राज्य-शक्ति द्वारा होती है। देश में लोकतंत्र हो, तो चुनाव द्वारा राज्य-सत्ता हाथ में लेकर उसके द्वारा समाजवाद की स्थापना की जाती है। इसमें

मुख्य रूप से कानून का सहारा लिया जाता है। साम्यवाद में एक दूसरा भेद यह है कि समाजवाद की स्थापना के लिए वह हिंसा का भी सहारा लेता है, जबकि सर्वोदय का कार्यक्रम है लोगों के विचारों में परिवर्तन लाकर उनके व्यवहारों में भी वैसा ही परिवर्तन लाने के लिए लोक-शिक्षण करना। वह कार्यक्रम बहुत व्यापक है और लोकशक्ति पर आधारित है।

इस प्रकार समाजवाद की तीन परिभाषाएँ की जा सकती हैं: (1) जो समाजवाद हिंसा से, बलपूर्वक स्थापित किया गया हो, वह तामसिक समाजवाद यानी 'साम्यवाद' है। (2) जो समाजवाद कानून से राज्य-शक्ति द्वारा स्थापित किया गया हो, वह राजसिक समाजवाद यानी 'लोकतान्त्रिक समाजवाद' है। (3) और जो समाजवाद स्वेच्छापूर्वक जनता के विचारों तथा व्यवहारों में परिवर्तन लाकर स्थापित होता है, वह 'सात्त्विक समाजवाद' यानी 'सर्वोदय' है। यद्यपि जैसे मनुष्य में उपर्युक्त तीनों गुणों का सम्मिश्रण होता है, उसी प्रकार इसमें भी होता है। किन्तु व्यवहार में जो गुण अधिक दीखता है, उसके आधार पर यह कहा जाता है कि वह अमुक प्रकार का है।

तो, ग्रामदान-आन्दोलन ऐसा सात्त्विक समाजवाद लाना चाहता है और वहीं असली समाजवाद होगा। मेरा यह दृढ़ विश्वास है कि भौतिकवादी दर्शन के आधार पर समाजवादी समाज-रचना कदापि नहीं हो सकेगी। समाजवादी तन्त्र के जो नमूने दुनिया में जहाँ-तहाँ दिखलायी पड़ते हैं, उनके अनुभवों से तो मुझे यह लगता है कि इस तरह राज्यवाद का ही विस्तार होगा, कोई समाजवादी समाज-रचना नहीं खड़ी होगी। क्योंकि आज समाजवादी आन्दोलन में मानव-निर्माण का कोई कार्यक्रम नहीं दीखता। समाजवादियों का ध्यान राजसत्ता पर अधिकार करके उसका उपयोग करने की ओर इतना अधिक केन्द्रित हो गया है कि लोकशक्ति खड़ी करके उसके द्वारा कुछ करने की बात उन्हें सूझती ही नहीं। किन्तु आज राज्यशक्ति द्वारा जो समाजवाद बना है या बनाने का प्रयत्न हो रहा है, उसमें अब पश्चिम यूरोप के समाजवादियों को कुछ कमी नजर आ रही है, कुछ दोष नजर आ रहे हैं। वे सब आज सोच रहे हैं कि हमने इतनी प्रगति की ओर यह सारी सफलताएँ प्राप्त हुईं, लेकिन समाजवाद के जो असली उद्देश्य थे, क्या वे हमें प्राप्त हुए। समाजवाद के कुछ नैतिक मूल्य (Spiritual values) थे। समाजवाद एक जीवन-पद्धति के रूप में था। वे मूल्य तो आज प्राप्त नहीं हुए हैं। वे सारी चीजें पीछे पड़ गयी हैं। इस तरह चिन्तनशील समाजवादियों के सामने अब यह प्रश्न है कि जो हमारे असली उद्देश्य थे, वे पीछे छूट गये हैं, उनकी प्राप्ति कैसे होगी।

ग्राम-भावना के बिना सारी कोशिशें गर्द पर पोताई के समान

हमारे यहाँ भी ऐसा ही अनुभव आया। पण्डित नेहरू राजसत्ता में गये। उन पर तो जनता का अपार प्रेम था। और उन्हें इतनी अधिक सत्ता प्राप्त की थी कि वे करीब-करीब देश के सर्वसत्ताधीश थे। गरीबों के लिए भी उनके दिन में दर्द था। फिर भी राजसत्ता द्वारा वे क्या कर सके, यह हम देख चुके। सामुदायिक विकास-योजना के द्वारा एक तरफ से पैसा फेंक दिया गया और दूसरी तरफ से पंचायतों के द्वारा सब उनके पास फेंक दी गयी। फिर भी हमने देखा कि जबतक गाँव में कोई मानसिक परिवर्तन नहीं होता, कुछ नया नहीं होता, नयी दृष्टि नहीं आती, तब तक सारी कोशिशें गर्द पर पोताई के समान हैं। एक बार तत्कालीन केन्द्रीय सामुदायिक विकासमन्त्री श्री एस० के० डे० साहब विनोबा जी से मिलने मद्रास गये थे। उन्होंने विनोबा से कहा कि "मैं कम्युनिटी डेवलपमेण्ट (सामुदायिक विकास) का काम कर रहा हूँ, लेकिन कम्युनिटी (समुदाय) की भावना तो गाँव में है नहीं। वह तो आपके ग्रामदान द्वारा ही लायी जा सकती है। ग्रामदान द्वारा गाँवों में कम्युनिटी (समुदाय) बनती है, जिसके आधार पर डेवलपमेण्ट (विकास) हो सकता है।"

गाँव में ऐसी पारस्परिक भावना हो कि हम सब मिलकर एक हैं, हम सब एक-दूसरे पर अवलंबित हैं, एक-दूसरे के सहयोग से हमें जीना है। विनोबाजी इसे ग्राम भावना कहते हैं और ग्रामदान द्वारा उसे लाने का प्रयत्न हो रहा है। **समाजवादी समाज-रचना करनी हो, तो वह भी इस ग्राम-भावना के आधार पर ही खड़ी की जा सकेगी।**

गाँधीजी भी गाँवों से ही शुरूआत करना चाहते थे

स्वराज्य मिलने के बाद आगे के काम के लिए गाँधीजी के मन में भी यही कल्पना थी। वह जोर देकर कहते थे कि भारतीय ग्राम और ग्राम-स्वराज्य ही उनके भावी समाज की बुनियाद है। वे भी अपना आगे का काम गाँव से ही शुरू करना चाहते थे। उन्होंने कहा था कि जब सात लाख गाँवों (उनके मन में हिन्दुस्तान-पाकिस्तान एक ही थे) का विकास होगा, तब उसका प्रभाव शहरों पर भी पड़ेगा। मैं यह नहीं मानता कि गाँधीजी शहरों के प्रति उदासीन थे। फिर भी उनके लिए बुनियाद ग्राम-स्वराज्य ही था। बिल्कुल इसी ढंग से विनोबाजी आज काम कर रहे हैं।

आज के शिक्षित लोगों को, उनकी आधुनिक दृष्टि से, यह एक अनोखी ही बात लगती है। हालाँकि इससे पहले भी चीन में माओ ने गाँवों के किसानों द्वारा क्रान्ति करके दिखायी है, इसलिए यह कोई अनोखी बात नहीं लगनी चाहिए। फिर

भी बुद्धिजीवियों को यह समझाना बहुत कठिन होता है कि भारत जैसे देश में क्रान्ति की शुरूआत गाँवों से ही हो सकती है।

और हमारे अपने लोगों के दिमाग में भी नया समाज कैसे बनेगा, इसकी कोई स्पष्ट कल्पना नहीं है, अन्यथा गाँव का महत्व हमारी नजरों में तुरन्त आ जाता। आज गाँवों की जो स्थिति है, उसका जो स्वरूप है, उसे तो हमें बदल ही डालना है। हमारी योजना में न तो आज के जैसे शहर रहेंगे और न आज के जैसे गाँव रहेंगे। हम दोनों को बदल देना चाहते हें। गाँधीजी तो गाँवों का शहरीकरण हैं और शहरों का ग्रामीकरण करने की बात करते थे। उनकी कल्पना यह थी कि समाज-रचना ऐसी हो, जिससे छोटी-छोटी 'कम्युनिटी' बने। लेकिन वह आज के गाँवों जैसी न हो। आज के गाँवों को तो गाँधीजी ने कूड़े-कचरे के ढेर की संज्ञा दी थी। उनके मन में कृषि-औद्योगिक छोटे-छोटे समुदायों की कल्पना थी। वे चाहते थे कि कृषि और उद्योग दोनों का समन्वय होना चाहिए, दोनों के बीच एक संतुलन रहना चाहिए। इसके लिए एक नये प्रकार की तकनालॉजी की जरूरत पड़ेगी, ऐसा भी वे मानते थे।

यह बात भी बुद्धिजीवियों के गले जल्दी नहीं उतरती। वे कहते हैं कि आज तकनालॉजी इतनी आगे बढ़ गयी है, तब भी आप लोग इन छोटे-छोटे समुदायों की बात क्यों करते हैं? अब समझने की बात यह है कि तकनालॉजी मनुष्य की सेवक बन कर रहेगी या उसके सिर पर चढ़कर बैठेगी? आज तो विदेशों में लोग यह अनुभव कर रहे हैं कि आज की तकनालॉजी का ढाँचा इतना भीमकाय हो गया है कि मनुष्य उसके नीचे दब गया है। क्या आधुनिक तकनालॉजी मानवीय पैमाने (human scale) में नहीं रह सकती? मानवीय सम्बन्ध भी विकसित हो सके, ऐसा कोई स्वरूप उसका नहीं हो सकता? तकनालॉजी का कोई मानवीय लक्ष्य (human purpose) है या नहीं? ये सब बातें यदि हम समझ लें तो गाँवों से क्यों शुरूआत करनी चाहिए, यह बार तुरन्त स्पष्ट हो जाएगी।

ट्राटस्की 'परमानेण्ट रेवोल्यूशन' (सतत क्रान्ति) की बात कहता था। किन्तु उसे तो उड़ा दिया गया। क्योंकि क्रान्तिकारी जब स्वयं गद्दी पर आ बैठता है, तब वह सतत क्रान्ति नहीं चाहता। किन्तु यदि बारीकी से देखें तो यह स्पष्ट होगा कि ग्रामदानी गाँव में ग्रामसभा बनती है और वह सक्रिय रूप से काम करना शुरू कर देती है, तो इस सतत क्रान्ति की प्रक्रिया शुरू हो जाती है। कितने ही प्रश्न होंगे, जिनका हल गाँववालों को ग्रामसभा में एक साथ बैठकर ढूँढना होगा। हाँ, देखना यह है कि सर्वानुमति के सिद्धान्त में जो एक रूढ़िवादिता का तत्त्व भी रहता है, उसका प्रभाव अधिक रहता है या क्रान्तिकारिता का। यदि क्रान्तिकारिता का प्रभाव

कायम रह सका, तो यह ग्रामसभा 'परमानेण्ट रेवोल्यूशन' (सतत क्रान्ति) के लिए एक उत्तम माध्यम बन सकेगी।

अपने समाजवादी मित्रों से

इस तरह, ग्रामदान-आन्दोलन भारत जैसे देश में गाँवों से शुरू होनेवाली एक क्रान्ति का स्वरूप हमारे सामने खड़ा कर देता है। यह एक प्रारम्भिक कदम है, लेकिन क्रान्तिकारी है। यह क्रान्ति अहिंसक पद्धति से होती है, स्वेच्छा से होती है, यह उसकी खूबी है। कानून द्वारा तो यह कभी भी संभव नहीं हो सकता।

इसलिए काफी चिन्तन के बाद मैं इस नतीजे पर पहुँचा हूँ कि इस ग्रामदान के कार्यक्रम में अपूर्व शक्ति है। मैं तो अपने समाजवादी मित्रों से हमेशा कहता रहता हूँ कि ग्रामदान-आन्दोलन से तो आपके लिए एक राजमार्ग खुल जाता है। इस आन्दोलन के विविध पहलुओं को समझेंगे और हृदय से इस ग्रामदान के कार्यक्रम को अपना लेंगे तो समाजवाद का या नयी समाज-रचना का जो सपना आप देखते हैं, वह धरती पर साकार होता देख सकेंगे।

डॉ० राममनोहर लोहिया से आखिर में पटना में हमारी मुलाकात हुई थी और काफी चर्चा भी हुई थी। सर्वोदय-आन्दोलन में हम क्या कर रहे हैं, मैं खुद क्या कर रहा हूँ, उसके पीछे क्या विचार है, क्या दृष्टि है, इसकी भी हम लोगों ने कुछ चर्चा की थी। मुझे लगा कि डॉ० साहब ने इसको न सिर्फ ध्यान से सुना, बल्कि उन्होंने अपने हृदय में लिया। इसलिए जब वे दिल्ली गये, तो पत्रकारों की मुलाकात में कहा कि हम लोगों की जो बात हुई, वह अच्छी हुई।

यदि समाजवादी आन्दोलन के अपने सभी साथियों को भी मैं इस नयी यात्रा में अपने साथ चलने के लिए राजी कर सका होता, तो मेरे दिल में बेहद खुशी होती। किन्तु ऐसा सम्भव नहीं हो सका। बल्कि आज तक बहुत सारे साथियों की ओर से यह शिकायत होती रही है कि जयप्रकाश नारायण ने हमें छोड़ दिया और उनके ऐसा करने से राजनीति को और खासकर समाजवादी आन्दोलन को भारी क्षति पहुँची।

किन्तु मैं यह कहना चाहता हूँ कि इस ग्रामदान-आन्दोलन की सफलता ही प्रत्यक्ष समाजवाद की क्रान्ति होगी। इस क्रान्ति से समाजवाद की इतनी शक्ति बढ़ेगी कि जितनी समाजवादी पक्ष के या पक्षीय राजनीति के दायरे में सीमित रहकर किसी प्रकार भी बढ़ना सम्भ्व नहीं है।

मेरे जो पुराने साथी अभी भी मुझसे नेतागिरी की अपेक्षा रखते हैं, उनसे मैं पूछना चाहूँगा कि आप कहते हैं कि जयप्रकाश नारायण आपका नेता बने, लेकिन नेता बनकर करे क्या? करे और कहे वह, जो आप चाहते हों! यानी जयप्रकाश

नारायण अपना दिमाग कहीं रखकर आये, उसे कहीं ताले में बन्द कर दे। आप उसके दिमाग को, कार्य-कलाप को, विचार को समझना चाहते हैं? वह क्या कर रहा है, वह क्या बोल रहा है, उसका समाजवाद से अथवा जनता के भविष्य के साथ क्या सम्बन्ध है? यह सब आप समझना चाहते हैं? क्या आपको कोई ऐसा नेता मिलेगा, जो आपकी शर्तों पर आपका नेता बनने को तैयार होगा? मैं तो अपनी शर्तों पर नेता बनने को तैयार हूँ। मानिये मेरी शर्त और चलिये गाँव में मेरे साथ। मैं जंगल में नहीं गया हूँ, हिमालय की गुफाओं में नहीं गया हूँ। गाँधियन इन्स्टीट्यूट में बैठा-बैठा किताब नहीं पढ़ रहा हूँ या शोध नहीं कर रहा हूँ। पहले जितना काम करता था, उससे ज्यादा ही कामकाज करता हूँ और वह भी जनता के बीच रहकर करता हूँ।

समाजवाद को सर्वोदय में विलीन होना ही पड़ेगा

इसीलिए मेरी सभी साथियों से प्रार्थना है कि मैं जो कुछ सोचता हूँ, अपने जो विचार आप लोगों के सामने रखता हूँ, जिस कार्यक्रम में आज मैं लगा हूँ, उसे समझने की कोशिश करें। मेरा यह अटल विश्वास है कि दुनिया में यदि कभी शान्ति, स्वतन्त्रता और बन्धुत्व स्थापित करना हो, तो समाजवाद को आखिरकार सर्वोदय में विलीन होना ही पड़ेगा। सर्वोदय-आन्दोलन के सम्बन्ध में प्राय: एक. शिकायत यह हुआ करती है कि वह राजनीति से अलग रहता है। आचार्य कृपालानी और ढेबरभाई जैसे सर्वोदय के मित्र भी हमेशा कहते रहते हैं कि आप लोग देश की 'मेन स्ट्रीम' से, मुख्य धारा से अलग हो गये हैं। किन्तु मैं इस बात से आज तक सहमत नहीं हो सका हूँ। मैं तो यही कहता रहा हूँ कि सर्वोदय का आन्दोलन, जो जनता के बीच चल रहा है, वही बुनियादी आन्दोलन है और वही देश की मुख्य धारा है। सर्वोदय-आन्दोलन राजनीति से अलग रहा है, यह ख्याल भी गलत है। उलटे हमने तो कमजोर और नकली राजनीति के बदले सशक्त और असली राजनीति ग्रहण की है। हम सर्वोदय-आन्दोलन में जो कुछ कर रहे हैं, वह गम्भीरतम अर्थ में राजनीति ही है, क्योंकि यदि हमें सफलता मिले तो हिन्दुस्तान की सारी सामाजिक-आर्थिक-राजनीतिक पद्धति में एक आमूल क्रान्ति आ जाय। इसलिए वास्तव में हम राजनीति से बाहर निकले नहीं हैं, उलटे राजनीति की गहराई में हमने प्रवेश किया है। इस बात का भावार्थ जनता समझे, यह बहुत महत्वपूर्ण है। इसलिए इस विषय में गहराई से विचार कर लेना चाहिए।

मेरी विचार यात्रा, भाग-1 1972 से उद्धृत।

45

रैडिकल सर्वोदय
(RADICAL SARVODAYA)

आचार्य राममूर्ति

राष्ट्र के पुनर्निर्माण की नैतिक धारा भूदान-ग्रामदान ह्रास की ओर जाने लगी तथा राजसत्ता लोकतंत्र-और राष्ट्र दोनों का अहित करने पर उतारू हो गयी। ऐसे संकट का समय था वह! एक प्रकार की शून्यता थी जिसमें प्रकाश की कोई रेखा दिखायी नहीं देती थी।

1973 का दिसम्बर महीना। जे.पी. ने भारत के युवकों के नाम अपील निकाला–'लोकतंत्र के लिए युवा' (यूथ फॉर डेमोक्रेसी) और यह कहा कि लोकतंत्र की पहली चीज है जिसकी रक्षा होनी चाहिए। संकट नैतिक है। यदि लोकतंत्र हाथ से निकल गया तो स्वतंत्रता निरर्थक हो जायेगी। जे.पी. पहले व्यक्ति थे जिन्होंने लोकतंत्र के राष्ट्रीय संकट को पहचाना, और उसे बचाने के लिए संघर्ष का आवाह्न किया।

यह आवाह्न युवकों के कानों में पड़ा। परिस्थिति की माँग तो थी ही। जनवरी '74 में गुजरात, और मार्च में बिहार में उफान आया। लगा, लोग आँखे खोल रहे हैं। मार्क्सवाद, समाजवाद की विचार-यात्रा से लौटे जे.पी. ने बीस वर्षों तक विनोबाजी का सिपाही बनकर भूदान-ग्रामदान के लिए गाँव-गाँव की खाक छानी थी। इतनी तपस्या करने के बाद उन्हें 1973 में लोकतंत्र की पुकार लगानी पड़ी और 1974 में निरंकुश सत्ता के विरुद्ध खड़ा हो जाना पड़ा, ठीक जैसे गाँधी 54 में पहिले ब्रिटिश सत्ता के विरुद्ध खड़े हो गये थे। बिहार में जे.पी. ने परिस्थिति के अनुसार गाँधीजी के क्रांति-दर्शन का संशोधित रूप प्रस्तुत किया। गाँधीजी का सत्याग्रही स्वराजदर्शन था। जे.पी. ने सम्पूर्ण क्रांति का ऐसा

दर्शन प्रस्तुत किया जिसमें उन्होंने अपने सत्याग्रही संघर्ष द्वारा लोकतंत्र के विकास तथा मानव की मुक्ति और उसकी नयी समाज-रचना के लिए मुक्ति का रास्ता दिखाया था। गाँधीजी ने रचनात्मक कार्य द्वारा पाश्चात्य अर्थनीति का प्रतिकार किया था, उसमें जे.पी. ने 1949 में भूमि के ग्रामीकरण (विलेजाइजेशन ऑव लैण्ड) की बात जोड़ी थी। सम्पूर्ण क्रांति में जे.पी. का मुख्य ध्यान लोकतंत्र, लोकतांत्रिक व्यवस्था, लोकतांत्रिक क्रांति तथा लोकतांत्रिक जीवन शैली पर था। 'जनता सरकार' के द्वारा वह क्रांति को लोकतंत्र की एक प्रक्रिया बना देना चाहते थे ताकि समाज अपनी गति तथा अपनी सम्पत्ति से आरोहण के मार्ग पर चल सके। इसमें राज्य का इतना ही काम रहे कि लोक-सम्मति पर कानून की मुहर लगा दे। गाँधीजी ने कल्पना की थी कि स्वतंत्र भारत क्रमशः ग्राम-गणराज्यों का महासंघ बने। जे.पी. ने भारतीय संविधान के अन्तर्गत छोटे राज्यों तथा स्थानीय इकाइयों का समर्थन किया ताकि सत्ता ओर जनता में सामीप्य बना रहे, और राष्ट्र ऐसे छोटे राज्यों का महासंघ बने। विनोबाजी ने दक्षिण एशिया में अफगानिस्तान, बर्मा, सीलोन (ए.बी.सी.) के त्रिकोण के देशों के महासंघ की कल्पना की थी।

जे.पी. के चिंतन में एक ऐसी गतिशीलता थी जो परिस्थिति के अनुसार उन्हें परिवर्तन की ओर मोड़ती रहती थी। दुख है कि उनकी सम्पूर्ण क्रांति को विनोबाजी द्वारा इस दृष्टि से देखा नहीं गया। इन्दिरा ने तो नहीं ही देखा। अगर जे.पी. की पहल को इस दृष्टि से दोनों ने देखा होता तो देश को एक नयी दिशा मिली होती, और लोकतंत्र की शक्ति पाकर राज्य और राष्ट्र दोनों शक्तिशाली हुए होते। यह नहीं हुआ। हुआ यह कि 'नेशन-स्टेट' की निरंकुश शक्ति दिनोंदिन बढ़ती रही, और समाज का ह्रास नहीं रोका जा सका। जे.पी. ने अहिंसा को मूल्य-निष्ठ लोकतांत्रिक प्रक्रिया का रूप देने की कोशिश की ताकि अहिंसा लोकतंत्र के द्वारा राष्ट्रीय जीवन और विकास में घुल-मिल जाये, किन्तु वह नहीं हो सका। अन्त में जेपी को अपनी वसीयत रैडिकल सर्वोदय के हाथों में छोड़ कर जाना पड़ा। रैडिकल सर्वोदय केवल शब्द नहीं है, एक नया दर्शन है जिसकी परतें समय के साथ खुलेंगी और उसका प्रकाश देश-विदेश तक फैलेगा। शायद तभी जे.पी. की 'विफलताओं की विरासत' सार्थक होगी।

सम्पूर्ण क्रान्ति का पहला अध्याय, जितना जे.पी. जीते जी लिख सके, वही आगे के लिए हमारी पूँजी है। 1974-75 में जो कुछ हुआ वह बहुत-कुछ उस समय की परिस्थिति से प्रभावित था। यों भी एक प्रारंभिक अभ्यास था। चार सौ पैंसठ दिनों के अभियान में जितना हो सकता था हो गया। उँगली पकड़कर जे.पी.

ने हमें 'जनता सरकार' तक पहुँचा दिया, तथा 'डबल फ्रंट स्ट्रैटजी'–संसद ऊपर, जनता सरकार धरती पर–का मार्ग दिखा कर गये।

बीसवीं शताब्दी में समाज और क्रांति के जो दर्शन विकसित हुए उनकी विभिन्न धाराओं ने बीसवीं शताब्दी में हमें प्रभावित किया है। हमारी सोच बदली है, हमारे काम करने की पद्धति बदली है। लोकतंत्र एक समग्र दर्शन के रूप में उभरा है। जिन मूल्यों के लिए कभी क्रांति की बात सोची जाती थी वे अब लोकतंत्र के दायरे के अंदर आ गये हैं। मानव–अधिकार, लिंग–समानता, सामाजिक न्याय, बुनियादी आवश्यकताओं की पूर्ति, बालिग मताधिकार राज्य के मुकाबिले नागरिक के अधिकारों के लिए संविधान में दी गयी गारंटी, अल्पसंख्यकों को संरक्षण, कानून का राज आदि विषय अब क्रांति के नहीं, लोकतंत्र के प्रश्न हैं। लोकतंत्र के क्रांतिकारी स्वरूप को निखारते जाने की चुनौती हमारे सामने है। जे. पी. ने उस चुनौती को पहचाना था, इसिलिए लोकतंत्र को 'प्राथमिकताओं में पहला स्थान' दिया था। लोकतंत्र परिस्थितियों के दबाव में, इस युग के प्रभाव में, स्वयं गतिशील होता जा रहा है।

सम्पूर्ण क्रांति के अगले अध्यायों को कौन लिखेगा? हर पीढ़ी अपना अध्याय लिखेगी। नियति को लेखनी कुछ लिखेगी, और लिखकर आगे बढ़ जायेगी। आरोहण की प्रक्रिया में कोई अंतिम अध्याय नहीं होगा।

जे.पी. ने सम्पूर्ण क्रांति को आगे बढ़ाने की जिम्मेदारी 'रैडिकल सर्वोदय' को सौंपी है। और उसे यह कह कहकर परिभाषित किया है कि रेडिकल सर्वोदय परिवर्तन–निष्ठ हो, केवल अच्छे काम करके संतोष न मान ले।

जीवन के मूल्य स्थायी हैं, सनातन हैं, काल के साथ उनके स्वरूप बदलते रहेंगे, किन्तु वे स्वयं अक्षुण्ण रहेंगे। रैडिकल सर्वोदय मूल्यों का वाहक होगा। उसकी शक्ति नैतिक होगी, राजनैतिक नहीं। वह लोकशक्ति को प्रेरित करेगा, स्वयं सत्ता से अलग रहेगा।

राजनैतिक शक्ति लोकनीति के अन्तर्गत होगी। इसलिए उसे भी 'रेडिकल' होना चाहिए। रैडिकल सर्वोदय तथा रैडिकल लोकनीति के मोरचे अलग होंगे, किन्तु अभियान एक होगा। सम्पूर्ण क्रान्ति की दोहरी रणनीति होगी नैतिक और लोकनैतिक (राजनैतिक)।

कार्यक्रम और कार्य–पद्धति, ये परिस्थिति–निरपेक्ष नहीं हो सकते, हमेशा परिस्थिति–सापेक्ष ही होंगे। गाँधी के सत्य–अहिंसा के मूल्य, मार्क्स का वर्ग–संघर्ष, विनोबा का ग्राम–स्वराज्य, जे.पी. का चतुर्विध संघर्ष, लोकतंत्र की सम्भावनाएँ, इन सबका समन्वय सम्पूर्ण क्रान्ति की कार्य–योजना में होगा। जे.पी. ने एक बार

समन्वय का रास्ता दिखा दिया है। कोई कारण नहीं कि आने वाले दिनों में समन्वय का क्रम तथा रेडिकल शक्तियों के कदम आगे न बढ़ें।

किसके हाथ में मशाल

जे.पी. से पूछा गया–"आपके बाद कौन आपका काम कौन करेगा?" जे.पी. का उत्तर था–"मैं सोचता हूँ कि क्रांति का काम फिर कौन शुरू करेगा। मैं इस नतीजे पर पहुँचा हूँ कि वह काम 'रेडिकल सर्वोदय ग्रुप' करेगा, जो क्रांति में विश्वास करता है, न कि नेकी, भलाई का कुछ काम कर संतोष कर लेता है।"

सर्वोदय का महत्व इस दृष्टि से भी है लोकतंत्र में एक तटस्थ नैतिक-शक्ति होनी चाहिए जो दल, धर्म, भाषा, क्षेत्र, जाति आदि संकुचित निष्ठाओं से ऊपर उठकर मनुष्य में निष्ठा रखता हो उसके आचरण का आधार सत्य और अहिंसा के शाष्ठवत मूल्य हों। जहाँ तक सत्ता (पावर) का प्रश्न है सर्वोदय राज्य-सत्ता के मुकाबिले लोक-सत्ता को बढ़ावा देता है, वह स्वयं सत्ता में नहीं जाता लेकिन लोक-शक्ति (पीपुल्स पावर) को प्रेरित करता है। पावर का प्रयोग करने का काम जनता का है, सर्वोदय प्रेरक शक्ति है।

जे.पी. की मान्यता थी कि समाज में मूल्यों के लिए खड़ी होनेवाली ऐसी तटस्थ नैतिक-शक्ति का सर्वोपरि स्थान है। भारत-जैसे विविधताओं से भरे देश में तो उसका स्पष्ट रोल है। ऐसे देश को तथा उसके लोकतंत्र को, 'सत्य की वाणी' की जरूरत है जो राज और समाज दोनों से ऊपर उठकर निर्भय, निर्वैर, निष्पक्ष सत्य का तथा समाज के जीवन में प्रचलित स्वार्थों से ऊपर उठकर मूल्यों का आग्रह रख सके।

सत्ता-परिवर्तन की प्रक्रिया जे.पी. के सामने पूरी हुई, किन्तु जे.पी. ने कभी नहीं माना कि एक पार्टी के स्थान पर दूसरी पार्टी के सरकार में जाने से या पश्चिम के रंग में रंगी विकास की योजनाओं से, क्रांति के लक्ष्य पूरे होंगे। वे पूरे तो तब होंगे जब देश के युवा और गरीब अपनी आवाज बुलंद करेंगे तथा राज्य की व्यवस्था और समाज की रचना में व्याप्त विषमताओं को निकाल फेकेंगे। वह दिन कब आयेगा?

उसने लाने की चुनौती हो जे.पी. की सच्ची विरासत है।

जे.पी. की विरासत, 1999 से उद्धृत।

46

सम्पूर्ण क्रांति का सैद्धांतिक गठन

के.के. सिन्हा

संपूर्ण क्रांति की अवधारणा अपने में संपूर्ण नहीं है, पर 1974 के आन्दोलन ने जब पूरे देश की राज्य-सत्ता को झकझोर दिया तथा यह सत्ता परिवर्तन का एक सफल प्रयोग सिद्ध हुआ तो परिवर्तन और संघर्ष के नए मान उत्पन्न हुए। गाँधी की आजादी की लड़ाई इतनी ही उग्र थी तथा उसके संघर्ष के तत्व भी जे.पी. आन्दोलन के समरूप थे। दोनों ने जनता की आवाज को उठाया तथा राज्य-विरोधी संघर्ष की रचना की। साथ ही साथ जन समर्थन के लिए सामाजिक संरचना के कुछ मुद्दों को भी संघर्ष का हिस्सा बनाया ताकि सत्ता जनता को लुभाने के कोई दाव न खेल सके। अहिंसा के बल पर लड़े जाने वाले संघर्ष के लिए संघर्ष और रचना की दुहरी आवाज एक साथ ध्वनित हुई जिससे संघर्ष में वह ऊर्जा आई जो किसी हिंसक क्रांति से कम उग्र नहीं थी। गाँधी ने अगर बुनियादी शिक्षा, चर्खा तथा अछूतोद्धार का शंख फूंका तो जे.पी. ने भ्रष्टाचार, महँगाई और कुशिक्षा को संघर्ष की चुनौती बनाया। छोटे लगनेवाले ये मुद्दे जमीन से इतने जुड़े थे कि राज्य का सिंहासन हिलने लगा था। राज्य विरोधी संघर्ष का मूल उद्देश्य सत्ता का परिवर्तन ही होता है क्योंकि राज्य-सत्ता का अतिरेक समाज में एक आत्मघाती स्थिति है।

गाँधी तथा जे.पी. दोनों ने बदलाव का पहला कदम सत्ता परिवर्तन को ही माना, इसलिए, यह कहना कि यह अराजकता थी–संघर्ष के मूल तत्व को नकारना है। इस अर्थ में मार्क्सवादी संघर्षों का भी चरित्र राज्य-विरोधी ही था। राज्य सत्ता निजी सम्पत्ति तथा धर्माडम्बरों के आधार पर अपनी सैनिक शक्ति का गठन कर लेता है तो एक यथा-स्थिति (थेसिस) का निर्माण करता है और मार्क्स इसके

साथ टकराव का संघर्ष का नाम देता है। यह टकराव अवश्यभावी है क्योंकि यथास्थिति से कुछ लोगों की सुख-सुविधा तो बढ़ती है लेकिन एक विशाल जनसमुदाय की शक्ति क्षीण होती जाती है।

ऐतिहासिक दृष्टि से मार्क्स ने इसे वर्ग संघर्ष का नाम दिया क्योंकि प्रताड़ित वर्ग राज्य-तंत्र और उसके वर्ग चरित्र से मेल नहीं खाता। इस वर्गों में गोलबंद होने की प्रक्रिया को मार्क्स ने औद्योगिक क्रांति के यूरोपीय परिवेश में देखा। पर वर्ग चाहे जितने हों और जैसे हों, राज्य की केंद्रित शक्ति के अधीन उनमें टकराव होगा ही। संघर्ष का यह सिद्धांत मार्क्स-लेनिन अथवा गाँधी-जे.पी. दोनों के संघर्षों के कहीं न कहीं समरूप है।

यह भी सत्य है कि ऐसे संघर्ष की उग्रता हिंसा में भी बदलने लगती है जैसा कि गाँधी या जे.पी. के आन्दोलनों में भी छिटपुट रूप में देखा गया। मार्क्स ने इसे शोषण की तीव्रता तथा मजदूर चेतना के गहराने की स्थिति बतलाया पर लेनिन अथवा माओ ने हिंसा को संघर्ष का सिद्धांत बना लिया। इसे पूर्णतः मार्क्स से जोड़ना गलत होगा। मार्क्स की पूर्व पुस्तक 'ग्रंद्रीस' अथवा उसकी अनुवादित पुस्तक 'आउट लाइन ऑफ नैशनल इकौनमी, 1930 में वर्ग-शोषण की जगह वर्ग-अलगाव (एलिएनेशन) की बात कही गई है जब अलगाव की स्थिति दबाई जा सकती है पर शोषण की स्थिति तो उकसाई ही जा सकती है। ऐसे में बीच-बचाव तथा दबाव द्वारा वर्ग-संघर्ष को हल्का बनाया जा सकता है, पर इसकी उग्रता शोषण के बढ़ते जाने तथा वर्गों में दोनों तरफ से सैन्य शक्ति के प्रयोग से हिंसक हो जाती है। लेनिन अथवा माओ के हिंसा का सिद्धान्त वास्तव में उन सैनिक जत्थों के मिलने के कारण बन गया जो राज्य की सैनिक शक्ति के विरोध में जन संघर्षों के साथ हो लिए थे। यह संयोग था और मार्क्स की संघर्ष रचना को ऐतिहासिक क्रम से हटाकर उसे आकस्मिक बना देता है जिसमें एक कठोर नेता तथा एक क्रूर पार्टी का वर्चस्व स्थापित हो जाता है।

गाँधी का संघर्ष लेनिन के काल में तथा जे.पी. का माओ के काल में हुआ पर दोनों ने हिंसा को संघर्ष का तत्व नहीं माना। वास्तव में गाँधी की अहिंसा कोई नैतिकता-जन्य नहीं थी बल्कि संघर्ष का व्यावहारिक नियम थी। जब राज्य के साथ सैनिक शक्ति खड़ी हो तब उसका विरोध किसी सैनिक शक्ति से नहीं किया जा सकता, वह तो युद्ध होगा, संघर्ष नहीं। साथ ही साथ हिंसा से जीती हुई लड़ाई के बाद एक हिंसक समाज की ही रचना होगी जो लेनिन अथवा माओ के बाद के दिनों में दिखाई पड़ने लगा।

संघर्ष का दूसरा चरण

राज्य सत्ता से लड़ना कुछ और बात है पर राज्य सत्ता के बदल जाने के बाद रचना काल आता है जब समाज की व्यवस्था से लड़ना होता है। इसके लिए अगर बदली हुई राज्यसत्ता समर्पित रहे तब तो व्यवस्था आसानी से बदलती है पर इस प्रक्रिया में राज्य को भी अपनी सत्ता में कमी करना होता है ताकि उसका लोकसत्ता में विलय होने लगे। पर ऐसा कहीं नहीं हुआ, न साम्यवादी संघर्षों के बाद न लोकतांत्रिक, क्योंकि संघर्ष तुरंत सत्ता का रसपान करने में लग जाता है। 1917 की लेनिन क्रांति के बाद जो सर्वहारा का राज्य बना वह अपनी शक्ति बटोरता गया तथा जो स्थानीय सोवियत जन स्तरों पर बने वे भी राज्य की सैन्य शक्ति का अंग ही बन गए।

रचनाकाल के लिए इसीलिए जे.पी. ने एक तीसरी अराज्य, सत्ता के बाहर की निर्दलीय शक्ति की बात की जो राज्य को अपनी शक्ति को जन-समुदायों में विलय करने के लिए दबाव डाले। पंचायतों का निर्माण हो जो इस प्रक्रिया में तेजी ला सकें। फिर व्यवस्था को जन-सम्मत बदलाव की स्थिति में लाने के लिए भी दबाव डाला जाए। पर रचना काल की ऐसी व्यूह रचना न गाँधी ही और न जे.पी. ही कर पाए।

रचनाकाल में तीन शक्तियाँ बदलाव में विघ्न डालती है—राज्य सत्ता का लोभ, निजी सम्पत्ति की कामना तथा धर्म के आडम्बर। राज्यसत्ता बदल जाने पर भी अपने को फिर खड़ी कर लेती है। वैसे ही निजी सम्पत्ति या धर्म की संस्थाएँ ध्वस्त होने पर भी नए चाले पहनकर उठ खड़ी होती हैं। इससे समाज के पिछड़े, दबे-कुचले वर्ग अलग-थलग पड़ जाते हैं तथा पिछड़ते जाते हैं। स्वाभाविक है कि परिवर्तन का संघर्ष जीत कर भी हारने लगता है। किसी न किसी रूप में साम्यवादी संघर्षों की नियति भी ऐसी ही रही तथा लोकतांत्रिक संघर्ष तो कुछ ज्यादा ही फीके पड़ गए।

रचना के चरण में साम्यवादी संघर्ष को जारी रखने के लिए सर्वहारा की तानाशाही को अन्तकार्लिक मान्यता मिली ताकि राज्य के विलय (विदरिंग अवे ऑफ स्टेट) होने तक तानाशाही राज्य व्यवस्था परिवर्तन के कार्य में ढील न आने दे। पर सत्ता के गलियारे में एक नयी शक्तिशाली शासक तथा सैन्य शक्ति का उदय हुआ जिसने स्थानीय सोवियतों को भी अपनी पार्टी के शिकंजे में जकड़ लिया।

इसमें आर्थिक स्वरूप भी मजदूरों के हित में नहीं उत्पन्न हुआ। मजदूर शिविरों में कृषि तो सिमटती गई, बड़े उद्योगों की ओर राज्य की पूँजी का प्रवाह बढ़ता गया और तथाकथित अर्न्तकालिक राज्य की शक्ति भी पूर्ण राज्य के रूप में बढ़ती गई। क्या ऐसे राज्य पूँजीवादी साम्राज्यवाद जैसे ही नहीं?

ऐतिहासिक दृष्टि से भले ही साम्यवादी राज्यविरोधी संघर्ष सफल हुए पर वे बाद में एक और निर्मम राज्य में ही बदले। ऐसी स्थिति में केवल निजी सम्पत्ति और निजी धर्म से मुक्ति तो मिल गई पर सम्पत्ति और धर्म से मुक्ति नहीं मिली क्योंकि सम्पत्ति राज्य के खाते में बढ़ती गई तथा धर्म भी एक साम्यवादी अंध-विश्वास (डॉग्मा) में बदल कर रह गया।

जे.पी. और गाँधी के रचना-काल में भी वह व्यूहरचना नहीं हो सकी जो राज्य की क्रांति-विरोधी ताकत को भेद सकती। गाँधी ने लोक सेवक संघ के निर्माण से सत्ता के नए बनने वाले गढ़ तो तोड़ना चाहा पर तब तक रचना कर स्वरुप ही बदलने लग गया जिसे गाँधी के संघर्ष ने बनाया था। जे.पी. ने भी गाँधी रचना के अनुभव के आधार पर सम्पूर्ण क्रांति के आयामों को बढ़ाकर संघर्ष को रचना काल मे लम्बा कराना चाहा, पर संघर्ष के बाद सत्ता की चाह इतनी बढ़ती है कि सामान्य जन पुनः अपने को राज्य के घेरे में बद कर लेता हैं सघर्ष के बाद अंतर्कालीन राज्य या संगठन का सिद्धांत सभी देशों में ढहता दिखाई पड़ता है।

राज्य-विरोधी कम्यूनवाद (एनार्किज्म)

यहाँ यूरोप के मार्क्स के काल में ही संघर्ष की एक समानांतर धारा की चर्चा आवश्यक है क्योंकि गाँधी ने अपने को एक राज्य विरोधी (एनार्किस्ट) कहा था। पियरे प्रूढ़ो (1809-65) फ्रांस के कम्यून आन्दोलन का एक हिस्सा था, जिसे पहला एनार्किस्ट कहा जाता है। उसने राज्य, निजी सम्पत्ति तथा धर्म, तीनों को परिवर्तन विरोधी तथा अन्यायपूर्ण तत्व माना। उसे 'सकारात्मक राज्य विरोधी' माना जाता है क्योंकि उसका राज्य-विरोध एक नए सामाजिक संगठन के पक्ष में था जो जनता से स्थानीयता के कारण जुड़ा होता और राज्य से संपोषित स्वार्थी तत्वों को तोड़ने में प्रभावी था।

कुछ एनार्किस्ट राज्य को तोड़ने के कड़े तेवर तथा विप्लवी दृष्टि के लिए इस शांत परिवर्तन के पथभ्रष्ट नायक माने जाते हैं जैसे वाकुनिन (1814-76) अथवा क्रोप्तोकिन (1842-1923) पर ये भी रचना काल में लेनिन की तरह के किसी तानाशाही राज्य के प्रबल विरोधी थे क्योंकि ये मानते थे कि संघर्ष के बाद की स्थिति बिल्कुल सहयोगी तथा समुदायी सूत्र में बँधी होती है।

इस अर्थ में गाँधी ने भी अपने को 'एनार्किस्ट' ही माना वे केवल राज्य विरोधी संघर्ष के काल में भी संयमित विद्रोह के पक्षधर थे, जबकि कई एनार्किस्ट राज्य विरोध को विप्लव एवं षडयंत्र में बदल देना चाहते थे।

पर रचना काल में बाकुनिन आदि का यह सोचना कि समाज की स्थानीय एवं सहकारी भावनाएँ अपनी को स्वयं खड़ी कर राज्य का विकल्प तैयार करती हैं– गाँधी और जेपी के विचारों से बहुत ही निकट हैं। शांति-पक्षीय एनार्किस्ट तो संघर्ष को 'शिक्षा, सुझाव तथा उदाहरण द्वारा प्रेरित करने की बात करते हैं। रचनाकाल के सहयोगी कम्यून, राज्य नहीं, राज्य से जन समुदाय को बचाने के संगठन मात्र थे। "राज्य को उखाड़ फेंको और उसके ध्वंस पर एक मुक्त समाज खड़ा हो जाएगा।" ये विचार जेपी की उस निर्दलीय तीसरी शक्ति के अनूकूल हैं जो सत्ता के बाहर रहकर ऐसी स्थनीय एवं स्वायत्त संगठनों का निर्माण करे। इस स्तर पर जो रचना होगी वह सामान्य जनता के हितों की रक्षा करते हुए एक जन-स्वराज्य अथवा जन-समाजवाद को खड़ा कर लेगी। संपूर्ण क्रांति इसी रचनाकाल के संगठन तथा संघर्ष को दर्शाती है।

जेपी के दुहरे दबाव की धारणा

यह भी विचारणीय है कि राज्यशक्ति का क्षीण होते जाना आकस्मिक नहीं होता। इस अर्थ में एक समर्पित राज्य का गठन जो अपनी शक्ति का विलय जन समुदायों और स्थानीय संगठनों में करने के लिए प्रतिबद्ध हो, जेपी के संपूर्ण क्रांति की एक आवश्यक शर्त्त है। जेपी के भारत की नई सरकार से, जो बिहार आन्दोलन के बाद 'बैलेट' की विधि से ही उत्पन्न हुई थी, ऐसा संकल्प राजघाट पर ही कराया था। साथ-साथ भूदानी पंचायतों को नये समुदायी स्वामित्व का आधार बनाने की भी पहल की थी।

गाँधी या जेपी का संघर्ष तबतक संपूर्ण नहीं होगा जबतक ऐसे ग्रामीण समुदायों और पंचायतों का गठन न हो जाए। रूसी विचारक तोल्सतोय (1880-93 के लेखक) जो एक शांति-पक्षी एनर्किस्ट थे, गाँधी के मजदूरों की श्रम-मानसिकता के साथ राज्य से लड़ते रहने के उग्र सत्याग्रह की प्रशंसा की और कहा कि 'आप (गाँधी) ऐसे आंदोलन को चला रहें जो धरती के दलितों के बीच नई आशा का संचार करेगा।' शांति से संघर्ष की ज्वाला निकलती रहनी चाहिए। जेपी के 'दोहरे दबाव' का बना रहना इस गुत्थी को सुलझा सकता है। शायद संपूर्ण क्रांति की आग इस अर्थ में कहीं न कहीं, किसी न किसी रूप में सुलग रही है और भड़क भी सकती है। यह जिम्मेवारी बुद्धिवादियों, युवाओं और छात्रों पर है तथा उन

शोषित वर्गों के संगठनों पर है जो एक दोहरे दबाव की रचना करते रहें। रचनाकाल की व्यूह--रचना में ही संपूर्ण क्रांति की संपूर्णता है। इसे एक राज्य-विरोधी समुदायवाद का सिद्धांत माना जा सकता है।

संदर्भ

1. मार्क्स के पूर्व के समाजवाद, बाकुनिन तक, सामाजिक परिवर्त्तन को कोई ऐतिहासिक प्रक्रिया नहीं मानते थे बल्कि अन्तर्चेतना, संकल्प तथा राज्य शक्ति को परास्त करने की इच्छा। (देखें जेपी-फ्रॉम सोशलिज्म टु सर्वोदय, चतुर्थ संस्करण, प. 22)
2. राज्य सत्ता के बदलने के बाद संघर्ष का दूसरा चरण तुरंत शुरू होना चाहिए। गाँधी के लोक सेवक संघ को काँग्रेस की जगह खड़ा करना चाहा। लेकिन गाँधी के "Last will and Testament' से नई राजनीति ने कोई सबक नहीं सीखा। गाँधीवाद सत्ता की राजनीति का विकल्प तैयार कर चुका था। एक सत्ता के बाहर की निर्दलीय शक्ति (देखें वही, प. 35-36)
3. सच्ची पंचायतें विधानसभाओं में नहीं, केवल अपने बनाए नियमों से चलती हैं। (देखें, वही, प. 37-38)
4. यद्यपि मैं मार्क्सवाद की बुनियादी मान्यताओं को छोड़ चुका था... मैं दृढ़ता से मानता रहा कि आदमी की आजादी केवल एक राज्यविहीन समाज में ही प्राप्त हो सकती है। (देखें, वही, प. 39)
5. गाँधी का सर्वोदय जन-समाजवाद है, न कि राज्य समाजवाद। ऊपर से बोझिल समाज तो केवल नौकरशाहों, प्रबंधकों और यत्र विशेषज्ञों का ही स्वर्ग होगा। (देखें, वही, प. 43)
6. ब्रिटेन में समाजवादियों का राज्यशक्ति पर कब्जा करने और उसी का उपयोग करने की मानसिकता ने उन्हें 'Validity of non-state forms of socialism' के प्रति अंधा कर दिया है। (हैरोल्ड कैम्पबेल, सोशलिज्म कमेन्टरी, जुलाई 1957, उद्धत, जेपी की उपर्युक्त पुस्तक, प. 41)
7. ऊपर के संदर्भ 3 और 6 मिलाकर देखने से जेपी भी गाँधी की तरह के 'एनार्किस्ट' हो जाते हैं। गाँधी ने माना था कि वे एनार्किस्ट हैं, कुछ दूसरे तरह का। (देखें, डी.जी. तेन्दूलकर, महात्मा, 1992 अंक 6, प. 143, 86-9, अंक-8, प. 37)
8. Grundrisse पुस्तक के संदर्भ के लिए, देखें डैनियल वेल, द ग्रेट आइडियाज टूडे, एनसाइक्लोपीडिया ब्रिटानिका, 1980
9. 'अगर मैं वर्ग संघर्ष को अपरिहार्य देखूँगा तब मैं मार्क्सवाद की शिक्षा और दीक्षा देने से भी नहीं कतराऊँगा' (देखें वी.बी. खेर सं. एम. के. गाँधी, इकोनोमिक एण्ड इण्डस्ट्रियल लाइफ एंड रिलेशन्स प. 74)
10. जेपी, वर्ग संघर्ष को कमजोर और मजबूत वर्गों के बीच देखते हैं। (देखें, ब्रह्मानंद, सं. टुवार्डस टोटल रिवोल्यूशन)

47

WELFARE STATE WITH A COOPERATIVE ECONOMY

V.M. Tarkunde

REVOLUTION FROM ABOVE

Communist revolutions succeeded in some underdeveloped countries like Russia in 1917 and China in 1949. Neither of these revolutions was brought about by the proletariat of those countries. Communist parties in both Russia and China were composed of persons from the middle class who had active sympathy and devotion to the cause of workers and peasants. Since both Russia and China were under-developed countries, economically as well as culturally, the dictatorships established in these countries consolidated themselves and refused to wither away. Obviously, if a dictatorship is imposed on a country where the prople do not cherish to an adequate extent the democratic values of liberty, equality and fraternity, it has an inherent tendeny to perpetuate itself.

I would go a step further and say that any revolution guided by the theory of economic determinism is bound to result in the setting up of a dictatorship which, by its very nature, would be a formidable impediment to social progress. This is because the theory of economic determinism assumes that ideas and ideologies arise from, and constitute a superstructure of, the basic economic reality which consists of the ownership of means of production and th social relations arising therefrom. Economic determinism postulates that, except in the case of a few de-classed intellectuals, liberating ideas would emerge in a society only after a liberal economic structure is created as a result of a revolution. Such a revolution is necessarily brought about from above, by a determined minority. It is not creatd from below, by an enlightened people who aspire for freedom and emocracy.

The stages of a revolution as visualised by the theory of economic determinism are that first a revolutionary party consisting of declassed individuals will capture political power, then the revolutionary party will expropriate the capitalist class of all the means of production and that thereafter an ideology suitable for a socialist society will develop among the people. Thus the sequence of communist revolutionary theory is–first a political revolution, then an economic revolution and thereafter a cultural revolution. Now a revolution brought about in this way cannot possibly result in the establishment of a democracy. The successful working of a democracy requires as a precondition that the people should cherish to an adequate degree the values of liberty, equality and fraternity. In the absence of these values, any political or economic institution, even if it is created with a democratic intent, will be perverted so as to subserve the interest of the ruling dictatorship.

Take the instance of the "soviets" in Communist Russia. A soviet was conceived as a basic organ of democracy, as an instrument of people's power. In the absence of the democratic values of liberty, equality and fraternity amongst the people, and with the imposition of the so-called "proletarian" dictatorship, the same soviet, instead of being an organ of people's power, became in Communist Russia an organ for the exercise of the State's power over the people. It became, in other words, an instrument of dictatorship.

Out of the three values of democracy–liberty, equality and fraternity–the values of equality are thus the basic components of the democratic ethos. When these values were pushed up into the "superstructure" and excluded from the basic reality, Communist practice became entirely unprincipled. Although Marx was himself a passionate moralist, Communist practice was guided by the dictum that the end justified the means. Morality was completely divorcd from the political practice of communism. Stalin secured the execution through fake trials of almost all the leading members of the Bolshevik Party who were Lenin's colleagues, and this inhuman conduct was justified on the ground that Stalin's aim was to achieve socialism in Russia. Stalin's pact with Hitler in 1939 for the division of Poland was justified on the same ground. Such a thoroughly amoral movement could not possibly create a free and moral society.

ECONOMIC DETERMINISM INCONSISTENT WITH MATERIALISM

Soon after his release from jail, M.N. Roy declared in a meeting held in Poona in December 1936 that "every worthwhile social revolution must be preceded by a philosophical revolution". He explained that a cultural transformation of society, a revaluation of the established values, was necessary before its political and economic liberation can be achieved. He had derived this conclusion from his study in jail for a period of about six years. He was of the view that modern democracy was born in Europe as a result of the Renaissance movement which generated among the people the values of freedom, rationalism and self-sustained morality. Although when I heard that speech I was already a fulfledged Marxist, I did not then realise that this statement of Roy was quite contrary to the theory of economic determinism. Roy was able to depart from the traditional Marxist view in this way because, as he often explained, he regarded Marxism as a way of thought and not a set of dogmas. The precedence which Roy gave to cultural transformation over the transformation of political and economic institution led him to the conclusion that, in India and elsewhere, a successful revolutionary transformation must start with the spread of the humanist value of freedom, rationalism and self-sustained morality, a movement which he called the 20th Century Renaissance. Such a movement, Roy felft, would lead to a "revolution from below" which would establish a genuine political, economic and social democracy.

Roy also explained in his writings that the theory of economic determinism does not necessarily follow from the philosophy of materialism. Roy fully appreciated the statement of Marx that "consciousness is determined by being". Marx used the word "being" to mean physical existence. Marx meant that consciousness is a property of life and that life emerged from inanimate matter. But this chronological sequence between matter and ideas did not justify the conclusion that the ideas and ideologies are a super-structure on the so-called materialistic foundation of society. The fact is that ideas are as materialistic as economic relations. Ideas are the product of the human brain and human beings are a part of nature. There is no reason why one part of material existence, such as the economic structure of society, should have greater influence in the making of history than another part, such as ideas and ideologies. The chronological sequence between matter and ideas cannot justify the conclusion that the ideas have a minor role in historical development than "material" existence. In fact, with the march of civilisation and with the shortening of the cultural distance between different societies, ideas are having an increasing influence in the shaping of historical events.

According to the theory of economic determinism, social evolution is determined, not by man's creative ideas, but by the development of the means of production. referring to that view, Roy raised the question: "Who creatd the first means of production and how?" He answered the question by pointing out that the first means of production must have been created by the human or sub-human brain. He observed that one can imagine an exceptionally clever anthropoid ape hitting upon the idea of breaking a branch and using it for beating down fruits, instead of taking the trouble of climbing to the top of the tree. Roy said that the first non-biological extra organic tool was thus created. He concluded that the main means of production is the human brain. It is thus clearly wrong to give precedence to the development of the means of production over the development of ideas in the theory of social transformation : In fact, ideas must have precedence in a worthwhile transformation of society because no political or economic institution can be run democratically unless the people who run that institution, and the people among whom the institution is run, cherish the values of democracy.

I have so far dealt with the first cause of the failure of communism which was the theory of economic determinism and dialectical development (often described conjunctively as "dialectical materialism") which led to the view that *historical changes were determined primarily by the development of the forces of production and not by the cultural and moral values of democracy and humanism.* I will not deal with the second cause of the failure of communism which consisted of the faulty assumption that social onwership of the means of production should be brought about by their nationalisation.

According to Marx and Engels, one of the contradictions of capitalism consisted of the socialisation of production while retaining individual appropriation of the goods produced. Before the emergence of capitalism, individual artisans worked with small implements belonging to them and they were also the owners of the goods produced. Under capitalism, increasing numbers of workmen worked with the aid of increasingly costly and complicated machinery belonging to the capitalist who was the owner of the goods produced. There was social production but individual appropriation. This contradiction, Marx and Engels observed produced by the economy and the requisite social appropriation could be secured if the ownership of the means of production was also socialised. This led Marx and Engels to the further conclusion, which had no justification, that the social ownership of the means of production should be brought about by the nationalisation of all industries. The contradiction between social production and individual appropriation could really be removed by ensuring that appropriation is socialised to the same extent to which production is socialised. This implied that the workmen who are engaged in the process of production should become the owners of the means of production which they utilise for producing goods and services. As I will presently submit, *this aim can be achieved by building up a cooperative economy.* Marx and Engels were, however, committed to the view that a proletarian dictatorship was necessary for expropriating the capitalist class and that was probably the reason why they equated social ownership with the national ownership of the means of production. This eventually led to the undoing of communism, both economically and politically.

Nationalisation of industry had initially the advantage of securing rapid industrial growth. In a few decades, however, the growth of industry in the Soviet Union came to a halt. This was for various reasons. Wholesale nationalisation of industry necessarily meant the absence of a free market. In the absence of a free market, there was no way to find out what the people wanted and what their relative preferences were. Prices of goods and services were therefore determined arbitrarily, without reference to the demands of the consumers. In the absence of competition, there was neither an incentive to increase the efficiency of State industries nor a dependable method of assessing their efficiency. Moreover, party bureaucrats who became the managers of State enterprises were not the best persons suited to the job.

Further, the alienation of the workers from their work and from the products of their work continued under State ownership as much as it was under capitalist ownership. In both cases, the workers never became the owners of the goods and services produced by them. *State ownership consisted of transfering the workers from the employment of capitalists to the employment of the State.*

Politically also, wholesale nationalisation of industry contributed to the consolidation of the dictatorship of the Communist Party. Nationalisation led to the concentration of all economic power in the same hands, in which all power was already centralised in accordance with the theory of proletarian dictatorship. This process was further aided by the State ownership of all the mass media and the business of publication of books, as well as the subjugation to the State of the judiciary, the legal profession and the profession of teachers in schools and colleges.

The contradiction between social production and individual appropriation could have been removed by developing an industrial structure in which the workers engaged in particular enterprises would be the owners of the capital invested in those enterprises. Such an industrial structure can be described as a cooperative economy. *A free market is not inconsistent with a cooperative economy.* A large number of cooperative enterprises producing the same or similar goods can compelete for the consumer's preference in a free market. The alienation of the workers from their work and from the goods they produce would also come to an and when the workers become the owners of the means of production and of what is produced by their work. In large corporations, the principle of cooperation can be implemented by ensuring that the shares in such corporations are progressively owned by the workers themselves. In enterprises where monopoly conditions are inevitable, the ownership can be placed, by appropriate statures in the hands of representatives of both workers and consumers. In such an industrial structure, all the workers are self-employed and the conflict of interests between employers and employees is eliminated. *A cooperative economy is clearly far more democratic and egalitarian than capitalism as well as State ownership.*

ALTERNATIVE TO COMMUNISM

It would follow that capitalism is not the only alternative to communism which has failed. A more democratic and egalitarian alternative to communism is a welfare State with a cooperative economy. A welfare State is characterised by social insurance against the various uncertainties and shortcomings of life, such as unemployment, accident, physical handicaps, sickness and old age. In a welfare State, equality of opportunity can be secured by making education equally available to all. Preventive and curative medical assistance can also be provided to all, irrespective of their economic means. A healthy cooperative economy can ensure that the State would eventually have the means to extend these facilities equally to all the members of the society. It is true that cooperative economy cannot succeed unless a culture based on individual freedom and purposeful social cooperation is developed in a society to an adequate extend. But that only means that a cooperative economy can only be developed gradually on the basis of the development of a cooperative culture.

CONCLUSIONS

We may conclude that a cultural revolution is a necessary pre-condition of a worthwhile political and economic transformation. So far we, the persons belonging to the middle class, have failed the Indian masses because we have either isolated ourselves from them, or else we have approached them for votes in favour of one party or another with the promise that the party of our choice will uplift them from their poverty and degradation. We have thus created an illusion amongst the people that somebody other than themselves would be their saviours. We should now go to the people with the message that they alone can help themselves and they alone are the makers of their future. We must awaken their urge for freedom and propogate among them the values of self-reliance, rationalism and self-sustained morality. On the basis of these *humanist values,* we can promote appropriate organisations of the people at the grass-root level so as to enable them to develop themselves and to fight for their rights.

Secondly, we should, I think, insist that capitalism is not the only alternative to communism. Another alternative is of a welfare State with a cooperative economy.

A third lesson of the failure of communism in Soviet Russia is the futility of centralisation of power in a nation which consists of a number of sub-nationalities. Even after 70 years of centralisation of power in Soviet Russia, the various sub-nationalities became separate States as soon as the dictatorship of the Communist Party came to an end. They would not be held together even in a loose federation as proposed by Gorbachev. India also is a nation of a number of sub-nationalities. We should not commit the mistake of continuing with the excessive centralisation of power which we have in the country today. We should have a genuine federation with the minimum power at the centre and the maximum power decentralised from the centre to the States and from the States to various zilla parishads, taluka samities, gram panchayats and Gram sabhas.

By courtesy, M.N. Roy Memorial Lecture, Indian Renaissance Instt. Delhi, 21 March, 1992

48

GANDHI AND MARX
(गाँधी एवं मार्क्स)

J.D. Sethi

[Mahatma Gandhi, who died some years ago is a much misunderstood man. The writer, a noted Gandhian scholar and a former members of the Planning Commission, chooses to examine in this article the Mahatma's philosophy of power.]

It is curious that Mahatma Gandhi's approach to power, particularly political power, is seldom made the subject of a serious study though he was for nearly four decades the most powerful central figure in the political struggle which removed the strongest imperial rule. Gandhi was a politician of the tallest order who refused to be even an ordinary member of the Congress. Yet he exercised enormous power. Had Gandhi instead of Nehru become the Prime Minister, India would never have sunk into the degradation she has.

Politics withot power is inconceivable though it is not always necessary to hold a state office to wield power. Yet it is no use pretending to study the nature of politics without studying the approach to power of the political figures, especially of the chief political figure.

No one was more acutely conscious of power than Gandhi. Any analysis of him that claims to study his philosophy and politics divorced from his power concepts, will amount to truncating him. Those who have tried to raise Gandhi to the level of an Avtar or a spiritual leader have committed the sin of making him irrelevant to the social, economic and political problems of the modern world. Gandhi was not a simple saint–if at all he was a Power Saint.

Gandhi's critique of power and its concentration in the state, the business and bureaucracy is well known but his dialectics, which predates Marx as it originates from Upanishads, is not so well known. The confusion arises because Gandhi himself did not make a specific theoretical statement. Indeed, the word power, i.e., political power, seldom occurs in his writings and speeches. The main dialectics was to pit the power of peaceful non-cooperation against the coereive and repressive power of the state. He called this dialectics an eternal law. He fought for power all his life, though not for himself in the sense of holding any state authority. His most remarkable exercise of power was that he moulded men of straw into national leaders. Paradocxically Gandhi fought for power for the sake of others who recognized his power but later betrayed him.

OPEN BOOK

Many Europeans and far more Indians, particularly the leaders of the Muslim League, called Gandhi a cunning man. Gandhi's politics was an open book but he was not a simpleton. Gandhi was his own moral Machiavelli, because he realised that truth was far more complex than a lie. If truth or a search for its is cunning then Gandhi was cunning. If the British leaders often got exasperated with him, it was not always because he used superior arguments or tactics. He could beat them with non-arguments which while irritating some, won the battle for him without a fight.

In this way he made the victims win over the victimisers and turned his and his countrymen's powerlessness into a giant power by means of which he remained the sole arbiter. Probably with the exception of early (not later) Mao Tse-tung, no other power figure in recent history had such a radical encounter first with himself and then with others, as Gandhi had. But unlike Mao, he ensured that power would not be misused so long as he remained on the scene.

SUPERIOR THEORY

Gandhi's theory of the state was superficially like that of Marx. The state has to wither away. We have seen how the communist countries have turned state into a monster with no signs of its power diminishing, let alone withering away. Gandhi's theory was much superior to that of Marx because the Gandhian polity and praxis ensured that.

The principal crisis and contradiction of India today is that the more the state and its organs accumulate power the more cynically they violate norms and use it for blackmail. Gandhi saw in the state power an evil as well as an instrument of social change. The structure of the state will be determined, he said, "not only by our definitions, but by our acts, voluntary or involuntary." No theory of speculation about the end product has meaning without identifying the nature and course of human action. In this context he was poles apart from Marx.

This indeed is the most critical and central component of Gandhian dialectics. So long as state power exists, the concentration of power needed to manage the system must be counter-balanced by a vast network of decentralized polities. People have misunderstood that concept of village which was an idealized political entity. Hagreed with G.K. Chesterton that "he who lives in a small community lives in a much larger world". It meant a series of concentric circles of direct democracy running parallel to institutions of representative democracies. State and political power was to be embedded in this system of parallel politics. To every theory there has to be an antithesis which in this case was that power must have transcended by moral practice.

The central themes of the Gandhian power can be culled from his practice as well as statements on related issues. First, a power struggle was not a two-person zero-sum game. The struggle for power as between two unequals and its inequality, though appearing profitable to one party in the narrow sense, was structured against the interest of both and had to be transformed from the negative to the positive. Hence the successful outcome of a power struggle would be ideal if it is resolved in the maximum interest of both parties. The party which is the stronger of the two, while giving up some of its economic and political power, will gain something else, self-actualizing power–spiritual or any other type of power–which is called power over the self. There will be a temptation to equate this view with the modern theory of consensual politics but such an equation has to be rejected because consensus can be about an unjust objective achieved with immoral means.

Second, in the Gandhian framework and assumptions, the question of power requires to be juxtaposed with political necessity, to find the relevance of both. At a pure philosophic level, there should be no difficulty in reconciling moral relativism with political necessity and even with political expediency. It is difficult to generalise because the problem is more specific than general. The most obvious case was of violence versus non-violence. The choice was obvious and unmistakable, but he was not blind to violence as an actual fact of life.

AMBIVALENT ROLE

The core of the arguent was that when the choice is between violence and non-violence, it is an absolute misuse of power to go for the former. However, in an existentialist situation of choice being limited to between two kinds of violence, the role of power becomes ambivalent. Other considerations will intervene. In other words, his approach to power, like his approach to morals, was also relativistic.

Third, Gandhi focussed on those attributes of power which focussed on his all embracing concept of Satyagraha: Power has the attributes of a force but it also had its antithesis, the soul-power, as defined by the Gita. In its dynamics, power was also a method or a technique which can be used for ill or good. Indeed, often power becomes power by the very method of its use. Finally power is both an end as well as a means. So long as it remains an end, power will tend to be corrupted. These attributes were discussed to focus on Satyagraha which is a unique concept standing in dialectical relationship with political power. Satyagraha is both power and an instrument for acquiring and using power.

Fourth, the most remarkable and critical aspect of Gandhian power was power over self. Indeed, the morality or ethics of power over others was determined in direct proportion to power overself. Gandhi built and acquired power over others at four different levels: In interpersonal relations; though communal living or Ashram life; through institutions or organisations ranging from as small as his own family to the biggest, the Congress; and by awakening the masses, fighting for their needs, bringing himself to their level and thereby acquiring charisma. His power was often invisible as he loathed all those symbols and manifestations which exhibited leaders' power over the led. He said he wanted to reduce himself to zero and by so doing he became extraordinarily powerful.

TWO ISSUES

Today almost every nation faces two major issues of politics and power. First, there is a general disgust with politics. Good and capable people have assumed a nihilistic view of it. Gandhi was totally opposed to this kind of approach. Gandhi's followers, particularly Vinobha and Sarvodya workers, made the mistake of walking out of politics. To them all politics appeared as power politics and hence evil. Gandhi's political philosophy of politics recognizes the inevitability of power and the political role of man at one end and the ultimate end of power politics at the other. But a perfectly non-violennt society would have to be thought of for the future.

However, in the end an element of irony or tragedy took over as reflected in three of Gandhi's mistakes. He should not have destroyed a lot of that correspondence which adversely reflectd upon the foibles and power weaknesses of his colleagues. There was also no reason to choose Nehru, whose view of power was rather romantic over Sardar Patel who was a realist. Finally, he could have avoided the tragic wilderness of Sarvodya workers by giving them clear lessons in how a moral minority can exercise restraining power over the power elite.

By courtesy H.T., Jan. 30, 1988.

49

KUMARAPPA ON GANDHINOMICS
(कुमारप्पा का गाँधीय अर्थशास्त्र)

B.R. Nanda

[Kumarappa's articles landed him in jail; this facilitated his decision to finally cast his lot with Gandhi. It was as a Gandhian economist that he was to occupy a unique position in the national scene]

It would have been difficult to think of a more unlikely candidate for the discipleship of Gandhi in 1929 than J.C. Kumarappa. He was 37 years old, a graduate of the Syracuse University in business administration, a chartered accountant, and a fellow of the Society of Incorporated Accountants and Auditors in England. For nearly 10 years he had been practicing as an auditor in Bombay, and had built up a lucrative practice. He had an affluent and westernised mode of life, and was popular among the local Europeans.

In 1928 Kumarappa had presented a dissertation on Public Finance and Indian Poverty for his master's degree in economics to the Columbia University, and was thinking of getting it published in India. With a formidable array of facts and figures. Kumarappa had exposed the financial jugglery of the British Treasury and the British War Office in unjustly heaping the costs of imperial wars on the Indian exchequer, and thus deepening India's poverty. Who could be a fitter person to appraise such a monograph than the pre-eminent leader of Indian nationalism? Kumarappa called at Mani Bhawan where Gandhi usually stayed when in Bombay. The Mahatma was busy in a meeting. Kumarappa left his monograph with Pyarelal, one of the secretaries. A few days later, he received a letter inviting him to meet Gandhi at Ahmedabad.

Dressed in a smart western-style suit, Kumarappa arrived at the Sabarmati Ashram on the afternoon of 9 May 1929, and then, in his own words:

> *"On the way I saw an old man seated under a tree on a newly-cleaned cow-dung floor, spinning. Having never seen a spinning-wheel before, I leaned on my walking stick, and standing akimbo, was watching as there were still ten minutes for the appointment. The old man after about five minutes opened his toothless lips and, with a smile on his face, inquired if I was Kumarappa. It suddenly dawned on me that my questioner may be no other than Mahatma Gandhi. So I in my turn asked him if he was Gandhiji, and when he nodded, I promptly sat down on the cow-dung floor, regardless of the well-kept crease of my silk trousers."*

Gandhi complimented Kumarappa on his dissertation, and offered to publish it in Young India in a series of articles. "You are almost the first economist I have come across, who thinks on the same lines as I do," he said and then made a proposition to Kumarappa. Would he conduct a rural economic survey for him in Gujarat? When Kumarappa tried to excuse himself by pleading ignorance of Gujarati, the local language, Gandhi offered to provide him assistance from the faculty and students of Gujarat Vidyapith, the national university at Ahmedabad.

The economic survey of Matar Taluka, which Kumarappa undertook, covered 50 villages in the Kaira district of Gujarat. Kumarappa had blazed a trail which few economists were to follow. What else the survey did or did not achieve, it converted him from an academic into a practical economist. His dissertation on public finance had acquainted him with the iniquity of Birtish rule.

Meanwhile events had moved to a climax in the political arena. Gandhi, who had embarked on the Dandi March, sent for Kumarappa, and asked him if he could help Mahadev Desai in running Young India. Kumarappa pleaded that he knew nothing about Gandhian philosophy, nor had any experience in journalism, and it would be more appropriate if he was given an assignment to fit in with his expertise in audit and accounts. Gandhi then came up with an ingenious–and irresistible–argument. He told Kumarappa that in Young India, the name of the writer was always published under each article. "If you write any trash," he said, "the public will say Mahatma Gandhi's paper publishes trash. But if you write anything that is appreciated, they will give all credit to this Kumarappa, who is writing in Gandhiji's paper."

Kumarappa's articles in Young India landed him in jail; this facilitated his decision to finally cast his lot with Gandhi. After his arrest and conviction for sedition, it was doubtful if his British clients would patronise his audit firm any longer. In 1934, he was appointed secretary of the newly set-up All India Village Industries Association at Wardha under Gandhi's aegis. It was, as a Gandhian economist that he was to occupy a unique position in the national scene.

Though Gandhi had written and spoken extensively on economic issues from time to time, he never had the time to evolve a coherent theory or a blue-print for its implementation. This task was undertaken by Kumarappa; in numerous articles and pamphlets, for more than 20 years, he expounded and developed Gandhi's ideas. In his Economy of Permanence, written in jail in 1944, he sketched a complete picture of life in a community working towards non-violence and peace. In another little book, The practice and Precepts of Juesus, written during the same jail term, Kumarappa linked the fight against economic exploitation to the highest religion. "Where God's will prevails." he asked, "can there be social inequalities of high and low... economic differences of rich and poor... and one nation lording it over the other?"

The years 1936-39 were halcyon years for Kumarappa's village economics. Unfortunately, the Second World War, the resignation of the Congress ministries and civil disobedience put the clock back.

There was again a ray of hope with the return of the Congress ministries in 1946, but the communal tension, the disturbances, and the turmoil preceding and following the partition of the country, hindered progress. Nor did the situation improve much after the attainment of independence in 1947.

The Gandhian model, which Kumarappa elaborated and advocated through hardhitting articles in the Harijan and Gram Udyog Patrika, aimed at a low-energy, low capital, nature-friendly and decentralised development. Some of its assumptions, such as self-sufficiency of the village and restricted trade with the outside world, seem hardly practicable in the fast changing world of today. Then there are the complex economic issues, such as inflation, balance of payments, internal trade and the underground economy, for which the Gandhian model may not have adequate answers. If Kumarappa were alive, he might well have argued that many of these problems would not have become so complex, but for the inordinate greed and indiscipline of individuals and sections of society entrapped in consumerism, and that after all, Gandhi's economic framework also postulated a moral base.

By Courtesy Times of India, Jan. 17, 1993.

50

SWADESHI, SARVODAYA AND GANDHISM
(स्वदेशी, सर्वोदय और गाँधीवाद)

K.K. Sinha

Swadeshi in the beginning was a political strategy against British trade and should not be taken as a purely economic concept. In free India Gandhi talked about Sarvodaya and not Swadeshi.

Gandhi spelt Swadeshi as 'that spirit in us which restricts us of the use and service of our immediate surrounding to the exclusion of the more remote. (M.K. Gandhi, 1957, pp. 67-8) It must not serve my distant neighbour at the expense of the nearest.' We may discuss some of the ingredients of Swadeshi here;

1. It concerned the unorganised sector in the main and gives a scheme of local income, employment and a circlar flow of goods within the unorganised rural sector.
2. It may out grow in the adjoining areas but without much cost on advertisements, transport or managerial expenditures.
3. Local employment and local demand created local supply so that the two balancd at an indigenous level.
4. There is greater emphasis on human factor of production than machine thus giving employment of men a priority over employment of machines.
5. Swadeshi is less disturbing to ecoogical balance, less exploitative and is non-violent and an economics of permanence and peace.

Thus Swadeshi does not negate the existence of an organised market economy but is an anti-dote to it. It counters the backwash effects of an over-centralised machine production based on markets and artificial demand, blind material consumption and profits. The technology of mass production is inherently violent, ecologically damaging, self-defeating in terms of non-renewable resources and stultifying for the human person. (Schumacher, small is beautiful, 77 p. 143) In such case supply does not create sufficient demand in view of increasing poverty areas. (Kumarappa, why the village movement, 1948, p. 125). Distorted advertisements are the bane of such production which only inflate prices. This leads to unnatural creation of demand with unnecessary goods and services. Thus an unnatural equilibrium is created which is unstable and violent. (Kumarappa, Economy of Permanence, 1984, p. 66).

Gandhi's Swadeshi is thus not just a boycott of British goods but a positive development of the village economy of indigenous lines. It is to create a necessary balance between the 'Videshi market sector' with a Swadeshi and wider village sector in the dualistic economics.

It is not just an economic concept but, like Marxism' hits at economic concentration of wealth and power.' It differs from Marxism because Marxism pleaded for just change of ownership of capital while Gandhism (Swadeshi) aimed at decentralisation of capital itself. Thus Swadeshi becomes a smoother and more humanistic system of development where as Marxism was highly material and dialectical. Fraud and speculation were the bane of both capitalism and marxism and both grew anti-human.

Gandhi accepts that a large industry sector would co-exist and there may be state and private monopolies in few areas but such areas must be guided by his Trusteeship concept when the rich sectors owed the surpluses to the society and when wealth was transfered from the rich to the swadeshi areas. This implied that trusteeship was not just a moral obligation of the rich sectors but which could be enforced by Satyagrah and pressure. In fact Bhoodan was application of trusteeship within the rural sector while a system of fiscal transfers could work as State regulated trusteeship.

SELF-RELIANCE: THE NEW NAME

Self-reliance was the new name given to Swadeshi in the post-Gandhian era characterised by a Nehruvian-Marxist planning.

Gandhi did want a non-dependent model of development. But it was not conceived in a narrow nationalist term, and not in terms of just boycott of foreign goods. 'All that swadeshi meant to him was a high degree of self reliance at various levels, individual, social, political and ofcourse, economic' (J.D. Sethi, HT, Oct. 2, 92).

The concept of Swadeshi first meant a self-reliant village economy, the basic units of Indian society. It was also to be designed so as to avoid flow of resources from villages to cities and to avoid the dominance of the former. In that sense Gandhi wanted to avoid the dominance and exploitation of other nations. This system does not negate cooperation and goodwill. What helped employment was good and so the norm of self-reliance was not just growth but employment. This naturally meant that swadeshi was against 'over-industrialisation'. The extent of capital heavy industries must be limited by the norms of trusteeship.

His scheme of industrialisation would surely start with the basic needs of life, i.e. Roti, Kapda and Makan and not those in developed capitalist or socialist countries. The needs of a poor society cannot be those in the rich ones. Swadeshi is thus not against modernism but actually for modernising first the villages with water, electricity and other needs. You cannot allow a consumerist culture without assuring a minimum consumption to the vast majority of people. You cannot be prematurely modern.

Nehru's self-reliance model meant import-substitution and export promotion. The first became very costly and actually highly dependent on foreign aid. A craze for technology must have its base at the indigenous qualities of life and society. Over-industrialism under market competition ignores this fact and may ignore that a vast area of development lies outside its scope.

THE NEW ECONOMIC POLICY VERSUS SWADESHI

The new competive market polity of 1991 was actually a reaction to the policy of self-reliance of forty years of planning and the 'commanding hieghts' of the public sector which was bearig no fruits. This was self-reliance without Swadeshi. The purpose of the new policy is to openly compete with the outer world without government protection, control and subsidy, and to give maximum premium to private initiative and enterprise. But the real problem is that in spite of this U-turn, will the new policy have a Swadeshi counterpart?

Most likely there will be absence of the swadeshi again. If the developing world cannot afford a war of competition with the developed, they must have to align with them. They cannot insulate their economy from outer competition nor can have regional trading blocks for themselves. They have to open their doors to participate vigorously in the global economy as the only course.

The justification for an open door economy is actually not against swadeshi if it does not divest all resources from the unorganised sectors to the organised. A swadeshi sector could grow and coexist with an open sector in a dualistic economy. The danger however is the inroad of developed technology to compete and all the indigenous resources may get exhausted just with the norm of gaining the markets. It can be nothing but a mad race.

The argument placed in favour of the NEP is that foreign capital today is not flowing for colonial interests as such flow is actually between the rich countries themselves. They are seeking low cost areas of production (Vivek Bharati, HT, 21 Aug. 92) and may flow to backward areas to the advantage of both. This is an opportunistic and happy assumption indeed. But increasing dependence on the World Bank or the IMF and even NRI.s or Multinationals would actually mean an over-growth of the non swadeshi sector.

THE FALL OF THE CONCEPT OF NATION-STATE

Capitalism has slowly liberated itself from ethics and from the limitations of a nation-state, and has become trans-national. Hedonism and populism have dominated the scene. Globalisation actually leads to flight of capital outside and inside the countries as in America and there has been unforseen wave of social disintegration (Girilal Jain, Times, Dec. 3, 92) and upsurge of ethnic hatred and recism with TV channels assaulting and disrupting societies.

After disintegration of communism, the post-cold war world has also lost its national fervour and is pretending to be a global village with the World Bank and IMF and Amnesty International to bring the world together.

But it is contended that the swadeshi spirit should not be lost sight of in a craze for globalisation. It must work as an effective anti-dote to globalisation. We may discuss the implications further.

NEP'S CONTRIBUTION TO UNEMPLOYMENT

It is estimated by some authors (e.g. Sudipta Mondal) that there was additional unemployment to the tune of 1 crore due to NEP (particularly by reduction of fiscal deficits) in 1993-94. This required a swadeshi sector investment of atleast 6000 crores (Rs.) a year and some structural adjustment loan of 500 million from the World Bank. But the National Renewable Fund concept in this regard provided not even half of the requirements. Swadeshi is the area where the state should get in. This is the area which may now be declared as the social sector, an engine of growth outside the global sector. Even Reganism in America is reverting back to it.

To myrdal, Gandhi's swadeshi was for an egalitarian society and a link between radicalism and rationalism. 'Political freedom must include real economic freedom for the starving millions and the poor villagers who are exploited by the foreign governments and by their own countrymen, the city-dwellers (Asian Drama, pp. 753-4) Swadeshi could wake up the poor and expect the rich sections to sacrifice their interest for them. This was a system of rural-oriented equality with some moral fervour.

It was a system of building from below. 'South Asian countries now run the risk of creating petty islands of highly organised western type industries that will remain surrounded by a sea of stagnation. (Myrdal, p. 1203). By itself industrialisation can do little to raise labour utilisation in the more tradition bound sectors, especially in rural areas.

The Swadeshi dilemma

Swadeshi may now be a genuine movement based on self-reliance and self-dependence. Its medium would be the self-governing panchayats and village cooperatives. Swadeshi discards the theory of 'trickle down' of the west, as voluntary participation does not emerge spontaneously in stagnant villages as it did in the western Europe. It needs to be fostered and directed by the state so that a multiplier effect is initiated and set in motion. Ofcourse it has not to be state-managed but the state has to see that villages grow into viable market units. (Myrdal, p. 880).

A building form below cannot be visualised without a swadeshi concept and there in no alternative to such development. Swadeshi is a means of generating competition among the weaker sections and surely has to be set apart from the competition between the giants. This becomes a dichotomy if the organised sectors are left free to develop in their own way. The two sectors can however co-exist in India if it is realised that India's problems can only be solved by certain types of idealism based perhaps on Gandhian principles of simplicity and austerity. (Tinbergen, Quoted Myrdal, p. 766 n) Some systematic thought should be given to this question.

51

मैं समाजवादी हूँ

स्वामी विवेकानन्द

भारतीय समाजवाद में विवेकानंद ने जिन वर्णों की बात की है, वे वास्तव में अपने कार्य विभाजन का बोध करते हैं। ब्राह्मण आज का बौद्धिक वर्ग, क्षत्रिय सैन्य बल, वैश्य व्यापारी वर्ग तथा शूद्र मजदूर का बोध करते हैं। व्यापारी वर्ग ही धनपति हुआ है और उद्योगपति भी। इस दृष्टि से विवेकानन्द का 100 साल पहले लिखा हुआ यह लेख भारतीय समाजवाद का अत्यंत यथार्थ चित्र प्रस्तुत करता है।

–सम्पादकद्वय

ब्राह्मण, क्षत्रिय, वैश्य और शूद्र–ये चारों वर्ण एक के बाद एक, संसार का शासन करते हैं। इनमें से प्रत्येक ने अपनी पूर्ण प्रभुता की अवधि में कोई ऐसे कार्य किये हैं, जिनसे लोगों की भलाई हुई है, और कुछ ऐसे, जिनसे उनको हानि भी पहुँची है।

जैसे पुरोहित समस्त ज्ञान एवं विद्याओं को एक साधारण केन्द्र–अर्थात् स्वयं में केन्द्रित करने में लगा रहता है, उसी तरह राजा स्वयं अपने को केन्द्रीय बिन्दु बनाकर, उसी में समस्त पार्थिव शक्तियों को एकत्र सन्निहित करने के लिए यत्नशील रहा करता है। यह सच है कि दोनों ही समाज के लिए उपयोगी हैं। एक समय की सार्वजनिक भलाई के लिए दोनों की आवश्यकता होती है, परन्तु वह केवल प्रारम्भिक अवस्था में ही।

राजा, जो अपनी प्रजा की एकत्रित शक्तियों का केन्द्र है, शीघ्र भूल जाता है कि ये शक्तियाँ उसके पास इसीलिए संगृहीत की गयी हैं कि वह उन शक्तियों को बढ़ाये और उन्हें सहस्त्र गुना अधिक बलशाली बनाकर पुनः अपनी प्रजा को लौटा दे, ताकि परिणाम यह हो कि वे शक्तियाँ सारे समाज की भलाई के लिए फैल जायँ। परन्तु होता यह है कि अपने अहंभाव के कारण, राजा वेण के समाज सम्पूर्ण

ईश्वरत्व का दावा करते हुए वह दूसरे लोगों के अति नीच समझता है और चाहता है कि वे दीनता प्रदर्शित करते हुए उसके सामने धरती पर लौटें। उसकी इच्छा का–चाहे वह भली हो या बुरी–विरोध करना प्रजा के लिए महापाप है। अत: रक्षण के स्थान में दमन–पालन के स्थान में रक्तशोषण होने लगता है।... जहाँ समाज सबल है, वहाँ शीघ्र ही राजा और प्रजा के बीच भयानक कलह उठ खड़ा होता है और उसके परिणामस्वरूप विप्लव में राजदण्ड और मुकुट दूर फेंक दिये जाते हैं और राजसिंहासन तथा राजसी साज-सामग्री आदि सब केवल अजायब-घर के तख्तों पर सुरक्षित रखी हुई भूतकाल की आश्चर्यजनक वस्तुओं के समान बन जाते हैं।

इस कलह का परिणाम–इसकी प्रतिक्रिया यह होती है कि वैश्य की प्रबल शक्ति प्रकट हो जाती है, जिसकी क्रुद्ध दृष्टि के सामने मुकुटधारी, शूरवीरों के अधिपति अपने राजसिंहासन पर पीपल के पत्ते के समान काँपने लगते हैं। गरीब और अमीर उसके हाथों स्वर्ण-कलश को पाने की व्यर्थ आशा लगाये हुए, विनीत भावों से उसका अनुकरण किया करते हैं, पर वह स्वर्ण-कलश मृगजल के समान उनकी पहुँच से सदा दूर-ही-दूर भागता जाता है।... वैश्य की शक्ति उसके पास के रुपयों में है, जिनकी झंकार की ध्वनि चारों वर्णों के मन को अनिवार्य रूप से आकृष्ट करती है। वैश्य को सदा डर बना रहता है कि ब्राह्मण उसकी इस एकमात्र सम्पत्ति को कहीं उससे हड़प न ले और क्षत्रिय अपने शस्त्रों की शक्ति से उसपर कब्जा न कर बैठे। अत: आत्मरक्षा के लिए वैश्यगण–सामूहिक रूप से–एक ही विचार के होते हैं।... वैश्य सदा इस बात की सावधानी रखता है कि राजसत्ता उसके द्रव्य के मार्ग में किसी प्रकार बाधक न हो। पर इस सब के लिए वह ऐसा कदापि नहीं चाहता कि राजसत्ता क्षत्रियों के पास से शूद्र के पास चली जाय। व्यापारी किस देश में नहीं जाता? स्वयं अज्ञ रहते हुए भी, व्यापार के साथ-साथ वह एक देश की विद्या, बुद्धि, कला और विज्ञान को भी दूसरे देश में ले जाता है।...

और वे लोग कहाँ हैं, जिनके शारीरिक परिश्रम के कारण ही ब्राह्मण को प्रभाव, क्षत्रिय को वीरता और वैश्य को धन प्राप्त होता है? उनका इतिहास क्या है, जो समाज का प्रधान अंग होते हुए भी सभी समय सभी देशों में 'नीच' कहलाये जाते हैं? .... भारतवर्ष को छोड़ अन्य देशों के शूद्र, प्रतीत होता है, कुछ जागृत हो चुके हैं; परन्तु उनमें समुचित शिक्षा का अभाव है और उनमें अपने ही वर्ग के मनुष्यों के प्रति पारस्परिक घृणा जो शूद्रों का स्वभाव-सा है, पायी जाती है। यद्यपि उनकी संख्या अन्य वर्गवालों से अधिक है, पर उससे उन्हें क्या लाभ?

वह एकता जिससे दस व्यक्ति में दस लाख की शक्ति इकट्ठी हो जाती है, शूद्रों से अभी बहुत दूर है। अतः प्रकृति के नियम के अनुसार सर्वदा शूद्र लोग ही प्रजा-वर्ग में रहा करते हैं।...

फिर भी एक समय ऐसा आयेगा, जब शूद्र अपने 'शूद्रत्व' के साथ ऊपर चढ़ेंगे। यह उत्थान आज के समान नहीं होगा' जबकि शूद्र वैश्यों या क्षत्रियों के विशेष गुण प्राप्त करके ही बड़े होते हैं, वरन् ऐसा एक समय आयेगा, जब प्रत्येक देश के शूद्र अपनी जन्मजात शूद्र प्रकृति और आचार के साथ ही–वस्तुतः वैश्य या क्षत्रिय बने बिना ही, एवं शूद्र रहते हुए भी–प्रत्येक समाज में पूर्ण प्रभुत्व प्राप्त करेंगे। इस नयी शक्ति की प्रभातकालीन किरणों का धीरे-धीरे फैलना पश्चिमी संसार में प्रारम्भ हो गया है और विचारशील लोगों की बुद्धि इस नयी घटना के अन्तिम परिणाम को सोच सकने में असमर्थ-सी हो गयी है। समाजवाद, विप्लववाद, शून्यवाद और इसी तरह के अन्य 'वाद' भविष्य में आनेवाली सामाजिक क्रान्ति के अग्रगामी सेनानी हैं। स्मृति-अतीत काल से शूद्र जिस दबाब और अत्याचार से पिसे जा रहे हैं, उसका परिणाम यह हुआ कि वे या तो श्वानवत् उच्च जातियों के पैरों को चाटनेवाले अधम दासवृत्ति के हो गये हैं, या हिंस्र पशुओं के समान निर्दय बन गये हैं।

पश्चिम में शिक्षा का प्रसार होने पर भी शूद्र-वर्ग की उन्नति के मार्ग में बड़ी भारी रुकावट है–और वह है, कम या अधिक, अच्छे या बुरे गुणों के आधार पर निश्चित होनेवाली जाति की स्वीकृति। प्राचीन समय में भारतवर्ष में इसी गुण द्वारा जाति-निर्णय प्रचलित था, जिससे शूद्र वर्ग को हाथ-पैर बाँधकर नीचे दबाकर रखा गया था। प्रथम तो, शूद्र को धन-संचय या यथार्थ ज्ञान या शिक्षा प्राप्त करने के लिए कदाचित् ही कोई अवसर दिया जाता था; फिर उसके ऊपर यह भी होता था कि यदि शूद्र जाति में कोई असाधारण बुद्धि और योग्यता वाला मनुष्य पैदा हो जाय, तो समाज के प्रभावशाली उच्च वर्गवाले व्यक्ति तुरन्त उसपर पदवियों द्वारा सम्मान की वृष्टि करके उसे स्वयं अपने वर्ग में उठा लेते थे। इस प्रकार उसकी सम्पत्ति और बुद्धि की शक्ति का उपयोग अन्य जाति के लाभ के लिए हो जाता था, जबकि उसकी अपनी जाति वाले उसके गुणों से कोई लाभ नहीं उठा पाते थे। और इतना ही नहीं, उच्च जातियों के निकम्मे लोग बाहर निकाल दिये जाते थे तथा शूद्रों के वर्ग में उनकी संख्या बढ़ाते हुए ढकेल दिये जाते थे।

वशिष्ठ, नारद, सत्यकाम जाबाल, व्यास, कृप, द्रोण, कर्ण तथा अन्य दूसरे, जिनके माता-पिता के सम्बन्ध में निश्चित जानकारी नहीं है, विशेष विद्वान, या पराक्रमी होने के कारण ब्राह्मण या क्षत्रिय पद पर प्रतिष्ठित कर दिये गये थे; पर

देखना यह है कि इस प्रकार उनके ऊपर चढ़ जाने से वेश्या, दासी, ढीमर या सूत जाति को क्या लाभ हुआ? फिर, इसके विपरीत, ब्राह्मण, क्षत्रिय या वैश्य वर्गों के पतित मनुष्य सदैव शूद्रो के पद पर नीचे उतार दिये जाते थे।

आधुनिक भारतवर्ष में शूद्र माता-पिता से जन्म लेनेवाले का, चाहे वह करोड़पति हो या महान् पण्डित, अपने समाज को छोड़ने का कभी भी अधिकार नहीं रहता; और उसका परिणाम यह होता है कि उसकी सम्पत्ति, विद्या या बुद्धि की शक्ति, उसी जाति की सीमा में आबद्ध रहने के कारण, उसके अपने ही समाज की भलाई के लिए काम में लायी जाती है। इस प्रकार भारतवर्ष की यह परम्परागत जाति-प्रथा, अपनी सीमा के बाहर कदम न रख सकने के कारण धीरे-धीरे, परन्तु निश्चित रूप से, अपने ही समाज के भीतर रहनेवाले मनुष्यों को उन्नत बनाने में सहायक हो रही है। भारतवर्ष के निम्नवर्गों का इस प्रकार सुधार उस समय तक चलता रहेगा, जब तक भारत उस राज-शासन के अधीन रहेगा, जो प्रजा से जाति और पद का भेद न रखते हुए व्यवहार करता है।

मानव-समाज का शासन क्रमशः एक दूसरे के बाद चार जातियों द्वारा हुआ करता है और ये जातियाँ हैं—पुरोहित, योद्धा, व्यापारी और मजदूर।... सबसे अन्त में मजदूर या शूद्र का राज्य आयेगा। उससे लाभ होगा—भौतिक सुख-साधनों का समान रूप से वितरण, और हानि होगी—(सम्भवतः) संस्कृति का अधःपतन। साधारण संस्कृति का विस्तार बहुत बढ़ेगा, पर असाधारण बुद्धिमान लोग अधिकाधिक कम होते जायेंगे।

यदि इस प्रकार का एक राष्ट्र बन सके, जहाँ पुरोहित का ज्ञान, योद्धा की संस्कृति, व्यापारी की वितरणशीलता और अन्तिम वर्ग की समता का आदर्श ज्यों-के-त्यों बने रहें पर उनके दोष अलग हटा दिये जायँ, तो वह आदर्श राष्ट्र होगा। पर ऐसा हो सकना क्या सम्भव है?

प्रथम तीन तो अपने दिन भोग चुके। अब चौथी अर्थात् शूद्र जाति का समय आया है। उनको वह मिलना ही चाहिए—उसे कोई रोक नहीं सकता। स्वर्ण-मान या रजत-मान सम्बन्धी सारी समस्याओं को मैं नहीं जानता (कोई भी शायद उसके बारे में अधिक नहीं जानता); पर यह मैं अनुभव करता हूँ कि स्वर्ण-मान गरीब को अधिक गरीब और धनी को अधिक धनी बना रहा है। ब्रायन का कहना ठीक था कि "हम सोने की सूली पर प्राण देने से इन्कार करते हैं।" रजत-मान गरीब को इस एक ओर भारी पल्लेवाले युद्ध में अधिक इच्छा अवसर देगा। मैं समाजवादी हूँ इसलिए नहीं कि मैं उसे सभी बातों में पूर्ण मानता हूँ, वरन् इसलिए कि 'अन्धे मामा से काना मामा अच्छा।'

दूसरी मत-प्रणालियों के प्रयोग किये जा चुके और वे अपूर्ण पायी गयीं। अब इसकी परीक्षा की जाय-और नहीं तो कम-से-कम उसकी नवीनता के कारण ही। इसकी अपेक्षा कि वे ही मनुष्य सदा सुख-दुःख भोगें, यह बेहतर है कि सुख-दुःख का नया बँटवारा किया जाय। इस दुःखमयी दुनिया में हर एक को अवसर देना चाहिए।

समाज के सभी व्यक्तियों को धन, विद्या और ज्ञान का उपार्जन करने के लिए एक समान अवसर मिलना चाहिए। .... हर एक विषय में स्वतन्त्रता अर्थात् मुक्ति की ओर प्रगति ही मनुष्य के लिए उच्चतम लाभ है। जो सामाजिक नियम इस स्वतन्त्रता के विकास के मार्ग में बाधक हैं, वे हानिकारक हैं और उनको नष्ट करने का उपाय शीघ्रता से करना चाहिए। जिन संस्थाओं के द्वारा मनुष्य स्वतन्त्रता के मार्ग में अग्रसर होते हैं, उन्हें प्रोत्साहित करना चाहिए।

स्मरण रहे, राष्ट्र झोपड़ियों में बसता है। भारतवर्ष के कृषक, चर्मकार, मेहतर तथा ऐसे ही अन्य निम्न जातिवालों में कार्य करने की शक्ति एवं आत्मविश्वास तुम्हारी अपेक्षा अधिक है। वे कई युगों से चुपचाप काम करते आये हैं और वे देश की सम्पूर्ण सम्पत्ति, बिना चूँ तक किये कमाते आये हैं। बहुत शीघ्र ही वे तुमसे ऊँचे पद में पहुँच जायँगे। क्रमशः पूँजी उन्हीं के हाथों में जा रही है। और आवश्यकताओं के बाहुल्य के कारण तुम्हें जितना कष्ट है, उन्हें इतना नहीं। वर्तमान शिक्षा ने तुम्हारा रहन-सहन तो बदल दिया है, पर धन-प्राप्ति के नये मार्ग, आविष्कारक बुद्धि के अभाव में, अभी तक नहीं खोजे गये हैं। इस सहनशील जनता का तुमने इतने दिनों तक दमन किया है; अब उनके प्रतिकार का समय आ गया है। और अब, तुम नौकरी को ही अपने जीवन का सर्वस्व बनाकर उसकी वृथा खोज में मर मिटोगे!

यदि मजदूर लोग काम करना बन्द कर दें, तो तुम्हें अन्न-वस्त्र मिलना भी बन्द हो जाय। और तुम उनको नीच जाति के मनुष्य मानते हो और अपनी संस्कृति की शेखी मारते हो! आजीविका के संग्राम में व्यस्त रहने के कारण उन्हें अपने में ज्ञान की जागृति का अवसर नहीं मिला। वे इतने दिनों तक मानव-बुद्धि द्वारा चलनेवाले यन्त्र के समान सतत् काम करते रहे हैं और चतुर शिक्षित समुदाय ने उनके परिश्रम के फल का सार-अंश ले लिया है। प्रत्येक देश में ऐसा ही हुआ है। पर अब जमाना बदल गया है। निम्न जातियाँ साधारणतः इस विषय की ओर जागृत हो रही हैं और अपना यथोचित स्वत्व बलात् ग्रहण करने के लिए इसका सामूहिक विरोध कर रही है।.... अब उच्च जातिवाले नीच जातिवालों को और अधिक समय तक दबा नहीं सकते, चाहे वे इसके लिए कितनी ही कोशिशें क्यों

न करें। उच्चतर जातियों का कल्याण अब इसी में है कि वे निम्न जातियों को उनके यथोचित अधिकार प्राप्त करने में सहायता दें।

जनसाधारण जाग उठेंगे, वे अपने ऊपर किये जानेवाले तुम्हारे अत्याचारों को जान लेंगे और तब उनके मुँह की एक फूँक से ही तुम पूरे-के-पूरे उड़ जाओगे! उन्होंने ही तुम्हारे बीच सभ्यता का प्रवेश कराया है और वे ही उस सभ्यता के ढहानेवाले होंगे। इस बात को याद करो कि 'गॉल' (Gauls) लोगों के हाथों से शक्तिशाली पुरातन रोमन-सभ्यता धूलि में मिला दी गयी! इसी कारण मैं कहता हूँ, इन निम्न जातियों को विद्या और संस्कृति प्रदान करके उनको निद्रा से जगाओ। जब वे जाग जायँगे–और एक दिन वे जागेंगे अवश्य–तब वे अपने प्रति की हुई तुम्हारी हितकारी सेवा को भूलेंगे नहीं और तुम्हारे प्रति कृतज्ञ रहेंगे।

भारतवर्ष के इन गरीब, निम्न जातिवालों के प्रति हमारे जो भाव हैं, उनका विचार करने से मेरे अन्तःकरण में कितनी पीड़ा होती है! उन्हें कोई अवसर नहीं मिलता, उनके लिए बचने का कोई रास्ता नहीं है और ऊपर चढ़ने का कोई मार्ग नहीं।... वे प्रतिदिन अधिकाधिक नीचे डूबते जा रहे हैं; निर्दय समाज के द्वारा अपने ऊपर होनेवाले आघातों का वे अनुभव करते हैं, पर वे जानते नहीं कि ये आघात कहाँ से आ रहे हैं। वे भी दूसरों के समान मनुष्य हैं, इस बात को वे भूल गये हैं। और इसका परिणाम हुआ है गुलामी का दासत्व। गत कुछ वर्षों के भीतर विचारशील पुरुषों ने इस बात को देख लिया है; पर दुर्भाग्यवश वे इसका दोष हिन्दू धर्म के मत्थे मढ़ते हैं; और उनको तो सुधार का एक यही उपाय दिखायी देता है कि संसार के इस महत्तम धर्म को कुचल दिया जाय। मेरे मित्रों, मेरी बात को ध्यान से सुनो, ईश्वर की दया से मैंने रहस्य का पता लगा लिया है। **दोष धर्म का नहीं है। इसके विपरीत, तुम्हारा धर्म तो तुम्हें यही सिखाता है कि प्रत्येक प्राणी स्वयं तुम्हारी आत्मा का ही नाना रूपों में विकास है।** पर दोष है व्यावहारिक आचरण का अभाव, सहानुभूति का अभाव–हृदय का अभाव। इस वस्तु स्थिति को दूर करना है–धर्म का नाश करके नहीं, वरन् हिन्दू धर्म के महान् उपदेशों के अनुसार आचरण करके और बौद्धमत, जो हिन्दू धर्म का तर्कसंगत विकास-रूप है, उसकी अद्भुत सहानुभूति को उस आचरण के साथ युक्त करके। लाखों स्त्री-पुरुष पवित्रता के जोश से उद्दीप्त होकर, ईश्वर के प्रति अटल विश्वास से शक्तिमान बनकर और गरीबों, पतितों एवं पददलितों के प्रति सहानुभूति से सिंह के समान साहसी बनकर इस सम्पूर्ण भारतदेश में सर्वत्र उद्धार के सन्देश का, सहायता के सन्देश का, सामाजिक उत्थान के सन्देश का, समानता के सन्देश का प्रचार करते हुए विचरण करेंगे।

वर्तमान समय में तुम्हारा कर्त्तव्य है कि तुम एक गाँव से दूसरे गाँव को जाओ और लोगों को समझाओ कि अब और अधिक समय तक आलस्यपूर्वक केवल बैठे रहने से काम नहीं चलेगा। उन्हें उनकी यथार्थ स्थिति का परिचय कराओ और कहो, "ऐ भाइयो! सब लोग उठो! जागो! अब और कितनी देर तक सोते रहोगे? अब तक ब्राह्मणों ने धर्म पर एकाधिपत्य कर रखा है; पर वे जब काल की प्रबल तरंग के विरुद्ध अपना एकाधिपत्य नहीं रख सकते, तब चलो, और ऐसे प्रयत्न करो कि देश भर में प्रत्येक को वह धर्म प्राप्त हो जाय। उनके मन में यह बैठा दो कि ब्राह्मणों के समान उनका भी धर्म पर वही अधिकार है। सभी को, चाण्डाल तक को भी, इन्हीं जाज्वल्यमान मन्त्रों का उपदेश करो। उन्हें सरल शब्दों में जीवन के लिए आवश्यक विषयों तथा वाणिज्य-व्यापार और कृषि आदि की भी शिक्षा दो। यदि तुम ऐसा नहीं कर सकते, तो धिक्कार है तुम्हारी शिक्षा और संस्कृति को, धिक्कार है तुम्हारे वेदों और वेदान्त के अध्ययन को! भारत की उच्च जातिवालों, तुम चाहे जितना भी अपने को आर्य पूर्वजों की सन्तान कहने का प्रदर्शन करो, चाहे जितना भी प्राचीन भारत के वैभव का रात-दिन गुणगान करो और अपने जन्म के अभिमान में अकड़ते रहो–पर क्या तुम ऐसा समझते हो कि तुम सजीव हो? तुम तो दस सहस्त्र वर्षों से सुरक्षित रखे हुए मृत देह (Mummies) जैसे ही हो! भारतवर्ष में जो थोड़ी बहुत जीवन-शक्ति अभी भी है, वह उन्हीं में मिलेगी, जिन्हें तुम्हारे पूर्वज 'चलते-फिरते, सड़े, गन्दे मांसपिण्ड' मानकर घृणा करते थे; और यथार्थ में 'चलते हुए मुरदे' तो तुम लोग हो। तुम्हारे घर-द्वार, तुम्हारे साज-सामान ऐसे निर्जीव और पुराने हैं कि वे अजायब-घर के नमूनों के समान दिखायी देते हैं; और तुम्हारे रीति-रिवाज, चाल-ढाल और रहन-सहन को देखकर कोई भी यही सोचेगा कि 'नानी की कहानी' सुन रहा है! तुमसे व्यक्तिगत परिचय प्राप्त कर लेने के बाद भी जब वह घर लौटता है, तो मानो यह सोचता है कि वह कला-भवन के रंगीन चित्र देखने गया था!

ऐ भारत के उच्च वर्गवालो, तुम तो माया के इस संसार में मानो इन्द्रजाल हो, रहस्य हो, मरुमरीचिका हो! एकत्र मिश्रित विभिन्न भूतकालिक क्रियाओं के तुम केवल द्योतक मात्र हो। तुमको अभी भी वर्तमान समय में कोई दिख रहा है–यह तो मानो केवल अजीर्ण के कारण होनेवाला भयानक दुःस्वप्न है। तुम तो भविष्य के शून्याकार, सारहीन, अस्तित्व-रहित पदार्थ हो। स्वप्न-राज्य के नागरिक! तुम लोग और अधिक समय तक क्यों भटक रहे हो? तुम भूतकालीन भारत के मृत शरीर के मांसहीन, रक्तहीन अस्थिकंकाल-जैसे हो–तुम शीघ्र ही अपने को मिट्टी में मिलाकर हवा में अदृश्य क्यों नहीं हो जाते? तुम्हारी अस्थिमयी अँगुलियों में

तुम्हारे पूर्वजों के संग्रह किये हुए रत्न की कुछ अमूल्य मुद्रिकाएँ हैं और बहुत-सी प्राचीन सम्पत्ति की पिटारियाँ तुम्हारे दुर्गन्ध-युक्त मृत शरीर की छाती से चिपकी हुई सुरक्षित रखी हुई हैं। अब तक तुमको उन्हें दूसरों को सौंप देने का अवसर नहीं मिला था। अब ब्रिटिश राज-शासन में प्रतिबन्धरहित शिक्षा एवं ज्ञान-प्रसार के दिनों में, उन सब वस्तुओं को अपने उत्तराधिकारियों को सौंप दो। यह बात यथासम्भव शीघ्र कर डालो। तुम अपने को शून्य में लीन करके अदृश्य हो जाओ और अपने स्थान में 'नवभारत' का उदय होने दो। उसका उदय हल चलाने वाले किसानों की कुटिया से, मछुए, मोचियों और मेहतरों को झोपड़ियों से हो। बनिये की दुकान से, रोटी बेचनेवाले की भट्‌टी के पास से वह प्रकट हो। कारखानों, हाटों और बाजारों से वह निकले। वह 'नव-भारत' अमराइयों और जंगलों से, पहाड़ों और पर्वतों से प्रकट हो। ये साधारण लोग सहस्त्रों वर्षों से अत्याचार सहते आये हैं–बिना कुड़बुड़ाये उन्होंने यह सब सहा है और परिणाम में उन्होंने आश्चर्यकारक धैर्य-शक्ति प्राप्त कर ली है। ये सतत विपत्ति सहते रहे हैं, जिससे उन्हें अविरल जीवन-शक्ति प्राप्त हो गयी है। मुट्‌ठी भर अन्न से पेट भरकर वे संसार को कँपा सकते हैं; उनको तुम केवल आधी रोटी दे दो, और देखोगे कि सारे संसार का विस्तार उनकी शक्ति के समावेश के लिए पर्याप्त न होगा। उनमें 'रक्तबीज' की अक्षय जीवन-शक्ति भरी है। इसके अतिरिक्त, उनमें पवित्र और नीतियुक्त जीवन से आनेवाला वह आश्चर्यजनक बल है, जो संसार में अन्यत्र नहीं मिलता। ऐसी शान्ति, ऐसा सन्तोष, ऐसा प्रेम और चुपचाप सतत कार्य करने की ऐसी शक्ति और कार्य के समय इस प्रकार सिंह-बल प्रकट करना–यह सब तुम्हें अन्यत्र कहाँ मिलेगा? भूतकाल के कंकाल देखो, तुम्हारे सामने तुम्हारे उत्तराधिकारी खड़े हैं–भावी भारतवर्ष खड़ा है। अपने खजाने की उन पिटारियों को और उन रत्नजड़ित मुद्राओं को उनके बीच जितनी जल्दी हो सके, फेंक दो और तुम हवा में मिल जाओ, फिर कभी दिखायी न दो–केवल अपने कानों को खोले रखो। अपने अदृश्य होते ही तत्काल तुम पुनर्जात भारतवर्ष का वह प्रथम उद्घोष सुनोगे, जिसकी करोड़ों गर्जनाओं से सारे विश्व में यही पुकार गूँजती रहेगी–"वाह गुरु की फतह!"

52

THE SOCIALIST SWAMI

(समाजवादी संन्यासी)

Nitish Sen Gupta

Swami Vivekananda, generally known as a religious leader, social reformer, spiritualist and humanist, was also one of the earliest socialist thinkers of our country. Indeed he described himself as a socialist (in a letter to his disciple Mary Hale in 1896) perhaps the first Indian to do so. Also, his perception of the class character of the society, the exploitation of the toiling masses by the feudal and capitalist classes, the inevitability of the former seizing power from the latter and his forecasting of the first proletarian revolution taking place either in Russia or China mark him as a true socialist.

Indeed proceeding from the economic analyses by Digby, R.C. Dutt etc. on the one hand, and from Marxian thinkers of Europe on the other, Vivekananda showed a rare insight to view India and the world on socialistic lines, diagnosed the ills of Indian society, and forcefully pleaded for policies and reforms analogous to those prescribed by scientific socialism.

As Subhas Chandra Bose said, in his address at a political conference at Rangpur on March 30, 1929, "Vivekananda's socialist ideas which did not come from outside, but have their roots in India's own intellectual and cultural traditions would do credit to a front rank socialist." One is surprised to see scattered in his writings statements which closely resemble Marx's typical comments such as the poor becoming poorer and the rich becoming ricer under the present social system or that the future culture of the Indian people can only be proletarian culture.

Romain Rolland also noticed the closeness between Vivekananda's social and economic thoughts and some aspects of Marxism. "On reading again the Real and Apparent an I admired how the institution of the Indian prophet had united without knowing it with the virile reason of the great interpreters of communism."

Unfortunately, his socialist thoughts are found scattered among his speeches, books and letters and also be passed away very early only after about 7 or 8 yeas of effective creative life before his ideas could be fully expanded.

For an understanding of Vivekananda's socialism, two points need to be emphasised. First, Vivekananda through his travels as an ordinary sanyasi between 1886 and 1893 through this country came to know the poorest and commonest Indian and the surroundings whee he lives and words as few Indian leaders have known. He saw poverty and exploitation in their most naked form and also the basic strength of the toiling masses and their potential for effective social and political action.

Secondly, he was an avid reader and undoubtedly became acquainted with contemporary socialist literature in Europe including Marxist literature. The following aspects of socialist can be identified from Vivekananda's writings:

(i) Concept of an evolutionary society constantly changing through the dilalectic principle of interaction by opposites.

(ii) Concept of a society being divided into classes based on control of the means of production and distribution and of the state apparatus, and the allied concept of class struggle. Using Indian nomenclature he divided history into four ages – the Brahan age, the Kshatriya age, the Vaishya age and the Sudras age (the last about to come) At least the last three ages approximate to the last three phases in Marx's materialsist interpretation of history, viz, feudalism, capitalism and socialism. Just as the Vaishyas had replaced the Kshatiryas through struggle, so also the Sudras were dstined to replace the Vaishyas through struggle.

(iii) Need for establishing a classless society through revolutionary action by the lower classes, for whom he used the term 'sudra'.

(iv) Concept of casteless society, an Indian variant of classless society. He held the caste system responsible for India's decline and bitterly opposed untouchability. He praised Islam as the most egalitarian religious system that had completely eliminated social differences, and longed for a combination of the Islamic body and the Vedantic soul.

(v) An all-pervasive concern for the poor, the exploited and the under priviledged. This is expressed in his repeated call for abolition of all privileges, social and economic, and all forms of exploitation. His stirring words are the most eloquent testimony of his deep concrn for the poor.

"So long as the millions live in hunger and ignorance, I hold everyman a traitor who having been educated at their expense pays no heed to them". "I do not believe in a God who cannot, give me bread here giving me eternal bliss in heaven." "I call him a traitor who having been nursed in luxury by the downtrodden millions of toiling poor never even takes a thought for them." His repeated announcement was that so long as the poor remained poor there was no point in practising religion or pursuing politics. "I do not believe in a God or religion which cannot wipe the widow's tears or bring a piece of bread to the orphan's mouth. Let the vedas, the Kuran, the Puranas and all scriptures rust now for some time". During a visit to Bombay in 1892 he came to know the conditions of textile labourers and the state of trade unionism. This cast a deep influence on him.

(vi) Running the economy–production; distribution and consumption–in the interest of the masses.

According to Sister Nivedita he was in favour of small-scale farming by peasant proprietors and small-scale agro-based enterprises as against largescale capital intensive projects.

He advocated small peasants' farm with the peasant having complete title on his land, the application of technology to agriculture, the setting up of small industrial workshops a a nucleus of agro-industries and technical education, the expansion of commerce, a socially controlled system of production and exchange.

(vii) Concept of creating mass consciousness and mass awakening with the implied possibility of mass movement which alone could change the face of society. According to him, all the social reform movements in India had suffered from a very narrow base in the sense that they were confined only to the very narrow upper strata of society. The society could never be revolutionised unless the bulk of the people lower down could be enthused into revolutionary action for social change.

(viii) Vivekananda's concept of universalism, a world order based on equality of nations and absence of all forms of chauvinism or hatred among nations. If one believes in the fundamental Vedantic assertion of unity of mankind, one has to accept that all nations are equal just as all individuals are equal. It was, therefore, a logial corollary to proceeding from this to the concept of a future universal order where there would be no domination of one nation by another. He therefore repeatedly emphasised that many of the problems facing mankind were beoming so much larger that they could no longer be solved nationally, but only on the larger international basis. He was convinced that a time will come when nations will cease to exist along with their differences, that India could never develop in isolation from the world, and that everything must be sacrificed, if necessary for that one principle–Universality.

(ix) He regarded labour as the chief factor of production and spoke about the harmful effect, casued by large-scale production and division of labour. "Excess of machines spoils man's intellectual faculty, and make inert objects out of man. In a factory men are doing the same work day after day, night after night, year after year. One group is making only a small part of an article–making the head of a pin, weaving threads or moving forward and backward along with the loom. He loses his job and then he is doomed. Working like inanimate object, he has become inanimate incapable of doing anything new."

(x) He also realised the true economic character of imperialism, "So many things are grown in India. Foreigners use that raw-material to make gold, and you are just carrying their burden like donkeys. Foreigners become richer and richer by taking primary goods from India and processing them by their intelligence, and you people have locked up your intelligence in a chest and are crying for bread after allowing others to take your own wealth."

Here, Vivekananda had shown how the imperialist country used the colony for procuring primary produces and utilising it as a market for its own industrial products. The colonial countries continue to suffer and economically decline and remain undeveloped. The answer therefore lay in the colonial country's undertaking processing of their own goods and selling them directly. Vivekananda, therefore, anticipated thoughts on the third world's economic development which became current long afterwards.

Almost anticipating Lenin, he stated that monopoly capital was utilising its unlimited power to exploit the toiling masses. When there was no further scope for exploitation in his own country the monopoly capitalist tries to grab other countries.

"These who have wealth are dominating the Government and are exploiting and plundering the commoners, who are thereafter being sent to other countries as soldiers to die. If there is victory the rulers will have more of wealth, and the commoners–soldiers are after all dead."

All this long before Lenin came out with his theory of imperialism. His deep conviction about the future scenario is also seen in the following prophetic statement quoted in Romain Rolland's Life of Vivekananda from the memories of his disciple, Sister Christine:

> *"In 1896, Vivekananda told me : "The next upheaval that is to usher in another era, will come from Russia or China. I cannot see clearly which, but it will be either the one or the other ... The world is in the third epoch under the domination ofVaishya (the merchant, the third estate). The fourth epoch will be under that of the Sudra (the proletariat)."*

Thus, at the end of the last century when the British Empire was at its zenith, when the Congress was just a body for petitions and prayers, and weli before our freedom movement was to commence, Vivekananda had the vision of a socialist India, and a socialist world to be acheived through mass movement and through uprising of the Sudra class. While the social order that he hoped for will be imbued with the Vedantic principles of unity of all men and universal brotherhood, this will also be a society where there will be no class, no caste, no social or economic privileges, but equal opportunity, complete freedom of religions and national respect for all religions. Also, there will be system of educating the masses through science, technology and professionalism and arousing a mass consciousness.

He had contempt for the parliamentary institutions of the West which were sham, only instruments of oppression for the upper classes. "The new order of things is the salvation of the people by the people." His method was that hundreds of thousands of young, poor but honest men and women should go to all corners of the country and impart knowledge to the toiling masses who will then become the instrument of revolution. "My young men will move across India like irresistible waves and will go to the houses of those who are the poorest, the meanest, and humblest and most exploited, carrying with them comfort, religion, morals and education. This is my dream and ambition".

This mission of Vivekananda is still to be accomplished.

By Courtesy Hindustan Times, 8 Nov. 1987

53

VEDANTIC SOCIALISM

Amiya Kumar Mazumdar

The most important contribution of the Vedanta philosophy, as Swamiji understood it, is the removal of all kinds of privilege. In Vedanta, which teaches oneness of existence, there cannot be any room for privilege. As Swamiji put it, 'The idea of privilege is the bane of human life.' Two forces are constantly at work, the one making for privilege, the other breaking down privilege. Swamiji speaks of four kinds of privileges which the Vedanta decries, time and again. The first idea of privilege is that of the strong over the weak. The strong man claims privilege over the weak because of his strength. The second kind is the privilege of wealth. If a man has more money than another, he claims a little privilege over the poor. The third is the privilege of intellect. If a man is more knowledgeable, he claims privilege over the ignorant. The last kind of privilege relates to spirituality There are persons who think that they know more about spirituality, God, immortality of soul and therefore claim privilege over those who are allegedly less spiritual.

Swamiji emphatically asserts that no person can be a Vedantist and at the same time claim privilege over any one, whether physical or intellectual or spiritual. According to the Vedanta, the same power is in every creature, the one majifesting more, the other less or, in other words, the difference between a man and away, a worm, is only a difference in degree. Given suitable opportunities, a worm also can develop itself to manhood. As Swami Vivekananda put it : "One atom in the universe cannot move without dragging the whole world along with it. There cannot be any progress without the whole world following in the wake and it is becoming clearer every day that the solution of any problem can never be attained on racial or national or narrow grounds. Every idea has to become broad till it covers the whole of this world, every aspiration must go on increasing till it has engulfed the whole of humanity, nay, the whole of life, within its scope."

Those who are wedded to the Vedanta view of life cannot admit of any kind of privilege in society. Following the ideal of the Vedanta, Vivekananda declared : "Our idea is the Brahman of spiritual culture and renunciation." By 'The Brahman ideal' Vivekananda means the ideal Brahmanness in which worldliness is totally absent and true wisdom is abundantly present. This, according to Vivekananda, is the ideal of the Hindu race. It does not require much logic to demonstrate that Vedanta paves th way towards socialism. When Vivekananda declared 'I am a socialist' all that he meant was the Vedantaic socialism which preaches oneness of existence and breaks down all artificial barriers between man and man, between race and race. It has to be borne in mind that Vivekananda did not subscribe to Marxian socialism because, (a) He did not believe in the inevitability of class struggle; (b) He did not believe in dialectical materialism as a philosophy of life; (c) Nor did he believe in materialistic interpretation of History. While Marx insisted upon the primacy of economic equality, Vivekananda looked upon man as an integrated personality and insisted on man's all round development, economic, moral, intellectual, political and lastly spiritual. This ideal, according to Vivekananda, can be achieved through practical Vedanta. His ceaseless exhortation to his countrymen was: 'The abstract Advaita must become poetic and practical in every day life.' By practical Vedanta he meant Vedantic principle as applied to everyday life. Vivekananda urged that the Vedantic truths must be brought out from the monsastery and broadcast to the people of the world.

By upholding that the individual Jiva and Brahman are basically identical, not only does Vedanta not encourage blasphemy, on the contrary, the Vedanta asks everybody to be sensible of his dignity, stature, heritage and destiny. As Vivekananda used to say : "Christs and Buddhas are but waves on the ocean which I am."

It has already been mentioned that Vedanta is both philosophy and religion, according to Vivekananda. Vivekananda speaks of 'The Religion' and 'Religions'. 'The Religion' is the perception, realisation and manifestation of man's real nature which is divinity. One cannot afford to forget the great saying of Vivekananda : 'Each soul is potentially divine.' The universal spirit which is man's essential nature manifests itself in various ways. In other words, the Religion which means oneness of existence manifests itself through various modes and media and these are called religions, such as Islam, Christianity, Buddhism, Hinduism etc. Religion, therefore is one in substance, but many in relation to forms. These forms may be compared to the different radii of a circle. The radii are so many paths meeting at the centre. When the centre is reached, all differences disappear. Even at th risk of repetition, it should be emphasised that religion is the realizationof this centre which embodies the essential truth. The radii are but different manifestations of the central truth. Religions are, therefore, many according to the different needs, capacities and surroundings of various groups of men. It is for this reason that Vivekananda affirmed : "We want to lead mankind to the place whre there is neither the Veda nor the Bible nor the Quoran; yet this has to be done by harmonizing the Vedas, the Bible and the Quoran. Mankind ought to be taught that religions are but the varied expressions of the Religion, which is Oneness, so that each may choose the path that suits him best." According to Vivekananda, *Vedanta alone under some form or other, is most suited to become the Universal Religion of man.* Vedanta, be it noted, is in consonance with the method and the results of modern science, particularly Quantum Physics. This has been proved, beyond doubt, by such eminent scientisits as Einstein, Heisenberg, Marx Planck, Milikan, F. Capra and others. Vedanta advocates, not levelling down of the higher segment of society to the lower, rather it recommends the levelling up of the down-trodden and the under-dogs to the highest cultural stage. Vivekananda's salutory advice to his countrymen was : "If anybody thinks that the difference between a Brahmana and a Sudra is insurmountable, then not a pie should be spent on the education of the Brahmanas but that all available funds of the country should be utilized for the education of the depressed classes." Anybody who cares to study seriously, the life and teachings of Viveknanda will not fail to notice that what was uppermost in his mind was uplifting of the masses, removal of poverty and the ignorance of the downtrodden. His historic utterence, 'I call that God, what ignorant people call Man, is too precious to be thrown away.

In regard to the role of Religion in social progress Vivekananda's views are clear and unambiguous. As he put it : "My Mission is to show that Religion is everything and in everything... Everything goes to show that socialism or some form of rule by the people, call it what you will, is coming on the boards. The people will certainly want the satisfaction of their material needs, less work, no oppression, no war, more food. What guarantee have we that this or any civilization, will last, unless it is based on Religion, on the goodness of Man? Depend on it, Religion goes to the root of the matter. If it is right, all is right." Again, "In all religions we travel from a lesser to a higher truth, never from error to truth. There is a oneness behind all creation, but minds are various. That which exist is one, sages call it variously. The worst religion are only bad readings of the truth."

Every improvement in India requires, according to Vivekananda, first of all, an upheaval in religion. That is why Vivekananda said, "Before flooding India with socialistic or political ideas, first deluge the land with spiritual ideas." To be sure, the spiritual basis lies in Vedanta only.

Since removal of poverty, ignorance and superstitition is the precondition of social progress in India, one may naturally raise the question, "Can Vedanta remove poverty?" Swamiji's answer is in the affirmative. Vedanta cannot directly remove poverty but certainly it teaches one to renounce one's narrow, selfish ego to serve man as the embodiment of God and to love one's neighbour as one's own self. Swamiji was keen on introducing modern techniques in agriculture as he was interested in India's industrial development. At the same time, he was anxious to see that there was equitable distribution of national wealth.

With unerring insight, Vivekananda saw that the upper classes will no longer be able to repress the lower. The well-being of th ehigher classes lay in helping the lower to get their legitimate rights.

Addressing the upper classes, Vivekananda said, "You merge yourselves in the void and dissappear and let New India arise in your place. Let her arise out of the peasant's cottage, grasping the plough, out of the huts of the fisherman, the cobbler and the sweeper. Let her spring from the grocer's shop, from beside the oven of the fritter-seller. Let her emanate from the factory, from marts and from markets. Let her emerge from groves and forests, from hills and mountains."

These common people have suffered oppression for thousands of years, suffered it without murmur, and as a result have got wonderful fortitude. They have suffered eternal misery which has given unflinching vitality. Living on a handful of grain, they can convulse the world; give them only half a piece of bread, and the whole world will not be big enough to contain their energy. Such peacefulness, such contentmen, such love, such power of silent and incessant work and such manifestation of lion's strength in times of action–where else will you find these?

Vivekananda's deep concern for the poor and the down-trodden is also manifest in his meditation at Kanyakumari, which is a land-mark in the life of the wandering Monk. After prostrating before theDivine Mother at the temple and crossing the sea, he sat on the last rock and fell into deep meditation. One would have naturally expected that the monk's meditation centered round his personal liberaion. But No!! He meditated on the past,the present and the future of his motherland and hit upon a plan to regenerate the masses from their poverty and squalor. This indeed is a unique meditation. Swamiji's concern for the poor and down-trodden has its roots in his Vedantic vision of spiritual unity of the universe and the basic equality of all creatures.

It was from the point of view of Vedanta that Vivekananda declared at the Parliament of Religions held at Chicago in September 1893: "We believe not only in universal toleration but we accept all religions as true." He proceeded to observe further: "I fervently hope that the bell that tolled this morning in honour of this convention may be the death knell of all fanaticism, of all persecutions with the sword or with the pen and of all uncharitable feelings between persons wending their way to the same goal." In his concluding address at the Parliament, Vivekananda observed: "If the Parliament of Religions has shown anything to the world, it is this : It has proved to the world that holiness, purity and charity are not the exclusive possessions of any church in the world and that every system has produced men and women of the most exalted character. In the face of this evidence, if anybody dreams of the exclusive survival of his own religion and the destruction of the others, I pity him from the bottom of my heart and point out to him that upon the banner of every religion will soon be written, inspite of resistance : Help and Not fight, Assimilation and Not Destruction, Harmony and Peace and Not Dissension."

There can hardly be a better exposition of the Vedanta.

By Courtesy, Vivekanand Kendra, 1991

54

KARMA YOGA AND MANAGEMENT
(काम का अधिकार एवं कर्मयोग प्रबंधन)

M. Lakshmi Kumari

The world has started acknowledging the scientific precision of our Jnana-Yoga, the mystic power behind Raja-Yoga and the extra ordinary charm and beauty of Bhakti-Yoga. The immense benefits that can accure to an individual and to the society through Karma-Yoga selfless dedicated work-are yet to be studied and experimented upon. For our countrymen, who have fallen very low in their work ethics, knowledge and practice to regenerate the glory of our Karmabhoomi through the lives and actions of each one of us and Karma-Yoga is the panacea for our present day social ills.

SWAMI VIVEKANANDA'S CALL

During his wanderings in the country from 1890-92 Swami Vivekananda experienced himself the deterioration in values and work ethics in our country. He observed that our people had become slaves in every sense of the term. The immediate emergency treatment that Swamiji could think of was to wake up our people from their centuries old lethargy and put them to right action through the time tested path of Karmayoga. Today we are in the last lap of 20th century. No doubt as our constitution puts it we are a Sovereign Republic. As a nation we are free. But as individuals we continue to be slaves. Self oriented work is all that we know of which as we become engaged in more and more, only add to the bondage, burden and misery instead of giving the taste of joyous freedom which is the natural flavour of good work well executed. The sum total-pursuit of excellence is a thing of past, honesty, truthfulness, dedication to work, so beautifully summed up in the word character efficiency are unknown. Understanding and sympathy for fellow human beings, have disappeared from the national scene. Even social service has become a paid job.

NATIONAL SCENE

At the national level we are fighting for our rights and privileges. There is no topic of discussion among the working groups other than pay, promotion, prospects, perks. Nobody is bothered about duty. The easiest and most practical path for our nation's regeneration is a reapprisal of this irrevocable and supremely relevant Karmayoga. To enrich and energise our national wealth of human resources which just cannot be done by creating new ministries and departments, our people should understand the fundamentals of 'Secret of action' and learn to suffuse their work with a new idealism of sacrifice and service, if not worship.

Management of finance, resources, personnel and of productivity in a system, etc are matters of study and discussion among the present day experts. What do our ancient seers have to say in this matter? A nation which excelled and created such marvels in study, philosophy, art, architecture and so on must have certainly evolved a philosophy of work too, for the individual, group and the nation. Not many of our experts have bothered to study this aspect of our great heritage. A country which was renowned by the name of Punyabhoomi, Tyagabhoomi, Dharmabhoomi, Karmabhoomi and so on, each epithet a pointer to a great philosophy, would certainly have something of value in this field of work as well.

The world at large is discovering in our Rajayoga–the royal path to self unfoldment–a science for total human development; in Bhaktiyoga, inexplicable heights of emotional fulfilment and in Jnanayoga, an absolutely scientific incomparable unified vision of the whole. We will be failing in our duty if we don't bring out the Golden Keys hidden in Karmayoga by which even the commonest among us can work one's way to deep satisfaction, discovering in our daily work an elixir for the growth and expansion of our total personality and to use the same as an instrument for the service of the nation and our people.

COUTOUR HERITAGE

Every human being must inherit the treasure which the cosmic Intelligence has made available to man from time to time. Swami Vivekananda was the foremost initiator of this world level interaction who with open heart and arms shared with the world outside as much as he could, of the invaluable science and technology of living which we had perfected as part of our spiritual heritage. His efforts uncovered for the world (including Indians) not ony the great beauty, scientific validity and practical relevance of the Indian vision of Reality but also made the world understand that progress, to be real and meaningful has to be achieved at two levels, internal as well as external, not separately but together. Science has progressed much since then and every one of its discoveries has only underscored Swamiji's observation.

KARMAYOGA

There are several definitions for Karmayoga. Karmayoga is the method of attaining perfection, freedom, bliss and blessedness thorugh work. Karmayoga is the union of our lower self with the Higher Self through work. In simpler terms Karmayoga is a purposeful action animated by a universal motive. But the best and most comprehensive of definitions has been given by Swami Vivekananda which we find incorporated in his famous words:

> *"Each soul is potentially divine. The goal in life is to manifest this divinity by controlling nature external and internal. Do it by work or worship; psychic control or philosophy, by one or more or all of these – and be free. This is the whole of religion. Doctrines or dogmas, or rituals, or books, or temples, or forms, are but secondary details."*

Each one of us has 3 facets to our personality – propelled from within by an infinite external spiritual force. It expresses itself in the intellect as intelligence (knowledge, wisdom), in our mind as emotions and the variety of feelings and at our physical level through our actions Sum total of our development should be also threefold. To:

1. Achieve the maximum perfection and development at the individual level.
2. Relate oneself with the whole of creation through our positive interactions and

3. Ultimately pave the way to reach out to the peak of evolution by realising oneself to be the part and parcel of that Ultimate Truth, Bliss, Godhood or by whatever name one may upto call it. Swami Vivekananda used the words "be free" with special emphasis and caught the attention of the West at one stroke. The idea was so appealing to them, all the more because they had just begun to taste, in a very elementary way, freedom from bondage, ignorance, wants and so on. That could indeed be a prime motivation to all of us, as it is truly freedom that every one is looking for through knowledge, through love or through action.

Of special significance is our work ethics as it is very pertinent in our national context, when, as mentioned earlier, inspite of being the citizens of a sovereign republic, our people have not learnt to shake off the shackles of slavery with the result they remain backward, weak, ignornant, poor and above all bereft of human dignity, plodding along a lack lustre life. All our problems are offshoots of this one malady.

KARMA TO KARMAYOGA

To illustate, let us take just one very very significant declartion fro Bhagavad Gita,

> *Karmanyevadhikaraste ma phalesu kadacana*
> *ma karmaphala hetur bhur ma te sango' stu akarmani.* 11, 47.

'To work alone you have the right, never to the fruits thereof. Let not your motive be fruits of action, nor let your attachment be to inaction.

It is easy to read the meaning of the sloka. It is more difficult to read into the meaning of it.

It is a life time's job to understand its full implications and put it into practice in our life as that demands a restructuring of our whole life-lock, stock and barrel – a great Sadhana indeed.

At the very elementary level we are warned of indulging in inaction. Action is the very insignia of life. Every atom in the Universe is in motion. Inaction is unnatural and almost impossible. Therefore one must constantly strive to be in the state of alert action thus making oneself part of the pulsations of the Universal rhythm. Inaction leading to lethargy and spiritual degradation robs man not only of his strength and vitality but his dignity as well.

Contributing nothing to national life, still our people are adept in asking for rights and privileges from the nation and in this both the governing and the governed are in wonderful collusion. *Making work a "fundamental right" will only help to bring more and more people into this organised form of colossal national waste.* That is all.

Even a tiny blade of grass raises its head and stands with a dignity of its own carrying out its bit of allotted work to the best of its ability demanding nothing for itself. Each is great in his or her own way. Truly speaking there is no one great or small. All have their unique place in the Universal scheme, in the totality of life.

Unfortunately, lethargy and laziness, wasting of energy, materials and time have asumed such enormous proportions in our country that one is habituated to look into the calenders, not for working days but for holidays. It is the 'off' periods one is worred about than 'on duty' timings' It is indeed a national calamity that work has lost its dignity and charm in this Karmabhoomi of ours.

Understanding of this basic fact of 'Karmayoga' will bring back dignity of work and realisation of the need for constant working.

WORK AND ITS RESULT

Second injunction calls upon man to give up his preoccupation with the result of the action. Why should not one get attached to the result? Firstly the real result of a work is subjective, in the reaction it creates in our mental stuff. Desire for a fruit disturbs the equanimity of the minds and slowly eats its way into our efficiency. Worries of the past, excitement in the present, anxiety for the future, all these side reactions are generated in the mind which gets result oriented. When there is desire for a particular result mind becomes attached to that and slowly the act of working looses its joy and charm and above all its purifying power. Net result is we are dragged into monotony, frustration and dissatisfaction not only with oneself but with the world around. On the other hand unburdened from the anxiety for the result one is able to express oneself in action more skilfully, systematically and fully. Every action then turns to be a subejctive exercise to gain inner strength, to grow inward towards the Infinite Self within.

When attention is shifted from the result (which implies taking) to giving and serving–action becomes a sacrifice, a yoga and whole life changes its colour. It adds to itself a new dignity, power, fulfilment and greatness. A new dimension is opened up. In fact that is the very purpose of living and working. With qualitative improvement in the 'subjective', there is a simultaneous betterment at the objective level. 'Yogah Karmasu Kausalam'–Karmyoga leads to a rare all round excellence. Even the most insignificant daily activity becomes an act of worship, of prayer, of meditation. Feelings of happiness, calmness and freedom pervade the mind. Thus just this one aspect of Karmayoga when practised sincerely makes one a Master of action, a force to be reckoned with and a benediction to the society.

MOTIVATION FOR WORK

The third point is what should be the motivation for work then? Let good actions flow out of us naturally say the scriptures. Right action should help us to manifest the best of qualities in us – or divinity as Swami Vivekananda puts it. An action is good if it uplifts the doer and produces maximum happiness to greatest number of people. It automatically becomes a tangible assertion ofTruth. If our thoughts, words or deeds put a wall of narrowness around us, making us aloof and separate from the rest of the world we deny our divine self no matter what that action is. Such actions are destructive and unspiritual. Our work should help us to remove the barrier of egoism, must help us to realise more and more the fundamental unity, the oneness which is behind the Universe. Swami Vivekananda therefore, says, expansion is life, contraction is death, Love is life hatred is death, knowledge is life, ignorance is death.

Selfish motivations hold within, anxiety and fear of disappointment. Fear makes us slaves. It is fearlessness, it is selflessness that makes us masters. Selfishness coupled with egoism have turned us today into a nation of cowards, slavish brutes.

The most important is the declaration with which the sloka starts, "you have right only to action." To understand this statement we have to understand something of the vedantic idealism, essentials of yogic or scientific approach to life.

WORK CENTRED IN TRUTH

Yoga helps us to synchronise our spirit, mind and senses. The idealism and understanding of our intellect should reflect the characteristics of the spirit, or Truth. What are these characteristics? At this point Indian philosophy puts to shame the discoveries of modern physics by its precedence of more than 5000 years. To mention just a few fundamental parellels–

1. Indivisibility of substance–Ekam sat–The material and efficient cause of the universe is one, matter, energy, mind, consciousness–all stand unified into one.
2. Universality: it is this one that has manifested into the many. Really speaking there is no creation of anything new. There are only manifestations – transformations of the one into many. That means everything in this Universe is interrelated.
3. Non objective–when there exists only one infinite unbreakable whole where is the question of subject or object. A new omnijective vision must replace the old approach based on subject/objec differences. *The word exploitation has no place in the dictionary of Karmayoga.*

These are the characteristics of the Truth, of the spirit, that should influences the thoughts of the mind, perceptions of the senses and action of our organs. Karmayoga thus becomes not only spiritualised activity but a truly scientific approach to work or action which, through directed externally is really a force operating within. In the fullness of spirit there is no time or place for desire. Desires make us move away from the subject to the world of objects, which have only a relative existence. When more and more of our actions conform to the characteristics of the spirit, more and more we move towards freedom and real happiness. Thus in Karmayoga we work outwardly but grow inwardly. Thus Karmayoga becomes a work, a prayer, a meditation, an yajna, all rolled into one, where there is neither a giver nor a receiver. One just excels in work deriving joy from the sheer act of working.

It is from this view point that Gita tells us that one has right only to work. It is just a statement ofTruth, a scientific fact. It is the whole that matters. "Particular" has no separate existence at all. From this height of awareness is there anything–material or work–that we can claim to be 'mine'. We are all–big or small, rich or poor–shareholders of tht one spiritual treasure –Omniscient, Omnipotent, Eternal and Infinite. That is why Upanishads called mankind as "Amritasya putrah"–children of immortality–a term which Swami Vivekananda used with so much of effectiveness in the lectures he delivered in the West.

At the same time there is a will in man to choose the right goal and the right means to achieve it. Thus every scope is provided for self effort, self unfoldment, self realisation–thus making human effort precious and valuable. We can make or mar our destiny. No God or extraneous power can interfere with it really.

CONCLUSION

Summing up, true reward of work is in the act of right working, in the act of right willing, in channelising the positive forces in us into one–in conformity with the Truth or Self within. Once one has made the right choice, fixed the right goal and decided on the right means there remains nothing more to be done. Education, guidance, upbringing, habits–all contribute towards this righteous living, in developing a really positive character.

Thus Karmayoga insists on a spiritual orientation. By its close association with ritualistic religiosity over the milenia unfortunately spirituality earned for itself a bad name. Buddha released it from the clutches of ritualistic religion and made it stand on its own. It was given to Swami Vivekandad to update it and project it to the world co-extensive with the modern scientific enquiry into the Unity of Existence and uphold it for one and all as a science for self management, self unfoldment, leading to health happiness and harmony within and peace without.

The mechanistic world of view of Cartesian–Newtonian Science is giving place to a new 'paradigm' of Reality–to a more holistic concept of Reality. To suit the emerging system view of life, mind, consciousness and evolution, a new conceptual frame work is to be created. This frame work will have to be necessarily spiritual in its ultimate nature, necessitating a restructuring of the human personality and our priorities.

In conclusion it is worthwhile recalling the words of that modern seer Fritjof Capra:

> "*........... the world view implied by modern physics is inconsistant with our present society, which does not reflect the harmonious interrelatedness we observe in nature. To achieve such a state of dynamic balance, a radically different social and economic structure will be needed : a cultural revolution in the true sense of the word. The survival of our whole civilization may depend on whether we can bring out such a change.*"

55

CAN ONE BE SCIENTIFIC AND YET SPIRITUAL?

Swami Budhananda

Now, at this stage of our deliberation arise two pertinent questions which were articulated by Swami Vivekananda in this manner:

> *Is religion to justify itself by discoveries of reason, through which every other concrete science justifies itself? Are the same methods of investigation which we apply to science and knowledge outside to be applied to the science of Religion?*

And, continuing, he himself gave this answer to these questions:

> *In my opinion, this must be so, and I am also of the opinion that the sooner it is done the better. If a religion is destroyed by such investigations, it was then all the time useless, unworthy superstition; and the sooner it goes the better. I am thoroughly convinced that its destruction would be the best thing that could happen. All that is dross will be taken off, no doubt, but the essential parts of religion will emerge triumphant out of this investigation. Not only will it be made scientific, as scientific, at least, as any of the conclusions of physics or chemistry, but will have greater strength, because physics or chemistry has no internal mandate to vouch for its truth, which religion has.*

So here we have, on the authority of a great spiritual teacher, the clear enupciation of the fact that by being subjected to scientific scrutiny and discipline, true religious spirit can only gain. This voice of religion vocalized by Vivekananda is singularly refreshing for two reasons : first, here religion shows true veneration for science, which though not unknown in oriental traditions, has been rarely shown in the Westernman's history; second, here religion challengingly comes out and bares its breast to any hostile arrow, confident as it is of its own indestructibiltiy.

When we juxtapose these two well-considered views, one coming form a great scientific leader, another from a great religious leader, we cannot have any reasonable doubt in our minds that one can be scientific and yet spiritual with enriching results for both the aspects of one's being.

To be convinced even theoretically of this possibility is itself a great help. For much work lies ahead of modern man, as far as solving problems of human existence is concerned. This conviction can be the resourceful basis of a new creative power wherewith he can attack the problems of today and tomorrow in a manner not hitherto possible for him, as he has been living in a house of knowledge divided against itself.

Great and many are the problems that are confronting us, but many also are the resources for solving them. The invaluable findings and realizations of man in the realm of the spirit are in our possession. So are the astounding discoveries of science. Unfortunately, however, these two mighty forces have thus far looked on one another with many misgivings and have often clashed to the detriment of man's best interest.

But today a time has definitely come, an urgency has certainly arisen when they should have a friendly and respectful encounter, in order to learn from each other, in order to profit from each other's association and to be strengthened by each other's powers. Otherwise, we shall not be able to solve the complicated problems of contemporary or future existence, either with the unaided wisdom of religion or the uninspired skill of science.

It is not an issue of scholasticism that we are discussing, the acceptance or rejection of which does not matter except in theory. What we are discussing is an issue of "to be or not to be" for man. Man will have to find the way to do this successfully or he will not survive. Of this one can be reasonably sure.

Something, therefore, will have to be done first in the very time spirit of today, which is dominated by the powerful overtones of the scientific spirit. These overtones, which create more problems than they solve, will have to be replaced by the conviction that it is possible to be scientific and yet spiritual. And if we understand all our problems at their roots, there is no greater urgency today than this.

It will, however, be a costly mistake to think that this encounter will hav to be brought about by sacrificing some grounds of both as a compromise settlement. If that is done, science will be less than itself and so will religion. And we cannot have much to do with science and religion that are not themselves. We want both science and religion to be full-blooded and vigorous in their own ways, and yet develop ways for helpful encounter.

How can we do it?

WHAT BEING TRULY SCIENTIFIC MEANS

This can be done only by preparing ourselves to understand as clearly as possible what it takes to be truly scientific and what it takes to be truly spiritual, and then by finding ways of being both in oneself, not theoretically, but in practice.

It should be a perfectly realizable ideal for the simple reason that in the human mind, which is the instrument for being both scientific are spiritual, there are no idea-tight compartments. Moreover, those who have known have told us that in the spirit there are no curtains or walls.

Now, what does it take to be scientific? Science, generally speaking, is "a description of the facts, with the maximum of completeness and maximum economy of thought." To be scientific we must accept the aim of science as our own, use its methodology, and also develop a scientific mood or temper. To be scientific requires regorous discipline of the mind. The aim of science is to describe impersonal facts of experience in verifiable terms as exactly as possible, as simply as possible, and as completely as possible. All its conclusions must be open to experiment and verification, besides being rational, and not subject to men's will or emotion.

Science aims at precisely describing things as they are, or seem to exist, in its scope science does not include transcendental concepts and offers no ultimate explanations. It deals with secondary causes and not ultimate causes. "It always seeks to reduce things to a common denominator and reduce the number of categories or necessary concepts."

It has been well said that 'laws of nature' are descriptive formulae in "conceptual shorthand" of the routine of our perception. Science does not pretend to know anything about God or ultimate reality. It cannot say that God does not exist, without being unscientific. And it need not say that God exists to be scientific.

> *The scientific mood is specially marked by a passion for facts, by cautiousness of statement, by clearness of vision and by a sense of interrelatedness of things.*
>
> *There is only one way of knowing how nature works the way of careful observation and experiment.*
>
> *Then you can begin to formulate hypotheses and theories, and from these again deductions can be made. Once more observation and experiment must be brought to bear on these deduction–so that in the end we get reliable theories which account for all the observed data. This sequence is called the scientific method.*
>
> *The fundamental postulate of science is the uniformity of nature.*

The important criteria of the scientific method are : dynamism and growth; reproducibility and reasonableness. Objectivity is the passion of science.

What is needed to be scientific is fidelity to facts and readiness to go with open eyes where facts lead, and ability to keep an open mind. Scientists must be absolutely unemotional in rejecting cherished theories when they have been proved wrong, and accepting a new one when it has been proved right.

WHAT BEING TRULY SPIRITUAL MEANS

Now, what does it take to be spiritual? In an absolute sense, spirituality denotes the illumined state of existence which one can have only after seeing God or realizing one's identity with the Supreme Spirit.

In a relative sense, to live a life of that kind of discipline which ultimately leads to the realization of God or experience of Atman, and thus brings about the liberation of the spirit, is also being spiritual.

In this way of living one has to find one's way to recognize a divine principle–whatever name one may give to it–which interprets, interpenetrates and undergirds the phenomenal world of which man is a part. When one continues to think at and grow with a progressive sense of relationship with that principle, one becomes more and more spiritual.

It has been said that the business of science is to deal with "facts". But what is a "fact"? That which exists or occurs may be defined as a fact. But how do we know what exists? Through our senses of perception directed by our mind we know what exists. Can there be no such case in which our senses of perception fail to apprehend something that exists? There can be such a case. For the blind man the tree in front of him does not exist. But, irrespective of his not knowing it, the tree exists. Thus we do not deal with facts as such even in science, but only with our awareness of what seems to exist. In man's dealings with facts, awareness is inseparable from the fact. Now this inseparable awareness is itself the great fact of life. Religion, in its finest reaches, deals with this fact. At one pole of existence is the awareness of fact, at another is the fact of awareness. The former is the subject matter of science; and the latter, of religion.

When the awareness of fact is polarized to the fact of awareness in a knowing person, if he is a scientist-like Sir Arthur Eddington-he begins to talk a language with strange accents, like the following:

> *The theory of relativity has passed in review the whole subject matter of physics. It has unified the great laws, which by the precision of their formulation and the exactness of their application have won the proud place in human knowledge which physical science holds today. And yet, in regard to the nature of things, this knowledge is only an empty shell-a form of symbols. It is knowledge of structural form, and not knowledge of content. All through the physical world runs that unknown content, which must surely be the stuff of our consciousness. Here is a hint of aspects deep within the world of physics, and yet unattainable by the method of physics. And, moreover, we have found that where science has progressed the furthest, the mind has but regained from nature that which the mind has put into nature.*
>
> *We have found strange foot-prints on the shores of the unknown. We have devised profound theories, one after another, to account for its origin. At last, we have succeeded in reconstructing the creature that made the foot-print: and lo! it is our own!*

If to be scientific is to deal with "facts", to be spiritual is also to be factual in another sense. Spirituality does not mean theorizing, but experiencing, seeing. Seeing what? Seeing what exists. And when one spiritually experiences a fact, unlike a scientific experience, it is no doubt a personal experience, but it is not a private fact. Such a fact is predictable and verifiable in the personal experience of others.

Patanjali in his Aphorisms on Yoga, and Narada in his Aphorisms on Devotion, clearly and precisely enunciate what kinds of disciplines, by what stages will lead to what experiences. In the Vedanta-sara, a textbook on non-dualistic Vedanta, four-fold disciplines are prescribed for the realization of Atman. Buddha codified his disciplines as the Noble Eight-fold Path, and clearly indicated by what stages one who practises these disciplines will attain nirvana. Given the same practices, the same experiences will be had.

If this approach to teaching religion is largely adopted, religion will stand on as sure grounds as science. Swami Vivekananda says:

Experience is the only source of knowledge. In the world, religion is the only science where there is no surety, because it is not taught as a science of experience. This should not be. There is always, however, a small group of men who teach religion from experience. They are called mystics, and these mystics in every religion speak the same tongue and teach the same truth. This is the real science of religion. As mathematics in every part of the world does not differ, so the mystics do not differ. They are all similarly constituted and similarly situated. Their experience is the same; and this becomes law...

> *Religion deals with the truths of the metaphysical world just as chemistry and the other natural sciences deal with the truth of the physical world. The book one must read to learn chemistry is the book of nature. The book from which to learn religion is your own mind and heart. The sage is often ignorant of physical science, beause he reads the wrong book–the book within; and the scientist too is often ignorant of religion, because he too reads the wrong book–the book without.*

There is some significant difference between two sets of disciplines, scientific and spiritual. To be scientific, it is enough if one sharpens one's intellect and observes the disciplines of the scientific method. Theoretically speaking, it is possible to be immoral and scientific simultaneously.

But it is impossible to be immoral and spiritual simultaneously. The scientist has to inform his mind in order to carry on his work, whereas the spiritual man has to transform his whole being. This is a great difference. This difference is due to the fact that basically science addresses itself to things within time-space-causality, and religion to things beyond time-space-causality. To know things beyond time-space-causality, we must transcend the barriers of time-space-causality. How do we do it? Here arises the question of moral perfection, by which is meant complete mastery over the senses and the mind ....

With some effort, it is possible for a single person to develop both the responses.

Extracts from author's book of the same title. We express our gratitude in procuring it from the publications.

56

BEYOND ECONOMICS

Hiranmay Karlekar

Reaffirming once again his commitment to economic reform, the Prime Minister told the Federation of Indian Chambers of Commerce and Industry (FICCI) last Saturday, "This is a one-way traffic., There is no return. There is no looking back and at the same time there is no relenting."

Mr. Narasimha Rao's words will dishearten those who believe that far from ushering in an economic millenuium, the proposed reform measures will cause disaster in the near future. Even if one does not share their apprehensions, one needs to ask, what is the wider philosophy behind the measures? Or are these regarded as ends in themselves in the belief that all India's ills will perish once these are successfully implemented?

Should one believe this to be the case, a look at the First World, which is reaping the fruits of the pattern of development which the Indian reform is trying to initiate, will be sobering. Continuously increasing affluence remains elusive. Witness the current recession in the United States, Japan and most European countries. Any attempt to dismiss it as the last of its kind will be laughable; there have been several similar ones since World War II, to say nothing of the ones before, including the Great Depression of 1929-32. This is not to suggest that the First World's economic system has not achieved anything. It has released productive forces on a scale undreamt of before. In the course of its evolution since the days of the embryonic emergence of capitalism, the geographical discoveries and the rise of the nation states, science and technology has taken several quantum leaps and human freedom has registered spectacular advances in terms of both personal space and insitutional guarantee and support.

Yet progress has been lopsided and its fruits most unevenly distributed. The poor acount for a significant and numerically growing minority in most First World countries. Worse, as productivity becomes more and more dependent on sophisticated technology, skilled workers command increasingly high premia; the unskilled slide deeper and deeper into unemployment and poverty.

Nor are the affluent in a state of bliss. They are haunted by the fear of crime, economic disaster, personal inadequacy and failure, and driven by a profound inner emptiness. The argument that we are far worse off in India and should first achieve what the First World has before looking at its warts is as engaging as it is untenable. The First World as it exists today has not emerged like Minerva from Seus head. The historical turning points which marked the beginnings of the evolutionary process shaping it, have been mentioned above. These in turn followed from two major developments. The first was the Renaissance which marked the re-emergence of humanism, with its emphasis on the sovereignty of the individual and reason, on the European horizon. The second was the Reformation, which marked the end of the spiritual dominance of the Papacy and in the long run, contributed to a climate that led to the decline of religiosity itself. If India embarks on a similar evolutionary process, it will be very difficult for it to have a society which is not made in the First World's image. The effort should be to examine what has gone wrong with the First World and how to avoid it.

Capitalism and the increasing dominance of reason in intellectual life have given the First World this character. Capitalism is a product of individualism which is at the root of individual enterprise. The Renaissance, which revived humanism in Europe, also resurrected individualism after centuries of suppression by the Church. Humanism, whose essence has been admirably encapsulated in Protagorus' celebrated aphorism, "Man is the measure of all things," portrayed the individual not as weak and powerless but as Prometheus unchained, the maker of destiny, the creator of history.

The rise of capitalim was also facilitated by the Reformation. Max Weber has argued persuasively in The Protestant Ethic and the Spirit of Capitalism that it was the Calvinist belief, that success in one's chosen calling was a sign of one being pre-destined to salvation, that enabled people to strive for success in commerce which was until then frowned upon by Christians. Puritan austeiry helped capital formation. His view has been questioned. But there can be no denying that the general weakening of the authority of the Church, which followed the Reformation, helped. In his classic Religion and the Rise of Capitalism, R.H. Tawney shows how the Church's injunctions against usury and profiteering were unceremoniously discarded as capitalism became increasingly assertive.

The sovereignty of reason, the cutting edge of protestant spiritual challenge to Rome, was heralded by the triumphant march of science and technology along avenues cleared by rational exploration. Anything not explicably its analytical methods became suspect. Among the latter was emotion which came to be looked down upon in intellectual circles as antithetical to reason.The same fate befell faith, the essence of religion.The latter also suffered as reason became the basis of new system of atheist thought.The process was aided by religion's failure to prevent catastrophes such as the two World Wars, the rise of Nazism, Fascism and Stalinism, the holocaust and the nuclear bombing of Hiroshima and Nagasaki in our times.

Karl Marx, who was highly critical of the role of religion in subjugating the masses, nevertheless once described it as the 'heart of a heartless world." This is because relgion provided succour to the troubled, and spiritual strength and sustenance in an uncertain world. The erosion of its inluence left human kind in a growing spiritual voild. The desiccation of emotion left its members alone, isolated even in a crowd, unable to reach out to other human beings. This led to the withering of compassion.

The de-spiritualisation and isolation of the individual was accelerated by economic success which became society';s dominant goal, greatly influencing the system of values. Human beings came to be regarded not as the measure of all things but resources for increasing production. Engrossed in the pursuit of wealth in an ambience of dog-eat-dog competitiveness, people became aggressive and self-centred. They had no time for reflection, sympathy or communication.Things have been made worse by the advent of the counsumer culture which has made self-indulgent consumerism the reward of success, and television, which has brought entertainment home thereby curtailing socialisation and communication with other human beings and intensifying the feeling of isolation.

Clearly, India must stop regarding economic growth as the predominant national goal if it is not to become an economic giant which is spiritually and emotionally a cripple. The emphasis should be on treating economic progress as a means of creating a compassionate and just society where the individual is the end of all ventures and is joined with other individuals in love and compassion. The need is for a philosophy which elaborates the view and a blueprint that translates it into action. The philosophy need not be religous; religion is a source both of succour and torment. Nor need it spurn reason, which is value neutral and has contributed greatly to the expansion of freedom. It must be a philosophy that upholds humanism and, in the present Indian context, prescribes that the burden of economic reform should be born not by the poor but those who can and that the reform should itself be jettisoned if it is not in the country's long-term interest.

By Courtesy Indian Express, Oct. 12, 1993.

57

SOCIALISM OF VIVEKANAND
(विवेकानन्द का समाजवाद)

K.K. Sinha

The paper reviews the growing element of Religion in Economics and its socialistic premises. After the collapse of Russian socialism, thinking on the subject has become strange admixture of material welfare and practical religion, what Vivekananda adumberated in Chicago hundred years back.

Such attempt dates back to 1270 when Thomas Aquinas tried to make a reasonable compromise between the laws of market and the concept of just prices for the salvation of man and his eternal life.

The trend drifted to material welfare with Industrial Revolution in Britain and self-interest was made a rational norm for growth of markets and material welfare. The merchants made a case for maximum earning from trade as a goal of national welfare. Adam Smith later on improved this dictum by some normative foundations of Natural liberty based on Reason, Morality and Competition. Thus the individualistic ego of the economic man could be oriented to fairness and social good.

This idea has prevailed over the western thinking as a classical and all-time truth. This gave the economic 'Nirvan' concept of happiness and bliss. Though there were always some doubts about this but they were solved by over-moralising and by substituting hedonism and self-interest with mystic utilitarianism, under the influences of Kant (1804) and Bentham.

Hegel (1831) gave a new turn to this Nirvan concept and found that Nirvan or synthesis came only after dialectical change. Marx interpreted it as a class struggle with a powerful state ending into the material Nirvan when the State 'withered away'. This was a Godless Nirvan.

Both the above views in the West wantd to prove logically what would happen in the market life. Compte's positivism stressed the need of historical investigations too whether some abstracted truths really happened. The stress was on social duty and moral ideas. But a science based moral order could not be a substitute for religion as it treated humanity an abstract idea of mind and body. Philosophy gave approximation about human nature but it remained hypothetial and what was actually happening in material life of man was different from what the economic axioms foretold.

VIVEKANANDA MOVEMENT

Accidently with the Chicago speech of Vivekananda, there was a tilt towards 'genuine religion' in economics. The christian socialists termed the utilitarian materialism of Bentham as a 'pig philosophy' while the humanist stance of the Marxists had to be oriented to, what Weber (1904) called, a Protestant work-ethics. They thus felt that socialism has ignored the spiritual needs of mankind. Among the Romantics, Marshall (a contemporary to Vivekananda) loved to preach the gospel of noble life and service to nation. This was true whether the system was capitalist or socialist.

Vivekananda preferred to be a socialist, beacuse 'equality' was more man-making than hedonistic pursuit of wealth and material prosperity. Further, equality had a spiritual content, i.e. the realisation that all souls were alike and God was nothing but the sum total of all souls. Material prosperity of a nation must be founded on this spiritual equality. Vivekananda called it practical vedanta, which entails four things–Gyan (knowledge), Bhakti (devotion), Karm (action) and Sadhna (self-searching).

Spiritual socialism denies all.privileges of strong over the week, of learned over the commoners, of priests over the believers and of the rich over the poor. It rests on patriotism and fellow feeling. It is a positive movement and not dialectical. Religion here concerns with soul and not social system. The base is not a rational man but a spiritual man.

Vivekananda created a movement not of Religion but of society. He brought religion to society as a practice and not something to be read in books : religion was, as if, a cream of all religions where God was to be seen in each soul and realising so was Religion. He therefore talked ofVedanta, the essense of all knowledge, a thing to be practised and realised in society. It was no dogma, no creed and no Ism.

Awareness of God was actually an awareness of the equality of souls. God could not exist in a differentiated, unequal world. When the Swami went to America, it was not to spread any religion but to know why was America so affluent and India so poor. He thought that the duty of a Sanyasin was not to preach religion but to work for the poor. To quote 'Sanyansin's duty is with the poor'. (Quoted Romain Roll and, p. 146) He could not shut his eyes to the material though his goal was spiritual. He therefore said 'I am a socialist not because it is a perfect system, but half a loaf is better than no bread'. (works, Vol. IV, p. 380-82).

What was to be fought was Inequality and it existed in spite of various religions in the world. He therefore declaed in the Parliament of Religions in Chicago that religion did not lie in differing but in accepting. If they differed, they were fanatics. So 'help, not fight, assimilation ot distruction and harmony and peace, not dissension' became the Swami's clue to a 'religious socialism'. Swami's address of the Parliament with 'Sisters and Brothers' was another concept of his socialism. It was not 'alienation' or exclusion which religions could thrive on. Swami Ji treated all religions preaching harmony and treated God the best unity solution, the one in many.

After returning fom Europe, he was actually getting fed up with too much of religion and said that he prefers an atheist to religious fanatics. He treated reform not only as a religious issue but of the whole system and a reform was in fact a social change where the miseries of the common man were removed. He therefore conceptualised the poor as the living Gods and service and sacrifice as the real worship. This naturally was not a process fo struggle of a physical world but of a spiritual world. Vivekananda therefore declared a war to deluge the land with spiritual ideas before flooding it with socialist or political ideas.' This requires a lot of restrospection.

The basic assumptions of Swamiji's world are three—1. Man is not just body but soul, 2. Each sould is potentially devine and 3. God is the sum total of all souls. It is a thesis and synthesis with no anti-thesis which the Marxists made the base of their dialectical change. What made Vivekananda's system revolutionary was his call for freedom from fear. Religion was not just a feeling of unity but a fearlessness to achieve it. 'Religion was the song of the soul' (Vol. 3

p. 179) It was a gradual upheaval of 'being and becoming' in one's own life time, when the self grows into one whole. (Vol. 3, p. 221).

Such change was not historical but just personal, what is known as a Man-making process. The process was not any dialectical materialism but a fine tuning of the material with the spiritual. It is a positive change or 'expansion' from the smaller to the bigger truths. Here there are no sinners but those who have to grow. Here there is no class conflict on that account but the progressive realisation of the unity and 'sameness' of all being.

(a) Such a realisation would not permit any type of privilege to any person or class. So nobody could have a privilege over others on account of wealth, physical strength, intellectual or spiritual power, and caste creed or even political status. Swamiji accepts that there are two forces, one making for privileges and the other breaking it down. The strong wants to have a privilege over the week, the more moneyed, over the poor, the more knowledgeable, over the ignorent and the ruler over the ruled, and even the priests over the followers. A spiritual movement would break such privileges as a natural consequence. Swamiji calls it a practical vedanta.

Vivekananda does not deny the existence of classes or castes which all are forces to obtain privileges. What breaks however, is not conflict but the realisation of the oneness of man. There are thus quite simple and practical tenets ofVivekananda's Socialism as given below:

(b) Practical Vedanta–Practical Vedant or practical religion is a process of change which has to be practised and the practice has to take account of the call of social reality. It is not just believing in a God but seing Him in every soul. Religion is not ritualism but doing somethig for the fellow beings.'Serve man, serve God.'

It is not priest craft either. It goes down where priestcraft arises. There could be no religion where there was priesthood. Religion negates privileges. religion comes when privileges go. Thus Vivekananda rescued religion from the onslaught of the Marxists by giving it a very practical import. He called it Vedant because it stopped nowhere and no priest could suppress anybody from telling the truth. Thus religion is brought out of temples and mosques to life and society. Religion is not moving from wrong to right but from low to high.

(c) Spiritualism–It is the opposite of materialism. It treats all souls as equals where as materialism is based on inequality of men.

It does not believe in super-natural because such beliefs belittle the devinity in every soul, and leads to superstitions. Spiritualism lies in upholding that the individual jiva and the Brahma are basically identical. To quote Vivekananda we are the greatest God that ever was or ever will be. Christs and Buddhas are but waves on the boundless ocean which I am! It is the faith in self which unites men and gives strength of a thunderbolt.

(d) Patriotism–Unlike the development of socialism in the West, the origin of socialism was love and not class conflict. It is why a concept of spiritual nationalism was developed by Vivekanand. It was not any pride for the heritage but a love for the people which made patriotism a necessary condition for a social change. It was the feeling in Heart of the pangs of the poor which made you a patriot. In fact the lack of this emotional fervour made the western socialism dry and short-lived.

We may here quote the last words of Swami Vivekananda – India is immortal if she persists in her search for God. But if she goes in for politics and social conflict, she will die. (Quoted, Rolland p. 168) This love for Mother India was not any animal pride in race or nation but to bring about within the disorganised Indian masses a sense of unity within the bounds of their own nation first. It was in no way a poltical process but an awakening.

Obviously a socialism of the type was not going to be a political process of fight for power, but a spiritual movement for freedom. Vivekananda would say – 'I have nothing to do with the nonsense of politics'.

(e) Karm Yoga–The 'Love India' theme could not be just Bhakti (devotion) but Karm (action). The search for God has a positive path–not to fly away from the wheel of the world machine but stand inside it and learn the secret of work. (Ibid. p. 193) It was thus going back to the material world but with a free mind and not as slaves. of passion and attachment.

Of the four paths of Love, Knowledge, Meditation and Work, Vivekananda found work most deep and moving. 'God is not a plaything in the hands of an imbecile' and that Bhakti is a sentimental nonsense, were uttered by the Swami when he thought of a practical religion 'for still my work for my motherland is unfinished'. He wanted a plan of his compaign and called his people to rise on mass and then he said that his country wanted 'muscles of iron and nerves of steel'. (Ibid pp. 107-25) It was invoking a religious power in India when Europe had political power as its vitality. Every human epoch has its own work and to Swami Ji 'our task is to raise the masses, so long shamefully betrayed, exploited and degraded.' It was the silent toiling mases whom Karm Yoga would make its heroes.

(f) Negation of class or caste – It is clear that Swamiji was looking at the mass and not class which divides men into superior and inferior or in ranks and grades. He would alow no castes among the workers but only different types of Karm Yoga. Karm (Work) has to be different and each man must learn his own work and try to accomplish it. (Karm Yoga, Chap. 1) And if superiority has to be given, it must be to the humblest and the lowest, not even to Christs and the Buddhas, but to the nameless, the silent ones, the unknown soldiers.

In fact castes as work groups are socialistic when the Western man is individualistic. It has given a social norm of collective behaviour and common good. But Swamiji finds it an imperfect institution and quite fluid. 'If ten thousand people in each caste put their heads together and say we will call ourselves Brahmins, nothing can stop them'. More over, caste system is opposed to the religion ofVedanta. It is simply a social custom and an out-growth of political institutions in India. It is a hereditory guild, and trade competitions are bound to break this.

The Brahma sutra does mention castes but it does not mean caste by birth. Spiritual oneness denies all such divisions. Except by way of Karm, any caste distinction, if made in books by priests, is madness and hypocricy. (Caste, Culture & Socialism, pp. 21-23, 49-53).

58

SPIRITUAL SOCIALISM

V.K.R.V. Rao

(Following is an extract of the paper which brings religion in the fold of economics in a most lucid and convincing way. This reprint (1991) was made available to us by courtesy ofVivekanand Kendra, Kanyakumari.)

Swami Vivekananda considered religion as co-extensive with life and wanted it to influence the social and economic ideals of the people and their daily conduct and activity. "Theory may be very good indeed but if it be absolutely impracticable no theory is of any value whatever except an intellectual gymnastics". He therefore called his religion "Practical Vedanta" This Practical Vedanta is synonymous with, to a great extent, what is known as socialism. Gandhian socialism leaned a lot on Swamiji's Practical Vedanta.

FELLOW FEELING

During his Parivrajaka days he saw for himself the trials and tribulations of the common people. It was this direct contact with the Indian masses, their poverty, illiteracy, superstitions and social degradation that moved him to fierce anger aat the social system that permitted the exploitation by a few of the many. He was appalled that there was no connection between the intellectual acceptance of the Advai8t doctrine and its application in day-to-day life of the people.

He was no mere theoretician or a platform speaker but a realist to the core and he gave vent to his feelings in a telling manner in all his writings and speeches. He even went to the extent of decrying people seeking personal salvation or moksha when their fellow beings were in need. He felt that if God was manifest in all human beings and especially so in poor and the down-trodden, then it was the business of the better persons to help the under-privileged. That was the best form of worship to God. He gave expression to this as "Serve Man, Serve God". He said : "I have lost all my wish for salvation. May I be born again and again and suffer thousands of miseries so that I may worship the only God that exists, the only God that I believe in, the sum total of all souls and above all, my God the wicked, my God the miserable, my God the poor of all races, of all species. Let each one of us pray day and night for the down-trodden millions of Indians who are held fast by poverty .. and tyranny. Feel for the miserable and look up for help....... In His name and with eternal faith in Him, set fire to the mountain of misery that has been heaped upon India for ages and it shall be turned down.

Where should you go to seek God? Are not all the poor, the miserable, the weak, Gods ? Why not worship them first?.........I believe in helping the miserable. I believe even in going to hell to save others. Know that service to these alone is the highest religion"

PATRIOTISM

His Vedantic socialism found expression in the formulation of the ideal of patriotism. While he was immensely proud of the country's philosophy and cultural heritage, he was also fully aware of the disastrous condition of the Indian masses. For him, the country was not just a geographical entity or a philosophic concept but essentially meant its people. People meant the vast majority of its masses. Patriotism according to him, should therefore show itself in what was being done to serve the interest of the masses and improve their social and economic conditions. Thus, the essence of patriotism was his great love for his people.

His patriotism needed three things for its practical implementation. One was passionate love for the masses. The second was finding practical solutions for their problems instead of paper reforms. The third was strength of will to overcome the obstructions to the implementation to these solutions.

He eloquently said : " Firsr feel from the heart. Do you feel that millions of the descendents of gods and sages have become next-door neighbours to brutes? Do you feel that millions have been starving today and millions have been starving for ages ? Do you feel that ignorance has come over the land as dark cloud ? Does it make you sleepless/Has it gone into your blood, coursing through your veins, becoming consonant with your heart beats ? Has it made you almost mad? Are you seized with that one idea of the misery of ruin and have you forgotten all about your name, your fame, your wives, your children, your property, even your own bodies ? Have you done that ? That is the first step to become a patriot. The very first step ."

Vivekanand did not believe in violent changes or revolution by coercion. He was willing to recognize that the past was a mixture of both good and bad. What was needed was to learn from the past mistakes and go forward from the good that undoubtedly came from the past of India. He said ; "If there are holes in the nation-ship, this society of ours, we are its children, let us go and stop the holes. Le us gladly do it with our heart's blood and if we cannot, then let us die. Say no one harsh word against this society." What greater love can there be than one that perceives the faults in the beloved land and would go all out to rectify them instead of condemning it because of the sins that one finds in her ? Reform, yes; but destroy never. This was the power and love of Vivekananada for his motherland and that was the message of patriotism.

SOCIAL CHANGES

His Vedantic socialism covered the social system and the need for reconstruction to enable the masses to play their rightful role in the society. When the needs of the times press hard on it, the society adopts certain customs for self preservation. If it be necessary to change any social custom, the necessity underlying it should be found first of all and by altering it, the custom will die of itself. He however felt that the desired social change would have been more effectively brought about if religion had been used as an instrument–a religion shorn of irrelevant accretions and reinterpreted in the light of its original exposition rather than attacking the religion itself at its roots.

CASTE SYSTEM

He was much concerned about the institution of caste which he disliked intensely but which continued to exist because of the mistaken notion of reformers that caste was a religious institution which led to their attacking religion in order to destroy caste.

Vivekananda denied the thesis of religious sanction for the caste system. He pointed out that the doctrine of caste in the Purush Sukta did not make it hereditary. He asserted: "The caste system is opposed to the religion of Vedanta. Caste is a social custom and all our great preachers tried to break it down. Caste is simply an outgrowth of the political institutions in India; it is a hereditary trade guild. It is in the books, written by priests, that madness like that of the caste is to be found not in the books revealed from God.

Religion has only to do with the soul and has no business to interfere in social matters. Caste is simply a crystallized social institution which after doing its service is now filling the atmosphere of India with its stench and it can only be removed by giving back to the people their lost social individuality."

PRIVILEGES

He was also a stout opponent of privileges in any form and took caste as the supreme illustration of the doctrine of privilege. Not that he was believer in arithmetical equality of all human beings. There were bound to be variations in the physical, mental and spiritual abilities of different human beings, but this gave no right for special privileges for those who had more of any such abilities. He pointed out: "The idea of privileges is the bane of human life. Two forces,as it were, are constantly at work. One making caste and the other breaking caste; in other words, one making privileges and the other breaking down privileges. Whenever privilege is broken down, more and more light and progress comes to a race.

The same power is in every man in one manifesting itself more and in the other less, the potential is in everyone. The work of Advait therefore is to break down all privileges." "Trampling on every privilege and everything in us that works for the privileges, let us work for that knowledge which will bring the feeling of sameness towards all mankind." The practical Vedanta he preached was thus even more radical in its implications for human relations than what we find even in the most radical social doctrines and its relevance for India today is even greater than when he preached it so many years ago.

WOMEN

Vivekananda was also a strong advocate for giving women their rightful place in the society, He said; 'If you do not raise the women who are the embodiment of the divine mother, do not think that you have any other way to rise." He wanted education to be made available as much for women as for men. "Once they are educated they could choose their role in their lives and not be dependent upon men as to what they should do." "Educate them first and leave them to themselves, then they will tell you what reforms are necessary for them.""No man shall dictate to woman nor a woman to man.

Each one is independent. Women will work out their own destinies much better too than men can ever do for them. All the mischief to women has come because men undertook to shape the destiny of women. His practical Vedant went even farther than socialism in the place it gave to women in society.

EDUCATION

About education he scoffed at the importance given to book-learning and memory training. "Education is not the amount of information that is put in your brain and runs riot there undigested all your life. We must have life-building, man-making, character building assimilation of ideas. If education is identical with information, the libraries are the greatest sages of the world and encyclopedias are the rishis.

FEARLESSNESS

Fearlessness was another thing he stressed. He was of the view that fear was the greatest enemy of self-development. It is fear and helplessness that dominated the Indian masses because of oppression and neglect of the power wielders of the land. He thundered "Strength is goodness, weakness is sin. If there is one word that you find coming out like a bomb from the Upnishads, it is the word Abhaya or fearlessness.

Either in this world or in the world of religion, it is true that fear is the sure cause of degradation and sin. It is fear that brings misery, fear that brings death, fear that breeds evil." He exhorted the youth to stand up and face the challenge of life and its many problems without fear.

INDIVIDUAL FREEDOM

While he was appreciative of the socialist doctrines which showed concern for the poor and the exploited, he was not in favour of depriving individual freedom. He pleaded for individual freedom, independent thinking and the development of individual will. He said : "It is more blessed in my opinion even to go wrong impelled by one's free will and intelligence than to be good as an automaton. How can that be called society which is formed by an aggregate of men who are like lumps of clay, like lifeless machines, like heaped up pebbles ?" He was not a blind patriot or an upholder of the status-quo but wanted fresh air to blow in and the individual to awake and assert himself.

ORGANISATION

But at the same time he was aware that while intellectual development might stimulate change, the change would not get implemented without organization and character. He was conscious of the deficiencies of the national character and its general spirit of inertia and passivity. This led to his critical analysis of the national weakness. He said "Jealousy is the central vice of every enslaved race. It is jealousy and want of combination which cause and perpetuate slavery.......... Let us wipe off first that mark which nature always puts on the forehead of a slave–the stain of jealousy. Be jealous of none .... " He often cited the Vedic quotation which ended "Let us not be jealous of each other".

But the need for organization and to work together was also stressed by him. "The faculty of organisatiion is entirely absent in our nature and this has to be infused. Cultivate the virtue of obedience. No centralization is possible unless there is obedience to superiors. No great work can be done without this centralization of individual forces."

He lamented; "Three men cannot act in concert together in India for five minutes. Each one struggles for power and in the long run the whole organization comes to grief." One should take charge not as leader but as servant. The least show of leading destroys everything by rousing jealousy. He exhorted "Do not try to lead your brethren but serve them. The brutal mania for leading has sunk many a great ship in the waters of life Do not fight with people, do not antagonize anyone. Bear with the opinion of everybody. Patience, perseverance and purity will prevail........... It is criticizing each other that is at the root of all mischief. That is the chief factor in breaking organizations

TO CONCLUDE

Vivekananda's socialism is not a political concept but a profound feeling of oneness which passed through the crucible of personal suffering and contact with the masses.. .... It has the added weight of true religion. It is applicable to all people and nations and at all times. This is the only way for human salvation. This identifies man with his Maker through inter-action with the fellow beings who area again the creation of the same great Maker.

"Everything goes to show that Socialism or some form of rule by the people, call it what you will, is coming on the boards. The people will certainly want the satisfaction of their material needs, less work, no oppression, no war, more food. What guarantee have we that this, or any civilization, will last unless it is based on religion, on the goodness of man ? Depend on it, religion goes to the root of the matter. If it it is right, all is right.." (Quoted Vivekananda)

INDEX

F

G

H